BOOKS BY JOHN KOBLER

Damned in Paradise: The Life of John Barrymore   (1977)

Ardent Spirits: The Rise and Fall of Prohibition   (1973)

Capone: The Life and World of Al Capone   (1971)

Luce: His Time, Life and Fortune   (1968)

The Reluctant Surgeon: A Biography of John Hunter   (1960)

Afternoon in the Attic   (1950)

Some Like It Gory   (1940)

The Trial of Ruth Snyder and Judd Gray   (1938)

DAMNED IN PARADISE

JOHN KOBLER

DAMNED
IN PARADISE

The Life of John Barrymore

ATHENEUM

New York

1977

Library of Congress Cataloging in Publication Data

Kobler, John.
    Damned in paradise.

    Bibliography: p.
    Includes index.
    1. Barrymore, John, 1882–1942.   2. Actors—United
States—Biography.   I. Title.
PN2287.B35K58   1977   792'.028'0924   [B]   77-76752
ISBN 0-689-10814-1

Published simultaneously in Canada by McClelland and Stewart Ltd.
Manufactured in the United States of America by
American Book–Stratford Press, Saddle Brook, New Jersey
Designed by Harry Ford and Kathleen Carey
First Edition

FOR JAY

This lovely light, it lights not me. All love-
liness is anguish to me, since I can ne'er
enjoy. Gifted with the high perception, I
lack the low, enjoying power; damned, most
subtly and malignantly! damned in the
midst of Paradise . . .

AHAB in *Moby Dick*

"I've been a reasonable figure of asburdity
for a number of years—Punchinello today,
Melpomene tomorrow, Benedick forever."

JOHN BARRYMORE

Introduction

═══════════

THE central mystery posed by the life of John Barrymore is his epic self-destruction. Barrymore, it would seem, willed, embraced the instruments of his own fall. Endowed with rare physical grace and beauty, surpassingly brilliant as both comedian and tragedian, wit, boonfellow, lover, a caricaturist of no mean ability, art collector, scholar, yachtsman, sportsman, he stood for a time at the pinnacle of both his professional and his social community. As one of the chief architects of his theatrical ascent, the stage designer Robert Edmond Jones, once told him: "Jack, you can do everything you want any way you want to do it. There is nobody in that position in the theater today." What Barrymore chose to do was to walk a steeply graded downward path—the process had begun even as his fame soared—into debasement and disintegration.

Through the peak era of silent films, through the early period of the talkies and still today in television and theater reruns, Barrymore occupies for me, and doubtless for untold others, a treasured niche. Probably none of his fifty-seven films belongs on any list of the world's best. Yet his personal constructions of cinematic characters have left an ineradicable stamp on the screen of my memory. The arrogant Beau Brummel, the elegant Don Juan, the indomitable Ahab, the grotesques—Hyde and Svengali—remain for me images inseparable from their Barrymore incarnations.

vii

Though I never saw John Barrymore on the stage, my schooling having kept me at a distance from Broadway, I can accept the verdict of theatergoers and critics on both sides of the Atlantic who acclaimed him as the greatest Hamlet of his generation. My fascination with Barrymore the actor was accompanied by puzzlement, then dismay and compassion as I followed the vicissitudes of Barrymore the man through four failed marriages, his self-deriding public capers, his suicidal dissipations.

Within two years of Barrymore's death Gene Fowler, who had intimately known and loved the man for almost three decades, published his affecting *Good Night, Sweet Prince*. By the author's own account, he had kept no notes on Barrymore during their long time together, had harbored no intention of serving as his Boswell. Only after the loss of his friend did he write a highly subjective, emotional memoir. But, sensitively as Fowler responded to Barrymore, he could not penetrate the heart of his mystery any more than could other close friends, mistresses, wives, family. "Setting down words to explain Jack Barrymore," said his brother, Lionel, "is like seeking the mystery of Hamlet himself in the monosyllables of basic English."

Why, then, this new biographical venture? Since Fowler's book a good deal of new material has become available. It is contained in unpublished letters, diaries, in autobiographies of Barrymore's colleagues and relatives, in the recollections of some who only recently have felt free to disclose their knowledge. Fowler himself accumulated and stored a quantity of research which, for various reasons, he did not wish to draw upon (see Acknowledgments). I have no pretensions to having lifted the veil from the Barrymore enigma. But these fresh sources, together with talks with more than fifty people who worked or played with John Barrymore, shed perhaps more light upon one of the most compelling figures in the history of the theater.

CONTENTS

ILLUSTRATIONS

(Following page 50)

━━━━━━

xi

PHILADELPHIA
1827–1895

1

The Duchess

O N May 11, 1827, the packet ship *Britannia* set sail from Liverpool for New York City. It was then standard practice among American theatrical impresarios, when they needed actors, to raid British stock companies, and the *Britannia's* passengers numbered eleven defectors who had been lured away by one John Hallam, the British agent for New York's Park Theatre. No transatlantic steamship had as yet come into regular service, and the packet's crossing under sail took four weeks.

Among the emigrating troupers was a child of stupefying precocity, Louisa Lane, age seven, the product of a long-established theatrical dynasty. Her grandparents, Thomas Haycraft Lane and Louisa Rouse, had been strolling country players, then actor-managers during the reign of George III. Their son, Thomas Frederick Lane, enjoyed success as a provincial mummer, though he never conquered London. He married Eliza Trentner, a "Sweet Singer of Ballads" as well as a comedienne. She was an Episcopalian so scrupulous in her devotions that, however needy, she shunned the stage on the Sabbath. Their only child, Louisa, born in Lambeth Parish, London, on January 10, 1820, made her professional debut at the age of twelve months in something called *Giovanni in London*. ". . . my mother took me on the stage as a crying baby," she recounted in her autobiography, published posthumously eighty years later; "but cry I

3

would not, but at sight of the audience and the lights gave free vent to my delight and crowed aloud with joy. From that moment to this, the same sight filled me with the most acute pleasure, and I expect will do so to the last glimpse I get of them, and when no longer to be seen, 'Come, Death, and welcome!' "

Louisa Lane uttered her first lines on a stage at the age of five in the principal role of a melodrama entitled *Meg Murnock; or, the Hag of the Glen.* The phenomenal mite next portrayed Dr. Frankenstein's hapless brother whom the Monster kills.

Thomas Lane died in 1825, when only twenty-nine, and two years later his young widow accepted John Hallam's offer to join the Park Theatre company with her daughter. En route to the Liverpool port they tarried long enough for little Louisa to make her farewell appearances at Cooke's Amphitheatre, famed for its elaborate spectacles that usually featured horses. Louisa drew the heroic role of Prince Agib in *Timour, the Tartar.* The climatic scene showed a cataract, center stage, with a prison cage to the right to which Agib's mother has been consigned by the barbaric Timour. Agib dashes across the stage on horseback, piping: "My mother, I will free you still!" and breaks open the cage. The mother (played by a circus equestrienne) leaps upon the horse behind her son and clasps him firmly around the waist while the horse carries them through the cataract, to wild applause.

New York in summer enchanted neither mother nor daughter, and they stayed there only a few days, "long enough to completely change my mother's appearance; the mosquitoes found her a very healthy English woman, and feasted at their will." Despite their arrangement with the Park Theatre, they were permitted to fill an engagement at Philadelphia's Walnut Street Theatre. There, on September 26, 1827, Louisa, not yet turned eight, began to enlarge her repertory of male roles. In Shakespeare's *Richard III* she impersonated the Duke of York. Richard was played by Junius Brutus Booth, father of Junius, Jr., Edwin and John Wilkes Booth.

Moving on to Joe Cowell's Theatre in Baltimore, Louisa was cast as Albert, the son of William Tell, played by the illustrious tragedian Edwin Forrest. Though she found Forrest "never a good-tempered man, and . . . apt to be morose and churlish at rehearsals," she esteemed him for his unwillingness to steal scenes from lesser actors. "If the character you sustained had anything good in it, he would give you the finest chance of showing it to the audience. He would get a little below you, so that your facial expression could be fully seen; he would partially turn his back, in order that the attention should be given entirely to you. This will be better understood by actors, who know how differently some players act."

Louisa's performance so impressed Forrest that he had a silver medal struck in her honor, with the inscription, "Presented by E. Forrest to Miss Louisa Lane as a testimonial of his admiration for her talents."

The Widow Lane, meanwhile, had married the stage manager of the Walnut Street Theatre, John Kinloch, and given birth to a daughter. At the time of the marriage, in 1828, child prodigies who could imitate adult characters were all the rage with American audiences. The craze had originated in London a decade earlier, following the appearance at the Drury Theatre of a six-year-old tot named Clara Fisher, who assumed such robust roles as Richard III, Shylock and the Scottish warrior hero Douglas.

Kinloch determined that his stepdaughter should surpass Clara Fisher (now well advanced into her teens and seeking, with scant success, to attract an American following). Louisa did not disappoint him. She not only specialized in adult roles, but would play several in the same production. In a farce entitled *72 Piccadilly*, she enacted five characters; in *Actress of All Work*, six; in *Winning a Husband*, seven. The program for *Four Mowbrays*, a one-act farce presented at Philadelphia's Chestnut Street Theatre on January 9, 1829, the eve of Louisa's ninth birthday, listed the four leading roles as follows:

Matilda Mowbray	Miss Lane!
Master Hector Mowbray	Miss Lane!!
Master Cobbleton Mowbray	Miss Lane!!!
Master Foppington Mowbray	Miss Lane!!!!

It was also at the Chestnut Street Theatre that Miss Lane portrayed the aged pedagogue of Voltaire's *Candide*, Dr. Pangloss. "As she stood by the orchestra," reported a reviewer named Allston Brown, "and looking around the pit, inquired if any one there wanted the instructions of an L.L.D. or an A.S.S., the effect was irresistible, and the house shouted with laughter."

Such dexterity moved another Philadelphia critic to comment: "This astonishing little creature . . . evinces a talent for and a knowledge of the stage beyond what we find in many experienced performers of merit. The entertainment of *Twelve Precisely* [in which the dauntless moppet played the entire cast of three women and two

men] is well adapted to the display of the versatility of her powers.
. . . Those who have a taste for the wonderful should not miss the
present opportunity of gratifying it. We promise ourselves a treat
of no ordinary kind when she appears as Goldfinch in *The Road to
Ruin.*"

During an engagement in Washington, D.C., shortly after
Andrew Jackson's inauguration, Louisa was invited to a presidential
reception. Upon her introduction to "Old Hickory" he kissed her and
observed: "A very pretty girl." ("Need I say," she noted, "that I was
a Jackson Democrat from that hour, and have remained one up to
date?")

Toward the end of 1830 John Kinloch, in partnership with a
New York entrepreneur named Jones, decided to form a new stock
company. They assembled nine players, counting Louisa and her
mother, and for their first stand they chose the British West Indies
colony of Jamaica. Disaster beset them from the start. Off the coast
of Santo Domingo their ship ran aground. The voyagers managed to
get to shore safely, only to discover that the nearest settlement lay
many miles away. Six weeks elapsed while they camped on the beach,
waiting for word of their plight to reach Santo Domingo City. A brig
finally took them aboard and conveyed them to the capital, whence
they embarked for Kingston, Jamaica.

Their arrival in Kingston coincided with a yellow-fever epi-
demic. It killed both Kinloch and his daughter, an infant in arms,
and nearly carried off his wife. Destitute, enfeebled and repeatedly terrified by rumors of a native uprising, the surviving Kinlochs remained
on the island two years, warding off starvation with an occasional
performance. When they finally returned to Philadelphia, cholera
was raging there. It spared them, and Louisa obtained work at the
flourishing Arch Street Theatre, a stately Greek Revival edifice with
broad stone entrance steps and a Doric colonnade supporting a gallery. It had the added distinction of employing an all-American company, the first theater of any consequence to do so. One of the co-
managers was William Forrest, who, with his brother Edwin's backing, produced all the plays written especially for the tragedian.
Louisa appeared in many of them.

Louisa's autobiography refers to two other half-sisters, Adine
and Georgiana or Georgia. Their origin poses a mystery. If Kinloch fathered them as well as the baby who succumbed to yellow fever,
he must have done so out of wedlock, for he had been married to
Eliza Lane less than two years before he died. Or were they the

fruit of a third marriage contracted by Eliza? Neither the autobiography nor the Kinloch-Lane genealogy yields a clue.

When, in 1833, Louisa and her mother, undaunted by the horrors of their previous expedition to the West Indies, joined a stock
company sailing to the Bahamas, they took Adine and Georgiana
along. They were shipwrecked again, cast up by a storm at night on
a sandbar off Egg Island. Adine displayed the true Lane spirit of
piety and resignation. "Mama," said she, as they awaited rescue, "if
we all go into the water, will God give us breakfast?" In the morning
the stranded actors were packed into a New York–bound "wood
boat"—that is, a freighter stripped of its bulwarks in order to carry
the maximum amount of lumber.

"At this time," Louisa recalled, "I was of a very unhappy age
(thirteen), not a child and certainly not a woman, so the chances
were against my acting anything of importance." She undertook
small parts for a season at New York's Bowery Theatre, then with her
mother was engaged for two seasons by Boston's Warren Theatre,
which paid them a joint salary of $16 a week. "I don't know how
we lived; but mother was a splendid manager at that time, a mar-
velously industrious woman, and we all lived at 'Ma' Lenthe's, at the
corner of Bowdoin Square, a gable-end. We had a large room on the
second story, a trundle bed which went under the other for the
accommodations of little children, a large closet in which we kept a
barrel of ale and all our dresses, and passed a very happy two seasons
in the enjoyment of that large salary. . . ."

In March 1836, at the age of sixteen, Louisa married Henry
Blaine Hunt, an English trouper twenty-four years her senior, whom
she later described, with the detachment of old age, as "a very
good singer, a nice actor, and a very handsome man of forty." Under
a succession of managements they toured the country—Louisville,
New Orleans, Vicksburg, Natchez. Unlike Clara Fisher, Louisa
underwent no decline of popularity. In addition to qualifying for
mature Shakespearean roles, she developed a mezzo-soprano voice enabling her eventually to sing Rossini's *Cenerentola*, and Rosina in his
Barber of Seville. She could also dance, and once in Louisville, when a
ballerina from Havana proved inept, replaced her as the second
Bayadère in *La Bayadère*.

Sunday performances became generally acceptable, but, to the
annoyance of stock-company managers, not to Louisa, reared as she
had been by a devout mother who had once been dismissed from a
company in New Orleans for refusing to act on Sunday. "I was too

good a Christian to do that, and as I acted in everything, there was a great trouble to get my parts studied for one night." Despite the inconvenience and extra expense this caused, the managers valued her abilities so highly that they promoted her to the rank of "leading lady," and in Natchez, in 1839, she played her first role as such— Pauline in Bulwer-Lytton's comedy *The Lady of Lyons*, following that with Lady Macbeth opposite Edwin Forrest.

Returning to the scene of her earliest triumphs as a child prodigy, Philadelphia's Walnut Street Theatre, she drew the highest salary it had ever paid a leading lady—$20 a week. Next season, at the Chestnut Street and Arch Street theaters, she played Ophelia, Desdemona and Beatrice. There and later in Pittsburgh, Cincinnati, Baltimore, Albany, Chicago, Buffalo and New Orleans (where her salary jumped to $35) she came to share honors with the foremost performers of the era. They included the English tragedian William Charles Macready during his third visit to America ("a dreadful man to act with; . . . he would press you down with his hand on your head, and tell you in an undertone to stand up!"); Edwin Booth, who had "a very sweet character and a charming manner at rehearsals, which he detested"; the Irish-born comedian Tyrone Power,* who confined himself chiefly to Irish character parts in such farces as *St. Patrick's Eve*, *Rory O'More* and *O'Flannigan and the Fairies*.

The combined salaries of Louisa and her husband, who usually appeared on the same bill, were never munificent, and some engagements left them with barely enough funds for fare to the next town. In Baltimore, one jobless summer, Louisa organized her own tiny company with Hunt and three other troupers and presented a repertory of one-act comedies. Her half-sister Georgiana was now old enough to peep through a hole in the curtain and count the house. After each performance the company would gather around a table and divide the profits equally. They seldom amounted to more than a few dollars.

At New York's Park Theatre, Louisa reverted to the tours de force of her infancy and essayed masculine roles such as Romeo and Marc Antony. But comedy was her forte.

Louisa parted from her husband after ten years. The cause of the divorce, an uncommon and scandalous occurrence in that day, has been suggested by a theatrical historian, Montrose J. Moses, writing at the turn of the century. "His dash, his spirit, his attractive

* Progenitor of a theatrical line culminating in the Hollywood star.

presence had in early years gained him a much coveted place among the fast set which George IV had assembled around the throne. So that when he found himself a married man, his nature was no more trained than was Louisa Lane's for the mutual duties imposed upon them."

Louisa remained single less than a year. Her next husband, George Mossop, was an Irish tenor and comedian with a paralyzing stutter who miraculously recovered normal speech whenever he set foot onstage. He was also an irredeemable tosspot. The Mossops had been married but five months when drink finished him.

During the first weeks of her bereavement Louisa began an engagement at the Albany Museum with a company that included another Irish comedian, John Drew, a slight, jovial man of twenty-three, to whom gossip ascribed a fondness for liquor rivaling that of his predecessor. He had a twin brother, Frank, also an actor, and they were so indistinguishable in appearance that either of them could play both Dromios in *The Comedy of Errors* until the scene of their meeting, with the audience none the wiser.

According to Montrose Moses, John Drew's "equipment as an actor consisted in a rich voice and a quick, sympathetic humor. His characters of Handy Andy and Sir Lucius O'Trigger were preëminent. . . . His O'Bryan in *The Irish Immigrant* was so perfect in its reality that one found it hard to cease identifying the role with the actor." A critic, Benjamin Rogers, observed: "With the discernment of a true artist, Mr. Drew applied himself to the requirement of old legitimate comedies, with a truthfulness of study, and an untiring research as to the spirit and purpose of a character that enabled him to present them with an individuality marked and effective." And the great actor Joseph Jefferson wrote: "I think it has been generally conceded that since Tyrone Power, there has been no Irish comedian to equal John Drew . . . but I doubt if he [Power] could touch the heart as deeply as did John Drew."

Louisa Lane in maturity cut a somewhat overpowering figure, ample and tending to masculinity, with a blunt chin and nose set in a round face. But intelligence, charm and an air of authority served her as well as beauty when it came to securing a husband. Georgiana, by contrast, flowered into a tall and slender belle. She captivated John Drew, who informed Louisa that he wished to marry her half-sister. Louisa imperiously brushed aside this declaration and not long after married him herself.

In 1852, Mrs. John Drew, as she now billed herself, bore her first child, Louisa, the only member of the family to prove too frail for the rigors of a theatrical career. A year later came John Drew, Jr., destined to become the peerless interpreter of drawing-room comedy, and three years after him, Georgiana, called Georgie, whom Otis Skinner would remember as "the funniest comedian I've ever seen; she made you hold your stomach laughing, but she was never distressing."

The Drews' relationship appears to have been amicable, if not exceptionally close. During the twelve years of their marriage they spent barely six together. Following a season in New York and Chicago, they settled in Philadelphia, where Drew shared the management of the Arch Street Theatre with a friend, William Wheatley. He relinquished his interest at the end of the second season to accompany Eliza Kinloch, his mother-in-law, on a tour of the British Isles, while his wife stayed behind as leading lady of the Walnut Street Theatre. No sooner home than he set out again on a tour of California, Australia and England that lasted four years. His earlier love, Georgiana, had not lost her appeal for him, and he took her with him, evidently causing Louisa no great concern.

Two years after his departure the stockholders of the Arch offered Louisa the lease of the property, and in 1861, at the outbreak of the Civil War, it opened as "Mrs. John Drew's Arch Street Theatre." The first woman ever to run an American theater of comparable importance, she struggled through the first season plagued by financial problems. She had insisted on adding expensive embellishments to the red-velvet-and-golden interior decoration. Though the annual rental of the building was $6,200, she kept the price of tickets within range of modest pocketbooks—balcony, fifteen cents; family circle, twenty-five cents; dress circle, thirty-seven and a half cents; parquet, half a dollar. She had to borrow money every week to pay her actors. She herself played forty-two roles during the 1861–62 season.

Drew and Georgiana showed up again in the early winter of 1862 and with them was a baby girl. Unperturbed, Louisa adopted her, naming her Adine after her younger half-sister. If she did not berate the errant couple, it may have been because of another addition to the family—a baby boy whom she claimed to have adopted during their absence. She said his name was Sidney White, which she changed to Drew. (Her grandson Lionel would declare: "I am proud to claim kin to him," and her granddaughter Ethel, too, would affirm the relationship: "Uncle Sidney may not have been the son of John Drew, but he was indubitably the son of Mrs. John Drew.")

The Arch box-office receipts improved when the wandering Irishman rejoined the company. After giving 100 performances he visited New York, where, according to rumor, he indulged himself in barroom carousals. A sudden illness, reportedly brought on by these excesses, felled him on May 18, 1862, and three days later, at the age of thirty-four, he was dead. Louisa wrote of him toward the end of her life as coolly and detachedly as she wrote of her first two husbands:

"I don't think there are many persons surviving him now who remember him well, and he was worth remembering; one of the best actors I ever saw, in a long list of the most varied description. Had he lived to be forty-five, he would have been a great actor. But too early a success was his ruin; it left him nothing to do. Why should he study when he was assured on all sides (except my own) that he was as near perfection as was possible for man to be? So he finished his brief and brilliant career at thirty-four years of age, about the age when men generally study most steadily and aspire most ambitiously."

Louisa proved herself as effective backstage and in the business office as she was onstage, and the Arch prospered, ranking second only to Lester Wallack's New York Theatre. She maintained the resident-company system, as it prevailed in most major theaters, personally directing every production. She was a severe taskmistress. Arriving in a glass-enclosed brougham from the white-shuttered house at 119 North Ninth Street where she lived with her four children and her aging mother, she began rehearsals at ten a.m., ending them four hours later. The actors were then expected to spend the rest of the afternoon studying their scripts. The curtain rose at eight and there was a performance every evening except Sunday.

The nucleus of "Mrs. Drew's Stock Company" did not change much from season to season, but Louisa often engaged celebrated outsiders to adorn a cast. Edwin Forrest, Edwin Booth, Fanny Davenport, Charlotte Cushman, Joseph Jefferson, to name but a few, all trod the boards under Louisa Drew's management. A performance of *Macbeth* starring John Wilkes Booth took place on March 13, 1863, two years before he assassinated Lincoln. Louisa treasured a letter the President wrote to her, dated June 25, 1864:

Madam, Please accept my thanks for the invitation given me to attend the Arch Street Theatre during my recent visit to Philadelphia—I also beg your pardon for having long delayed the acknowledgment.

Yours tr.

A. Lincoln.

With the exception of the fragile Louisa, each Drew child joined the Arch company soon after entering adolescence. They would have done so earlier had not their mother compelled them to experience at least a primary-school education, such as she herself had never had. The first child to go on the stage was Georgie, a gay, radiant blonde with enormous blue eyes and a natural comic sense. In 1872, when fifteen years old, she made her debut at the Arch, playing a minor role in a comedy entitled *The Ladies' Battle*. The following year it was John's turn. His introductory vehicle consisted of a one-act farce, *Cool As a Cucumber*, by the British humorist W. Blanchard Jerrold. To give him confidence, his mother took a walk-on part. The gesture proved superfluous. Her eighteen-year-old son exhibited such cocky self-assurance that she felt constrained to ad lib a couple of lines of admonition. "What a dreadful young man!" she exclaimed, to the delight of the knowing audience. "I wonder what he will be like when he grows up."

John incurred his mother's further displeasure by his antics off-stage. Between the prompter's box and the orchestra conductor's podium ran a speaking tube. One evening John filled it with face powder. As the orchestra was about to strike up the overture, he decoyed the prompter away from his post and blew through the tube. The conductor's sudden ghostliness brought gales of laughter from both musicians and audience. But Mrs. John Drew was not amused.

Sidney White or Drew was the last of the brood to take to the stage. He also became adept at pool and billiards and enriched himself as a poolroom hustler. Lying in wait for unskilled players, he would fleece them by professing to be a feeble novice, losing small bets to them the first few games, then proposing higher stakes. He usually walked off with a bundle.

The fragile Louisa Drew married an actor from Boston, Charles Mendum, whom her mother briefly employed as an assistant manager. He was also heir to a banking fortune. Louisa bore two children, Edmund and Georgie Drew Mendum, who became a musical-comedy performer.

Of Mrs. John Drew's many attainments the most surprising was her impeccable status in starchy Philadelphia society. Despite a pro-

fession which was widely regarded as Satan's snare, despite three husbands—two of them notorious topers—a divorce and a son of doubtful legitimacy (not to mention the senior Drew's Adine, whom she
adopted), she commanded a deference accorded to the city's most rep-
utable citizens. Both her children and the members of her company
referred to her, without mockery, as "the Duchess." A younger actress,
Clara Morris, left this portrait: "What a handsome, masterful young
creature she must have been in the days when she was playing the
dashing Lady Gay, the tormenting Lady Teazle, and all the swarm
of arrant coquettes! Her high features, her air of gentle breeding, the
touch of hauteur in her manner, must have given the same zest to
the admiration of her lovers that the faint nip of frost in the autumn
air gives to the torpid blood. And, good heavens! what an amount of
work fell to the lot of the stately gentlewoman! . . . She was always
a wonderful disciplinarian; hers was said to be the last of those
greenrooms that used to be considered schools of good manners. Some
women descend to bullying to maintain their authority—not so Mrs.
John Drew. Her armor was a certain chill austerity of manner, her
weapon a sharp sarcasm, while her strength lay in her self-control,
her self-respect."

Under the Drew matriarchy the household exemplified the Victorian proprieties. Mrs. Drew never permitted her daughters to receive a male visitor unchaperoned. Their admirers had to converse
within range of the Duchess' frosty gaze while she sat on the opposite
side of the parlor and, in Georgie's phrase, "snowed on us."

On Sunday, books, games, even sewing were taboo. An exception was a ponderous and pious work, *The Spirit of the Missions*,
which Grandmother Kinloch never wearied of rereading. The family
attended St. Stephen's Episcopal Church, occupying a pew reserved
for it. By maternal decree Georgie taught Sunday school at St.
Stephen's.

One weekend in the autumn of 1875 there burst upon this sedate
and godly menage a spirited, dazzlingly handsome young actor, recently arrived from England, who wore a monocle and a silk topper
and spoke with an Oxonian accent. His assumed name was Maurice
Barrymore.

2

"The Most Effulgent Man . . ."

H ERBERT Arthur Chamberlain Hunter Blyth was born during the month of September 1839 (exact date unrecorded) at Amritsar in the northern Punjab. His father, like his grandfather, had served under the British government in India. John Blyth had been a warrant officer in the Bengal Army until he died in his fiftieth year at Allahabad, leaving a totally destitute widow and eight children. The eldest of those children was Herbert's father, William Edward Blyth. At the age of sixteen William went to work as a civil assistant in the survey of India.

Herbert's mother, Charlotte Matilda Chamberlain, was only sixteen when she married. She bore Herbert ten years later and died soon after. His father eventually married Mrs. Sarah Hunter, a widow of Irish Catholic extraction. Herbert's baptism took place on June 13, 1852, at Fort Agra, where he spent the next several years, a good deal of them behind defensive sandstone walls seventy feet high. Among the familiar sights of his boyhood were the white marble Pearl Mosque, which the Shah Jahan erected inside the fort, the Jahangiri Palace and the matchless jewel of imperial Indian architecture, Jahan's Taj Mahal. In later life Herbert would enchant his friends and family with descriptions of these marvels and of the mystery, magic and violence he had witnessed in India, embroidering the recital with figments of his soaring imagination. He went so far as to claim

14

his mother delivered him in the dungeon of the old fort, built by the Emperor Akbar, that being the safest refuge against a threatened attack by Sikh insurgents. His parents raised him on goat's milk, he also maintained, out of respect for the Hindu sanctification of the cow. This nourishment, he pretended to believe, partly explained the peculiarities of his own progeny.

Herbert Blyth was expected to follow his antecedents into the Indian Civil Service and though the prospect bored him, he dutifully began to study for the qualifying examination. Scarlet fever intervened. An older sister, Eva, meanwhile had married into the influential Wace family. Her brother-in-law, the Reverend Henry Wace, was a prebendary of Canterbury Cathedral (of which he later became dean) and when Herbert recovered, he advised him to study law. The youth complied and again endured boredom, yet passed his bar examinations. But he never practiced. What he longed to do was act.

In London, at loose ends, he resumed boxing as a middleweight and in 1872 won the Marquis of Queensberry Cup, awarded annually to the best amateur boxer in any class. At Windsor that year he also managed, to the dismay of the Blyths and the Waces, to obtain a part in *Cool As a Cucumber*, the same comedy in which John Drew would make his bow the following year.

A chance encounter in Brighton, not long after, fortified Herbert's determination to pursue a theatrical career. Sauntering along the boardwalk one evening, he came upon an elderly comedian, Charles Vandenhoff, exchanging hot words with a pair of ruffians. Vandenhoff had a pretty young girl on his arm and the ruffians were trying to take her away from him by force. Without so much as wrinkling his sleeves, the amateur boxing champion of England knocked their heads together and sent them flying.

The grateful old actor invited his rescuer to join him and his fetching companion at dinner, and in the course of a convivial evening Blyth confided his ambition. Vandenhoff not only exhorted him to persist, but offered him a berth in his own stock company. Starting with the role of Cool in Dion Boucicault's *London Assurance*, Blyth toured the provinces for two years under Vandenhoff's management. To spare his family further shame, he adopted a pseudonym, retaining Herbert as a middle name and preceding it with Maurice, probably for euphony.

Concerning the source of the surname there have been several conflicting versions. Both of Maurice's sons, John and Lionel, would claim it to have been their paternal grandmother's maiden name. Mrs. Blyth, however, was born a Chamberlain. Maurice's daughter, Ethel, would promulgate a genealogical myth of her own—to wit, that she was descended from a sixteenth-century buccaneer, Sir Philip Blythe. According to what John told Gene Fowler, his father took the name from an old playbill exhibited in the foyer of London's Haymarket Theatre. A "Mr. Barrymore" did perform at both the Haymarket and the Drury Lane theaters during the late eighteenth and early nineteenth centuries. His real name was not Barrymore either, but William Henry Blewitt. Again, John Barrymore, talking to an *American Magazine* ghost writer, doubtless with tongue in cheek, traced his ancestry to the Earls of Barrymore, a succession of Georgian rakehells. He embossed his silverware and other accouterments with what purported to be his ancestral crest—a crowned serpent regnant on a golden field. But the device was conceived and sketched by none other than John. No connection whatever existed between Blyths and Barrymores, though the earls' wild antics, their love of sport and their lavish amateur theatricals must have struck a sympathetic chord in the frolicsome Herbert Blyth if he chanced to have read about them. Their biographer, John Robert Robinson, prefaced his chronicle thus:

"I record the doings of this curious family in no sympathetic spirit, nor would I have undertaken what has proved a most laborious task did I not think some good might be effected by this disastrous example of folly and extravagance."

The earls were profligate spenders and gamblers, patrons of the track and ring. Richard Barry, the seventh Earl, founded the Bothering Club, devoted solely to practical jokes. Before he reached his majority he built on the ancestral estate at Wargrave-on-Thames a 400-seat theater considered the loveliest, most luxurious in all Britain, and a scarcely less sumptuous one in London's Savile Row. For a while Blewitt alias Barrymore belonged to the peer's private troupe. The seventh Earl squandered £300,000, exclusive of gambling debts, before he was killed in an accident at the age of twenty-one when a gun went off in his face. Henry, the eighth Earl, turned out to be equally reckless.

It may well have amused Herbert Blyth to borrow the name of such devil-may-care roisterers.

Vandenhoff brought his company to America in the spring of 1875, but the tour he had planned never came off, for lack of enough bookings. He acted without his company wherever he could find a theater willing to employ him and, finding few, returned to England, leaving his protégé to fend for himself.

Maurice was down to his last cent before he finally persuaded Augustin Daly, a playwright and producer, to give him a chance at acting. A Boston benefit performance of Daly's melodrama *Under the Gaslight* introduced Maurice Barrymore to an American audience. It also featured a spectacular innovation, often to be imitated, that raised a storm of gasps, boos, hisses and applause. In the climactic scene the leering villain lashed an ally of the hero (played by Maurice) to a railroad track while offstage the whistle of an approaching locomotive grew shriller. Then, just as the locomotive chuffed into view, the heroine snatched the intended victim from the jaws of death.

Maurice's single Boston performance sufficed to satisfy Daly, who engaged him first for his road company and a few months later for his resident Fifth Avenue Theatre company. At this period of his career, when he was twenty-seven, the Briton's chief assets as both actor and boulevardier consisted of an unshakable poise, magnificent looks and a lightning wit. Standing five feet eleven inches tall and weighing 170 pounds, he had an ideal athlete's physique, lightly built but powerful, broad-shouldered and narrow-hipped, enhanced when he chose to dress conventionally (which was infrequently) by such sartorial elegance as London's best clothiers had been able to provide. "In romantic costume or in evening dress on the stage he had the grace of a panther," wrote the playwright Augustus Thomas. "On the street or in the club or coffee-house he was negligent and loungy and deplorably indifferent to his attire. In the theatre a queen could be proud of his graceful attention. Outside, a prizefighter or a safe-blower was of absorbing interest to him unless some savant was about to discuss classic literature or French romance."

With his Apolloesque profile, wavy, silken locks worn long, his sensual brooding mouth and cleft chin, Maurice could overwhelm almost any woman he fancied, and he fancied many. "To look upon, to watch, to listen to Maurice Barrymore in a congenial part is to behold nature in her liveliest temper of pleasantness," raved Amy Leslie, the Chicago *News* drama critic. "He is about as near a desirable man to see across the footlights as the stage shall ever grant us."

Nine months after Maurice began performing under Daly's aegis the playbill outside the Fifth Avenue Theatre proclaimed:

"Mr. Daly has pleasure in introducing Mr. EDWIN BOOTH, for the First Time in this Theatre, and for the First Time in New York since 2 years. Monday Evening, Oct. 25, 1875, will be presented, after elaborate and costly preparation, Shakespeare's Tragic Play, in 5 acts, entitled HAMLET! With Mr. Edwin Booth as Hamlet, Prince of Denmark and the following very strong distribution of the other characters . . ."

Maurice Barrymore was cast as Laertes and John Drew, who had been a Daly regular for almost a year, as Rosencrantz. Of the latter the prestigious critic of the New York *Tribune*, William Winter, reported that he "evidently had an engagement with a friend after the performance, so hurried was his speech and so evident his desire to get through with his part." Winter ignored Maurice altogether.

The two young novices took to each other, and when the run of the play ended, John brought Maurice back home with him to Philadelphia. The dashing stranger did not impress the Duchess favorably. She considered him a fop, a poseur and, as an actor, beneath notice. But Georgie, who was then nineteen, by no means shared her mother's antipathy, and when upon short acquaintance Maurice proposed to her, she eagerly accepted. Despite persisting maternal opposition, they were married on New Year's Eve of 1876 and went to live and act in New York. When, a year later, Georgie became pregnant, Mrs. Drew relented to the extent of sheltering the struggling couple, who between them had seldom earned more than $60 a week, but her glacial attitude toward her son-in-law never thawed. She spoke to him no more than necessary, and Maurice addressed her like royalty as "Ma'am."

The Barrymores christened their first child, born on April 28, 1878, Lionel. "Yes, I'm proud of him," said Maurice when a friend congratulated him. "The newspapers always accuse me of taking things from the French. This is one time they cannot say that." By the following winter Georgie was pregnant again and obliged to drop out of a small road company her husband had organized with another actor, Frederick Warde, and return alone to Philadelphia. The company's only production was Victorien Sardou's *Diplomacy*, which had scored an immense success when Lester Wallack presented it in New York. The principal barnstormers included John Drew, one Benjamin Porter and a pretty substitute for Georgie named Ellen Cummings. It was very nearly Maurice's last tour.

In the frontier town of Marshall, Texas, whose Opera House they had just played, the troupers were waiting at the railroad depot for a train to take them to their next destination, Texarkana. Barry-

and Maids as They Are, by a Mrs. Inchbald. "Don't go to bed, John," commanded that redoubtable woman, handing him the script. "You play this tonight." His role, Mr. Bronzley, was an exceptionally long one, but by dint of studying it for eight hours without so much as a catnap and attending a ten a.m. rehearsal, he sailed through the night's performance, letter-perfect.

The second Barrymore baby, a girl, made her appearance at the Ninth Street house on August 15, 1879. She was named Ethel after the heroine of one of her father's favorite novels, Thackeray's *The Newcomes*.

Financial disaster, meanwhile, was threatening the Arch Street Theatre. Public tastes had changed, but Mrs. Drew had failed to change her policies with them. Philadelphia audiences were growing tired of seeing the same resident actors so often; they wanted more visiting stars. Too late Mrs. Drew painfully "concluded to follow the example of all the other theatres in the city, and ceased to have a stock company, and called the theatre a 'combination theatre'; but it never did so well as before. The public seemed to miss the old favorites and not to care for the new ones. I clung with such tenacity to the old customs that we were the last to take up *matinées*. There were two new theatres on Chestnut Street and one on Broad Street. They eventually became as one, having the same manager. Thus they and the old Walnut and new Park got all the best stars or combinations, and we were obliged to put up with what they kindly left."

She continued to manage the Arch, reluctantly making compromise after compromise. But profits steadily dwindled. At the same time the indomitable Duchess entered upon the period of her greatest personal triumph. As Mrs. Malaprop in Sheridan's *The Rivals*, with Joseph Jefferson playing Bob Acres, she toured the country for twelve seasons, traveling almost 20,000 miles, and became as closely identified with the role as Jefferson was with Rip Van Winkle. In the first performances at the Arch, Maurice portrayed Captain Absolute. But he never succeeded in conciliating his mother-in-law. She once vented her displeasure by handing him a copy of the play from which she had expunged all his lines. He retaliated with a gift of peanuts, a food he knew she abominated.

Maurice did not long remain on tour with *The Rivals*. Instead he moved effortlessly into the ranks of matinee idols, where at $300 a week he was among the highest-salaried performers of his day. Galaxies of leading ladies wanted him as their leading man, and he

more and Porter escorted Miss Cummings to the Statioı
lunchroom, the only one open at that hour. Drew stayed be
the hotel lobby. As the trio ate, they were visible from the ac
saloon, where Jim Currie, a two-gun badman with a knife
in his belt, sat swilling whiskey and itching for action. Des
reputation as the killer of at least six defenseless victims,
had been entrusted with the duties of both railroad engine
deputy sheriff. Upon glimpsing Ellen Cummings, he began
passing obscene remarks. Maurice sprang up and ordered him
his tongue.

"I can do any of you up," Currie bragged.

"I suppose you could with your pistol or knife," said M

"I'll do it with my bunch of fives," and Currie brandishec
Maurice shed his coat. "Then I'll have a go at you."

As the former boxer advanced, the desperado lost his ne
drew one of his guns. The bullet struck Maurice's upper arı
Porter, rushing to his aid, took a second bullet in the abdom
staggered out to the station platform and fell dead. Drew, hear
shots, ran into the lunchroom and grappled with Currie. Bef
killer could wrench himself free, the sheriff of Marshall a
disarmed his deputy and marched him off to jail.

The company stayed at the hotel several days while N
recuperated. The bullet had lodged in a back muscle, and ↑
doctor extracted it, Maurice announced: "Ill give it to my son
to cut his teeth on." (That the infant actually did teethe
bullet was, according to Lionel's memoirs, "another of those fi
about the Barrymores too happily told for me to deny at th
date.")

Currie was twice tried for murder, and both times Maur
turned to Marshall at his own expense to testify. In the first tı
jurors, eleven of whom were rumored to have committed m
accepted the gunslinger's plea of self-defense. A key witness
shooting, the lunchroom waiter who served the actors, had vaı
The second trial ended the same way. Yet rough justice prc
in the end. A year later, in New Mexico, Currie picked a quarrc
a man who happened to pack a gun, too, and was shot to deatł

John and Maurice got back to the Ninth Street house in
delphia, dog-tired and dispirited after a largely profitless tou
Diplomacy, at two o'clock on a winter morning. John's ı
opened the door to their knocking, a candle in one hand and
other, the script of an old English comedy, *Wives as They*

came to support such stars as Fanny Davenport in *As You Like It* and *Twelfth Night*, Rose Coghlan in Oscar Wilde's *A Woman of No Importance* and the fiery-haired Mrs. Leslie Carter in David Belasco's *The Heart of Maryland*, a melodrama of the Civil War wherein the Southern heroine, to save her Northern lover's life, scales a bell tower and silences the clapper, which is to signal his death, by clinging to it as it swings to and fro. Maurice's longest theatrical association was with Countess Bozenta Chlapowska, née Opid, known to American audiences as Helena Modjeska.

A native of Poland and once an ornament of Warsaw's Imperial Theatre, Modjeska had had to flee the country with her husband in 1876 because of his anti-Czarist liberalism. Drifting to Southern California, they joined a group of Polish émigrés in an attempt to establish a Utopian commune. Their doctrine embraced free love, in exemplification of which the Countess permitted herself a brief fling with Henryk Sienkiewicz, author of the historical novel *Quo Vadis*. The commune collapsed within a year and she resumed her profession at the California Theatre in San Francisco. Despite her Polish accent, she played Juliet and Ophelia with sensational success, then embarked on a triumphal cross-country tour, the Count now serving as her manager. She became the first star to travel in her own private railroad car.

Of Maurice Barrymore, whom she alternately pampered and upbraided, Modjeska later wrote that he was "one of those handsome men who have the rare gift of winning all hearts. . . . He was equally liked by men and women. Sentimental girls used to send him flowers, to his great amusement. . . . [He] was too intellectual to be a mere matinée idol."

Maurice never realized his potential. He shone mainly by the reflected light of the actress he supported rather than as a star in his own right. Indolence, among other deficiencies, marred his career. He often failed to study a role hard enough to master all the lines and when stuck during a performance would interpolate words of his own. "Barry," said Count Chlapowski reproachfully after an opening in New York, "you didn't speak your lines tonight."

"Oh, yes, I did," said the offender, "*my* lines."

He devoted a great deal of time and energy to drinking, revelry and the pursuit of women. Otis Skinner called him "the Bedouin of Broadway." Georgie, who had some of her mother's acerbity, was not deluded about her husband's behavior away from home. According to a frequently retold bit of Barrymore domestic history,

Maurice, returning one Sunday morning from a night of dissipation, encountered Georgie just leaving the house. "Where are you going, my dear?" he inquired.

"I am going to Mass," said she, "and you can go to hell."

Following another all-night bender, Maurice persuaded a fellow delinquent to accompany him home, hoping his presence would deflect Georgie's anger, but it only exacerbated it. "So you've brought your squarer with you, have you?" she said.

"No, my dear," Maurice replied, "my rounder."

The children, too, sometimes caught the rough side of their mother's tongue. During a birthday party for Uncle Jack Drew, at which he was to cut the cake with a sword he had worn on stage, John became so excited that he loudly broke wind, a lapse that reduced the gathering to awkward silence. "Very nice, my child," said his mother. "With a little more practice you'll be able to use the bathroom."

In the cafés and bars where show folk congregated, in theatrical clubs like New York's Players and Lambs, Maurice was surrounded by a coterie of affectionate, attentive colleagues. To the comedian Nat Goodwin, he was "the most effulgent man whom I have ever met. A brain that scintillated sparks of wit that Charles Lamb or Byron might envy, a tongue capable of lashing into obscurity any one who dared enter into verbal conflict with him (yet always merciful to his adversary), with the wit of Douglas Jerrold without the cynicism, the courage of a lion, the gentleness of a saint—there you have but the faint conception of this child of Bohemia."

Maurice became as famous for his repartee as for his acting. It is doubtful that any of his contemporaries, with the exception of Oscar Wilde, uttered so many widely circulated bons mots. If not always hilarious in themselves, his style of delivery, languid, sonorous, mock lordly, made them seem so. A sense of fun rather than malice prompted his sharpest sallies, which in another mouth might have given offense, as when Steele Mackaye, a playwright and actor of note, told him: "You'll never become a great actor unless you have a great sorrow or a harrowing experience," and Maurice riposted: "Then, my dear Steele, write me a play and I shall have both." Augustus Thomas attested, "I never heard him speak a line that left a scar. . . . His smile and manner, true declarations of his intent, made the most acid speeches amiable."

At the Lambs, viewing a new member who had more money than charm, Maurice remarked: "He looks like a sin I wouldn't commit."

Edwin Booth and Lawrence Barrett formed an alliance as co-stars to double the price of orchestra tickets, which was then $1.50. At about the same time the Players hung a full-length portrait of Booth in the role of Bulwer-Lytton's Richelieu, right arm uplifted, three fingers extended heavenward. Upon first seeing it, Maurice drawled: "Ah, there's the old man raising the price to three dollars."

Joseph Jefferson donated to the Lambs Club a painting from his own amateur brush, depicting a landscape in summer, the actors' worst season before air-conditioning, when the heat forced most theater managers to curtail the run of a play, however successful.* "Summer," murmured Maurice as he inspected the landscape through his monocle, "isn't as bad as it's painted."

A pompous millionaire, up from the slums through shady business methods, was boasting to Maurice: "I am a self-made man, Mr. Barrymore. Yes, sir, a self-made man."

Maurice trained the full power of his luminous eyes upon the braggart. "Who interrupted you?"

Under an iron-clad rule of the Lambs, theater critics could not cross the threshold. Maurice tried to make an exception for James Huneker and got him as far as the door.

"Look here, Barry, this won't do," Huneker reminded him. "I can't go in. No dramatic critics are allowed."

"That's all right, old chap, go in," said Maurice. "No one ever mistook you for a critic."

Upon being introduced in a café to a critic who had consistently disparaged his performances, Maurice feigned surprise. "Oh, you're the one?" he said. "Ah, well, now that I have seen you, all resentment ceases. Have a drink."

During a later engagement in London Maurice was sharing a hansom cab with a critic on the way to the theater when he spied a process-server waiting for him at the stage door. Maurice shoved the critic out of the cab, shouting: "Run, Barrymore, run," and made off in the opposite direction.

A woman for whom he ordered absinthe in a café complained of the taste. "It's like something I had when I was a child," she said. "I mean it's like paregoric."

"Yes," Maurice agreed, "absinthe is the paregoric of second childhood."

A friend reproved him for refusing to attend E. H. Sothern's

---

* Among the early efforts to cool theaters was to keep huge electric fans blowing over cakes of ice.

Hamlet, which the tragedian was playing for the first time at the Garden Theatre in New York. "Go and sit out only one act," the friend suggested.

"My boy," Maurice replied, "I never encourage vice."

In a Broadway barroom Maurice fell to quarreling with a visiting Texan. "If I had you in Texas," the latter blustered, "I'd blow your head off."

"Then your courage is a matter of latitude," retorted Maurice.

Steele Mackaye held a table of Lambs Club diners enthralled with a reading of his latest drama. Maurice seemed to be the most enthusiastic listener of all. At the end of the recital he rapped his knife against his plate, applauded wildly and bellowed: "Bravo! A hundred times bravo! Mackaye, you ought to have been an actor."

Maurice detested puns to such a degree that people who uttered them in his presence risked physical punishment. He was tippling with friends at the Morton House café one night when a pugnacious vaudevillian known as Robby dropped in, already crocked. At sight of Maurice he launched into a litany of imagined grievances, concluding with a threat to tear Maurice apart.

"Robby," said Maurice coolly, "behave yourslf. You appear to be burying a lot of dead tonight."

"That's all right," said the vaudevillian, grinning idiotically. "I'll Barrymore."

Maurice gazed at the culprit with an expression of utter disgust. "Even the excuse of drunkenness is no condonation for such an unspeakable lingual profanation," he said, caught him around the waist, slammed him face down on a table and spanked him.

When finally allowed to regain his feet, Robby stared ruefully at his chastiser. "Maurice Barrymore," he said, "I wouldn't have your disposition for all the world."

A new entry on the flyleaf of the Barrymore family Bible announced the birth of "John Sidney son of Georgiana Blyth Philadelphia Feb. 15, 1882." The birth registration, however, gave the date February 14. Considering the number of feminine hearts that John Sidney would flutter, it is pleasant to accept the latter date—St. Valentine's Day.

3

Exits and Entrances

═══════

Long before John's birth the Duchess' Ninth Street house had
become too populous for comfort when every member of the
Barrymore-Drew clan was in town at the same time, what with Grandmother Kinloch, now in her dotage and ministered to by Adine
(known as "Aunt Tibby"), Maurice and Georgie Barrymore, John
Drew ("Uncle Jack"), Sidney Drew ("Uncle Googan") and a
platoon of servants, comprising Lily Garrett, Mrs. Drew's dresser;
Lily's mother, who did the laundry; her daughter-in-law Kitty, the
children's nurse; a cook and a maid, who, like every cook and maid
Mrs. Drew ever employed, were Irish and, whatever their real names,
addressed as "Mary Aggie."

The Duchess leased a larger house at 2008 Columbia Avenue,
where John Barrymore was born, but this, too, proved inadequate
and she soon made a second move to 140 North Twelfth Street, a
three-story red-brick structure which Georgie dubbed "The Tomb of
the Capulets" because it stood opposite the studio of a tombstone
sculptor. Ethel Barrymore would remember it as "enormous—with
large rooms and cavernous halls and most alarming echoes. I can
see now the Victorian landscapes on the wall, the gold-colored sofa,
the music box on the table which Grandmother magnificently wound
up so that it might unwind 'The Carnival of Venice,' and the square
piano upon which were pictures of Edwin Forrest and his wife. There

was a sturdy solemnity about the place which made me seem very tiny . . . on the second floor there was the sitting room, then the bathroom, and then . . . our playroom. Then there was the big front bedroom which was a little frightening to pass, for in it dwelt my great-grandmother, who was ninety-five. . . . Then there was the long flight up to the third floor, rather dark at night. . . ."

That flight, which led to the boys' bedroom, intimidated John during his early childhood, and when ordered to mount it, he would fortify his courage by muttering, "You can't hurt me. I have a wonderful power!"

The family fortunes fluctuated violently according to the earnings of its acting members and the receipts of the Arch Street Theatre, and at times the money ran out altogether. While watching a child of his own play "Bean-porridge hot, bean-porridge cold," John told the friend at his side: "I used to play that game with Ethel when I was a child, and it recalls to my mind how hungry I used to be in those days when we were so poor and often with not enough to eat. And when the last words were said with the hands extended, 'Bean-porridge in the pot, nine days old,' I used to feel as though I were pushing away with my hands the hunger that I felt, for there was sometimes no porridge in the pot for us, even *one* day old!"

Maurice turned to playwriting. His first effort, in 1880, was *A Bitter Expiation*, a blood-and-thunder melodrama that never reached the stage. The following year he translated a French play under the title *Honor*, took it to London and offered it to the Court Theatre as his own original work, a deception that was exposed before rehearsals began. Rewritten by another playwright and properly credited to the French authors, *Honor* ran for 100 performances, though critics condemned it as "dreary" and "repulsive." Next, during the year John was born, came *Homeward Bound* in collaboration with a Julian Magnus. This as well as *Blood Will Tell* and the libretto of a comic opera, *The Robbers of the Rhine*, with music by one Charles Puerner, garnered neither critical laurels nor substantial profits. Maurice planned to dramatize Victor Hugo's *Les Misérables*, but was soon discouraged by the lack of enthusiasm among New York showmen. "You mean none of them will produce it?" a friend asked him. "Produce it?" said Maurice. "They can't even pronounce it."

He suffered his worst critical drubbing as a playwright with *Roaring Dick*, a melodrama whose title role he took himself, but the assault failed to dim his sense of humor. Following the closing performance, he ran into one of the other actors, Harry Bagge, at the

Lambs Club. After chaffing him awhile, he said: "You shouldn't mind me, old chap. I've always been your friend. I was with you in *Roaring Dick*, and for that I love you. For that I regard you as one of my best friends."

"Why are you so fond of me just because I was in *Roaring Dick?*" Bagge asked.

"Because, old man, you're my only excuse."

For Modjeska, Maurice rewrote *A Bitter Expiation* and entitled it *Nadjezda*. Laid in Poland, it revolved around the machinations of a lecherous, malevolent political leader to whom the heroine gives herself to save her lover, then commits suicide. Sworn to vengeance, her daughter (meant to be played by the same actress), whom the villain also lusts after, pretends to yield and stabs him to death. A tryout took place in Baltimore on February 8, 1884, followed four days later by the première at New York's Star Theatre. The double feminine role, with its opportunities for flamboyant histrionics, tempted a number of leading ladies besides Modjeska, among them Emily Rigl, who performed it at London's Haymarket Theatre with the author as the hero and Herbert Beerbohm Tree as the villain. In both America and England the critical consensus was generally favorable. In an Australian production the second Tyrone Power impersonated the hero.

Maurice sent a copy of *Nadjezda* to Sarah Bernhardt, who kept it for two years before returning it without comment. Soon after, she appeared in Sardou's *La Tosca* (which Puccini later converted into an opera). It was now Maurice's turn to cry "Plagiarism!" for the basic plot of *La Tosca* was similar to his. He filed suit against Sardou. The reaction of the "Divine Sarah," as friends reported it to him, was to remark that an obscure source might indeed suggest the germ of an idea to a great playwright; Sardou was such a playwright and his adversary a nobody.

Said Maurice: "I hold a man no less a thief if he steals from his own hat rack my cane, which I have confidently placed there, and proceeds to build upon it an umbrella."

Nothing came of the suit.

The deepest emotional attachment of John Barrymore's formative years, perhaps of his whole life, was to his grandmother, whose grandchildren called her "Mum Mum." During the frequent absences of their parents on tour, she served as their surrogate mother. The rigorous demands she made on them, her insistence on decorum, her outward reserve never concealed from them the essential sweetness of her nature. "She was fond of me," John recalled, "fonder, I think I may say, than of any of her other grandchildren." He would sit spellbound at her knee while she reminisced about the vicissitudes of life on the road, of the theaters she had graced and the notable actors she had played opposite. "To my mind, my grandmother typified everything that an actress should be." For John, Ethel and Lionel some of the most memorable moments of their childhood were when Mum Mum allowed them to watch from her private box or from the wings at the Arch a Forrest, a Jefferson, a Booth—a thrill often capped after the performance by the sight of such legendary personages conversing in Mum Mum's drawing room.

Between Maurice Barrymore's out-of-town theatrical commitments and his sprees he found little time to spend at home. Fond of his family though he was, he became more and more a transient whom nobody knew when to expect, a fascinating transient to his children as he regaled them with readings, recitations and jokes, with gripping tales of his boyhood in India, of the exotic and dangerous fauna, of mutinies, strange customs and religious wonder-workers. In his recollections of gurus and magicians he imparted to John a sense of the occult which deepened as he grew older.

Maurice doted on animals, all kinds of animals, and as he journeyed through the country by train, he acquired a motley collection that crowded baggage cars and obliged him to put up at squalid hotels because no decent ones would admit his pets. They came to number seventy-eight and included kittens, rabbits, mice, beavers, coyotes, mountain lions, weasels, two skunks whom Maurice named Minnehaha and Molly Bawn, seven Japanese spaniels, a black chow, two huge Eskimo dogs, Kimo and Rita, an enormously valuable prize Clydesdale terrier, Belle of Clyde, and a bear who opened beer bottles with his teeth and quaffed the brew. When a friend asked him what he intended to do with them all, Maurice replied: "Why, bless their hearts, just make every one of them happy."

Belle was his favorite. A young actress, Virginia Tracy, who traveled from New York to San Francisco during the summer of 1893 with a road-company production of Bronson Howard's hit *Aristocracy*, of which Maurice was the star, recounted:

"The trip was a horror of dirt, and heat, and alkali. There weren't even train window-screens in those days. Crossing the desert, everybody's skin got discolored and sandpapered with alkali—the suit I wore on the train smelled so of it that it had to be thrown away. There was one member of the company, however, whose toilet was always carefully made. This was Belle Barrymore.

"Every morning, while the rest of us were still yawning and throwing paper dishes out of the windows, a table would be brought forth and set up in front of Mr. Barrymore; Belle would be placed on it. Then would begin the hour-long business of combing that curling silk, which even twenty-four hours had matted into one snarl. There was never anything like the patience of it, the infinite subtlety of little careful strokes."

Eventually Maurice housed his zoo on a rundown Staten Island farm he had bought. An unknown arsonist set fire to the barns. Only Belle escaped alive. Maurice wept inconsolably.

Another of Maurice's passions was baseball. When in New York, if no matinee intervened, he would board the "El" for the Polo Grounds and pass the afternoon, jacket slung over his arm, shirt collar open, munching peanuts from a bag. He was a perfervid Giant fan. After one of their defeats, which Ethel, then seven, witnessed with him, he paced the El platform, arms raised to heaven, crying: "God, how could you do this to me, how could you?"

Parental responsibility seldom weighed heavily on Maurice. As often as not, he would forget to send money home from the road, if he had not already squandered his salary on his pleasures. He once took the infant John to the Lambs Club and checked him in the cloakroom while he sought relaxation at the bar.

An unlooked-for and, to Mum Mum, appalling spiritual influence was exerted upon Georgie by Modjeska. As "leading lady to the star" (to use the then technical designation of Georgie's theatrical status), she admired everything about the magnetic Polish actress, including her ardent Catholicism, and upon returning from a tour she whisked Ethel and Lionel off to a Catholic church and had them and herself re-baptized. Ethel saw to John's conversion when he was a little older, and he served as an altar boy. Though divorce and remarriage in his early manhood would automatically excommunicate him, he would continue to wear religious medallions on a gold chain around his neck and in his various homes burn votive candles before a statuette of the Virgin Mary.

Maurice remained a lapsed Episcopalian. For a time he evinced a mild interest in Christian Science. When a doctor, attacking the validity of that religion, argued: "I suppose you would throw physic to the dogs," Maurice retorted: "Not to good dogs." A fellow guest at a dinner table in San Francisco expressed surprise that he professed no religion. Maurice hastened to disabuse him. "Yes, sir, I most certainly do—but I'm afraid God doesn't know it."

In 1885 a substantial inheritance from an aunt enabled Maurice to take Georgie and the children to London. They stayed there two years, during which Maurice starred in *Diplomacy*, *A Woman of No Importance* and his own *Nadjezda*. On fashionable St. John's Wood Road he rented a spacious house and garden standing behind a high brick wall, and installed cages full of dogs, birds and monkeys. The children's rooms at the rear of the third floor commanded a distant view of the famous old Lord's cricket ground and they would watch championship matches through field glasses. A red-headed young woman named Polly took charge of them. Maurice swore she looked like the bewitching American actress Mary Anderson, but was even more beautiful. On Sunday afternoon Georgie presided over a salon attended by actors, artists and writers. "Everything about those two years was magical," Ethel remembered. "Those London days are clear and shiny in my mind."

Lines from plays were common currency in the Barrymore household. If left to themselves, the children would stay up all night—a family friend called them "owlingales"—and at the ordained bedtime Georgie or Maurice would quote Lady Macbeth: "Stand not upon the order of your going, but go at once." Or if they bolted their food, it was Friar Laurence warning Romeo: "Wisely and slow: they stumble that run fast." A precept issued to Pauline, the heroine of Bulwer-Lytton's comedy *The Lady of Lyons*, had a special application to Ethel. Acutely shy as a child, she tended to cast her eyes down in the presence of visitors. "Look up, Pauline!" her parents would admonish her. One Sunday afternoon a particularly glittering flock of celebrities thronged the drawing room of the St. John's Wood house, and when tea was served, Ethel passed the sandwiches and cakes, keeping her eyes fixed upon the floor all the while. As she approached a large man with a long, oval, fleshy face, Georgie called to her: "Look up, Pauline!" Obeying, Ethel beheld Oscar Wilde. She shrieked, dropped the plate and fled.

What became a family saying was first heard at a children's party Lionel went to. When Polly came to take him home, his small host shouted across the room: "Barrymore, you're fetched!"

The children's language, like Maurice's, was at times salty, and when they visited their strait-laced British kin, the Blyths and the Waces, it shocked them. Georgie's quick-wittedness somewhat softened the effect. "Maurice," she said, "I'm always telling you not to let those children into the coachman's quarters."

By the time the Barrymores returned to Philadelphia, Maurice's inheritance had been exhausted. Both parents rejoined the Modjeska company and were soon earning enough money to avoid serious privation. In line with Georgie's insistence that the children attend Catholic institutions, Lionel's elementary education, already begun at London's Gilmore School, continued at St. Aloysius Academy in Yonkers, New York (whose graduates, it was said, entered either the priesthood or the Eastern Baseball League), then Mount St. Vincent nearby, where Eugene O'Neill was a classmate, and in 1889 Seton Hall in South Orange, New Jersey. Ethel was enrolled in a Philadelphia convent school, the Academy of Notre Dame, where she studied music and resolved to be a concert pianist. One Sunday at home she played a Beethoven sonata for her father. Tears sprang into his eyes. She must go to Vienna, he declared, she must study with the great teacher Theodor Leschetizky. No prospect could have delighted Ethel more. But Maurice never mentioned it again.

John went as a day pupil to the convent's kindergarten annex supervised by a Sister Vincent, a merry, rosy-cheeked little woman whom he would remember with tenderness. All three children endured a good deal of derision at the hands of their schoolmates because of the English accents they had picked up during their two years abroad.

Though barely five years old, John showed a proclivity for sketching. His subjects were mainly demons and monsters. When Sister Vincent asked him why, he said he saw them in his dreams.

In a fury kindled by the taunts of a classmate, John hurled a hard-boiled egg at him, smiting him on the ear. "One day you might become an actor yourself," said Sister Vincent, "and an egg may come back to you." As punishment, she restricted him to an empty schoolroom for the rest of the day and gave him an enormous, heavily illustrated book to reflect upon. The punishment missed its mark. The book was Dante's *Inferno* with Gustave Doré's grisly illustrations, and they inspired John. "It opened up wide fields for me, things I had never dreamed of," he recalled. "It made such a lasting impression upon me that when I followed my own bent some years later and took up drawing, I tried to draw like Doré. And this incident, I think, accounts for much that is macabre in my character."

The last decade of the century brought manifold sorrow to the

Duchess. Returning to the Arch Street Theatre in 1892 after months on the road as Mrs. Malaprop, she found the box-office receipts so meager that she decided to abandon her managership and confine herself to such acting with other companies as her seventy-two years would permit.

The North Twelfth Street house had gradually emptied. Both Grandmother Kinloch and Aunt Tibby were dead. Maurice and Georgie had moved with John to New York, while Ethel continued her convent studies and Lionel remained at Mount St. Vincent. Uncle Googan, having acquired a solid reputation as a comedian, married Gladys Rankin, the actress daughter of McKee and Kitty Rankin, a distinguished acting couple. John Drew, already acclaimed for the suavity of his performance in drawing-room comedy ("He doesn't act, he just behaves," wrote one critic), had also married an actress, Josephine Baker—"Aunt Dodo" to his niece and nephews—and gone to New York, where they kept a suite in the Sherman Square Hotel at Seventy-first Street and Broadway.

Maurice and Georgie first occupied a brownstone house at 1564 Broadway* and sent John to Seton Hall, where Lionel had studied for a year. John continued to sketch at every opportunity. Lionel, too, acquired some skill as a draftsman and years later, as an etcher and painter, developed an artistry far superior to his brother's. Neither John nor Lionel showed any other aptitude except for sports. Their scholastic grades hovered around the average.

Like Lionel, John stayed only two semesters at Seton Hall, perhaps because the tuition strained his parents' finances. He attended New York public schools for a while. Among his classmates at P.S. 43 was Raoul Walsh, a future film director. The Walsh family had a well-stocked library in their Riverside Drive house, and John passed blissful hours there, browsing.

Following a successful run at the Madison Square Theatre in a thriller called *Captain Swift*, Maurice met a young dramatist who would not only become a devoted friend, but would write parts specially tailored to his style in four plays, all of them hits. This was Augustus Thomas, whose output during his long, prosperous career totaled sixty-one plays. The meeting took place in the office of an entrepreneur named William Smythe, who proposed to produce a play by Thomas, *The Burglar*, and wanted Maurice in the lead.

* On the site of which, in 1913, Martin Beck, head of the Orpheum vaudeville circuit, built one of the world's most famous vaudeville theaters— the Palace.

When introduced, Maurice held Thomas' hand in an iron grip and eyed him narrowly as if sizing up a boxing opponent. "Somewhat of a husky, eh?" he said and, still grasping Thomas' right hand, jabbed him playfully in the ribs. Thomas broke away, ducked and held up his fists. "Know something about that, do you?" said the former amateur boxing champion of England. Thomas recalled years later: "I have seen boys of ten begin acquaintance in similar pretense. That meeting characterized the intercourse between us that covered the next twelve years or more—the last of his active life."

The Barrymores' tenancy of 1564 Broadway was brief. Maurice's nomadic nature led him to maintain four separate addresses. When Georgie went on tour without him, he shared a Fourth Avenue flat with some other actors. On Twenty-eighth Street just off Broadway he kept a sparsely furnished hall bedroom solely as storage space for his costumes and props. To write plays, he preferred to use a room on Twenty-fifth Street near Broadway. When Georgie returned from the road, they took a hotel apartment, usually in the Sturtevant House at 1586 Broadway.

In 1893 Georgie contracted tuberculosis. On her doctor's advice she set out for the warm climate of Santa Barbara, California, accompanied by Ethel. During the voyage Ethel awoke one night to hear her mother crying over and over: "Oh, my poor kids, what will ever become of them?" Georgie died in Santa Barbara in July, and Ethel, not quite fourteen, took the coffin to Philadelphia for burial in the family plot in Greenwood Cemetery.

Wild grief, heightened no doubt by twinges of remorse, shook Maurice to the core. If eleven-year-old John did not appear as distraught as his father, it was perhaps because he had seen so little of his constantly barnstorming mother. "Of my mother I remember very little," he wrote years later.

Within a few months of the funeral Maurice found consolation in the arms of Mamie Floyd, the daughter of the stage manager at Wallack's Theatre. He married her without notifying his children. Ethel, whom he had sent back to the convent, learned of it from a newspaper clipping the mother superior showed her. ". . . it was years, really years, before I could take it in stride."

The following June, at fifteen, Ethel stepped onto a stage for the first time. From Montreal, where Mum Mum was again portraying Mrs. Malaprop under Sidney Drew's management, came word to join them. They cast her as Julia, "a young lady of fashion." "I had never known I was to go on the stage. I had thought I was going to be a great pianist. . . . But suddenly there was no money, no Arch Street Theatre, no house, and I must earn my living."

The Rivals had served as an introductory vehicle for Lionel, too, the year before when he was fifteen. The place was Kansas City and the role that of Thomas, the coachman, in a brief "front" scene— that is, played before a curtain—usually considered dispensable. When he got back to his boardinghouse room that night, he found a note on the dresser:

> My Dear Lionel: You must forgive your Uncle Sidney and me for not realizing that when Sheridan wrote the part of Thomas he had a much older actor in mind. We feel that we were very remiss in not taking cognizance of this—although we are both happy that you are not at the advanced age you would have to be in order to be good in this part.
>
> We think, therefore, that the play as a whole would be bettered by the elimination of the front scene and have decided to do without it after this evening's performance. Sincerely and with deep affection, your Grandmother,
>
> Mrs. Drew.

Far from feeling injured, Lionel rejoiced. He had no more desire to act than Ethel did, and for the next three years he studied happily at New York's Art Students League, with occasional modest theatrical stints as economic necessity dictated.

Not long after Georgie died, Mum Mum lost her other daughter, Louisa Mendum. "The Duchess" was the last to leave Philadelphia. John and Josephine Drew made room for her in their hotel apartment.

Years later nostalgia brought John Barrymore back to Philadelphia. He called at the Notre Dame kindergarten. Sister Vincent was still in charge. He flung his arms around her and gave her a hearty kiss. Too flustered to speak, she fled, fingering her rosary.

Disillusionment awaited John when he revisited the Tomb of the Capulets. "It had seemed such a wonderful place to me, and the rooms had been so big; but now it was all drab and dreary. I do not know of what substance those conventional white Philadelphia steps are made, but they were being washed by a slatternly woman, and they did not seem to get much cleaner in the process. Those three steps that Ethel, Lionel and I had jumped up and down on in our countless trips in and out of that house. John Drew had crossed them to see his mother. Grandmother, with her stately dignity, had left them to go to the theater. Jefferson, in his calls upon her, had walked there. . . . I went into the house and looked at the old rooms where I had played, and of which I had such deathless memories. They were cramped and fusty. . . . I did get back something of the personality of that wonderful old actress. Somehow I sensed the aura of Mrs. John Drew, even in that mean, shabby house. I felt something of her personality and austerity which she ever carried into the theater. . . ."

PART
II

NEW YORK AND
LONDON
1889–1901

4

Feeling Safe

=========

J OHN exhibited at an early age a waywardness not surprising in a son of Maurice Barrymore. On October 16, 1895, in his thirteenth year, Maurice delivered him to the preparatory-school division of Georgetown University, a Jesuit institution in Washington, D.C. The priest who greeted them, Father Richard, showed them through the various buildings. As they entered the gymnasium, John asked permission to test his skill on some horizontal bars. The priest readily granted it and John executed a neat handstand, forgetting what his pockets contained. Out tumbled a pair of brass knuckles, a pack of cigarettes and a half-pint flask of whiskey. Maurice was not greatly perturbed by this evidence of precocious turpitude, and the Jesuit fathers, while troubled, decided to admit the boy in the hope of reforming him. They failed.

One night, returning to his dormitory from a clandestine visit to Harvey's Old Oyster House, flushed with liquor, John proceeded to entertain his schoolmates with imitations of drunken actors. A preceptor interrupted the performance. "I suppose you know you're going fast to perdition," he said.

"No," John retorted, "but I'm sure I'm going back to New York."

He was right, though two and a half years elapsed before his final fall from grace.

Jack S. (for Sidney) Barrymore, as he then signed himself, achieved distinction in several areas. He was president of Georgetown's junior tennis team, an assistant editor of the school magazine, *The Academic*, and an outstanding student in the "English branches," scoring on his examinations as high as ninety-four and a half points out of a possible ninety-five.

The March 1897 issue of the magazine carried a short story by John; also a poem, "To Aurora," adapted from a translation of Ovid:

Aurora! Lovely Goddess of the Dawn,
Upon whose wings bright health and beauty borne
　　Sweep with delicious fragrance o'er the earth,
　　And gently waft to mankind joy and mirth.

Stay, heavenly Virgin, stay! Cannot our love
Constrain thee from our bower above?
　　Cannot our admiration of thy face
　　Prolong thy stay from thy celestial place?

Expectant nature hails thy bright approach,
And smiles all radiant at thy gentle touch.
　　On high the song-bird, fain thy face to see,
　　Pours forth his soul in maddening rhapsody.

How often have I wished that western night
Would tarry and retard thy rosy flight,
　　That Heaven's gems around their King would cluster,
　　Afraid, lest you would rob them of their luster.

Or that thy span of winged steeds would flag,
Or trip, afrighted, o'er some treacherous crag.
　　Ah, stony-hearted Maid! that thou mightest fail!
　　But prayers, entreaties, threats, are no avail.

Like arch coquette she hides her blushing face
Amid the mazy folds of vapory fleece.
　　In high disdain she closely wraps her veil,
　　And turns deaf ears to Man's and Nature's wail.

Referring to the author as "the *infant* [*sic*] *terrible* of our class," the editor commented in the next issue, ". . . reaped a harvest of praise from the story he wrote. . . . Well he deserved it. It was certainly a clever thing and remarkably good for a boy of fourteen. Those, however, who know our Jack intimately are not surprised, for a more omnivorous reader does not exist in the school. . . . The poem, *Ad Auroram*, is the maiden effort of a boy of fourteen, who received his first ideas on metrical composition the day he wrote these lines."

Another Barrymore poem published by *The Academic* was entitled "Rondeau":

> Sweet Spring has come! The robins sing!
> And from the South the soft wings bring
>   To teeming Nature warmth and fill
>   Of grateful moisture. Now each hill
> And dale proclaims the approach of Spring.
>
> The fields their hue recovering,
> Their snowy mantles shed. Each thing
>   Of life awakes, that slept until
>   Sweet Spring has come.
>
> In dell and dingle blossoms fling
> Their lovely petals to the King
>   Of Day; and beg the kisses he will
>   Bestow. And to the murmuring rill
> The gentle breeze is whispering,
> "Sweet Spring has come."

When the juniors presented a "public specimen" marking "the awakening to consciousness of the genius of our class," John recited Ovid's "Orpheus and Eurydice," which, according to *The Academic*, was "exceptionally well-done, and won him the hearty applause of an attentive audience."

One evening in May 1898 the suspicions of a faculty member were aroused when he detected a group of boys sneaking out of their dormitory under the cover of dark. Following them, he saw them enter a bordello. The only boy he had been able to recognize was John. Next day when John, who had not in fact transgressed, refused to identify his companions, he was immediately expelled.

Maurice was more amused than upset. "What were you doing in such a place, son?" he asked.

"Nothing," John swore, "absolutely nothing."

"Then what the devil was the matter with you? Aren't you a Barrymore?"

During the summer, with Maurice on the road, the Barrymore children were shunted back and forth between the country retreats of relatives, such as Uncle John Drew's cottage in Westhampton, Long Island, and Uncle Googan's house in Long Branch, New Jersey. Sometimes the brothers stayed on their father's dilapidated Staten Island farm under the care of an aged Negro tenant farmer, Edward Briggs, whom the family referred to as either "the Black De Reszke" because of his stentorian voice or "Edward, the Black Prince." When Maurice received a letter in California from a meddlesome friend, reproaching him for entrusting his offspring to such hands, he wrote to them and demanded a report. John penned the reply, but the Black Prince dictated it. The boys, the letter ran, were in splendid health, their comportment exemplary "and as for Edward Briggs, he is a noble fellow and I love him."

The last words were no exaggeration. The brothers did indeed find Briggs lovable. "He never made us wash our faces," John recalled, "we never made our beds or washed the dishes, and we had a magnificent summer—the three of us and thirty-five dogs."

The dogs were huskies, four of them a gift to Maurice from the Arctic explorer Robert Peary the other thirty-one their young. "They swarmed through the house, sharing our beds, chasing cats, and yelping at the moon. It was a glorious existence. . . ."

During periods when Maurice neglected to forward enough funds, "Edward, through the terrific force of his personality, would wangle enough stuff from the grocery stores to keep us alive. Now and then, passers-by would offer us a dollar—once the offer was five dollars—for a dog, but no matter how much we needed food we wouldn't part with one. Only in a family of irresponsible actors could such a situation occur—two kids, thirty-five dogs, and an old Negro left to shift for themselves. It was grand.

"Edward was devoted to us, and there grew up between us an attachment not unlike that between Huckleberry Finn and the Negro Jim in Mark Twain's great book. *Huckleberry Finn* is my favorite of all books and I read it at least once a year, and, in reading it, live over with real affection that summer with Edward, the Black Prince."

Another summer haven for the young Barrymores was a boardinghouse not far from the farm, run by a landlady of French descent,

Mme. Bourquin. Wherever they were placed, Mum Mum would usually go along to watch over them unless a theater engagement called her away. Beyond range of her vigilant eye they were apt to court trouble. John once fell out of a tree head-first onto a flower pot. The wound left a small, triangular scar above his left eye which would turn white when he lost his temper.

Uncle Googan's country neighbors included Oliver Doud Byron, a prosperous actor and playwright of patriarchal presence, whose son Arthur, a future star, had become a friend of the Barrymore children during their visits to Long Branch. Indelibly stamped on Arthur's memory were the sight and sound of the three Barrymores as they swung on his father's garden gate, chanting:

> Little drops of water,
> Little blades of grass,
> Once a haughty actor,
> Now a horse's ass.

It was at Mme. Bourquin's establishment that Ethel, Lionel and John appeared together in the same play for the first and only time in their lives. Ethel conceived the enterprise, chose the play, *Camille*, in a muddled version of her own which she based on hearsay, never having seen or read the original. She cast Lionel as her lover, Armand Duval, and John as the evil Comte de Varville. Behind a locked bathroom door she practiced the heroine's consumptive cough with a vigor that caused Mum Mum, whom she had kept in the dark about the approaching performance, to exclaim: "Something must be done about that child! She has started to bark like a dog," and as the cough worsened: "My God, she's got a bone in her throat!" Ethel finally explained, obviating the need of a doctor's attention. Admission to the Bourquin parlor, where she rigged up a little stage, was a penny, and from boarders and some curious neighborhood children the Barrymores collected thirty-seven cents.

Maurice tried to draw closer to his children during their adolescence. Ethel remained aloof, unable to forgive him for marrying again so soon after her mother's death. The boys often accompanied him to the zoo, to sporting events, theaters and cafés, Ethel only occasionally and with scant enthusiasm. She was, moreover, frequently in rehearsal or on the road. John, at fourteen, bore a resemblance to his father which increased startlingly as he grew taller and filled out—the classic profile, the cleft chin, the full, moody mouth. He had Maurice's large, deep, gray eyes, and, like him, was lightly built, strong and agile. An elderly actor of deviant tastes, struck by the boy's comeliness, half jestingly told Maurice he would like to adopt him. "Do you wish to adopt my son, sir," Maurice asked, "or adapt him?"

Father and sons would stroll through the wonderland that began close by his lodgings—Broadway's pleasure sector, which then stretched from the mid-Forties, with their opulent hotels, gilded saloons and lobster palaces, down to the Academy of Music on Fourteenth Street. Cable cars teetered up and down the center of the thoroughfare over newly laid tracks. Hansom cabs disgorged bustled, fur-enveloped belles, their hands tucked into muffs, escorted by men crowned with derbies or silk high hats. At rare moments a Duryea, the first American gasoline-powered car, a buggy-bodied two-seater on four spindly wheels, would rivet all eyes.

Maurice knew everybody of interest and everybody knew him, and the awed boys would find themselves shaking hands with John L. Sullivan, who only a few years earlier, in 1889, had won the last world's heavyweight bare-knuckle prizefight from Jake Kilrain; with "Gentleman Jim" Corbett, who had defeated Sullivan three years later in the first championship match requiring boxing gloves; with the mighty wrestler William Muldoon, one of Maurice's earliest American friends, whom Modjeska had cast, at his urging, as "Charles, wrestler to Frederick" in her production of *As You Like It*.

John and his father once dined with William Cody—"Buffalo Bill"—and his worshipful friend and press agent, "Major" John Burke, who had proclaimed after their first encounter: "I have met a god." They were about to take their Wild West Show on a tour of thirty-one one-night stands. Rosa Bonheur had painted Buffalo Bill's portrait in Paris, and the Major, a bull-voiced talker wearing mutton-chop whiskers and reeking of whiskey, unrolled a poster depicting Napoleon astride a horse on one side, on the other a mounted Buffalo Bill, and between them, at her easel, Rosa Bonheur. Under Napoleon, Burke had written: "The man on the horse of 1795—from the Seine to the Neva, from the Pyramids to Waterloo," and under Buffalo Bill: "From the Yellowstone to the Danube, from Vesuvius to Ben Nevis." Indicating the latter, he remarked to John: "The finest figure of a man that ever sat a steed."

Perhaps the greatest single attraction of the Wild West Show had been Sitting Bull, the Sioux chieftain who led the massacre of General Custer's detachment at the Little Big Horn River in 1876 and fourteen years later was himself murdered by federal officers lest he foment another uprising.

"What did Sitting Bull look like?" John asked.

"The living image of Daniel Webster," boomed the Major.

At the beginning of the meal John started to giggle, and his father, sensing the reason, dragged him out to the washroom. "You'd better be goddam careful," he warned him. "Just because Buffalo Bill has long hair doesn't mean he's effeminate. He'll carve your heart out if you don't stop it."

John kept a straight face for the rest of the evening while Buffalo Bill, shoulder-length locks jouncing up and down and mustache and goatee waggling, described his triumphs abroad, the two command performances he gave before Queen Victoria, how much Sir Henry Irving relished the spectacle, how Chief American Horse, Sitting Bull's replacement in the show, shook the Princess of Wales' hand.

The most arresting architecture on Broadway was Oscar Hammerstein's mammoth citadel completed in 1895, "the grandest amusement temple in the world," with its Indiana-limestone façade, its polished granite pillars and ponderous carved portals opening into a marble foyer illuminated by a chandelier composed of 600 arc lights. Nearly every one of the countless recesses and niches held an oil painting or a sculpture. Covering the entire Broadway side of the block between Forty-fourth and Forty-fifth streets, it embraced under one roof the mammoth Lyric Theatre for plays, the Music Hall for vaudeville and the Concert Hall for musical productions. An elevator wafted customers to the tiers, of which there were eleven with 124 boxes. The three orchestras had 6,000 seats among them. The price of admission ranged from fifty cents to $1.50.

The Barrymores might interrupt their peregrinations to drop in on the studio of Augustus Saint-Gaudens on West Thirty-sixth Street and watch him at work on one of his public monuments. Or they might pause for a seidel of beer in the rathskeller of the nine-story Pabst Hotel, straddling the crossroads at Forty-second Street, an area known as "Long Acre" (later Times Square). The hotel towered over the neighboring buildings, few of them higher than three stories, their walls masked by billboards advertising such attractions as the Madison Square Garden Electrical Show, the Castle Square Opera Company, the melodrama *Shenandoah*.

Every available Barrymore and Drew would attend Charles Frohman's Empire Theatre at Fortieth Street for the première of whatever new production starred John Drew, "The First Gentleman of the Stage," an event that usually signaled the opening of the fall-winter theater season. In John's fourteenth year the play was *Rosemary*, by Louis N. Parker and Murray Carson, with Ethel playing a small role, the year after, *A Marriage of Convenience*, adapted by Sydney Grundy from the French *Un Mariage sous Louis XV*, both airy trifles. In response to critics who chided his uncle for seldom attempting more challenging roles, Lionel said: "He deserves the highest honors of all the male members of our family, for it's much harder to be a great gentleman than a great actor."

During John's boyhood, Broadway below Long Acre was more variegated and exciting than the segment above it. There were more theaters and bright lights. On the Thirty-ninth Street stood the Metropolitan Opera (choicest seats: five dollars) and six blocks farther south the Weber and Fields Music Hall, where burlesque originated—not the kind later popularized by Billy Minsky, but parodies of theatrical hits to which one could safely expose one's maiden aunt. Four blocks away, facing Madison Square, the north wall of the Cumberland Hotel had displayed, in May 1892, the city's first spectacular electrical sign, 1,475 light bulbs flashing ads for "Manhattan Beach Swept by Ocean Breezes," Sousa's Band and Pain's fireworks. Upon learning that the Cumberland was to be torn down to make way for the Flatiron Building, H. J. Heinz, the pickle king, rented the space, and until the end of the century the myriad lights, operated by an attendant with a hand switch from an adjoining roof, spelled out a limping verse of Heinz's own composition beneath a gigantic reproduction of his product:

> Here at the death of the wall of fame
> We must inscribe a well-known name
> The man whose varieties your palate did tickle
> Whose name is emblazoned in the big green pickle.

Nothing so quickened Maurice's pride in his sons as evidence of athletic prowess. One day, in Old Wood's Gymnasium on East Twenty-eighth Street, Lionel was sparring with Hobart Bosworth, a young bit player and a bigger, brawnier, more experienced boxer. Lionel wove and ducked so adroitly that Bosworth, aiming a blow at his jaw, hit the top of his head instead. The impact scarcely bothered Lionel, but it broke Bosworth's right hand. When Lionel gleefully reported the encounter to his father, the latter expressed some skepticism, aware as he was of Bosworth's physical superiority. But a few days later at the Players Club Maurice saw Bosworth sitting across the grill room, his arm in a sling. Maurice pantomimed "Broken?" Bosworth nodded. Maurice executed elaborate gestures, indicating "My son?" Bosworth nodded again, whereupon Maurice raised his hands to heaven in a dumb show of gratitude and joy until Bosworth protested: "Oh, come, Mr. Barrymore, isn't it rather unkind of you to be thanking heaven for my misfortune?"

"Oh, my dear Bosworth, no, no!" Maurice reassured him. "I am very, very sorry for you, but in this hour of fatherly emotion even my sympathy for you is forgotten, for at last, dear boy, I have detected my son in a truth."

During the late spring of 1896 Maurice was again floundering in a sea of financial troubles when Oscar Hammerstein came to his rescue with a contract to headline the bill at the Music Hall in some sketch of his own choice. Maurice's friends tried to dissuade him, arguing that vaudeville would be infra dig. But the money—$500 a week—proved irresistible. As his vehicle, Maurice selected *A Man of the World*, a "comedietta" by Augustus Thomas. The minor characters included a youth with no words to speak, and Maurice enlisted John.

On opening night Maurice reached his dressing room tardy as always, with only minutes to put on his makeup before the curtain rose. Too hurried to pay attention to John, he pasted on a handlebar mustache according to the requirements of the playlet and rushed toward the stage. In the absence of any specific instructions as to makeup, John applied an identical mustache and entered the scene behind his father. The laughter that burst from thousands of throats as he appeared, the image of Maurice Barrymore in a smaller package, would long re-echo in his mind's ear, stifling what little interest in acting he had. Like Lionel, he far preferred art.

It was during the year of his theatrical blooding, while still at Georgetown, that John began to drink heavily. A Los Angeles physician, Dr. Samuel Hirshfield, who treated him in middle age and was familiar with his earlier medical history, noted in a diagnostic report: "Since the age of 14 has been more or less a chronic drunkard."

At fifteen John was seduced by his pretty young stepmother. Passionate and sexually versatile, Mamie Floyd initiated him into varieties of love-making not normally experienced by a boy his age. It is probable that the relationship profoundly affected his sexual development, engendered conflicting emotions toward his father and produced a trauma that contributed to his increasing alcoholism.

Many years later John confided the details of the affair to Gene
Fowler, who, out of consideration for people still living, glossed over
them in his biography and disguised Mamie Floyd's identity. But
John indicated to Fowler that he had suffered pangs of guilt for
cuckolding his father and had ever since tended to mistrust all attractive women. The second Mrs. Maurice Barrymore eventually
obtained a divorce.

John would love many women, but would like few. His obser-
vations about the sex, conveyed in a lapidary style reminiscent of his
father's, reflected a cynical view. "It's slander to say my troubles come
from chasing women. They begin when I catch them. . . . The way
to fight a woman is with your hat. Grab it and run. . . . When
they find the arms of Venus de Milo, they will discover boxing gloves
on the hands."

He was prey to violent seizures of sexual jealousy. Those women
who commanded his affection and respect, whom he truly liked, were
almost all precluded from any sexual involvement with him by reason
of age difference, lack of physical appeal or a close family relationship—certain kindly old landladies, his voice teacher, his mothers-in-
law.

Concerning his feelings for his father, another physician who had
had John as a patient, Dr. Harold Thomas Hyman, a psychiatrically
oriented New York internist, wrote to Fowler after reading *Good
Night, Sweet Prince* and ventured the hypothesis that John hated his
father. In Fowler's reply* he wrote: "All this may, I concede, sub-
stantiate your position that Jack hated his own father. . . . I can
only say, 'I do not know,' when the scientist gives me his opinion.
This is the decent view a non-professional should take. My own impression, however, was and is that he adored his father. He remembered his mother hardly at all. Lionel and Ethel (and Ethel *did not*
adore her father) concur in this. Also, the testimony of men who
knew both Maurice and Jack during Barrymore's boyhood have told
me at great length of the tender relation between father and son. . . ."

During the winter of 1896 Mrs. John Drew went touring again
in an all-star revival of *The Rivals*. The following January she appeared briefly on the road in *The Sporting Duchess*, "the Great
Drury Lane Melo-Drama" by Cecil Raleigh, Henry Hamilton and
Sir Augustus Harris. It was her last engagement. Seventy-seven years

---

* On the file copy of which he noted, "Not to be published unless all of
us have been dead for thirty years—and perhaps not even then."

old, afflicted with kidney and heart ailments, her legs swollen from edema, she withdrew to Bevan House, a boardinghouse overlooking the Sound at Larchmont, New York. But she refused to consider her retirement permanent. When Lionel repeated to her the doctor's pessimistic prognosis, she rejected it. "The typical nonsense of his deplorable trade," she said. "There is nothing the matter with me at all. I am merely resting between plays. And I must be up soon for a new rehearsal."

Her family was, as usual, scattered far and wide. Son John Drew was on the road out west with *Rosemary*, son Sidney touring Australia under McKee Rankin's banner. Grandson Lionel, in need of money, had temporarily left the Art Students League to try the stage again, this time with slightly more encouraging results. Son-in-law Maurice had taken his vaudeville sketch to distant cities. Granddaughter Ethel, after three years of haunting Broadway casting offices and finally settling for insignificant roles that Uncle Jack offered her in his successes, had joyfully departed for London with the cast of *Secret Service*, headed by its author, William Gillette.

But Mum Mum still had John to lean on. He stayed with her at Bevan House through most of the summer of 1897. They occupied cramped top-floor quarters because those were the cheapest. Mum Mum's swollen legs made it painful for her to go up and down stairs and so she spent the entire day in a rocking chair on the veranda. "I can see her now," John wrote thirty years later. "She had innumerable paper-backed books, and there was always one in her hands, but she seldom read. She sat gazing out across the Sound, but she was really gazing at old half-forgotten things, things that once seemed important and which were now becoming confused in her mind. Sometimes she would . . . break into the middle of a topic as though we had left it but a minute before. Mostly, she spoke of other times and other manners in the world of the theater. . . . At night when she went to bed I helped her to her room. I waited to be there to do this, though I wanted to go about nights and stay out until any hour."

By August she was bedridden and had to have a nurse in attendance. On the morning of the 31st she and John talked at length. Toward noon she felt sleepy, silently patted his arm and dozed off. While he was away she slipped from sleep into coma. He returned a few minutes before three in the afternoon to find the nurse and doctor at her bedside. She had gone into a convulsion and was now barely breathing. John saw her die.

"He never felt safe after that," Lionel said in his old age. "I am inclined as the shadows grow longer to the theory that he was in revolt against the whole insecure pattern of life, and that the insecurity sprang from the collapse of his frame of reference when Mum Mum died when he was fifteen."

In accordance with his mother's wishes, John Drew had inscribed on her tomb in Greenwood Cemetery a stanza from a poem by Anna Barbauld:

> Life! we've been long together,
> Through pleasant and through cloudy weather;
> 'Tis hard to part when friends are dear;
> Perhaps 'twill cause a sigh, a tear;
> Then steal away, give little warning,
>   Choose thine own time;
>   Say not Good-Night, but in some brighter clime,
>   Bid me Good-Morning.

The Barrymore / Drew Dynasty

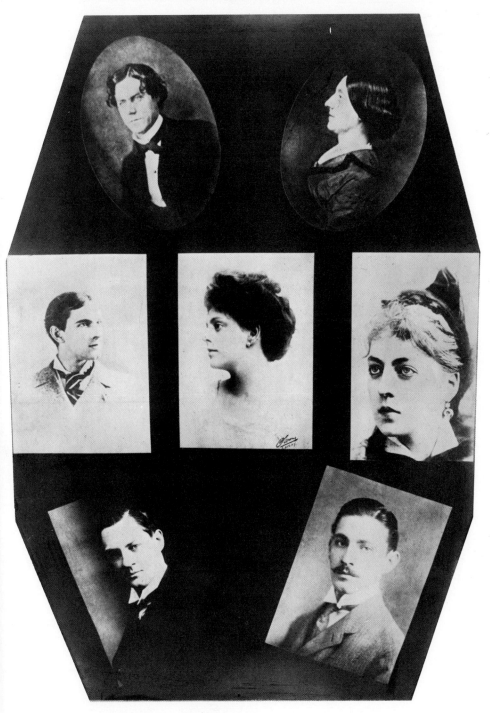

TOP ROW: *Grandfather John Drew, Grandmother Louisa Lane*
MIDDLE: *Father Maurice Barrymore, Daughter Ethel, Mother Georgie Drew*
BOTTOM: *Sons Lionel and John*

The matriarchal Mrs. John Drew as Mrs. Malapr[e]

Maurice Barrymore in the title role of
Haddon Chambers's Captain Swift,
which opened at New York's Madison
Square Theatre, December 24, 1888

Georgie Drew Barrymore

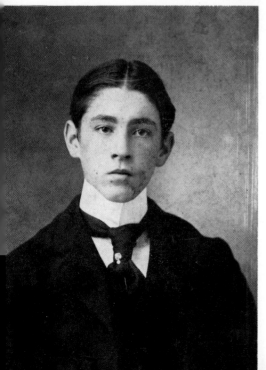

John, aetat 15

The staff of the Georgetown Preparatory School magazine, The Academic, *in 1897. John stands second from the left in the middle row.*

A scene from Raffles, *John's ninth movie, shot in 1917 in front of The Players club. The actor on the left is Frank Morgan.*

Katherine Corri Harris, the first Mrs. John Barrymore

As Falder in John Galsworthy's Justice

In the title role of George du Maurier's Peter Ibbetson, *with Lionel Barrymore as the villain*

Hamlet

Fedya in Tolstoy's Redemption

Richard III

The Moscow Art Theatre company visits Hamlet.
BACK ROW, L. TO R.: *Nikita Balieff, Olga Chekova (widow of the dramatist)*
FRONT ROW, L. TO R.: *Morris Gest, Ivan Moskven, John Barrymore, Vassily Katchaloff, Constantin Stanislavsky (director of the company), Ethel Barrymore, Arthur Hopkins, Robert Edmond Jones*

With many a take to come, but probably John's finest film

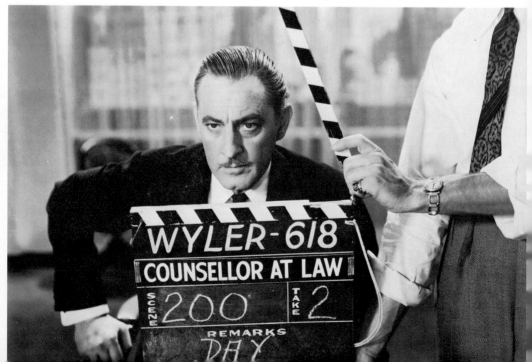

John with the second Mrs. Barrymore, the former Mrs. Leonard Thomas, née Blanche Oelrichs, nom de plume *Michael Strange*

John and friend on the set of The Man from Blankney's

Honeymooning in the Galapagos with the third Mrs. Barrymore, Dolores Costello. The iguana was the bride's quarry.

Home movies on Guadalupe Island. The newlyweds film a herd of elephant seals.

Dolores, sister Ethel and John by the swimming pool of John's Beverly Hills estate, Bella Vista

The Barrymores at home in 1933 with daughter Dolores ("Dede") and son John, Jr.

At Sport

RIGHT: *With fellow skeet shooter, Clark Gable, on John's private range*

ABOVE: *Alaska: John bags a Kodiak bear*

RIGHT: *Aboard John's yacht,* The Mariner, *with Clementine*

At New York's El Morocco, John with the fourth Mrs. Barrymore, the former Elaine Jacobs (who changed her name to Barrie in his honor), entertains his mother-in-law and father-in-law, Edna and Louis Jacobs.

Caliban and Ariel

A foursome of Bundy Drive boys. L. TO R.: *Sadakichi Hartmann, John Barrymore, Gene Fowler, John Decker*

John, the unquenchable

John's caricature of his own duality: the romantic idealist vs. his wild, aberrant self.

As Allan Manville in My Dear Children, *his last stage appearance, John travesties himself.*

In wet cement, in the forecourt of Hollywood's Chinese Theater, where normally the footprints of stars are preserved, the owner, Sid Grauman, subjects John's profile to the ceremony.

June 2, 1942. At rest.

5

"I Must E'en Fly"

———

I N the fall of John's sixteenth year his father found himself solvent enough to send him to England for further schooling. Ethel, he expected, would keep her eye on her brother and open all kinds of doors to him. Certainly, to judge by the society news from London, she was in a happy position to do so. No longer shy, of princessly grace, versed in literature and music, a gifted pianist, she had, during the year since she crossed the Atlantic, won numerous admirers in both Mayfair and the West End. A friend of Uncle Jack's, the war correspondent Richard Harding Davis, had written ahead, urging his English friends to extend their hospitality to Ethel, and she met such luminaries as Sir George Lewis, one of the country's foremost solicitors, who was reputed to know the skeletons in the closets of every notable British family; Wilfred Grenfell, the medical missionary; Anthony Hope, the novelist. . . . Dining in the home of the publisher William Heinemann, she sat next to James A. McNeill Whistler. Dinners, parties, balls, sometimes two or three an evening, crowded her social calendar. The eldest son of the Marquess of Dufferin and Ava (soon to die in the Boer War) called her "Cinderella." Lord Kitchener, the hero of the Sudan, asked her to dance with him. The Duke of York (King George V to be) had the actress Cissie Loftus present the lovely American to him. After John Hay was installed as the new American Ambassador to the Court of St. James's, Ethel went to the embassy on Thursday afternoons to help Mrs. Hay

51

pour tea. Rumor had Ethel betrothed to Anthony Hope, to the Duke of Manchester, to Prince Kumar Shri Ranjitsinhji, Cantabrigian, cricket captain and future Maharajah of Nawanagar, to Winston Churchill. "No one has ever done anything like what Ethel's done in London," remarked the acidulous Margot Asquith.

Ethel's progress as an actress was less brilliant, though no cause for discouragement in a novice of only nineteen. The reigning stars of the British stage petted her. To Ellen Terry she was "little Bull-finch." Sir Henry Irving took a personal interest in her career. When *Secret Service* ended its London run and Ethel was about to return to America for lack of funds, Sir Henry offered her a prominent part in his melodramatic specialty, an English version of Erckmann-Chatrian's *Le Juif Polonais*, retitled *The Bells*, and to follow, the feminine lead in his son Laurence's *Peter the Great*. Her starting salary was £10 a week, the equivalent of about $50.

"People will never say I am a great actress," she told Irving. "They'll only say I'm a personality, that I'm just Ethel Barrymore."

"See to it that is all they ever say," Irving advised her.

While rehearsing *Peter the Great*, Ethel and Laurence thought themselves in love. Ethel cabled her father, care of the Lambs Club, announcing her engagement. He cabled back: CONGRATULATIONS LOVE FATHER. But ten days later, before the play opened at the Lyceum Theatre, she fell out of love. To her second cable, rectifying the first, Maurice replied: CONGRATULATIONS LOVE FATHER.

When John arrived, Ethel was sharing a flat at 21 Bedford Street with another young American actress, Suzanne Sheldon. The logical choice of an institution for his higher education was King's College in Wimbledon since his father's brother-in-law, the Reverend Henry Wace, was then the headmaster. He lived with the Waces and felt a surge of family pride when, in English history class, reading an account of the Indian Mutiny, he learned that "the first man over the battlements of Lucknow was a young subaltern, Richard Wace." He drew incessantly in the margins of his books. He was often truant, disappearing into the pleasure haunts of nearby London. When Ethel asked "Aunt Eva" Wace how her brother was faring, she answered: 'Oh, he's quite happy, fluctuating between the deanery and the beanery."

Like most Americans of that era, John was a stranger to Association Football, or soccer, a game then limited mainly to the British Isles. But having determined to try out for the King's College team, he proved so adept that the coach assigned him to the crucial position of goalkeeper. There is no indication that John ever played soccer again after quitting King's College a year later, though opportunities were not lacking. Indifference succeeded achievement, a pattern that would recur throughout his private and professional life. Hardly any challenge would daunt him, whether big-game hunting, mountain climbing, yacht racing, laying siege to an intractable woman or playing Hamlet. But once he had surmounted it, his interest would tend to slacken. Repetition bored him. In his declining years, when Otto Preminger, who directed John's last play, asked him why he alternated good performances with wretched ones, he explained: "Boredom, dear boy, boredom." Art was an exception, but then he never achieved distinction as an artist.

From King's College John transferred to London University, where he attended a course of lectures in English literature under a Professor Kerr. With Ethel's financial aid he then reverted to his first love at the Slade School of Art.

Another betrothal which Ethel recognized as a mistake decided her to put time and distance between herself and her fiancé. He was Gerald du Maurier, the younger son of George du Maurier, the illustrator and author of the novels *Trilby* and *Peter Ibbetson*. Ethel believed she still loved him, but foresaw intolerable conflict with her prospective mother-in-law. Scraping together her last few pounds, she booked passage for America after commending John to the care of Ben and May Webster, an acting couple with a theatrical ancestry antedating that of the Barrymores, while he continued his education. The Websters' daughter, Margaret, who was to carry on the family tradition as both actress and director, recalled: "The fraternity found it hard to understand what further education was supposed to be acquired by a youth whose extensive knowledge of life left them gasping."

Ethel had deposited a small sum with May Webster for her to dole out to John as pocket money, thus guaranteeing that he would often report to the Websters. This was no burden to him. He relished their company. He would sit talking to them by the hour, then, recalling some appointment, would announce: "I must e'en fly," only to to linger for another hour or so.

When the pocket money finally ran out, John drafted a cable to Ethel: FOR CHRIST SAKE SEND ME FIFTY DOLLARS. The cable clerk told him he could not transmit such a profane message. "Why not?" said John. "It's the name of my manager—George W. Christ."

Ethel had reached New York with twenty-five cents in her purse.

The next day Uncle Jack arranged an interview for her with Charles Frohman, then, at the age of thirty-eight, on his way to supremacy as a theatrical producer in both America and England. On the mantelpiece of his mammoth office at the Empire Theatre stood a marble bust of Napoleon, whom he vastly admired and fancied he resembled. Frohman was a stubby, paunchy little man with a head shaped like a cantaloupe and a wide mouth that broke readily into a smile of good humor and bonhomie. Born to a German-Jewish dry-goods peddler and raised on New York's lower East Side, entirely self-educated, he had, like his older brothers Gustave and Daniel, been involved in some phase of show business since boyhood.

Frohman developed a laconic style of communication that could sting or stroke as the occasion demanded. To an English playwright, George Sims, who cabled him after the Broadway opening of his comedy called *Fanny:* HOW IS FANNY GOING, Frohman replied: GONE. Explaining to the American actor E. H. Sothern how he wanted him to play certain scenes in a new play, he condensed his instructions for the entire third act into three words: "Court. Kiss. Curtain." Illness once forced the popular American comedian William Collier to drop out of a Frohman production at his Garrick Theatre. The day Collier rejoined the cast happened to be Frohman's birthday, and Collier wired: MANY HAPPY RETURNS FROM ALL YOUR BOX OFFICES. The producer assured him: MY HAPPIEST RETURN IS YOUR RETURN TO THE GARRICK.

He usually had a crisp reply to reporters' questions. What were the best seats in the house from which to view a play? "The paid ones." What was the difference between New York and out-of-town audiences? "Fifty cents." Whom did he consider to be the greatest American dramatist? "The one who writes the last great play."

When Frohman's London manager, W. Lestocq, notified him that a Scottish woman author whose play they were considering for production on Broadway wanted an advance of $10,000 and a fifteen-percent royalty, Frohman asked him: "Did you tell her not to slam the door?" Infuriated when "C.F.," as he came to be known throughout the theatrical world, dared criticize her performance, the tempestuous Mrs. Patrick Campbell informed him: "I want you to know that I am a great artist." "Mrs. Campbell," he rejoined, "I will try to keep your secret." Georgie Barrymore once matched his terseness when he answered her telegram from San Francisco requesting new costumes with the single word NO. She sent another telegram: OH.

Frohman saw in Ethel qualities reminiscent of her mother, and he gave her a part at $35 a week in a confection by a French play-wright, Henri Lavedan, entitled *Catherine*. Though she had less than a dozen lines to speak, her fresh, delicate beauty, in addition to the glamour with which the press reports from London had invested her, roused audiences to tumultuous applause.

Catherine kept Ethel on the road during the winter and spring of 1898–99. By summer she had saved enough of her salary to pay for a return trip to England aboard the American liner *Paris* and she cabled John the date of her debarkation at Southampton. Borrowing two pounds from the Websters, John started for the port. He missed the rendezvous, turning up at the Websters' three days later, bleary-eyed and bedraggled, with the lame explanation that he had got as far as Southampton all right, but there had fallen in with some sailors and tarried to play billiards.

It was the summer of Ethel's social apotheosis. She became a protégé of Millie, Duchess of Sutherland, frequently visiting Stafford House, the Sutherlands' historic London mansion, and Dunrobin, their seaside castle in northern Scotland. She was welcome in the homes of Margot and Herbert Asquith, the Liberal statesman (and future Prime Minister), of the modish painter Sir Lawrence Alma-Tadema, of Joseph Jefferson's clever grandchildren Eleanor Farjeon, who was to be celebrated for her children's stories, and her brother Joseph, a future popular writer of mystery novels.

Ethel introduced John to many of her fashionable friends, some-times to her regret. In swift succession he had affairs with a duchess and an actress. The actress's aged husband learned of her infidelity and wanted to divorce her, naming seventeen-year-old John as co-respondent, but fear of ridicule restrained him.

In the course of a house party at Dunrobin Castle, to which both Ethel and John were invited, two girls, expert high-divers, enter-tained their fellow guests (among them a gorgeously kilted Scottish peer, the Earl of Mar and Kellie, and Winston Churchill) with an exhibition of their skill. "Jack . . . had never dived from any great height before," Ethel recalled, "but he could not bear to see two girls doing it, so off he went one day and made the best dive of anybody—a way Jack had."

Ethel rented a summer cottage for herself and her brother at Cookham, a village on the Thames from which droves of punters launched their craft. One afternoon John was watching a friend, E. H. Sothern's brother Sam, punting with his wife. Mrs. Sothern clung to her pole too long and was pulled overboard. Instantly diving in after her, John almost bashed his head against the bottom of the river, for at that point the Thames was scarcely three feet deep. Mrs. Sothern walked out of the water, laughing, but Sam rewarded John's chivalry by giving him unlimited access to his extensive wardrobe, a godsend since John then possessed but a single suit and that threadbare.

Not long after, he went swimming naked across a secluded stretch of the river, having left his clothes in Sam Sothern's punt. Sam absently let himself drift away while he fished and forgot to return for hours. Bare as Adam but nonchalant, John sauntered back to Cookham past clusters of gaping villagers.

The summer depleted Ethel's savings and reluctantly she prepared to leave England again. Lestocq advanced her the money for steamship fare. In New York she had to pawn a diamond belt buckle. She was able to retrieve it when C.F. began paying her $80 a week to play Stella de Gex, the heroine of another airy romp by Robert Marshall, *His Excellency the Governor*, in a road-company production. "There's going to be a big development in one of my companies before long," C.F. predicted. "There's a daughter of Barry who gets a big reception wherever she goes. She's got the real stuff in her."

Ethel was never to rank among the world's greatest actresses, but, as numerous drama critics on both sides of the Atlantic would agree, she projected a personal magic that transcended bad plays. "Miss Barrymore evidently depends very much on her personality," wrote the astringent Max Beerbohm in the *Saturday Review*, "and very little on her instinct for the art of acting, and very little on her experience in that art. . . . The only question is whether she is a fascinating person on the stage. And the only answer to that question is a prompt, loud, unqualified 'yes.' " And Brooks Atkinson, formerly of the New York *Times*, concluded in his history of Broadway: "Ethel was a personage first and an actress second. . . . In some elusive way, she had a particular gleam that captivated audiences. It seemed compounded of radiance held in reserve, mocking eyes, light and spontaneous movement and personal grandeur. . . . When she was beginning in the days of make-believe theater, she played comedy parts with grace and subtlety, and she became a vogue actress. She could do no wrong; thousands of theatergoers were more interested in her than in the plays she acted. . . ."

Critical reservations probably did not wound Ethel as deeply as they would a single-minded, more aspiring performer. She shared her brothers' ambivalence toward the theater. All three Barrymores not only denigrated acting, but belittled themselves as actors. Under ideal circumstances, Ethel claimed at the end of her career, she would have pursued a different profession, that of a pianist. "I went on the stage because I did not know how to do anything but act—and I did not know how to do that. I had not become an ambitious actress. In fact, I never have."

Lionel compared himself to "an amateur fireman who got thrown in with the professionals early, failed to find his métier anywhere else, and had to keep running to various theatrical conflagrations because he couldn't get out of the way. . . ." He maintained: "I didn't want to act. I wanted to paint or draw. The theater was not in my blood. I was related to the theater by marriage only; it was merely a kind of *in-law* of mine which I had to live with. . . . The reason I worked in the theater was that I had nothing else to do, and the reason I worked in motion pictures was that I had nothing else to do. Anyone can be an actor."

And John insisted: "I didn't want to be an actor. I was there merely because it was supposed that any member of a theater family ought to have something in him that would carry him through a crisis on the stage; at least he might be expected to possess a certain adaptability to the medium. . . . I wanted to be a painter. . . . I only went back to the theater because there is hope—at least money—for the bad actor. The indifferent painter usually starves. . . . Ambergris brings a great price by the ounce. It comes from the stomach of the diseased whale, but who would wish from choice to be the whale who makes this contribution? . . . If there were no such thing as acting, if it were all wiped out, it wouldn't make a particle of difference to the sort of people who really matter."

Years later John was discussing the nature of acting with a playwright. The playwright insisted: "An actor is the only man in the world who can do anything. Because his art is to use emotions rather than be used by them."

"Acting is not an art," John countered. "It's a junk pile of all the arts. But in behalf of my scavenger profession I'll make this boast. An actor is much better off than a human being. He isn't stuck with the paltry fellow he is. He can always act his better and non-existent self."

In the fall of 1900, following another summer sojourn in England, Ethel brought John back to New York with her. They both took rooms at Mrs. Wilson's, a theatrical boardinghouse on West

Thirty-sixth Street opposite the Lambs Club, Ethel footing the bill. At Oscar Hammerstein's brand-new Republic Theatre, Lionel was playing a juvenile in a comedy of rural life, *Sag Harbor*, his eleventh role but his first on Broadway.

Mrs. Wilson's was a garden of rare blooms and John found himself in a constant state of bedazzlement. As the first prospective amour among his fellow boarders he fixed upon the shy and wispy Maude Adams, who had been John Drew's leading lady for five years and would consolidate her fame with her portrayals of Sir James Barrie's fey heroines. But Maude Adams, who was John's senior by ten years, took only a minimal interest in men of any age, and rebuffed his advances. On the rebound John laid siege to Ida Conquest, a svelte enchantress who customarily came down to dinner wearing full evening dress. "Where are you going?" Ethel once asked her. "Nowhere," Ida replied with hauteur, "I always dress for dinner." She, too, had played opposite John Drew, was twelve years older than John and treated him like a schoolboy. The beginnings of romance began to flower between John and a third boarder, Margaret Bird, a tiny creature with eyes like saucers, a cascade of wild curls and a small figure so perfectly proportioned as to win her the sobriquet "The Pocket Venus." John had barely started his amorous campaign when Margaret left Mrs. Wilson's and the theater to marry Samuel Insull, the Chicago utilities nabob who eventually fled the country to avoid prosecution for mail fraud.

"Ethel," C.F. announced when she called on him shortly after her arrival, "I have a nice part for you at last." The part was the leading one of a prima donna, Mme. Trentoni, in *Captain Jinks of the Horse Marines*, "a fantastic comedy" that the prolific Clyde Fitch had just finished writing. The story of an Italian diva courted by three American marine officers, it called for her to sing and dance as well as act.

While Ethel started rehearsing, John badgered his father for tuition money at the Art Students League, where Lionel had studied. Maurice yielded, though not without scorn. "Do you want to be an artist and daub," he asked, "or an actor and make love?"

The League disappointed John, and he attended only one class. "Boy, what defeats me is how you happened to go to even one," said Maurice. The art school run by the painter George Bridgman, in which John enrolled next, proved more fruitful. "He took an especial interest in me, and helped me out of all proportion to what my demands upon his time should have been. I saw a good deal of him out of classes, and then he taught me more of life, observation and art than there was time to teach in the school."

Through Cissie Loftus, who was playing opposite E. H. Sothern in a play by her husband, Justin McCarthy, about François Villon, *If I Were King*, John sold a work of art for the first time—a poster advertising the play. At Miss Loftus' suggestion, Frohman commissioned it and paid John $5. "I have no embarrassment in mentioning how good this drawing was," said John. "Bridgman did most of it."

John also exhibited some drawings at the Press Artists' League, a gallery which divided the purchase price, if any, equally with the artist. One of the drawings depicted a hangman walking along a road, the shadow of the gallows at his feet and floating above his head the faces of the condemned he had hanged. It went for $10. The purchaser was the steel magnate Andrew Carnegie.

Cosmopolitan published a series of macabre, Doré-esque pen-and-ink drawings by John with the titles "Fear," "Unrest," "Jealousy" and "Despair." An accompanying commentary by an art critic named Hjalmar Hjorth Boyesen 2nd set forth: ". . . his work is of interest not only because he has left the beaten paths, but also because he displays considerable power of thought and technique. Any one might tell that the anatomy of his figure is correct and that his work is well ordered. But it is more than that. It has strength of the kind that arrests and holds the eye.

"All of the emotions portrayed by Mr. Barrymore are the strong emotions of strong men. Take, for instance, his 'Fear.' . . . It is the fear which must be met face to face, such as one feels seated at the bedside of one's dearest friend whose doom the doctor has whispered above the labored breathing: the fear of the end which seizes the man of ill-spent power. Tense, inevitable, awful Fear . . . The lonely figure on the promontory, stealthily approached by 'Unrest,' is that of a man, good or bad, who lived according to his own clearly defined obstacle-overcoming plan. . . . His 'Jealousy' is the insidious possessing force which tortures a man. . . . It taunts with helplessness, inactivity, indecision. . . . 'Despair,' too, is a crushing Titan in whose grasp the pigmy, man, is powerless.

"Mr. Barrymore's pictures give great promise for his future."

When *Cosmopolitan's* art editor restored the originals to John, he prophesied: "They're going to be collectors' items."

"They are now," said John. "Garbage collectors. I know a junk art dealer who'll give a dollar each for them, and I can always use the money."

"They'll fetch a hundred times that when you're famous and in your father's shoes."

"Me act? Not on your life."

"Speak up, Ethel!" a voice cried from the balcony of the Walnut Street Theatre (where Mum Mum had made her American debut at the age of seven) as she struggled, terror-stricken, with her first major role, Mme. Trentoni, in a tryout performance, before the New York opening, of Clyde Fitch's comedy *Captain Jinks of the Horse Marines*. "You Drews is all good actors." And another voice rang out: "We loved your grandmother, Ethel, and we love you."

But the reviews were brutal. "If Miss Ethel Barrymore were as graceful as she is pretty," wrote one Miriam Michelson, "if she were possessed of a well-trained, flexible, resonant voice, she might act. . . . She poses very prettily and very stiffly, for what might be labeled 'Portrait of a Young Lady During the Grant-Greeley Campaign.' . . . She acts not at all. She sings a bit and very badly. . . ."

She implored C.F. to close the play, but he kept it going for two weeks in Philadelphia despite meager audiences, then took it on the road for three weeks and finally opened it at his Garrick Theatre in New York on February 4, 1901. Uncle Jack had a red apple delivered to Ethel's dressing room, thereby instituting a family tradition. It was meant to evoke the old-time rural schools whose teachers used to tell their pupils: "Speak your piece good and you'll get a big red apple." Ever after, when any Barrymore or Drew opened in a new play, some relative would send a red apple.

For Ethel the première was excruciating. "I kept saying to myself, as I have done on every first night since, 'Why am I doing this? Why didn't I try to do something else?' I would have been glad of an earthquake or some other great calamity that would stop people coming in or me from going on."

But this time her panic proved groundless. The New York audience adored her, if not the foolish play. So did the majority of critics. The New York *Sun* reported: "Her inheritance of a gift of comic expression that betrays no effort, her beauty of a type that imparts an aspect of refinement to her form, and her sufficient skill to utilize her natural advantages effectually in serio-comic scenes, makes her the full equal of Georgie Drew Barrymore as a comedienne and of Maurice Barrymore as an exposition of debonair sentiment." *Harper's Weekly* pronounced her "a delight," and the New York *World* said: ". . . a little lady of the finest theatrical stock aimed at a shining mark last night and hit the bullseye."

With Ethel's name in electric lights above the marquee of the Garrick, *Captain Jinks* lasted until October—seven months—and on the road all through the 1901–02 season. She remained under C.F.'s management to the end of his days, eventually receiving as much as $2,000 a week.

Ethel had not laid eyes on her father for many months before *Captain Jinks*. His career meanwhile had suffered severe setbacks. He made his last appearance on the New York stage in 1899, playing Rawdon Crawley to Mrs. Fiske's Becky Sharp in a dramatization of *Vanity Fair* by Langdon Mitchell, with such élan as to bring him a brief resurgence of glory. Thereafter he confined himself almost exclusively to vaudeville sketches which profited neither his pocketbook nor his reputation.

Unknown to his daughter, Maurice had watched, weeping, from the back of the house when she made her Broadway bow. After the final curtain, he fought his way to her dressing room through the dense crowd of admirers, kissed her, murmured, "It was wonderful, darling," and slipped away.

Two months later Maurice Barrymore was in no condition to appear ever again on any stage.

6

"It Was a Lovely Day in June"

================

At some indeterminable point in the course of his amorous adventures Maurice had contracted syphilis. He may never have realized it. The primary surface lesions at the site of the infection, sometimes so slight as to escape notice, may soon heal, but the microorganisms causing them continue to attack the system, producing symptoms easily confused with those of many other diseases. If not correctly diagnosed and treated—and in Maurice's day the diagnostic techniques and treatment for syphilis were undependable—an invasion of the brain may lead in months or years to paresis. The symptoms of paresis, punctuated by periods of remission, commonly include an incapacity to work, erratic judgment, memory failure, delusions, homicidal rages. Maurice eventually exhibited them all. His condition was not improved by the quantities of absinthe he consumed.

An early manifestation of derangement may have been his increasingly bizarre garb. He would roam Broadway in moccasins, a dinner jacket, striped pants, a soiled, collarless shirt. But if his wits were addled, his wit was still intact. "Wearing it on a bet, old man?" inquired a Shakesperean actor, encountering him in a particularly outlandish ensemble.

"Yes, I am," said Maurice.

"You must have given the man long odds, Barry."

"I did. I wagered him that you were not the most mediocre reader of blank verse now alive on the globe, and he proved me wrong and won."

Maurice first suffered a mental collapse in 1898. He recovered temporarily under the care of Dr. Robert Safford Newton, an alienist attached to Bellevue Hospital and a friend. His children knew nothing about it at the time, Ethel and John being abroad and Lionel barnstorming.

The following year Maurice left vaudeville to support an actress named Marie Burroughs on the road in a melodrama, *The Battle of the Strong*. During rehearsals in New York he regularly missed his cues, driving the director, Daniel Arthur, to distraction. He once arrived for rehearsal wearing pajamas under his overcoat. "You will pardon me," he said, "but I overslept and could not wait while I dressed." Maurice soothed the director with the assurance that he never did everything expected of him until the first night. But when the play opened in Louisville, Kentucky, he showed no improvement and steadily deteriorated on succeeding nights.

Holbrook Blinn played the villain of the piece, with whom the hero fights a sword duel while carrying a small girl on his shoulders. One night Blinn noticed to his consternation that Maurice had removed the guard from the tip of his sword and seemed intent upon running him through. Defending himself as best he could without ruining the scene, Blinn sustained a slashed hand. The precariously balanced infant was Blanche Sweet, age four, who grew up to become a star of silent films.*

Arthur gave Maurice two weeks' notice, but Maurice did not wait that long. Barely able to walk through his part, fumbling nearly every line, he quit the cast a week later in St. Louis. *The Battle of the Strong* ended his career in the legitimate theater. During the next three months he regained control of himself sufficiently to fill a few more vaudeville engagements. He gave his final performance on March 28, 1901, in a Harlem theater, the Lion Palace, interrupting it with a torrential outburst against theater managers.

In this Maurice was voicing the grievances of the White Rats ("Star" spelled backward), a forerunner of Actors' Equity, formed to fight a powerful coalition of theater managers. In 1896 a group of the latter, dominated by Abraham Lincoln Erlanger, an obese, cruel,

---

* At the time I write she is the last survivor of Maurice Barrymore's era to have appeared on the same stage with him. She retains a vague memory of delight as she was whirled around the stage while hero and villain dueled.

foul-mouthed predator, organized themselves into "the Syndicate" with the initially praiseworthy object of bringing order out of the then chaotic booking system. Within a few years efficiency became tyranny. A star who balked at signing an exclusive contract with a member of the cartel would find it hard to book a New York theater or arrange a national tour.

Prominent among the stars who resisted the Syndicate were Joseph Jefferson, Nat Goodwin, James O'Neill (the father of Eugene O'Neill), Minnie Maddern Fiske, Sarah Bernhardt and Maurice Barrymore. When the Syndicate blacklisted Sarah Bernhardt, she played in tents. In an effort to cow Mrs. Fiske's husband, Harrison Grey Fiske, a publisher whose New York *Dramatic Mirror* relentlessly denounced the Syndicate, it posted the following enjoinder on the call boards of all the theaters controlled by its members: "Notice is hereby given that under pain of dismissal members of the cast are forbidden to advertise in, buy or read the New York *Dramatic Mirror*." After seeing the decree backstage at Boston's Hollis Street Theatre, Maurice immediately got off a telegram to the Syndicate: HAVE RARELY READ A DRAMATIC NEWSPAPER BUT WILL READ THE DRAMATIC MIRROR REGULARLY HEREAFTER.

He bombarded the press with letters pleading the cause of the White Rats. He delivered speeches at their meetings and wrote propaganda leaflets which he had printed and circulated throughout the theater district. But as mental illness overtook him he began to perceive the Syndicate as a force dedicated to his personal ruin. Part way through his performance at the Lion Palace, he stepped down to the footlights and launched into a savage, semi-coherent tirade against all theater managers. Many of them were Jews, and he reviled them with anti-Semitic gibes.

Walking out on the stunned audience, he retreated briefly to a small property he owned across the Hudson River in New Jersey. He reappeared at the Lambs Club with an account, wholly imaginary, of how a policeman had attacked him on the Fort Lee ferry, how he had fought back and killed a passenger who interfered. Maurice's fellow Lambs held him in such affection that they would have sheltered him indefinitely had they not feared a rampage that would injure members and demolish furniture. As it was, he stayed three days, restlessly pacing the rooms and projecting grandiose schemes: he would erect the world's biggest theater; he would plaster all New York with placards exposing the villainy of the managers who sought his annihilation because they envied "Maurice Barrymore, who has brains." Occasionally, flashes of his old gaiety and wit would recur.

One morning he crossed the street to Mrs. Wilson's boarding-house and broke into Ethel's room, crying: "Death to the Syndicate!" He then forgot his obsession long enough to declaim passages from old plays he had acted in. The next moment: "Charles Frohman is dead. The White Rats have killed him. The trust is doomed." Ethel, faint with horror, forced a smile, pretended to agree and otherwise tried to humor him. In his delirium he seized her by the throat. Before he could harm her, John arrived. Suddenly calm, Maurice described a play he intended to write, then quietly returned to the Lambs Club.

With Ethel too distraught to act on her own and Lionel out of town, it fell to John to decide what to do. His father, he realized, must be placed under restraint lest he endanger himself or others. A lawyer whom he and Ethel consulted undertook to obtain a legal commitment from a magistrate. John meanwhile adopted a ruse suggested to him by a Lambs Club member. He offered to accompany his father in a cab to police headquarters, there to file charges against the officer who Maurice said had assaulted him on the Fort Lee ferry. John took him instead to Bellevue Hospital. When Maurice understood where he was, he remarked, smiling: "My son has an exaggerated idea of my condition."

Neither the medical nor the journalistic ethics of the period prevented the public disclosure, day by day, of Maurice's plight. Following his dismissal from the *Battle of the Strong* company, the New York *Telegraph* had proclaimed in bold headlines: RUMOR THAT ACTOR HAS RETURNED A WRECK—TALK OF HIS BREAKDOWN. Now Maurice's children endured the ordeal of reading: MAD BARRYMORE A STAR THO' IN LUNATIC'S CELL and NOTED ACTOR AND WIT COMMITTED TO BELLEVUE HOSPITAL FOR EXAMINATION AS TO HIS SANITY.

Ethel tried to conceal the truth with a statement to the *Journal:* "My father has not been well for a year. He has never fully recovered from a severe attack of the grippe at Baltimore last year. So my brother and I thought it better to send him to a hospital."

A franker statement appeared in the *Journal* under Augustus Thomas' byline: "There are breakdowns and breakdowns. Some are little jolts in a rut. Some are like that of the deacon's One-Hoss Shay. There's nothing left to build a new one. That's the way with Barry. Poor Barry. There is very little hope, I am afraid. Poor old Barry!"

And the *Journal* quoted the Bellevue doctors as ascribing Maurice's collapse to "absinthe and incipient paresis."

During the five days Maurice spent under observation in what Bellevue termed "the Insane Pavilion" he imagined himself once again before the footlights, reenacting the roles of his heyday—Captain Absolute, Orlando, Romeo. His ward became for him a stage and the other inmates and their attendants, supporting actors awaiting their cues. At three o'clock the first morning, unable to sleep, he roused them all, crying: "You must take your parts in this play. I am the author," and pointing to an attendant dozing on a bench: "There's Claudius, the King of Denmark, asleep." At times he fancied he saw his daughter, her demeanor cold and reproachful, and he would whimper: "Oh, Ethel, Ethel, don't talk to your father that way."

He had been assigned a large room to himself with a desk and chair and he started to write a play which he called *The White Swan* after the heroine, a Shawnee princess. Every so often he would drop his pen and stretch like one awakening from a deep slumber and plaintively exclaim: "They are gone!"—then, reaching out his hand as if to clasp another's: "White Swan, where art thou? Let me have your hand again."

In his blackest moods he would plot the extermination of the Syndicate. He swore to kill Abe Erlanger on sight. During an ophthalmic examination, a strapping attendant approached to assist the doctor. Maurice grabbed him around the waist, lifted him off his feet and slammed him to the floor, shouting: "This is how Orlando takes the first hold." He hit another attendant over the head with a table. Injections of sedatives finally averted his rages.

Maurice's former wife, Mamie Floyd, who had been traveling abroad, visited him. He bore her no rancor, seemed, in fact, overjoyed to see her, and they chatted like fond old friends.

The doctors' final prognosis was categorical: the patient was in an advanced, irreversible stage of paresis. Dr. Newton gave him no more than six months to live. For her father's permanent confinement Ethel chose the Long Island Home at Amityville, Long Island, a private sanitarium about thirty-five miles from Manhattan, whose outward aspect had none of the usual institutional grimness. With its neat, comfortably furnished villas scattered over an expanse of trim lawns, shade trees and flower beds, its tennis courts, gymnasium and other recreational facilities, it looked more like a country club. The director reserved for Maurice a combination living room and bedroom on the ground floor of one of the larger villas. Ethel and John signed the commitment papers and Ethel assumed the payments of $20 a week, a burden lightened by Charles Frohman, who raised her weekly salary to $125 and a little later doubled that figure.

Believing Ethel's explanation that he was going to Philadelphia for the tryout of a new play, Maurice allowed himself to be transferred to Amityville without a struggle. In lucid intervals, when he grasped the reality of his situation, he would say resignedly: "I never thought this would be the end."

Dr. Newton had erred. Maurice did not live six months longer, but four years. John and Lionel visited him occasionally as their work allowed. Ethel, in whose heart compassion had supplanted resentment, was the most faithful visitor.

Among the few old friends for whom Maurice still existed were Augustus Thomas, William Collier, Nat Goodwin and Frank Case, the owner of the Algonquin Hotel, the celebrity haunt of which Maurice had been an habitué. They would sometimes find him at a desk, pen in hand, frantically covering sheet after sheet of foolscap. He was, he explained, writing a new play. Case once glanced at the sheets. They bore a single sentence endlessly repeated: "It was a lovely day in June." Nothing more.

As John saw his father slowly sink into idiocy, the fear possessed him, never entirely to leave him, that he might finish the same way, a fear intensified through the years with the growing realization of how much more than skin deep was his resemblance to his father— the sexual voracity, the compulsive drinking, the spells of indolence and boredom that followed achievement. At times he was terrified— groundlessly, as doctors would prove—lest a legacy of poisoned blood doom him, too, to paresis.

John turned to pictorial journalism. The New York *Morning Telegraph* gave him his first job. It lasted twenty minutes, the time it took him to execute the art editor's order for a line drawing of Gainsborough's Duchess of Devonshire. The drawing failed to please the editor, who fired him forthwith.

During the next few months John's life was an unremitting scramble for food and shelter. He borrowed what small sums she could spare from "Ee-thel," as he playfully called her—she called him "Jake"—"the only member of the family [according to Lionel] who managed in any way to look after any other member. . . . bless her, [she] was always on hand when the chips were down." He posed for artists, among them Rip Anthony, an emaciated beanpole of a man with a pointed black beard, who seldom had enough money to feed himself. Two friends served as Anthony's salesmen, dividing the proceeds equally when there were any. Exhibiting portfolios of his wash drawings, they would try to melt the resistance of prospective purchasers by telling them that the poor artist was dying of tuberculosis. (Ironically, he *did* die of tuberculosis.) John was the model for each of the dying officers in a panoramic representation of Custer's Last Stand, and for a Roman matron mourning at the grave of her son. By way of compensation Anthony let him have sleeping space in his one room at the antiquated Aulic Hotel on Thirty-fifth Street and Broadway.

John also wheedled endorsements out of celebrities for Shaeferine, a face lotion, earning five dollars per endorsement. Ethel was on the road when he started this enterprise, and by telegraph he urged her cooperation. Western Union duly delivered the following message to the Schaeferine Company: DEAR SIRS I RECEIVED YOUR I CAN'T REMEMBER THE NAME OF THE DAMNED THING BUT IT'S THE BEST TABLE WATER I EVER DRANK.

John Drew and Nat Goodwin responded to John's solicitations somewhat more helpfully, though Goodwin wrote to him after applying the lotion and contributing his testimonial: "I have used your Schaeferine. My lawyer will see you in the morning."

The second newspaper to employ John was Hearst's New York *Evening Journal* and he survived there eighteen months, eventually drawing a weekly salary of $50. But he brought scant joy or comfort to the prim, teetotaling managing editor, Arthur Brisbane. It was the dawn of the roughneck era in American journalism, of a roughneck mystique, when reporters wore their hats on the backs of their heads, kept their neckties loosened, imbibed Niagaras of liquor, perpetrated rowdy practical jokes and stopped at nothing to score a scoop. Sometimes leading, sometimes led, John happily immersed himself in this raffish milieu and there, as well as on the fringes of the art and theater worlds, accumulated a collection of adoring cronies. "Jack was one of the high spots of my life," said the hell-raising illustrator James Montgomery Flagg. "Oh, what a guy! The best company in the world. They busted the mold when they made Jack," and Guernsey Palmer ("Jack") Prescott, an actor fond of mixing bourbon and absinthe, who joined the pack a few years later, remembered John as "the sweetest guy who ever lived." Yet John could scarcely have chosen more pernicious companions. He needed no encouragement to drink, and with rare exceptions they were men dedicated to the bottle.

A couple of John's early Katzenjammereien involved public monuments. Cresting the sculpture-encrusted plaster Dewey Arch in Madison Square, hastily erected to honor Admiral George Dewey, who had defeated the Spanish fleet at the battle of Manila Bay, was a figure symbolizing Victory, a shield in one hand, a spear in the other. Egged on one night by Rip Anthony and Frank Butler, an alcoholic *Telegraph* reporter, John scaled the arch, filched the spear and with his fellow reprobates marched up Broadway, pausing at every bar en route to drink and boast of his feat. Some months later John and Cleon Throckmorton, a scenic designer, leaned a ladder against the Washington Square Arch, ascended, pulling the ladder up after them so that nobody could interfere, and sat on top of the arch, roasting hot dogs.

When exceptionally hard pressed, Rip Anthony and John resorted to a stratagem they had perfected to ensure their next breakfast. They would seat themselves at a restaurant table and pocket the bread as soon as it was placed before them along with the salt and pepper shakers, then, after a decent interval, they would summon the maître d'hotel and instruct him as follows: "If Mr. Vanderbilt comes in asking for us, please tell him we couldn't wait any longer and have gone on to Sherry's." In the morning, hot water seasoned with the salt and pepper made a bouillon of sorts to wash down the bread.

Frank Butler devised another artifice enabling two to assuage their hunger as cheaply as one. At most cafeterias ten cents would buy three filling hot cakes and a cup of coffee. Butler would go in first, leaving John outside to observe him through the window. He would pay his dime, eat exactly one and a half hot cakes and drink half the coffee. Now John would enter, pretend surprise upon seeing Butler and dash over to him to whisper in his ear. "My God, how terrible!" Butler would exclaim, hurrying out of the cafeteria and leaving John to finish the hot cakes and coffee.

To John, "Frank Butler was, I think, the most extraordinary man that I ever met. He was the son of a nephew of General Butler, of Civil War fame,* and his mother was Rose Eytinge, at one time the leading woman of the Union Square Theater and a great favorite in New York. . . . he was what is usually described as a character,

---

* Benjamin Franklin "Beast" Butler, the scourge of New Orleans, who ruled the city after its fall to his troops, hanged a resident for tearing down the U.S. flag, confiscated the property of Confederate sympathizers and posted a warning to the effect that any woman bothering Union soldiers would be treated as a whore.

and in any age the designation of him would probably have been the same. . . .

"Somehow Frank Butler had managed to lose a front tooth, and in its place there was a detachable gold one. If his smile flashed the gold tooth he was to be trusted, he was affluent. If the gold tooth was not in sight it was pawned. . . . The limit of borrowing with this security was seventy cents. We often tried to get more but never did. It was his last asset and he never let it go without trying everything else to get money."

What bemused John was a quality of Butler's mind that transmuted ordinary experiences into fantasies. At the outset of his journalistic career John rented a hall bedroom on Fourteenth Street which he was too poor to furnish even with a bed. He slept on the floor and proffered the same accommodation to friends with no better place to rest their heads. There were books, however. John never lacked books, and hundreds of them cluttered the place, some belonging to his father, some bought by John secondhand. One overnight guest was Frank Butler, who heaped books around his body for warmth. When he awoke in the morning, he described to John a dream in which all the authors had come to life to solace them in their penury, saying: "We were poor ourselves until we gained recognition. You little know in what good company you find yourselves and how much better bedfellows you have than if you had more money. It's not at all bad to be poor when you can have such distinguished company."

Butler sold his dream to the *Telegraph* for $15. Three years later he died insane after his removal to Bellevue Hospital from Central Park, where he had been telling passers-by that he was Nebuchadnezzar and, like the king of Babylon, "did eat grass as oxen and his body was wet with the dew of heaven."

For a while John shared a room above an Italian restaurant in Times Square with a red-headed young New York *Herald* reporter from St. Louis. Herbert Bayard Swope (later executive editor of the New York *World* and a journalist of international repute) had a weakness for women and gambling, but, in contrast to most of the newspaper fraternity, he drank sparingly, wore spats and a Homburg, carried a cane and comported himself with such a patrician air that many doors closed to his rough-and-ready colleagues would open to him. His major spheres of interest were crime and politics.

Now and then John would accompany his roommate on his reportorial rounds. The assignment one evening was an interview with a minister. A saloon stood opposite the rectory, and John elected to wait there. When Swope finished the interview, he found John in front of the saloon's swinging doors, surrounded by a ring of snarling toughs. "Hey, I got us a fight lined up!" John yelled. With a sinking heart, Swope recognized several members of the Hudson Dusters, a West Side gang of eye-gouging, skull-cracking thugs. As they started to close in, the minister emerged from the rectory, indicating to Swope that he had some additional information for him. In the reverential lull that greeted the churchman's appearance the besieged friends stole away.

John's first serious clash with Arthur Brisbane was occasioned by Ella Wheeler Wilcox, whose mawkish doggerel the Hearst newspapers had been featuring for years. Her effusions radiated sweetness and light, but John, when requested to illustrate them, produced a Doré-influenced gallows scene. Though the art editor passed it, Mrs. Wilcox was incensed. Never again, she vowed, would such a morbid artist be permitted to pervert the spirit of her work. Brisbane dispatched John to the Hoffman House, where the versifier then resided, to placate her. The mission was readily accomplished. Her ire evaporated before John's Byronic allure and, to Brisbane's bewilderment, she reversed herself, insisting that thenceforth none other than Barrymore was to illustrate her poetry.

> Tell me, pretty maiden,
> Are there any more at home like you?
>
> There are a few, kind sir,
> But simple girls, and proper too.

It was the smash musical-comedy hit of the 1900–01 season. Opening on November 12, 1900, at the Casino Theatre on the corner of Thirty-ninth Street and Broadway, *Florodora* ran for 547 performances before going on the road. What entranced the gay blades of the city, such as the architect Stanford White, "Diamond Jim" Brady, the Tammany sachem Richard "Boss" Croker, William Randolph Hearst, were six pretty maidens, all the same height and shape, each a flawless little goddess. The turnover was tremendous because nearly every one was soon swept by some panting swain into either marriage—five members of the original *Florodora* sextette became the wives of millionaires—or into an informal arrangement.

During the first year seventy-three chorines pranced across the stage of the Casino Theatre as *Florodora* maidens.

Of these replacements few surpassed the appeal of a sixteen-year-old girl from Tarentum, Pennsylvania, named Evelyn Florence Nesbit. Nobody could quarrel with her descripiton of herself. "My face," she wrote years later in her memoirs, *Prodigal Days*, "was a faintly olive-hued oval crowned by lustrous copper curls. My eyes were hazel and very brilliant, my nose was straight and almost Irish in its slight upward tilt, and my mouth very red—a bit full, the lips pouting."

She was the mistress of the great architect Stanford White, a tall, handsome satyr three times her age, who designed some of the most imposing buildings in New York. Evelyn's widowed mother had sold her to him. Mother, daughter and a son, Howard, occupied a suite in the Hotel Audubon, opposite the Casino Theatre, provided for them by White.

Among White's architectural masterpieces was Madison Square Garden, with its central tower 300 feet tall, modeled after Seville's Giralda Cathedral tower. At the top stood a nude bronze Diana by Augustus Saint-Gaudens. "Madison Square is now thronged with clubmen armed with field glasses," a reporter noted when the building was completed in 1891. "No such figure has ever before been publicly exhibited in the United States."

Beneath the scandalous Diana, White maintained a studio apartment where he gave dinners and parties for a select group of sculptors, painters, architects and assorted celebrities. He often included John, whom he admired and wanted to encourage as an illustrator. It was at a small luncheon in the tower that John first beheld Evelyn Nesbit. The sight stunned him. He had grown an elegant mustache like his Uncle Jack's and throughout the meal he kept stroking it and sneaking longing glances at Evelyn.

When White was called to the telephone, John bent forward and whispered urgently: "Quick! Your address and phone number!" She gave him both and he scribbled them on his cuff. That night she received an American Beauty rose buried in a cluster of violets with a card reading: "To a quivering pink poppy in a golden, wind-swept space."

Not long after, White left the city for a two-week fishing trip and John openly courted Evelyn. Every night he waited for her at the stage door and took her to supper. Once, at Rector's, he plucked a rose petal from the table decor, floated it on the surface of a glass of milk she had ordered, and murmured: "That is your mouth."

"She was the most maddening woman, the most utterly distracting woman I have ever known," John recalled. "She was the first woman I ever loved."

According to the story Evelyn repeated on numerous occasions, she and John consumed such quantities of red wine in an Italian restaurant one night that they could barely stagger out of the place. Rather than face Mrs. Nesbit in that condition, they decided to go to John's wretched little hall bedroom and rest there until they recovered. Evelyn complained of the cold, so John enveloped her in an old cloak his father had worn as Orlando. Then they both fell into a deep sleep—"the heavy dreamless sleep of youth," as Evelyn put it—not to awake until eleven o'clock next morning.

Neither Evelyn's mother nor her paramour, who were waiting at the Audubon in a state bordering on frenzy, believed the story. "How could you forget your mother, your name, your future!" Mrs. Nesbit cried and, as though Evelyn's position as White's mistress carried no stigma, added: "Your reputation is ruined!" But she did not blame Evelyn. The fault, she insisted, was John's and she swore to make him suffer for it.

White now took a curious step. He drove Evelyn to his physician, Dr. Nathaniel Bowditch Porter, with instructions to keep her under lock and key and give her neither food nor drink. Throughout the day Dr. Porter plied the starving girl with questions on behalf of White. "Is it true? Did Barrymore seduce you?"

The next day White summoned John and Evelyn to the tower. Under cross-examination John said the only thing a gentleman could say: his relations with Evelyn had been strictly platonic. He then turned to Evelyn and asked her to marry him.

"Good Lord, no!" White shouted, livid with rage. "You two kids can't marry. What would you live on?"

"Love," John replied.

She was sitting beneath a lamp that heightened the coppery tones of her hair. "Don't move, Eve," John entreated her. "You look beautiful there. Why not marry me, Eve?"

"I don't know," she said teasingly.

Every day thereafter her mother would ask her if she really intended to marry "that little pup" who didn't have a cent. She told White she was sure they planned to elope. White raised a more alarming objection than John's poverty. "Barrymore is a little crazy," he warned Evelyn. "His father is in an insane asylum. The whole family is queer."

To remove her from John's orbit, they sent her to the De Mille School at Pompton, New Jersey.*

But Mrs. Nesbit had no cause to fear that Evelyn would throw herself away on a penniless artist. After a brief stretch at the De Mille School, she became first the mistress, then the wife of the psychotic millionaire Harry Kendall Thaw.

For John the episode scarcely dispelled his mistrust of women.

John's career as a pictorial journalist came to an abrupt halt on May 12, 1902, three days after the novelist Paul Leicester Ford was shot to death by his brother Malcolm, who then killed himself. The tragedy prompted Brisbane to compose one of his gaseous, platitudinous commentaries. A large space was left on the editorial page for John to fill with an edifying illustration. But John, having caroused all the previous night, reached the *Journal* in disarray with but minutes to spare before the deadline. He dashed off a sketch depicting a brutal, hulking figure, the mark of Cain upon his forehead. It was too late for the photo engravers to make a careful reproduction, and the resulting half-tone looked like a sand drawing after a windstorm.

At sight of the botch Brisbane summoned John to his office and suggested that perhaps he should follow his family's example and try his hand at acting.

Many years later, in a letter soliciting John's support for a fund-raising campaign to rebuild the Shakespeare Memorial Theatre at Stratford-on-Avon, Brisbane wrote: "I remember very well your newspaper work when you were so young. If you had stuck to it, you would of course have gone into painting, but not even the Angel Gabriel knows whether you might have in that direction made an even bigger name than you have made in pictures that move."

John agreed to do his bit for Shakespeare and added: "I am glad you remember my old days on the paper. Why in the name of Heaven the editorial axe did not descend sooner on my jejune and careless head, I realize now in later manhood was due entirely to your tolerant good nature and innate sense of whimsical philanthropy. I have not forgotten it."

John's love of art never waned and his failure to rise above mediocrity as an artist saddened him, if, indeed, the frustration was not a factor in his self-destructiveness. He kept on sketching and oc-

---

* Run by Mrs. Henry Churchill De Mille, the mother of the film director Cecil B. De Mille and the playwright William C. De Mille.

casionally attempted watercolors. He posed as his own model for a series of dramatic character studies, caricatured various celebrities, decorated the margins of his letters to friends with roguish little cartoons. "I might have been," he told Gene Fowler, speaking of his artistic aspirations, "but I wasn't."

PART

III

POINTS WEST
1901–1917

7

Running Easy

ACT One. The Landing Dock of the Cunard Steamship Company.

Captain Robert Carrolton Jinks and his comrades, Lieutenants Charles Lamartine and Augustus Bleeker von Vorkenberg, ablaze with gold braid, each holding a shako in one hand and a nosegay in the other, are waiting for Mme. Trentoni, the rich and famous diva, to descend the gangplank. Under the terms of the scheme they have concocted, they will pool their resources, $4,500 altogether, and Captain Jinks, who has undertaken to capture Mme. Trentoni's affections, will draw upon the money pool to further his courtship. If he succeeds, he will share his wife's fortune with his co-conspirators. But in the end true love intervenes and the Captain renounces the deception.

As the first act gets under way, Lieutenant Lamartine begins to recapitulate the terms of the contract. . . .

It was John's first speaking role and he owed it to Ethel. During a return engagement of *Captain Jinks* at Philadelphia's Garrick Theatre in October 1901, the actor playing Lamartine, Francis Byrne, had to leave the city to attend his mother's funeral and Ethel, having persuaded the stage manager to let John replace him, summoned her brother from New York by telegraph with instructions to memorize his lines en route.

"Agreement made this day of October in the year 1872," says

John onstage, then stops dead, staring blankly at Captain Jinks. "I've blown up," he announces without noticeable distress. "Where do we go now?"

For the rest of the act he improvises, throwing the cast into utter confusion. (Maurice redivivus.) His impudence strikes Ethel, watching from the wings, as so comically outrageous that she can barely contain herself when she makes her entrance. To cap the mischief, as the curtain rises to applause after the second act, John advances to the footlights and bows deeply as if the applause were meant for him. He then leads Ethel forward, bows to her and bows again to the audience.

The audience laughs indulgently. Despite the hash he has made of the play, they cannot help but respond to his gaiety, his insouciance, his verve—assets that would sustain him as an actor for years to come. Charles Frohman, who happens to be in the theater, tells John: "With a better memory, you might make a comedian someday. As a matter of fact, your own lines got more laughs than the rest of the show."

Francis Byrne returned for the next performance and John did not get another chance to act for two years. He sold an occasional drawing. He painted some murals for Murray's Roman Restaurant in New York. He undertook a number of endorsements for commercial products, including Never-Split Linings. But mostly he depended on Ee-thel's largesse, as did Lionel. When, during one of her summer jaunts to England, she was rumored engaged to an impecunious captain of the Cold Stream Guards, Harry Graham, the question arose in international social circles: "Who's going to support them?" "Don't worry," said the Chicago humorist Finley Peter Dunne, an old friend of the Barrymores, "Lionel and Jack will support them on the money Ethel gives Lionel and Jack."

In June 1902, when *Captain Jinks* ended its tour, Frohman tendered Ethel a bonus in lieu of a raise. She declined. Ever solicitous of her brothers' careers, she demanded instead a character part for Lionel in a play Frohman was to produce in the fall, *The Mummy and the Humming Bird* by Isaac Henderson. John Drew was the star, and the part Ethel had in mind for Lionel was the exacting one of a Neapolitan organ grinder, which required him not only to play the instrument but to speak English with a convincing Neapolitan accent. Lionel got the part and made a great success of it.

Through family connections John, too, again obtained work in the theater. Uncle Googan's father-in-law, McKee Rankin, was

touring the West with a repertory that included Hermann Suder-
mann's drama *Magda*, starring Nance O'Neil. Rankin cast John
in the minor part of a young officer, Max von Wedlowski. The
opening date, on which John received his first red apple, was October 31, 1903, and the place, W. S. Cleveland's newly constructed
theater on Wabash Avenue in Chicago. Amy Leslie, the Chicago
News critic who had extolled Maurice Barrymore with such
fervor, found less to applaud in the son's performance. "The part of
Max," she wrote, "was played by a young actor who calls himself
Mr. John Barrymore. He walked about the stage as if he had been all
dressed up and forgotten."

Following Lionel's tour de force as a Neapolitan organ grinder,
Augustus Thomas wanted him for a major part in his new comedy
The Other Girl. This necessitated a good many dinner-table con-
ferences and John was often invited to join them. The playwright,
who had a strong feeling for the occult, noted: "There is in both the
boys a deep hospitality for everything approaching mysticism, and
the forceful side of telepathy had for them a profound attraction."

One evening, at the Café Boulevard on Second Avenue and
Tenth Street, Thomas proposed an experiment in thought trans-
ference. "I was referring to . . . the possibility of making a person
in front of one in an audience conscious of the gaze of another at a
distance behind him." John, long convinced of the validity of such
phenomena, was enthralled. Sitting at a table in the extreme rear of
the restaurant, they chose a woman in the far front, her back squarely
toward them. "Instead of merely commanding the lady to look around,
we in our minds definitely dramatized her doing so and focused
thought and attention on her." Ten seconds later, with a gesture of
annoyance, she faced about and glared resentfully at the trio.

Few events in the career of a young American actor are more important than his first Broadway appearance, and Frohman, with, one
suspects, a nudge from Ethel, arranged for John's debut at the Empire Theatre. The play, by the incessant scribbler Clyde Fitch, was a
verbose comedy set in a department store entitled *Glad of It*. The casting was largely a family affair. John's cousin Georgie Mendum enacted an important character. So did his uncle Sidney's sister-in-law,
Phyllis Rankin. John had to content himself with the modest role of
Corley, a press agent. Another inconsequential part was portrayed by
Thomas Meighan, who would one day achieve celebrity as a star of
the silent screen.

As theatrical entertainment, *Glad of It*, which opened on De-

cember 28, 1903, was catastrophic. The New York *Dramatic Mirror*
reflected the critical consensus with its pronouncement that "it was
one of the gabbiest plays ever seen and heard, here or in a lunatic
asylum." The *Evening Sun* reported: "It isn't a play at all. It is a
series of scenes with the same characters running through them, and
the curtain did not fall on the last scene until very nearly 12 o'clock."

For John the critics had kinder words, especially from those who
remembered Maurice Barrymore. "His resemblance in voice and
manner to his father of twenty years ago," reported the New York
Telegraph, "his walk and features, smile and look was startling. He
was only in the second act when he could, advantageously to himself
and Mr. Fitch, have been in all four acts."

John was fortunate in his next play, deriving from it a rare
technical training in the art of comedic acting and ad libbing. It was
a farce, *The Dictator*, by his sister's friend Richard Harding Davis,
and another Frohman production, with William Collier the star.
John used to say in later years that he learned from Collier more
about how to raise a laugh than from all the Barrymores combined.
His role in *The Dictator* was that of a drunken wireless operator and
he often staggered onto the stage authentically stewed, yet able to
get through his lines almost as written.

The opening of *The Dictator*, in the spring of 1904, coincided
with preparations for a momentous domestic event among the Rankins,
the Drews and the Barrymores. The first two families had already
been united through the marriage of Sidney Drew and Gladys
Rankin. Then Phyllis Rankin, the second of McKee and Kitty Rankin's
daughters, married the actor Harry Davenport. And now Lionel was
enraptured by the youngest daughter, Doris Rankin. She was sixteen
years old. They were married on June 19, 1904, in New York's St.
Xavier's Catholic Church.

On March 25, 1905, John was still impersonating the alcoholic
telegrapher of *The Dictator*, Ethel was playing a comedy, *Sunday*,
in Philadelphia, and Lionel was on the road in *The Other Girl*, when
word reached them from the Long Island Home at Amityville.

Long before, in a saloon, Maurice had borrowed a pen from a
bartender and written this quatrain as his own epitaph:

> He walked beneath the stars
> And slept beneath the sun;
> He lived a life of going-to-do
> And died with nothing done.

When Ethel and John arrived at Amityville, Maurice had been dead for hours. In despair over the spoiled relationship between herself and her father, she asked John, as the bills were handed to her: "Do you think I ought to give this room up?"

She recounted later: "He and I telegraphed Uncle Jack to ask if we might bury father in the Drew family plot in Philadelphia and he said we might. So we brought father back to Philadelphia, and only Jack and I and some old family retainers . . . were at the cemetery. [Lionel couldn't get there in time for the funeral.] This ended a chapter in my life that has always seemed tragically incomplete."

Almost from their wedding day Lionel and Doris had been debating the course of his career. Lionel wanted to quit the stage and return to the Art Students League.

"Why go there?" said Doris. "Go after the real thing. You've *been* to the Art Students League. Go to Paris."

When Lionel consulted Ethel, she used the identical argument. "Well, why the League? You've been there. Why don't you do it right and go to Paris?"

Because, Lionel explained, he didn't have enough money.

"All right, I'll lend you the money."

And so the newlyweds departed for Paris. They stayed there for almost four years, living la vie de Bohème while Lionel happily painted.

Ethel, now a full-fledged star, was rehearsing James Barrie's *Alice Sit-by-the-Fire*, which, together with his curtain-raiser *Pantaloon*, was scheduled for a Christmas-night opening at the Criterion. She talked Frohman into engaging John for the former and both brothers for the latter. She herself appeared only in *Alice Sit-by-the-Fire*. Lionel, in his last stage appearance before sailing to Europe, played a character part, a clown, and acquitted himself brilliantly. But John, who was drinking as heavily as usual, gave his sister cause for regret. One night he failed to enter on cue. Ethel tried to save the situation by ad libbing: "Here he comes. . . . He's walking up the path. . . . He's ringing the bell. . . ." She ad libbed in vain. The stage manager, James Kearney, found John sprawled across a couch in his dressing room, dead drunk and without a stitch on. Kearney had to play his role for the rest of the performance.

On the road with the twin bill John comported himself well

enough until the company played the Grand Theatre in Chicago. During *Alice Sit-by-the-Fire* the leading man, Bruce McRae, standing in the wings with a supporting actress, May Seymour, chanced to look behind him. "Don't turn around," he cautioned her. But curiosity prevailed and, turning, she beheld John stark naked, holding up a pair of shoes and demanding in a stage whisper: "Who'll polish them for me?"

William Collier should have known better. After two years with *The Dictator*, first in New York, then in London, he was accustomed to John showing up drunk at curtain time or not showing up at all. Several nights the stage manager had to play his part. In desperation Collier told Frohman that, much as he loved John, he would have to get rid of him. "Don't do it, Willie," the producer pleaded, "it'll break Ethel's heart."

"If I keep him," said Collier, "it will break mine."

And now the entire company, all except John, was assembled at Grand Central Station, ready to take off on the longest stretch of the tour thus far—Australia, with a stopover in San Francisco. Collier had implored John to leave a call at his hotel in case he overslept. But there was no sign of him. "All aboard!' cried the conductor. At the final warning John at last sauntered onto the platform. He was wearing evening dress.

"Why," Collier raged, "why didn't you leave a call at your hotel like I told you?"

"I did," said John, "but I couldn't tell where I would stop last night, so I left calls at six or seven hotels, only I didn't hit the right one."

During one of their last conversations at Amityville in 1905 Lionel told his father he was under contract for a tour that would take him across the country to San Francisco.

"You're a God-damned liar!" said Maurice. "Everybody knows that San Francisco has been destroyed by earthquake and fire."

A year later, on the night of April 17, 1906, John was sitting in a box at San Francisco's Grand Opera House, listening to Olive Fremstad, Bessie Abott, Enrico Caruso and other members of the Metropolitan Opera Company sing *Carmen*. He was to sail for Australia next day.

A supper party after the performance lasted until four a.m. of the 18th and John accompanied a fellow guest to his home. John had a room at the St. Francis Hotel, but at that hour he was glad to accept his companion's invitation to stay the night. Before retiring, his host insisted on showing him his priceless collection of antique Oriental glass.

John had been in bed but a few minutes, lying in full fig on the coverlet, a carnation in his buttonhole, when at about 5:12 a.m., the first shock of the San Francisco earthquake hurled him across the room. It is unlikely that amid the falling plaster, the screams of terror and flaming chaos in the streets John recalled his crazed father's precognition, but it must have come back to him later, strengthening his belief in the occult.

John hurriedly tried to rouse his host. The collector slumbered on as if nothing more than a gentle rain had fallen upon the city. John finally jolted him awake by shouting: "Come see what's happened to the Ming Dynasty."

When John got back to the St. Francis Hotel, he found it intact and heard Willie Collier calling to him from Union Square across the way. "Go West, young man," said the comedian, who was perched atop a pile of debris clad in a flowered dressing gown and bedroom slippers, "and blow up with the country."

Nearby, shivering in the early-morning cold, an opera soprano sat on her trunk. John found a saloon that had not been totally demolished, filled a glass with cognac and gallantly pressed it upon the freezing soprano. He passed Diamond Jim Brady, who never tired, after he returned East, of telling people how John Barrymore dressed for an earthquake.

A slight split had developed meanwhile in the façade of the St. Francis. It was then past eight a.m. and John's body ached for sleep. He asked the desk clerk if he considered it prudent to retire to his room.

"Perfectly," the clerk assured him. "There isn't the slightest chance in the world of it ever happening again."

The words had scarcely left his mouth when the second shock shook the city. Yet the hotel stood firm, and John, worn out, tumbled into bed to awaken hours later to the stench of a burning city. He found refuge with some friends living in the suburb of Burlingame, where he stayed a week before he could rejoin the Collier troupe on the Oakland ferry, sail to Vancouver and thence to Australia aboard the liner *Moana*.

With $10 left in his pockets and no clothes other than a blue serge suit a size too small, he wrote Ethel a long letter. "I wanted to

make it a good one and worth at least a hundred dollars, so I described in great detail what I had seen in those harrowing days and
what I had myself been through. I confessed to having seen people
shot in the street, spiked on bayonets and other horrors so great that
the imagination was almost blunt from contemplating them. I wrote
that I had been thrown out of bed by the earthquake and almost
miraculously escaped injury from falling bricks and plaster, and then,
with much pathos and resignation, I described the terrible scene at
the Oakland ferry where, weak from exhaustion and privation, I had
been put cruelly to work sorting stones by the soldiers."

Ethel showed the letter to John Drew, who read it so contem-
platively that she asked him: "What's the matter, Uncle Jack? Don't
you believe it?"

His reply became the definitive character assessment of the
young John Barrymore. "I believe every word of it," he said and
added the epigram that was to sweep through the theatrical world:
"It took a convulsion of Nature to make him get up and the United
States Army to make him go to work."

For a man of John's tastes, and of Willie Collier's too, Australia
was no Cockaigne. In Melbourne, for example, they failed to find a
single café, bar or restaurant of the sort where they could eat and
drink away the tedious hours between shows. They finally persuaded
the owner of a delicatessen, which was illuminated by one gas jet,
to let them use his establishment for their festivities.

Their spirits were considerably lifted as they left the theater one
night when they discerned not far ahead a towering figure in a high
hat, an Inverness cape and across his shirt front an advertisement
for Hoffman House cigars. He was spectacularly drunk, a condition
the two actors were also approaching. As they neared the formidable
figure, he stopped, flung out a mighty arm and, in the rolling tones
of a third-rate Shakespearean tragedian, cried: "Birds of the night,
whither away?"

Loath to part with so rare a specimen, they insisted he share
their supper table at the delicatessen. But no sooner was he seated than
he fell into a profound torpor. The conversation among the conscious
drifted around to other American actors who had fared poorly in
Australia. Somebody mentioned Nat Goodwin. The slumbering giant
immediately awoke. "Goodwin!" he roared. "Goodwin! Nat Goodwin
was once preeminent in sententious comedy, but now—if you will
permit me to say so—he is—erstwhile!" And he fell asleep again, not
to emit another sound for the rest of the night.

Such was the rigor of law and order in Melbourne that John and Collier were arrested one night, when there was no performance, for laughing too boisterously in the street after nine p.m. "That's what's the matter with our audiences," said Willie. "They're afraid to laugh after nine."

As John was rattling across the Australian continent on June 26, 1906, the American press carried a jolting story of lust and crime. The night before, Harry Thaw and Evelyn Nesbit, his wife of a year, had seated themselves at a table on the Madison Square Garden Roof for the opening of a musical comedy, *Mamzelle Champagne*. Not far off, the architect of the Garden, Stanford White, occupied a table of his own. Thaw walked over to him, whipped out a pistol and shot him dead. "He ruined my wife," Thaw told the policeman who arrested him a few minutes later.

In Australia John did manage to find sweet diversion in the companionship of a musical-comedy soubrette known as "The Gaiety Girl." Grace Palotta was a joy to behold and the popularizer of a song from a burlesque show, *A Runaway Girl*, whose endearingly inane verse went like this:

> Oh, listen to the band—
> How merrily they play!
> Oh, don't you think it grand?
> Hear everybody say,
> "Oh, listen to the band."
> Who doesn't love to hark
> To the shout of "Here they come!"
> And the banging of the drum?
> Oh, listen to the Soldiers in the Park.

The Collier troupe toured the continent for a year, playing *The Dictator* as well as Augustus Thomas' comedy *On the Quiet*. When the time came to sail home, John was saddened to leave his Gaiety Girl, whom he often referred to thereafter as one of the loveliest creatures on earth.

John had barely shown up in the East when the Manhattan District Attorney, William Travers Jerome, subpoenaed him as a witness in the trial of Harry Thaw. The defense was temporary insanity brought on by his wife Evelyn's confession to him of how Stanford White had debauched her in her girlhood. The Thaw family spent a fortune to besmirch the murdered man's reputation, while Evelyn herself received $200,000 to testify in behalf of her husband.

To counter the defense strategy, Jerome proposed to show that there had been other men in Evelyn's life before she married Thaw, John Barrymore among them.

John's testimony was not yet needed and the court excused him. He finished a short Boston run of *Captain Jinks* with Ethel, then, pleading grippe and a nervous breakdown, retreated to a sanitarium in Poland Springs, Maine. By the time he recovered, the Thaw defense had won—that is, instead of sending him to the electric chair, the jury found him "not guilty as charged on the ground of the defendant's insanity," and he was committed to the State Asylum for the Criminal Insane at Matteawan. Seven years later, after an attempted escape and two more trials, he was declared sane and acquitted of all charges.

The nature of the questioning to which John would have been subjected began to emerge when Jerome summoned a Dr. Carlton Flint to the witness stand. Rumors had been rife for months that John took Evelyn to this physician for an abortion. Surgery had indeed been performed on Evelyn at the De Mille School, but it was supposedly an appendectomy. Curiously, Evelyn was reported to have undergone two other appendectomies before.

She blanched when Flint entered the courtroom.

"Did you ever see this gentleman before?" Jerome asked her.

"No," Evelyn swore.

"Are you sure?"

"I am quite sure I never saw him before."

"Did you never go to that gentleman for medical treatment in this city?"

"No, sir."

"Did you not go with Jack Barrymore to this Dr. Carlton Flint's office in his house in New York City?"

"No, sir."

"Was the operation performed on you at Pompton a criminal operation?"

Thaw's lawyer, Delphin Michael Delmas, known as "The Napoleon of the Western Bar," who was receiving a fee of $100,000, successfully objected that Evelyn had been anesthetized and so could hardly have known what kind of operation it was.

Jerome had another go at Flint, but it proved no more revelatory than the first.

"Did this young woman, in the company of Jack Barrymore, come to your office for treatment in 1901 or early 1902?"

If Flint should answer, Delmas protested, he would be violating a professional confidence.

No real theater-lover, none who prized artistry, good language and fresh ideas in a play, could have quarreled with the Boston critic Henry Clapp when he complained in 1900: "Our drama has no permanent literary value and produces nothing that is going to remain in the intellectual stock-in-trade of our race." The American theater during the first decade of the twentieth century had a simplism verging on idiocy. Successful playwrights like Fitch and Thomas were mechanics who knew down to the last nut and bolt how to construct a melodrama that would shake the rafters with roars of excitement or a romance that would set flowing a flood of tears.

Few people took the theater seriously, unless the dramatist was Shakespeare. Shaw was widely viewed as a sneering, venomous radical, Ibsen as a morbid desecrator of moral values. Personality was what counted. No matter what claptrap might star a James O'Neill, a William Faversham, a Mrs. Fiske, the play was not the thing. *Captain Jinks* may have been one of the most foolish farces ever written, but Ethel Barrymore played the lead and it was this young, dewy, regal beauty the audience came to see. "We regard the workman first and the work second," said Charles Frohman. "Our imaginations are fired not nearly so much by great deeds as great doers."

John's professional equipment was now extensive. He had not only mastered Willie Collier's bag of comic tricks and flair for ad libbing, but he could do a fair imitation of Uncle Jack, lighting a cigarette or twirling a glass of wine with aristocratic elegance, and when required to draw a sword in a costume piece, he had all his father's bravura. At this stage of his career he wore a trim mustache. His otherwise Praxitelean symmetry was marred by slightly crooked, almost clawlike fingers on short, stubby hands, but his instinctive manipulation onstage lent them a grace, a force, a humor, as the occasion demanded. Nicotine stained the sides of his right middle and index fingers, for he was a chain smoker.

The plays in which he appeared when he returned to the States did nothing to raise the prevailing theatrical standards. The first was *The Boys of Company "B,"* a comedy about the National Guard* which opened at New York's Lyceum Theatre in April 1907 and

* One of the Guardsmen was Mack Sennett.

then embarked on a nationwide tour. "A drama of the chocolate éclair variety," so one Broadway reviewer described it. The Baltimore *American* summarized the plot in a fashion to stir every red-blooded male in the audience: "The hero is such a one as is dear to the American heart—energetic and ardent in his love-making and determined past all opposition to come out a winner in getting the girl he loves."

Compared to John's next vehicle, *The Boys of Company "B"* was a masterpiece. Clyde Fitch adapted it from a farce by the Parisian wit Tristan Bernard, calling it *Toddles*. "It is easy enough to spoil a French farce," commented *Theatre Magazine*, "if adapter, stage manager and actors unite their incapacities. . . . Mr. John Barrymore as Toddles was not without the comic spirit, justifying a hopeful view of his possibilities for the future, in an atmosphere depressing enough to nullify the efforts of the best possible comedian. . . ."

The majority of critics both in the city and on the road agreed. After dismissing *Toddles* as "stupidly puerile," the New York *Globe* observed: "The excellence of the work he [Barrymore] did only increases our disappointment in the meagre opportunities given him by the author."

John shrugged and noted, as he normally did when theatrical discussion assumed too lofty an altitude: "There's a lot of talk about the art of the theater. The truth is it's just one way to make a living." Shortly before the San Francisco earthquake, he had admitted in an interview with an *Examiner* critic: "If I had a choice, I'd give up the stage."

One December evening in 1908 found John broke, jobless and dining alone in style at an Atlantic City restaurant when he recognized a producer from Chicago, Mort Singer, who specialized in musical comedies. In the ensuing shop talk Singer disclosed his plans for an extravaganza to be called *A Stubborn Cinderella*. "Would you like a part in it?" he asked John unexpectedly.

Rarely, if ever, had John brought off a more persuasive performance. "Oh, I don't know," he drawled. "I've got something in mind I'm considering."

All he had in mind was how to pay for the shrimp bisque he was savoring, not to mention his hotel bill.

"How would a hundred and fifty dollars do?" Singer suggested.

John had yet to earn more than a third of that. Singer mistook his gasp for outraged refusal.

"Well, then," said the producer, "make it a hunderd and seventy-five. If you want some money, here's a hundred dollars."

A Stubborn Cinderella brought John more than money. It brought him in the person of its slim, sprightly leading lady, Sallie Fisher, a playmate who remained so for the run of the show—almost six months in Chicago alone. John sang, danced and clowned and, according to the Chicago press: "Your matinee audiences beat their breasts in admiration." Of his dancing John Golden, the producer, still remembered decades later: "He had a trick of stepping up in the air that seemed to surprise and please the ladies."

Amy Leslie continued to be John's severest Chicago critic—but not for long. "He is not a good actor," she had concluded after sitting through *The Boys of Company "B."* . . . "He has twenty faults which he can, but probably will not, correct, because the Barrymores never correct anything."

A personal encounter a month later radically altered this view. "To meet him casually or at a table," she told her Chicago *News* readers, "is to come across a lighted taper of inexhaustible humor—a humor sweet, bubbling and irresponsible as the flight of a zephyr and quite as harmless. He is one of those well-bred surprises who by no manner of means could ever trespass upon the estate of a listener's sentiments or blunder into a faux pas for the sake of a laugh. He is always kind, boyishly courteous and full of laughter and quick replies. He does not philosophize, but thinks only effervescent and evasive things, avoids burdens of mental, moral or social strain. . . ."

"I am so good these days," he smilingly told Miss Leslie, "so good my halo pinches."

She concurred, and when *A Stubborn Cinderella* opened in Chicago on December 16, 1908, she wrote: "He has developed into a capital actor."

Between *A Stubborn Cinderella* and Winchell Smith's *The Fortune Hunter*, John's greatest success up to then, he attempted another musical comedy, *The Candy Shop*, a calamity, but such was the spell he had cast over Amy Leslie that she wrote: "Jack Barrymore is running easy in the straight and narrow path of the steady musical comedian and though fretting at the bit a little and wanting to break away and join something else, anything so it is a change, he must be credited with the hit of his life and handed much advice to stick around a while."

In Chicago as well as in every other major city on the theatrical circuit, critics and audiences were beginning to applaud John regardless of the merit of the play. Since *Magda*, which he stumbled through at the age of nineteen, he had enacted twelve roles in comedies and farces which were almost uniformly trash. It scarcely mattered. What brought the fans flocking to the box office were the same qualities that had attracted them to John's father—the verve, the dash, the physical beauty.

8

Women

S HE was blonde and small, weighing barely ninety pounds. Born Irene Frizzell in Chicago, she started her theatrical career at the age of sixteen under the management of Henry W. Savage as a chorus girl in a Broadway musical show, *Peggy from Paris*. Within a month she was promoted to leading lady. At about this time she and John became lovers.

The affair was short-lived. Irene left John for a prosperous Wall Street investor, Jay Ward, then left Ward to marry a multi-millionaire real-estate operator, Felix Isman. She never abandoned the theater, but, under the pseudonym Irene Fenwick, specialized in the portrayal of such sinful women as Sylvia Futvoye in *The Brass Bottle*, Ki Ki in *The Zebra* and Anne Grey in *The Co-Respondent*. "I know people will hate me for saying it," she said archly, "but I do enjoy playing these parts. I can't help it. So many of the interesting heroines of history have been wicked."

Isman divorced her, charging her with adultery and naming John, among others, as co-respondents. But she was not long alone. She soon married another substantial Wall Streeter, James F. O'Brien. Isman, meanwhile, married a chorine named Hazel Allen.

In the procession of showgirls and actresses who brightened John's nights, the second Mrs. Isman figured almost as prominently as the first. Hazel Allen (sometimes billed as Pinkie Evans) was featured in a Ziegfeld revue, *Midnight Frolic*, at the time she married Isman and in another musical, *Aphrodite*, when they were divorced. According to a Broadway commentator, Hazel was "quite familiar to . . . the patrons of lobster palaces."

John's tireless pursuit of women was sometimes hampered by his financial condition. He could now afford to treat a companion to a bottle of champagne and a lobster at Rector's or Delmonico's, but furs and diamonds still lay beyond his resources. It may have been this deficiency which so quickly lost him the exquisite little Margaret Bird (stage name: Gladys Wallis) to Samuel Insull.

On the road John often found himself playing the same town as Elsie Janis, a gifted singer, dancer and mimic. (Her most famous impersonation came to be Ethel Barrymore purring her renowned exit line: "That's all there is. There isn't any more.") But for the vigilance of Elsie's mother, Mrs. Bierbower, the relationship might have grown considerably closer. John, Elsie confessed in her middle years, had been "my first love, I hasten to add that he will probably be my last—for once you start loving any of the Barrymores you find that, like jungle fever or lumbago, 'it' comes back on you every now and then."

Elsie kept a diary. In a 1909 entry she noted: "Chicago. Nothing exciting, except that Jack Barrymore is in town."

A New York entry: "Rector's. Jack Barrymore was there. He came over to our table. He is wonderful."

John gave her a de luxe edition of *The Ancient Mariner* illustrated by Gustave Doré, which they read together aloud while the watchful Mrs. Bierbower sat in the adjoining room with the door between wide open.

When he was in New York, John's first-line consorts included Lotta Faust, Vivian Blackburn and Bonnie Maginn. Lotta, a former cashier in Brooklyn's Abraham & Straus department store, made her theatrical debut in 1897 and proceeded to scandalize audiences by dancing clad in diaphanous veils. She had jet-black hair, a buxom figure and a back as shapely as Juno's, if somewhat plumper. "The 'Lotta Faust back,' " reported the New Jersey *Review*, "will be mentioned for many years wherever the beauty of women is discussed. Marblelike in its firm whiteness, it became famous on both sides of the Atlantic. Miss Faust esteemed lightly that back, but she gave credit to the person who discovered its artistic possibilities. 'It was my dressmaker,' she said. 'She was trying on an evening gown and said:

"You ought to have your gowns cut down to the waist behind. . . ." The back immodest? Fudge! If a stranger came into the room while one was dressing, what would she do? Turn her back, of course.' " John once confessed: "I like to grab a handful of back."

Now it was the season of Bonalin ("Bonnie") Maginn, a wriggling mass of golden curls and curves and the most conspicuous of the Weber-and-Fields Music Hall showgirls. She eventually married John T. Davis, whose multimillionaire father, Henry Gassaway Davis, was the unsuccessful Democratic candidate for vice-president in 1904 at the age of eighty-one. John was next distracted by Vivian Blackburn, who combined the skills of model, showgirl and professional fencer. In her fencing gear, a red heart sewn to her white blouse, Vivian reigned as the queen of the cigarette-picture girls.

And then came Katherine.

It was a family of some substance and distinction. The late John R. Brady had been a New York State Supreme Court justice. Of his two daughters, each of whom inherited half a million dollars from their uncle, the younger, Kitty, married a corporation lawyer with an international practice, Sidney Harris. His mother, Miriam Coles Harris, produced a spate of novels celebrating the rewards of virtue and piety. Among the most widely read were *Louie's Last Term at St. Mary's* and *Dear Feast of Lent*. The older Brady girl, May, married Albert Stevens, a wealthy man of impeccable pedigree and thereby succeeded to the eminence of chatelaine of Stevens Castle, which had stood on the west bank of the Hudson River for generations. Widowed, she married Herbert Harriman, an influential figure in the world of high finance.

Sidney and Kitty Harris had been divorced for ten years. Kitty's avuncular inheritance, augmented by alimony, enabled her to live grandly on Long Island with her daughter, Katherine. In 1910 Katherine was formally introduced to New York society, and at a coming-out party she met John Barrymore. He was then twenty-seven and had been playing the hero of Winchell Smith's *The Fortune Hunter*, his most profitable role to date. Katherine had just turned seventeen, a lithe, doe-like belle with a corona of honey-hued hair and a faint lisp. After a dance or two John was bewitched.

As the courtship progressed, Sidney Harris raised furious objections. He wanted no actor for a son-in-law, let alone one ten years older than his daughter who had been running around with such wantons as the unspeakable Evelyn Nesbit. He compelled his ex-wife, under threat of holding up her alimony, to take Katherine to Paris and enroll her in the Convent of the Assumption.

Secretly, Mrs. Harris was on her daughter's side. Stagestruck from girlhood, she had once played a part with John Drew in *Rosemary*. Her lovelorn daughter had an even more ardent champion in Judge Brady's widow, Katherine Lydig ("Gabbie") Brady. She passed John in the street one day. It was the first time she had ever seen him. She immediately wrote to her granddaughter:

> Don't let your father keep you over there. Come back with your mother. You cannot be shut up. The more he is against Jack Barrymore, the more you will like him. Do not be afraid of Mr. Harris. He helped to bring you into the world. That was all.
>
> Aunt May and Uncle Herbert [Harriman] are bitterly against Jack, but don't you care. Come home to see him. A lady told me today that the Barrymores go everywhere in Philadelphia. Excellent family. Excellent position.
>
> Jack looks as if he wants a woman's care. I saw him in the street. He is so handsome. If I were a young woman, I could be crazy about him myself.

Thus fortified by maternal support, Kitty Harris delivered her daughter back to New York and the arms of John Barrymore. Sidney Harris raged, but had no power to intervene since Katherine was now of age. A month later, on September 1, 1910, Father Thomas Harlin married John and Katherine at St. Xavier's, the same church where Lionel and Doris Rankin had been united. The bride's father refused to attend.

Swift vengeance fell upon those who had abetted the romance. Kitty Harris was forced to sue for unpaid alimony. The Harrimans, who had been supporting Grandmother Gabbie, sharply reduced her allowance.

The year before Ethel, too, had been married. The groom was Russell Griswold Colt, whose father, Samuel Pomeroy Colt, headed the U.S. Rubber Company, among others, and whose grandfather had invented the Colt revolver. Ethel bore him three children—Samuel, Ethel and John. At Samuel's baptism the godfathers were Finley Peter Dunne and John Barrymore. The priest assumed that they both knew the Apostles' Creed and at the appropriate moment he instructed them to recite it. John began: "I believe in God, the Father Almighty,

Creator of heaven and earth—" Then dropping his voice: "That lets me out."

Ethel's marriage brought Lionel and Doris home from Paris, where they had been living happily among artists, musicians and poets. As Lionel put it, "When Ethel was married . . . it seemed only appropriate and decent that I cease being a remittance man."

He had no wish to return to the stage. But after discovering that he could not earn a livelihood as either a painter or a magazine illustrator, he found himself, in the fall of 1909, under the Frohman banner, impersonating "Abdulla, a dragoman" in *The Fires of Fate*, "a modern morality play in four acts by Arthur Conan Doyle."

It garnered no laurels. Nor did any of the four endeavors that followed, including some vaudeville sketches thrown together by Lionel and Aunt Gladys Rankin. In his need he turned to the despised infant industry then burgeoning in New York—moving pictures. He approached a former stock-company actor he knew slightly, David Wark Griffith, now a director for the Biograph Company at 11 East Fourteenth Street.* Griffith hired him for $10 a week and in 1912 Lionel stepped in front of a camera for the first time in a one-reeler, *The New York Hat*. A twelve-year-old girl named Anita Loos wrote the story and was paid $25 for it. Mary Pickford played the heroine.

The following year Ethel made her screen debut in *The Nightingale*, written for her by Augustus Thomas. "Those of us who are well-known are constantly being approached by the various companies," she commented at the time, "and they make such attractive propositions!" The producers of *The Nightingale*, All Star, paid her $15,000.

There was no honeymoon for John and Katherine. Within a few days of the wedding breakfast at Delmonico's, John took off on a tour

---

* The motion-picture industry began in the East, with nearly every studio situated in or near New York City. The first public commercial projection took place on April 23, 1896, at Koster and Bial's Music Hall on West Twenty-third Street. The projector was the Vitascope invented by Thomas Edison. The series of short subjects flashed on the screen showed a seascape and a dancer billed as "Annabelle." Among the movie studios that developed during the first decade of the twentieth century were, in addition to Biograph, All Star, Vitagraph (later absorbed by Warner Brothers), Famous Players—all situated in New York City. Between 1906 and 1909 a few small studios opened in Los Angeles, but none existed in Hollywood until October 1911, when two English brothers, William and David Horsley, established a California branch of their Centaur Company.

with *The Fortune Hunter*. The senior Colt had bought his son and daughter-in-law a big, old house in Mamaroneck, New York, and the couple persuaded Katherine to live with them during John's absence. To her embitterment, the tour kept him away, except for brief visits, almost a year.

When John finally returned to New York, it was to rehearse a road-show production of a comedy called *Uncle Sam*. As stagestruck as her mother, Katherine clamored for a chance to act with him. This was a privilege that all of John's wives and several of his mistresses would demand, and he seldom disappointed them. Billed as "Katherine Blythe"* and assigned a small part in *Uncle Sam*, Mrs. Barrymore drew faint praise from the Chicago critics for her aplomb and graceful carriage. In New York the play closed after the first night.

The next play employing both husband and wife was *Princess Zim Zim* in 1911. A comedy about a young millionaire who falls in love with a Coney Island snake-charmer, it met a harsher fate than any of the fifteen previous productions involving John. Its reception at the Boston tryout was icy and it played only 48 performances in New York. But in one respect *Princess Zim Zim* proved transcendently important to John, for it brought him into close communion with a man who would reshape his entire career and, in the words of the producer-director Arthur Hopkins, take him "up to the high mountain."

---

* To the original family name of Blyth, John, for unknown reasons, had added on "e."

9

Ned

Why did one feel this way about him? How explain this extraordinary influence over other people? In what resided his power? The question is not answered by any listing of his qualities, saintlike though they were. Of course, all who knew him were fired by his sustained gallantry, were quickened by the unquenchable flame of his spirit, were overcome by his princely prodigality of heart. . . .

He saw you whole, and in his presence you felt whole. The beautiful prayer from the *Phaedrus* was answered: "The outward and the inward man were at one."

. . . his genius was for seeing *through* the outer man to the inner one. It was his understanding of the inner man that was the most miraculous and for which one was most grateful. . . . He saw people with love, all of them, even the newcomers like myself. He saw them, therefore, creatively; not only as they were, but as they strove to be, as they were meant to be. He became for many people the creative observer in their lives.

—Anne Morrow Lindbergh

Edward Sheldon was twenty-two, a Harvard postgraduate working toward a master's degree, when a play he had completed as an undergraduate, *Salvation Nell*, opened on November 18, 1908, at

New York's Hackett Theatre with Minnie Maddern Fiske as the anguished heroine. Nell Sanders, a saloon scullion (and perhaps Mrs. Fiske's most affecting role), has an illegitimate child by her brute of a lover, Jim Platt, whom she supports with her pitiful earnings. When Jim goes to prison for killing a man during a drunken brawl, Nell joins the Salvation Army as her only escape from a life of misery and squalor. There, through religious conversion, she is redeemed and goes forth to preach salvation in front of the saloon where once she slaved. Hearing her impassioned sermon, Jim, now free on parole, sees the light, and the purified lovers are reunited.

Salvation Nell was a hit, "the most daring play New York has ever seen . . . not only dramatizes the Salvation Army, but serves up Hell's Kitchen piping hot." It ran for seventy-one performances* at the Hackett Theatre before taking to the road, and the young Harvard scholar, a product of Professor George Pierce Baker's renowned playwriting course, became an instant celebrity.

He was born on February 4, 1896, into a wealthy and highly respected Chicago family. His father, Theodore Sheldon, made his fortune as a real-estate operator, acquiring in the process a solid reputation for both integrity and shrewdness. The son attended two select Eastern schools, Hill and Milton Academy, before entering Harvard at eighteen. Breezing through the curriculum for a bachelor's degree in three years instead of the usual four, he graduated magna cum laude.

He was a slim, handsome youth, reserved yet genial, modest, poised, gentle and affectionate. The warmth of his personality, his ready laughter, his genuine concern for the troubles of others attracted to him professors as well as classmates. He was one of the most popular students who ever went to Harvard, despite an innate fastidiousness reinforced by a measure of familial Puritanism that led him to eschew the traditional collegiate dissipations. "Though no hail-fellow-well-met," wrote his biographer, Eric Wollencott Barnes, "Ned had a distaste for horseplay because it affronted his sense of human dignity, and the usual undergraduate experiments with alcohol he found dreary. But he was no teetotaler, and he was always ready for a party, particularly if it promised good talk. . . .

"One of Sheldon's most graceful talents was his ability to parry the heaviest onslaught of feminine emotion with skill and effectiveness

---

* Enough to return a healthy profit, unlike today's Broadway productions, which, because of soaring costs, may run a year or more before netting any profits.

and yet somehow leave the lady in full possession of her self-respect, and incidentally of her admiration for him.

"It was not that women lacked attraction for him. On the contrary, he felt himself drawn all too easily to a pretty face and a softly curved figure. But passion with Ned was inevitably tinged with romanticism. . . . From his mother he had acquired the idea that the only definitive relationship between men and women was marriage. Obviously he could not marry all the beautiful women who came his way, and this prevented him from plunging into any affair that could not be ended without undue complications."

Salvation Nell had barely started its run before Ned went to work on another play. For audiences of that epoch the theme of *The Nigger* was profoundly shocking: the governor of a Southern state learns, after marriage to a white woman, that he has Negro blood. Nevertheless, *The Nigger*, with all its references to racism and lynch law, was chosen in 1909 as one of the first repertory productions of the mammoth New Theatre on Central Park West. It packed the house at every performance and two road companies took it on tour.

In January 1911, at the Astor Theatre, William Brady and Holbrook Blinn, who played the title role, presented Ned's third play, *The Boss*, an arraignment of political corruption and business greed. Its success topped that of *Salvation Nell*, with eighty-eight performances. At the age of twenty-five Ned Sheldon was rich as well as famous.

None of his plays were great plays likely to outlast his generation.* But in an era when artifice and triviality typified the American theater, Ned broke new ground by dealing seriously with serious issues. Many years later Eugene O'Neill wrote to him: "Your *Salvation Nell*, along with the work of the Irish players on their first trip over here, was what first opened my eyes to the existence of a real theatre as opposed to the unreal—and to me then, hateful—theatre of my father, in whose atmosphere I had been brought up."

Princess Zim Zim was one of Sheldon's few total failures.† But he found compensation in the friendship with John Barrymore that began during the Boston tryout—perhaps the strongest friendship either of them ever formed and for John the most inspiring. According to Arthur Hopkins, writing after both men were dead, "Sheldon had

* The Chelsea Theater Center, one of New York's leading repertory groups, revived *The Boss* in 1976 as its contribution to America's Bicentennial.

† Of the twenty-three plays he wrote alone or in collaboration, all but six were commercial, if not artistic, successes.

put the finger of destiny on John Barrymore. He foresaw all that he was to become. His determination for Jack never wavered. . . . The true director of John Barrymore's rich career was Edward Sheldon."

At first blush the friendship struck those familiar with the two men as singular, the dissolute, mercurial actor and the temperate, stable playwright five years his junior. When Ned's mother, who disapproved of John, asked Ned to explain the attraction, all she could elicit was, "I like to be with him."

Mrs. Sheldon failed to grasp the scope of the common interests and enthusiasms drawing Ned and John together. They were both zestful men who shared a catholicity of tastes that embraced art, architecture, literature, music, philosophy, mysticism. They would sometimes prolong their discussions through the night and beyond dawn. Ned tried to steer John away from liquor and predatory women, with only spotty success. John feared his bad opinion and, in an effort to prevent him from discovering his delinquencies, devised elaborate stratagems, which, to Ned's amusement, he invariably saw through.

"No one ever stood in greater need of Sheldon's gift of human understanding than did John Barrymore," Barnes perceptively wrote, "and no one ever received it in fuller measure. . . . Barrymore had grown up in a world of total insecurity—emotional, financial, and moral. . . . Throughout the years Sheldon's affection was Barrymore's chief anchor in normal life. He looked upon Sheldon not only as someone with whom he could share his fun, but also as one on whose understanding and unselfish interest he could always count. Though Barrymore was five years older, his attitude toward Ned was that of a son to a far-seeing and always forgiving father."

Ned was the first to discern in John latent qualities which, if developed, could make him a great actor. But to realize this potentiality, Ned felt, John needed the challenge of good, strong plays instead of the featherweight drivel that had occupied him thus far, and he persistently prodded him toward a change of direction.

At the crest of his career, in a surge of loving recognition of how much he owed to his friend, John said: "All I want on my tombstone is, 'This goddamned son of bitch knew Ned Sheldon.' "

During the winter of 1911 Ned began work on a play inspired by the Italian opera singer Lina Cavalieri. He did not finish *Romance*, as he entitled it, until the summer of 1912. It was a love story pure and simple, unweighted by any social significance, in which a diva named Cavallini arouses the passion of a young clergyman, Tom Armstrong, to such fever heat that he is ready to abandon the cloth.

Though Cavallini requites his passion, she cannot accept the sacrifice of his promising clerical career and so rejects him. The renunciation scene reaches its climax to the accompaniment of Christmas carols sung offstage by Tom's congregation.

In the spring of 1911, shortly before sailing to Europe, a holiday trip he now took every year, Ned disclosed a happy prospect to John and a few other cherished friends: he was to marry Doris Keane. While writing *Romance*, he envisaged his betrothed as Cavallini incarnate, and when the Shubert brothers, Lee and Jake, contracted to produce the play, he would hear of no other interpreter, though a good many better actresses were available. To portray the Reverend Armstrong, Ned proposed John, who declined, saying he could not picture himself as a clergyman in love. The role went to William Courtenay. It was a lost opportunity John would regret.

Opening on February 10, 1913, at the Maxine Elliott Theatre, *Romance* was the crowning success in the careers of both playwright and actress. Following 160 performances on Broadway, the original cast toured America until 1915, the second year of World War I. In London *Romance* ran for almost three years, chalking up 1,049 performances, some of them interrupted by Zeppelin raids. This was only the beginning. In translations *Romance* moved audiences to tears all over the world. A Russian company, headed by the wife of the novelist Maxim Gorky, played it throughout Russia over a period of five years. Revivals, road companies and a musical version kept *Romance* alive for nearly three decades. In 1920 Doris Keane starred in a film version. Ten years later Greta Garbo was Cavallini, her second role in talking pictures.

But for Ned the triumph was bittersweet. Doris had broken her engagement, a blow from which he never entirely recovered. They remained close friends, however, even after she married her London leading man, Basil Sydney. Ned, in fact, wrote a play for Sydney, *The Lonely Heart*, and when, after the Baltimore tryout, the producer concluded that Sydney was wrong for the part and demanded a change of cast, Ned withdrew the play altogether.

Katherine went on tour again with John in another perishable production, *Half a Husband*. In Rochester, following a dress rehearsal, John, Katherine and two other actresses were approaching their hotel when a trio of mashers accosted the women, using unseemly language. The blood of battling Maurice Barrymore in John's veins boiled over. After seeing the women safely into the hotel lobby, he reappeared, hatless and coatless, and landed such punishing blows on the mashers that one after another turned tail and fled.

John acquired a considerable reputation for pugnacity during that tour. His wrath, possibly kindled by liquor, erupted again in a San Francisco barber shop. The casus belli was the length of his hair. After shaving him, the barber, Martin Bergman, insisted he needed a haircut. Deaf to John's explanation that the role he was then playing called for longish hair, Bergman approached him, scissors in hand. Springing from the chair with a blistering oath, John knocked him flat. Bergman filed a damage suit for $1,550. The court awarded him $800.

John and Katherine also appeared together in a comedy by John Frederick Ballard, *Believe Me, Xantippe* and, on a vaudeville tour, in one of seven sketches written by the Austrian dramatist Arthur Schnitzler under the title *The Affairs of Anatol*. In the Schnitzler sketch the feminine lead fell to Katherine. On Broadway John played five of the sketches with various ladies, Katherine not among them. His contract guaranteed him a sum unequaled in his career up to then —$1,500 a week, and *Anatol* ran nine weeks.

These joint appearances soothed but failed to heal the hurt John had caused his wife by his prolonged absences at the outset of their marriage. Their relations steadily deteriorated. Neither understood the kind of life the other wanted. In John's case it included a large measure of domesticity, alternating with nights of unbridled revelry among his old Bohemian friends in journalism and the arts like Frank Butler and "Monty" Flagg. Few actors interested him outside the theater. Once the curtain had rung down, he put his profession behind him. The social gatherings of his colleagues, formal sociability of any description tended to irritate him and induce acerbity. Though a clubbable man, he frequented the Players and the Lambs less than most members. (The Players once dropped him for not paying his annual dues, but reinstated him a year later after he repaired the omission.) A pungent and inexhaustible conversationalist, drunk or sober, he preferred the company of men for good talk, considering them more stimulating intellectually than women. An exemplar of male chauvinism, he once complained: "She looketh well to the ways of her household and eateth not the bread of idleness. That was the ideal of Biblical days. But the modern woman has boiled all that down to a trip to the beauty parlor and the first three words. She looketh well."

John's earnings were now averaging $600 a week, enabling him
for the first time to indulge his cultural tastes, which were as expensive as they were eclectic. He shared with Katherine a snug little
apartment at 36 Gramercy Park and he embellished it with etchings
and paintings, old silver, period bric-à-brac and rare books (he eventually acquired a first edition of *Alice in Wonderland*). He liked to
antique furniture. "I've made a lot of these antiques," he disclosed. "I
see an old chair that's good and then I get to work and make it all over
again. You don't know how much fun it is to bore worm-holes into a
chair with an ice-pick." He was a self-teaching student of medieval
history.

Nothing so contented John as to pass an evening in slippered
ease at home among his treasures, reading or sketching, a bottle at
hand, unless it was to carouse with Flagg and kindred drinking companions. In the latter case Katherine might not see him for days.

In 1913 Adolph Zukor, the founder of Famous Players and the
progenitor of the screen's star system, persuaded John to follow the
example of his brother and sister and venture into motion pictures.
John agreed as much from curiosity as from his chronic need of
money. Under Zukor's initial policy Famous Players concentrated on
the conversion of established stage hits into screen fare. Charles
Frohman was an associatae. John's first film was a four-reel reworking
of a sentimental old drama, *An American Citizen*. He portrayed
Beresford Cruger, who, when obliged to leave his native country for
England, fondles a portrait of George Washington and passionately
embraces an American flag.

The film, directed by one of Famous Players' key figures, J.
Searle Dawley, was shot at its studio on Manhattan's West Twenty-
sixth Street. The fourth day Zukor asked Dawley what he thought of
John's screen capabilities. "Mr. Zukor," replied Dawley, "he's the
best actor I've ever had the privilege to handle."

"You think we ought to put him under contract?"

"If you don't, you're losing a great opportunity."

Zukor took the advice.

Famous Players released *An American Citizen* on January 10,
1914. *Variety*'s evaluation of John's performance did not differ sub-
stantially from that of the rest of the cinematic press. "The . . .
play . . . is admirably suited to the Barrymore unction and magne-
tism. . . . Young Barrymore is at home in its every scene and im-

parts to the play a light touch. . . . It's all very natural, romantic and at times touching. . . . The Barrymore personality made it joyous."

Fascinated by the medium (and the easy money when compared to the monotony of a long Broadway run and the discomforts of the road), John proclaimed it an art form superior to the theater. "The film determines an actor's ability, absolutely, conclusively," he declared. "It is the surest test of an actor's qualities. Mental impressions can be conveyed by the screen more quickly than vocally. The moving picture is not a business. It is an art." Yet he later told Flagg: "Acting, all you have to do is to put red paint on your nose and walk on," and he complained: "In the silent days I found myself making frantic and futile faces to try to express unexpressible ideas—like a man behind a closed window on a train that is moving out of a station who is trying, in pantomime, to tell his wife, on the platform outside, that he forgot to pack his blue pajamas and that he wants her to send them to him care of Detwiler, 1032 West 189th Street, New York City."

Zukor extended to John the privilege of passing on the scripts intended for him. He would call at his dressing room to outline the story. John would listen reflectively and let the producer depart without committing himself. A day or two later one of John's friends would bring Zukor the decision.

"Once on the set, Barrymore was all business," Zukor said later. "He insisted on his way of doing things and sometimes there were flare-ups of temperament, but he gave his best and demanded that everybody else do the same. He preferred a story which combined romance, swashbuckling and comedy."

But despite this preference for swaggering roles, he usually accepted the scripts Zukor offered him. He made ten movies altogether for Famous Players (in three of which Katherine appeared). The majority were slapstick farces.

In *Are You a Mason?*, a typical specimen, John, drunk, comes weaving along a Manhattan side street and approaches an antique shop with a replica of the Venus de Milo standing by the door. When the first take was being shot, a couple rounded the corner. They recognized John, but failed to see the camera. The slightly addle-pated woman clasped her companion's arm in dismay. "Oh, look," she cried. "It's poor Jack Barrymore! Look what he's come to. I wonder what his daughter Ethel would think."

In another early film John was required to jump through a stained-glass window to escape a husband he had cuckolded. Zukor's scenic designer, Richard Murphy, painted the window on a paper panel. John balked. He refused to jump through a fake window. If he had to act, he was going to act realistically. A compromise was reached. Murphy built a window, using an unresistant resin composition instead of glass. From a distance it was indistinguishable from the real thing. But not to John. Finally, Murphy, hoping that a last-minute access of prudence would save John from injury, set up both windows side by side, leaving it to John, when the time came to jump, to take his choice.

Confident that his star would choose the commonsensical course, Zukor retired to his office. A moment later he was jolted out of his chair by a deafening crash. Dashing out to the set, he beheld John shedding shards of real glass, a smile of triumph on his face and not a scratch anyplace.

The only serious clashes between Zukor and John occurred over John's casual life style. "Once in bed, Barrymore was never in any hurry to get up. And when he did get up, he was likely as not to forget all about the film and begin to paint. Al's job [Al Kaufman, Zukor's brother-in-law] was to go down to Barrymore's Greenwich Village studio, plead with him to arise if he were still in bed, and try to get him in a mood to come in. He was not always successful.

"After Barrymore had been missing both from our studio and his for a few days, I would say to Murphy and Riley [William Riley, the studio property man], 'Go over to the waterfront and see what you can do.'

"Their custom was to begin at a favorite saloon of Barrymore's on Twelfth Avenue. If necessary they traced him from dive to dive. The effect on the prop and scenic departments was not good, but they often brought their man back.

"It is possible to look back with amusement at these things. But at the time they could bring us close to disaster, for money was short, and often we were working on a picture that had been sold to the distributors in order to get funds to make it. . . ."

John once not only disappeared, but, in effect, shanghaied the director-actor and a boon companion, James Kirkwood. With the picture, *The Lost Bridegroom*, almost completed and noon long past, John was still absent. Kirkwood went in search and shortly phoned Zukor: "I've got him and he's coming back with me."

Three days elapsed and nothing more was heard from either man.

John, as Zukor subsequently discovered, had promised to return with Kirkwood if they could stop at the Hotel Biltmore to drink one for the road. John ordered absinthes—doubles, as the Biltmore bartenders always served them when they saw John approaching. Kirkwood was at the time unaware of the devastating effects of absinthe (a beverage later outlawed). Thus, three days of oblivion.

When Katherine married John, she expected to meet through him the great figures of the theater—to her the most glamorous creatures on earth—to attend round after round of theatrical parties and, in her turn, to show off her dazzling mate to the elite of Newport and the Hamptons. Her disabusal was painful and the couple had ferocious quarrels. A resident of their Gramercy Park apartment house recalled: ". . . their voices could be heard all over the building. When the contretemps became too frequent, several of the tenants held a meeting to discuss what must be done. It was eventually decided to write a letter of complaint to the landlord, which was to be signed by the tenants. The letter was written, but the very next day the two young Barrymores were seen, arm in arm, as if nothing had ever happened to disturb their connubial bliss, and as happy as two lovebirds. The letter never got mailed."

But these arm-in-arm truces seldom lasted long. The furnishings of Katherine's mind were sparse and when she ventured some fatuous opinion, John did not conceal his amused contempt. He referred to her as "the mental giantess." At the same time he was wildly jealous. If a man so much as glanced at her appreciatively, as most men did, he would snarl: "He has a light in his eye!"

Flagg and his wife, Nell, twenty years older, counted the Barrymores among their dearest friends. Sunday supper together at the Claridge Hotel became a tradition. Now and then all four would spend the night in Flagg's studio apartment. Following one party there, during which the copious supplies of hard liquor were gone by dawn, John, who would drink practically anything containing alcohol, was found in the bathroom, emptying an eight-ounce bottle of spirits of peppermint.

Flagg was not immune to Katherine's sexual appeal. He became infatuated with her. "Her lanky, blonde beauty was accompanied by a decided body urge," he wrote years later. "After one look at her I had to paint her portrait. After that she posed a lot for me in illustrations. . . . I have known some beautiful women who were not 'photogenic'—which is always a surprise. I think it is because the camera is mindless. Katherine was one of these women. In her photos and snaps she was nothing. But in reality . . . irresistible! Lovely! So much so I wanted to draw her all the time. She had a lovely figure, or blueprints for same, a bit too skinny for my taste, but wide-shouldered, willowy—beautiful ends. But her face—enthralling!"

A quivering Katherine once arrived at Flagg's studio carrying a two-handed medieval sword. During the night, she told him tearfully, she had fled the apartment house in her nightgown and hidden in the small park opposite after John threatened her with the weapon. He then tore through the building, pounding on every door and bellowing: "I want my wife!" Meantime, a policeman to whom Katherine appealed for protection was making advances to her. She managed to escape his clutches, sneak back into the apartment and finally pacify John. She wanted Flagg to keep the sword lest John chase her with it again. It remained among the illustrator's most prized possessions.

Katherine spent so much time at Flagg's studio that John, who trusted no beautiful woman, protested. His suspicions were not groundless. Friendship had not inhibited Flagg. The upshot was a row between the two men in which John flung at the artist: "You've been living with my wife!"

Flagg's rejoinder was brutally direct: "No, John, you've been living with her. I've been sleeping with her."

There was, surprisingly, no violence. But they did not speak to each other for years. After they finally made peace, John said: "You know, Monty, I can't really blame her. I was drunk most of the time."

Flagg's portrait of Katherine no longer existed. He had destroyed it upon discovering that he was not her only extra-marital lover.

The first producer to offer John a serious stage role—serious, that is, as opposed to comic or farcical—was one of the most picturesque figures ever to enliven Broadway. Born in Budapest and raised on the Bowery, a tall, disheveled man, his big head crowned with a mat of untended hair, semi-literate and loquacious, A. H. ("Al") Woods—originally Aladore Herman—would sometimes buy a play without reading it simply because he fancied the title. "Sweetheart," he said (he called everybody, friend and foe alike, "Sweetheart"), "I'll always take a chance on an unknown author if he smells right."

Al Woods' earliest production sprang from a title that happened to pop into his head—*The Bowery After Dark*. He had posters printed showing a slavering fiend in hot pursuit of a luscious girl, then commissioned a hack playwright to fashion a melodrama around the title and the poster. With the world's lightweight champion, Terry McGovern, in the lead, *The Bowery After Dark* opened on Christmas night of 1899 at the Star Theatre, Broadway and Thirteenth Street, ran for two years and netted Woods $75,000. Presently Woods had twenty-three productions on the road. They were all the same play. Only the titles varied.

"Art is all right," Woods observed, "but I frankly confess that the theatrical business appeals to me not a little as a business proposition." Though he eventually backed plays of distinct merit for many years, he staked his money on lurid thrillers and bedroom farces. The most facile writers of the genres in his stable were Owen Davis and Avery Hopwood. Davis wrote *Queen of the White Slaves, Her One False Step, Edna, the Beautiful Typewriter Girl* and countless more like them before he turned to dramas of quality like *Icebound*, which won the 1923 Pulitzer Prize. Perhaps the most unconsciously hilarious line ever uttered by a Woods author occurs in Davis' *Edna, the Beautiful Typewriter Girl.* After the villain has attempted unsuccessfully to kill Nellie by shoving her down an elevator shaft, throwing her off Brooklyn Bridge and tying her to railroad tracks, he asks her plaintively, "Why do you fear me, Nellie?"

For bedroom farce, Woods' most dependable contributor was Hopwood. From his pen flowed *Ladies' Night in a Turkish Bath, Up in Mabel's Room, Getting Gertie's Garter*

Woods was an honest, loyal and kindly man, not nearly as cynical as his often expressed view of human endeavor would indicate. "It's all applesauce," he would say. During the Actors' Equity strike of 1919 (which the moral and financial support of John Drew and the Barrymores, especially Ethel, helped to win) he approached a group of chorines picketing in the rain. "Hello, sweethearts," he said. "Where's your raincoats?"

"We didn't expect this weather, Mr. Woods," their leader replied.

Woods pointed to a nearby women's-clothing store. "You go there," he said, "and buy raincoats and charge them to me. I don't want you to get pneumonia because when all this is over I'm going to need you again."

Woods cast John as Julian Rolfe, the leading role in a tinny melodrama, *The Yellow Ticket* by Michael Morton, which opened at the producer's Eltinge Theatre on January 20, 1914. A young American foreign correspondent stationed in St. Petersburg, Rolfe loves a beautiful Jewish woman, Marya Verenka (Florence Reed). The title of the play refers to the identification cards prostitutes were obliged to carry if they wished to move about Russia freely. Though chaste, Marya once obtained such a card as her only means of leaving the "Pale of Settlement" to which the Czarist laws relegated all Jews, and of reaching New York in time to see her immigrant father, who lay dying there. At sight of her yellow ticket, the American immigration agents refused to admit her. Back in Russia, she has assumed an alias in order to live outside the Settlement. A libidinous government official, learning her secret, demands the surrender of her virtue as the price of his silence. She rejects him, they struggle and she stabs him to death with a hatpin. She is about to be sent to Siberia when Rolfe, with the aid of the American embassy, rescues her from the clutches of the police and promises to accompany her to America.

The nightly repetition of lines, especially inane ones, always exasperated John, and partway through the long run of *The Yellow Ticket* (183 performances) he came onstage drunk, ad-libbed words of sympathy to Miss Reed because she lacked transportation for getting around Russia, and thrust into her hands a batch of New York subway tickets. Down went the curtain and when it rose again an understudy had replaced him.

The obloquy the boozy prank incurred, along with his crumbling marriage, so depressed John that he sought relief in a trip to Europe. This was during the spring of 1914, three months before the outbreak of the First World War. Fortuitously, in Venice he found Ned Sheldon, the friend most likely to lift his spirits. John poured out his troubles, and Ned, without mentioning his own sorrow over losing Doris Keane, comforted him. John was soon restored as together they journeyed from Venice to Rome to Florence, feasting their eyes on the art treasures of museum, cathedral and palazzi, going to operas and concerts, whiling away the balmy nights in open-air *trattorie*.

Before checking out of the Grand Hotel in Venice, John berated a desk clerk for what he deemed generally dilatory service. To distract him, the clerk indicated a slight, aging woman of doleful expression sitting by herself on a lobby settee. "Do you know who that is, signor?" he asked John and, lowering his voice to a whisper, reverently uttered the name of one of the world's greatest actresses, Eleonora Duse, whom ill-health had forced into temporary retirement.

John strode over to her, knelt, kissed her hand and murmured:

"Madame, forgive my temerity. I am but a poor young actor, a fledgling daring to address an eagle."

Duse spoke no English, but she caught the drift of the tribute and invited John to sit beside her. With a smattering of Italian and French and eloquent pantomime, he made himself understood. He had seen her, he said, in *Magda* at the Metropolitan Opera House during her fourth American tour eleven years before. He had never forgotten how, in a scene with her lover, she appeared to blush. "Would you explain the illusion, madame?"

"It is no illusion," Duse replied. "I blush. That is the way I am supposed to feel."

Did she mean she could blush at will?

"It is necessary to the scene."

Ned and John parted in Italy, Ned to proceed to London, John to sail home full of high hopes. Ned was still in London when a Serbian terrorist brought Europe to the brink of war by assassinating the Archduke Franz Ferdinand, heir to the Austrian throne, and his wife. Not until late July was Ned able to obtain passage aboard a west-bound liner.

Shortly after John's return, Al Woods, having overlooked his misconduct, offered him the principal role of Chick Hewes, a rehabilitated ex-convict, in Willard Mack's *Kick In*. It was another "serious" play, a slight cut above *The Yellow Ticket*. Katherine obtained a fifty-percent interest and a role.

No producer except Woods had as yet imagined John capable of any but frothy characterizations. John himself said later: "People thought Woods was crazy to trust me with the part. His friends—perhaps they thought they were my friends, too—remonstrated with him, told him he was a fool himself and would make a fool of me. . . . They flourished the usual theatrical measuring stick of 'personal limitations.' According to them, mine were marked out by my previous parts from the good-for-nothing who gaily and facetiously wins out in *The Fortune Hunter* down to *Anatol* of the lively Parisian adventures. These, it appeared, were the limit for me and Woods was besought to leave well enough alone and not try to make a poor character actor out of a fairly good comedian. That he did not yield to their protests showed a confidence in me for which I shall always be grateful."

The confidence of "Saint Al," as the *Herald Tribune's* reviewer, Percy Hammond, somewhat hyperbolically dubbed Woods, was not misplaced. While the play itself merited no critical accolades, John achieved a resounding personal success, which he owed in part to sheer physical dexterity. The third-act climax of *Kick In* came when Chick and Detective "Whip" Fogarty closed in hand-to-hand combat. One night they staged it with such realism that they tumbled into the orchestra pit. "Keep it in, sweetheart," Saint Al urged, "it's marvelous." So in subsequent performances the grunting, grappling, fist-swinging actors rolled across the boards and over the footlights until Woods decided that the cost of replacing smashed light bulbs was becoming excessive.

When admirers flocked backstage to congratulate him, John tended to revert to self-deprecation. "I'm no actor," he told one such group. "I'm just a ham. They're merely cashing in on the family reputation."

Ned Sheldon considered *Kick In*, which chalked up 188 performances at the Eltinge, a step for John in the right direction away from farce and low comedy. He could not say the same about his friend's fifth movie, *The Incorrigible Dukane*,* which the New York *Review* described as "the best acrobatic show in town." As the hobo Dukane, John took a blow on the jaw, was ejected head-first through the swinging doors of a saloon, hurled into a heap of slag, flung across a camp table, kicked by a gigantic Westerner, trampled by a horse, chased by a mob, attacked by a construction gang, given a black eye by the foreman, beaten with a lead pipe, blown up with dynamite, dragged around by the neck and knocked flat twenty-two times.

In the spring of 1915 Sheldon was planning his seasonal trip abroad, undaunted by the perils at sea of German submarines and on land of Zeppelin raids. Charles Frohman, equally unconcerned despite Germany's threat to sink all ships, neutral as well as enemy, sailing through waters surrounding the British Isles, booked passage to England, where he had urgent business. Due to embark on May 1, he pressed Ned to accompany him. Ned agreed, but at the last minute a Harvard classmate about to be married asked him to serve as best man and he felt he could not refuse. Six days later, eight miles off the southeastern coast of Ireland, a U-boat torpedoed the Cunard liner *Lusitania*, taking 1,198 lives, among them Charles Frohman's. One of the 761 survivors reported that as the ship went down C.F. said,

---

* The earliest John Barrymore film of which prints are extant. The author knows of one owned by a private Connecticut collector and another in the George Eastman House at Rochester, New York. Of the fifty-seven films Barrymore made altogether, thirteen have been lost, including the first four—*An American Citizen* (1914), *The Man from Mexico* (1914), *Are You a Mason?* (1915) and *The Dictator*, an adaptation of the Richard Harding Davis play (1915).

smiling: "Why fear death? It is the most beautiful adventure of life."

Fate had spared Ned the horror of the *Lusitania*'s last voyage only to subject him to a terrible lifelong ordeal. During the summer of that year he was troubled by an inexplicable stiffness in his knees, especially after exercise. Within a few weeks his shoulders and hips underwent the same strange change and any movement of the afflicted parts caused him intense pain. The doctor he consulted diagnosed his condition as rheumatoid arthritis with ankylosis—that is, a fusion of bone joints, producing a complete fixation, etiology unknown. It was a progressive, irreversible disease and in Ned's day there were no drugs, such as cortisone, to control it. By the fall of 1915 he could no longer climb in or out of taxis unaided.

He convinced himself that the disease would ultimately respond to treatment and, for all his suffering, he was more concerned with John Barrymore's career, seeking a play worthy of what he believed to be his friend's unrealized potential. He thought he had found it when he read John Galsworthy's *Justice*. The plot was simple. William Falder, a well-meaning but weak young clerk in a law office, loves Ruth Honeywill, the wife of a drunkard who brutalizes her. To enable them to escape together to another country, Falder raises a check. Arrested on the eve of flight, he is sentenced to three years' imprisonment. "The rolling of the chariot wheels of justice" drives Ruth into prostitution and Falder, after he has served his term, to suicide.

A powerful indictment of England's penal system, *Justice*, when originally staged in 1910 at London's Duke of York Theatre, aroused such indignation among humanitarians as to move the Home Secretary to institute prison reforms. Against all indications to the contrary, Ned insisted that John could portray Falder, even though the role was totally unlike any he had ever attempted. While doubting his ability to switch from light comedy to grim tragedy, John agreed to try. For a producer Ned turned to another Harvard classmate, John Williams, who had just entered the field.

Following a New Haven tryout, *Justice* opened at the Candler Theatre in New York on April 3, 1916, within two months of John's thirty-fourth birthday. Seldom had he ever felt so insecure. "When we came into New York for a few rehearsals before opening, I found that in front of the . . . theater . . . and in the lobby, there were bills and posters featuring my name. I went round with strips of paper and pasted out this display. For a short time I was given credit for modesty, but it was not that. It was shrewdness, I think, for I wanted no extra advertising if I were to fail."

A red apple from Uncle John Drew was delivered to his dressing room.

Next day John had the strips of paper removed.

PART

IV

NEW YORK AND LONDON

1916–1925

10

Justice

I N retrospect, twenty-five years later, Brooks Atkinson wrote: "As the plot closed around Falder, looking down from the second balcony was a little like looking at a flame. For the lean, handsome, magnetic Barrymore was giving a burning performance in his first serious role, and I could feel the heat of it at the top of the theater. . . . Other actors had more surface, but Barrymore cut through the darkness of the theater like a sharp, glittering penknife."

With that single portrayal John vaulted from the populous sphere of clever light comedians to an eminence where, according to Lloyd Morris' history of the American theater, "he had no equal on the American stage." As the inarticulate Falder, he spoke comparatively few lines. He conveyed emotion for the most part silently through gesture, facial expression and stance.

The scene that one critic found "almost too horribly realistic to be endurable" takes place in a solitary-confinement cell without a word uttered. Falder, pallid and stooped, his hair close-cropped, stands motionless near the cell door with its barred opening, trying desperately to hear a sound outside. He stiffens, as if he does hear something. Then, frustrated, he slouches back to his assigned task, stitching buttonholes in a shirt. His face a mask of infinite sorrow, he sews a stitch or two, stops abruptly, begins to pace the cell, listens again at the door, forehead pressed against the bars. Still hearing nothing, he moves toward the window, raises the lid of a can of food perched on the sill, peers into it. The lid slips from his hand and falls to the floor with a clangor that jolts him. Presently, there sounds a distant noise like fists beating on metal. At first he shrinks back, alarmed. The noise swells. Seemingly hypnotized by it, he creeps closer to the door as, one after another, his unseen fellow prisoners join in. At length Falder, lifting both hands, fists clenched, hurls himself against the door and is pounding on it frantically when the curtain falls.

"Everyone who saw *Justice* realized that this scene was one of the great experiences afforded by the modern theater," Morris wrote. "Some surmised that the attribute which made it luminous and never to be forgotten was genius."

Little did audiences suspect the mischief John wrought onstage from time to time to alleviate what was for him the exquisite boredom of repetition. During the concluding moments he was supposed, as the corpse of Falder, to lie motionless, his back to the footlights, while Cathleen Nesbitt, playing Ruth Honeywill, knelt beside him, sobbing, and the elderly head clerk, Cokeson, played by O. P. Heggie, a superlative British character actor, said: "Don't cry, my pretty. No one will touch him now, never again. He's safe with gentle Jesus." To avoid bathos, such a line calls for the utmost skill and control. John would murmur obscenities, wriggle his nose as if about to sneeze, whisper that a cockroach was crawling toward him. After a particularly unsettling prank, Heggie stalked out of the theater without waiting for curtain calls. He left a message for John: unless he apologized and swore to mend his ways, Heggie would quit. Refusing to take the threat seriously, John said: "Tell the old boy I'll be good next week." Next week an understudy had to play Cokeson. Conscience-stricken, John sent Heggie a note, pledging his oath to reform. "I'll present it to you on my knees, with humble apologies, in your dressing room if you'll only come back." Heggie reappeared to be greeted with champagne by John, who thereafter behaved himself unexceptionably when the older actor was onstage.

At John's urging, the twelve jurors in the second-act trial scene were recruited from the ranks of needy, unemployed actors. One night when John under cross-examination faltered between questions, creating a sudden, unexpected pause, one of the supernumeraries was clearly heard to inform the aged actor beside him: "I know where you can get the best ham and eggs in town." The stage manager wanted to fire the offender, but John would not stand for it.

By June, after 103 performances, John felt so drained of energy and so sick of his lines that he demanded a respite before resuming his role on the road come September.

"In Genesis it says that it is not good for a man to be alone," he once observed, "but sometimes it is a great relief." Since the spring he had been living apart from Katherine in Ned Sheldon's apartment on East Fifty-fourth Street. Ned's condition was worse. He could neither bend at the waist nor cross his legs without racking pain. The doctors thought that perhaps a milder climate might give him some relief. So John accompanied him to California. Katherine went along, but with a different objective. In California one year sufficed to establish legal residence and obtain a divorce. Accordingly, when John rejoined the cast of *Justice*, she remained in Santa Barbara.

Outside New York the play fared poorly. To attract audiences in Grand Rapids, Michigan, its press agent proposed a stunt: would John be willing to sit in the window of a department store, autographing copies of *Justice*? John would not. "I suggested to them that it would also be good advertising if I, like Lady Godiva, and in the same costume, were to ride through the town on the back of an elephant painted blue, holding in one hand the scales of Justice and in the other a placard with the name and location of the theater."

The profitless tour ended in November. The following month, while John was completing his ninth film for Famous Players, *Raffles, the Amateur Cracksman*, Katherine was telling a Santa Barbara judge:

"When he arrived home after a performance, he had exhausted his humor and his interest, and spent all the rest of his time in reading books and sleeping. Jack read all night frequently while I watched and waited for recognition; and he slept all day, leaving a call for just before the time the curtain was scheduled to rise. I thought it would be grand to be the wife of such a man before I married him and even later when he told me we were to part forever, I tried to win him back. His only response was that our temperaments were too different, and further living together was impossible."

Apprised of this statement, John did not contradict it. "Katherine was much younger than I, a charming, delightful, ingenuous person," he told reporters. "She looked upon Broadway as something not unlike the Promised Land. To her, actors were jolly fellows whose amusing monkeyshines continued after the theater in gay restaurants, in Bohemian studios, and even at the breakfast table before the coffee was served. Like most bums, I had a secret passion for domesticity. To me, marriage meant escape from Broadway. To Katherine's intense bewilderment and dismay, this supposedly glamorous Broadway party hound turned out to be a dull goof who at once bought himself a pair of carpet slippers and put his dress suit away in mothballs. It is not fair to Katherine to indicate that this was her only complaint against me. I know that often I was a very trying person and even now I cannot reasonably explain my irritatingly inconsistent conduct. I don't know why a guy thinks he wants to be domestic and who revolts against going to parties with his charming wife feels that she is quite unreasonable in raising merry hell when he comes home unsteadily at five a.m. after an innocent night out with the boys."

The Santa Barbara judge granted Katherine an interlocutory decree on the technical grounds of desertion and a year later pronounced the decree final. John had agreed to pay her $350 a month. Alimony, as he defined it, was "the most exorbitant of all stud fees, and the worst feature of it is that you pay it retroactively."

Still stagestruck, Katherine performed in an Al Woods production, *The Big Chance.* Then Ethel Barrymore, who liked her and agreed that her brother had ill-used her, saw to it that she got a part in one of her greatest successes, Zoë Akins' *Déclassée.* In 1921 Katherine married Alexander Dallas Bache Pratt, a stockbroker whose financial and social position met her father's standards. They were divorced in 1923. The same year Katherine married Leon Orlowsky, then secretary of the Polish Legation in New York. Like many of the women John loved, she retained his friendship and solicitude. He was at her bedside the day she died of pneumonia at the age of thirty-six.

With *Raffles* in the can, John was wondering what to do next. Ned Sheldon told him.

11

Peter Ibbetson

=====

A L," said John, "I've got a play, but I don't want you to read it."
"I suppose you just want me to give you the theater and pay the
bills," Al Woods said.

"Yes, that's about what I want."

"What's the play like, sweetheart?"

"Oh, you wouldn't like it. It's called *Peter Ibbetson*. . . . I'm
going to play Peter, Constance Collier is going to be the Duchess of
Towers and Lionel is coming back from the movies to the theater, and
he's going to play Colonel Ibbetson, my uncle."

"That's pretty good. Can't you tell me anything about it at all?"

"Well, there's one scene where Lionel calls me a bastard and I
hit him over the head with a club and knock him cold. It's the end of
the third act."

"You're on, sweetheart. I'll take it."

A dramatization of George du Maurier's late-nineteenth-century
best-seller *Peter Ibbetson* doubtless appealed to the romantic, the sentimental and the mystical in John's nature. The young man of the
title, "slender, refined, sensitive . . . inclined to be dreamy," has
never ceased to cherish the memory of the sweetheart he loved in
childhood, "Mimsey" Serasquier, whom he has not seen since and
believes dead. At a ball he is introduced to Mary, Duchess of Towers, "tall, beautiful, stately and gracious." She reminds him fleetingly

123

of Mimsey, while he reminds her of "Gogo," her beloved playmate of the distant past.

The truth dawns upon them in the second act when they compare memories: Mary is indeed Mimsey and Peter is Gogo. Mary loves him still, but tells him they must not meet again, for she is not free, being a married woman. But both the lovers are able to "dream true" —that is, to meet in each other's dreams and thus, no matter what the vicissitudes of their earthbound existence, to share an ineffable joy.

The bane of Peter's existence is his uncle, Colonel Ibbetson, "a big, strutting braggart" whose ward he has been since the death of his parents. No love is lost between them, and when in a rage he boasts that Peter's mother was his mistress and that Peter is his natural son, a fight ensues, during which Peter smites him with a cane, killing him.

Condemned to life imprisonment, Peter, dreaming true, rejoins Mary. Their love even defies death, and after he has breathed his last, thirty years later, their spirits are united for eternity.

The play's author, an English journalist named John Nathan Raphael, had submitted *Peter Ibbetson* to every London producer in vain. Following a chance encounter with the actress Constance Collier and the discovery of a mutual fondness for the Du Maurier novel, he sent her his dramatization written twenty years before. The same night Miss Collier read it twice through, ignoring the air-raid sirens, and finished it at five o'clock in the morning. "By that time," she recounted later, "I had made up my mind that if I never did anything else in my life, I would produce *Peter Ibbetson*."

An opportunity arose in July 1915 to stage it at least once when she was asked to raise money for the benefit of the Allied Base Hospital at Etaples. With the author's permission, she rewrote many scenes, obtained the services gratis of some of England's best actors and the free use of His Majesty's Theatre. The performance netted almost £2,000 for the Base Hospital. But when Miss Collier tried to arrange a regular production, she was no more successful than the playwright.

At about this time the Triangle Corporation, which D. W. Griffith, Thomas Ince and Mack Sennett had established in Hollywood to screen adaptations of theatrical hits, offered her a contract, and so, braving the perils of U-boat-infested waters, a life-preserver strapped around her torso, she crossed the Atlantic. She took Raphael's brainchild with her. As soon as she finished her Hollywood stint, which included playing Lady Macbeth opposite Beerbohm Tree, she went to New York, her faith in *Peter Ibbetson* undiminished. Like countless other friends of Ned Sheldon, she sought his advice. He liked the play, though he felt it needed further overhauling, and he agreed with her that John Barrymore would make an ideal Peter Ibbetson. If John would consent, Ned knew, they would not have much trouble finding a producer. He not only prevailed upon his friend to tackle a role as remote from Falder in *Justice* as Falder had been from everything John had done before, but he interrupted work on a play of his own to revise the Collier revision, a task that occupied him for weeks. He and John also persuaded Lionel, who was contentedly making movies and had no desire to return to the stage, to portray the loathsome Colonel Ibbetson.

Al Woods put up $12,000, all he could spare at the time, and got the Shuberts to furnish the balance of the sum required, bowing out in their favor as the titular producers. Rehearsals began in the late winter of 1917. Saint Al attended many of them and never failed to weep. "I don't know what it's about," he said, "but I can't help myself."

When, on April 6, 1917, the United States entered the war against Germany, John nearly renounced the theater for the duration. He and Jack Prescott hied themselves to a recruiting station and applied for officer's training. Prescott passed the physical examination, but John, to his astonishment and chagrin, flunked because of a leg slightly dilated by varicose veins.

Some months later, while exhibiting the afflicted leg to one of his warmest admirers, the drama critic Ashton Stevens, he said with a show of lightheartedness he did not feel: "I got it standing with one foot on the rail," and he added: "Some winter's night in the years to come, when children sit on my lap and say, 'Granddad, just what did you do to lick the Kaiser?' I'll throw out what's left of my chest and say, 'I put greasepaint on my nose and made faces.' "

He read to Stevens a cablegram from E. H. Sothern and the producer Winthrop Ames: " 'Our soldiers in France vitally need entertainment from home to combat homesickness and keep them fit. This need is emphasized by every important officer.' But acting isn't important. Acting isn't important anywhere."

The time spent at the recruiting station whetted the applicants' thirst and they repaired to the nearest saloon. Hungry after several rounds of strong drink, they headed, half-seas over, for the Astor Hotel at Broadway and Forty-fourth Street. Mounting the marble stairs to the dining room, John, aflame with patriotism, stopped every few steps to deliver anti-German imprecations. "This place is run by

Germans!" he shouted. "Every damn waiter is a Hun." Another step
and: "It's nothing but a meeting place for spies!"

The spacious dining room had a relatively sparse clientele,
so that there were two or three waiters to every table, a good many
of them German, to judge by their accent. When the befuddled pair
had seated themselves and the headwaiter approached to take their
order, John lashed out: "See that coward? He's a spy—a German
spy!" The headwaiter backed away. John picked up a plate and
heaved it at him, missing him by inches. He seized every piece of
china within reach and let fly. Pandemonium reigned. The waiters
closed ranks and advanced, blood in their eyes. The plate-hurler and
his abetter took shelter under the table, then fled back down the
marble stairs. Upon reaching the street, John announced to passers-
by: "We're the two musketeers, fellows—the two musketeers!"

When sober again, John thought of a way to accompany Prescott to war symbolically. He gave him a silver-mounted cane with
both their names engraved on the handle, explaining: "You must
have a cane, old boy. Every officer uses one. You're going to war as
my guest."

As the first night of *Peter Ibbetson* drew near, grave doubts
assailed John. There was a side of him to which acting appeared
narcissistic and unmanly. The blond wig he had to wear, the Victorian
dress with its frilly shirt front and flowing cravat, he felt, feminized
him. He spoke of himself as "a marshmallow in a blond wig . . . a
sweet-scented ass." It discomforted him further to utter such lines as
"Dream true. Mother—Mimsey—I'm coming to you. . . . Mother
—Mother darling! I am in great trouble. I want you so terribly.
Can't you come out of the past just for a moment? Just time to take
me in those dear, dear arms and say, 'I love you, Gogo.'" To look
more virile, he grew a mustache and goatee, but removed them after
Beerbohm Tree, who was impersonating Thackeray's Colonel New-
combe at the New Amsterdam Theatre, remarked: "The fellow looks
so like a dentist. If you don't shave him instantly, the romance will
fly out the window."

Long afterward Lionel, seeking to elucidate his brother's character, said: "He was continually afraid of being dubbed a pretty boy,
and possibly it is valid to suggest that in doing so many of the things
that pretty boys should not do he was working out some embarrassed
defense mechanism."

Lionel, who regretted his promise to Ned Sheldon, had problems of his own in coming to grips with the ungrateful role of the

malevolent Colonel Ibbetson. What should he look like? How should he carry himself? One day, as Lionel stood behind a piece of scenery, he overhead John and Miss Collier talking about him on the other side. "But Jack, dear," Miss Collier was saying, "the dress rehearsal is almost upon us and so far he has done absolutely nothing."

"Yes, yes, Constance, quite so. Well, perhaps that personage you are always calling upon will be able to help us. Let us hope so."

"Personage I am always calling upon? Who?"

"God."

But once the curtain had risen at the Republic Theatre on the opening night of April 17 the Barrymore familial sense of histrionics reasserted itself. *Peter Ibbetson* marked the beginning of amicable scene-stealing battles which the brothers would wage both on the stage and in movies. While the critical response to *Peter Ibbetson* ranged from cool to lukewarm, John's standing as the country's matinee idol nonpareil was consolidated and Lionel was hailed as one of its foremost character actors. The audience adored both play and actors. The mere sight of John at his first entrance drew a collective sigh from the women. When part of the scenery collapsed, a mishap that recurred the second night, nobody laughed, nobody uttered a sound.

After fifteen curtain calls Miss Collier said to John: "It was beautiful, and if there is such a thing as a spirit coming back, then I know Du Maurier was here tonight."

"If he was," said John, "he got hit on the head."

Between the Broadway run of seventy-one performances and a nationwide tour *Peter Ibbetson* lasted a year. One New York woman proudly declared that she had sat through the play forty-five times, sobbing each time. Another woman was rushed from the Republic Theatre to a hospital suffering from "an unaccountable weeping hysteria." A panel of twelve women voted John the second most fascinating man in the world after the Prince of Wales.

John never hesitated to step out of character to reprove a spectator who disturbed him. Miss Collier left this account:

"At the end of the first act John had to pick up the Duchess of Towers' bouquet and, after looking at it a moment tenderly, put it to his lips and kiss it as he murmured 'L'Amour.' It used to thrill the ladies in the audience. This particular night some girl in the gallery giggled. Jack suddenly got furious and threw the bouquet with all his force, into the face of a lady who had nothing to do with it. Then he let out a string of profanity, ending with, 'If you don't like the way I do it, you can bloody well come on and do it yourself,' and he stalked off the stage.

"The curtain was lowered. The manager rushed round to me, as I was responsible for the finances of the company, and said that he would bring a damage suit against me.

"John had locked himself into his dressing room and by this time was beginning to feel ashamed of himself. I begged him to come out and talk it over and eventually he emerged. There had been half an hour's wait. The manager insisted we should make a speech and return the money to the audience, but in spite of him we took the curtain up. The first surprise was that few people had left the theater, or asked for their money back, but there was an ominous and sinister silence.

"Jack did not come on till we were halfway through the act. The scenes that preceded his entrance were received in stony silence. We were terrified. The dread moment arrived. He entered, and to our amazement received the biggest round of applause you can imagine.

"You see, there was no way of disciplining him, because the public loved him so much they let him do anything he liked."

Lionel dropped out of the touring company in January 1918 to accept Augustus Thomas' offer of the title role in his Civil War drama, *The Copperhead*. An obscure actor named Edward Elton replaced him. *Peter Ibbetson* was to have played Hartford, Connecticut, on February 18, the day scheduled for the opening of *The Copperhead* at the Shuberts' Broadway theater, a red-apple occasion John did not intend to miss, but so that the Shuberts should suffer no financial loss he proposed to buy out the entire Hartford house, the sum —about $3,000—to be deducted from his pay. "Forget it," said Lee Shubert, whose brother Sam had died in a train accident. "I had a brother once. I was very fond of him."

Lionel's performance as Milt Shanks, an Illinois farmer who poses as a Confederate sympathizer—a "Copperhead"—in order to gather intelligence for the Union Army and thus incurs the scorn of his family and his neighbors, crowned his stage career. None of his few subsequent theatrical characterizations surpassed it.

Soon after *Peter Ibbetson* reached Chicago, John, succumbing as usual to the boredom of achievement, notified Miss Collier that he must withdraw. With both Barrymores out of the cast, it seemed hopeless to continue and so the play died on the road.

In October 1917 John had signed a lease on a top-floor apartment at 132 West Fourth Street, just off Washington Square. With his indulgent landlady's sanction, he now proceeded to have the roof covered with tons of topsoil in which to plant flowers, shrubbery and trees. The apartment itself he crammed with objects of virtu and books. He liked to stretch out full-length on the floor, half a dozen volumes before him, and skip from one to another, finishing them all at about the same time. "A woman is only a woman," he said, "but a book and especially a fine, first edition, bound in calf—oh, that is a voluptuous pleasure."

This placid bachelor existence was soon to be disrupted by a violent emotional upheaval.

12

Redemption

========

After several dollops of absinthe, consumed in the privacy of her studio, Blanche Thomas and her English friend Iris Tree ambled along Fifth Avenue through a heavy snowfall, pausing occasionally by a lamppost to steady themselves. A raven-haired woman of twenty-seven with enormous dark eyes, married to a millionaire banker thirteen years her senior, the mother of two small boys, Blanche was bemoaning the dissatisfaction, the ennui, of her life. She felt the necessity, she said, "to bite into something real—even if the core should be bitter."

Iris, a lemon-yellow blonde, moon-faced and generously proportioned, who sometimes accompanied her father, Beerbohm Tree, on his tours, said (as Blanche reconstructed the conversation long afterward in her autobiography): "Well, you ought to meet Jack Barrymore. He wouldn't bore you."

"Oh, yes, he would," Blanche assured her. "I don't care for him on the stage or off it. Why, when I was only fourteen years old, I was lunching with my mother at the Hotel Knickerbocker, and there he was with his drooping mustache and his dazed eyes, *vis-à-vis* of an awfully made-up-looking woman, years older than himself and all dressed in black."

"You seem to have remembered it pretty well. And he is not a bit like that now. He is absolutely fascinating."

A few weeks later, at a party given by the Theatre Guild, one of the directors, Philip Moeller, asked Blanche if he might present John Barrymore, who, he added, was eager to meet her. She said he might, and shortly John was pressing her hand, "bowing and smiling, looking very slim and nervously poetic, with greyish greenish hazel eyes of immense fascination, because they seemed to mirror back oneself in flattering mischievous terms.

"He looked elfin and forsaken, an intriguing combination! but very highly strung too. His walk, slanted, oblique, seemed to say that his clothes irked his skin; but what a metamorphosis from the dazed individual I had seen at the Hotel Knickerbocker!"

At this initial encounter John and Blanche kindled fire in each other.

Blanche exemplified the "New Woman," the "Free Soul." She was in the audacious minority of those who bobbed their hair before the style became generally acceptable. She smoked cigarettes publicly. A suffragette, she was chosen in 1915 from among numerous "American Junos" to lead a parade, Washington Square to Fifty-ninth Street, bearing the yellow standard of the movement. Paul Helleu, a fashionable portraitist, pronounced her "America's most beautiful woman." She wrote free verse, short stories and plays. Her somewhat overwrought poetry bristled with metaphors whose meaning was often elusive, such as:

O our love is like a rainbow
Shooting up from chasms of incredibly scarlet glee—
Yet illuminating suddenly the far blonde face of a placid star—
O our love is like a bridge fountaining its iridescent strength
From across some chaos of claw-sprawly spaces—
Towards a columned brightness of strangely perfected measure—

And again our love is like Death—
Seeming ever to culminate in total cessation—
As a beautiful dual merging—folding in behind shadows—
To an increasing surge of song.

She affected mannish clothes à la George Sand and adopted a man's name, "Michael Strange," as her nom de plume.

She was born, the youngest of four children, into a socially elite family, well known on the Newport–Palm Beach circuit. Her father, Charles Oelrichs, a stockbroker, was descended from Bremen stock, her mother from petty Austro-Hungarian nobility. Her older sister,

Lily, became the Duchess of Mecklenburg-Schwerin, a branch of the Hohenzollern dynasty. Rebellious since early girlhood, Blanche was expelled from the fashionable Brearley School at age fourteen after she organized an offensive against authority, waged in emulation of the Russian Nihilists she had read about in the Sunday supplements. She planted explosive caps under the teachers' chairs, sounded false alarms for fire drill, once laced her math teacher's tomato soup with Irish whiskey stolen from her father's supply. At the Manhattanville Convent, to which she was sent next, she lasted three months. The misdeed that resulted in her expulsion was eating foie-gras sandwiches in bed.

Blanche met her husband while traveling abroad with her parents. Leonard Thomas had been Second Secretary of the American Embassy in Rome, then Secretary of Legation in Madrid. His avocation was composing music, mainly hymns, but he also dedicated a waltz to his betrothed, calling it "The Blanche." They were married in 1910 and had two sons, Leonard, Jr., and Robin.

The Thomases maintained homes in New York and Newport, and Blanche's nonconformity manifested itself in both places. A *bal masqué* she contrived was denounced from the pulpit by Newport clergymen. Starting on a Saturday night, it did not break up until six o'clock Sunday morning when a masquerader named Moncure Robinson, in the feathers and beads of an Apache chieftain, led his fellow merrymakers across a golf links and past a church where sober folk were at prayer.

When the United States declared war on Germany, Leonard Thomas was commissioned a first lieutenant and shipped overseas. It was at about this time that his wife began to see a great deal of John Barrymore. They addressed each other by the same nickname, "Fig"—why, neither of them ever disclosed.

During the early phase of John's development as a serious actor there formed around him a coalition of some of the theater's most creative figures with the object of advancing his career. This "Barrymore Board of Regents" consisted of Ned Sheldon, the producer-director Arthur Hopkins, the scenic designer Robert Edmond Jones and the superlative voice teacher Margaret Carrington.

Arthur M. (for Melancthon) Hopkins belonged to that rare theatrical species, the producer who places quality above profit. "Honesty! Honesty! Honesty!" he once said. "That is all we want.

Do things as they should be done and let the results take care of themselves. I want no praise for bad work. I scorn the man who offers it. I want always to have my intent examined, my execution scrutinized. If they find me stooping to sham devices, if they find me careless or cross, cheap or vulgar, my head is on the block for them."

Brooks Atkinson remembered Hopkins as "the most modest and lovable little man who ever produced on Broadway." Rotund, stubby and rubicund, customarily wearing a wide-winged bow tie and a derby, he was so laconic and poker-faced that the theatrical press conferred upon him the epithet "The Sphinx of Forty-fifth Street" after the location of his Plymouth Theatre. When job-seeking actors appeared at his office, a tiny, crescent-shaped cubicle off the stairs to the first balcony, and he had none to offer, he would sadly waggle his head without uttering a syllable. Taciturnity evidently ran in the Sphinx's family. According to legend, when one of his seven brothers visited him, half an hour elapsed before they greeted each other.

Hopkins also observed an economy of words at rehearsals. For the first week or more he would straddle a chair at the rear of the orchestra or stand in the wings, smoking, while the cast read and reread the script until he felt that everybody understood it. Only then would he allow any acting. He rarely told a performer what to do, only what not to do. If he had a criticism to make, he would gently draw the actor aside to spare him humiliation before the others. He was the first director to let actors speak with their backs turned to the audience. While rehearsing Elmer Rice's *On Trial* in 1914, he conceived of the revolving stage, permitting changes of scene in less than a minute.

The son of Welsh immigrants, Hopkins started out in his native Cleveland as a reporter for the Cleveland *Press*. He distinguished himself by roaming the city's Polish district until he had established the identity of Leon Czolgosz, the anarchist who assassinated President McKinley. From reporting he switched to press-agentry for vaudeville theaters, then became a talent booker. In the last capacity he handled William S. Hart, Vernon and Irene Castle, Harry Lauder, Will Rogers.

"Keep in your souls some images of magnificence. . . . The artist should omit details, the prose of nature, and give us only the spirit and the splendor."

These were axioms of Robert Edmond Jones, America's foremost scenic designer, whose approach to theater went deep below surface effects, however arresting. One of six children born to a New Hampshire farmer, he was copying illuminated lettering from a Doré Bible at the age of ten. Color, light, paint obsessed him from the start. He worked his way through Harvard, as a postgraduate attended the Department of Fine Arts and then taught there. Traveling to Europe, he seized the opportunity to watch the rehearsals of the prodigious Austrian director Max Reinhardt. When he returned to New York, he designed sets for the Stage Society's production of Anatole France's *The Man Who Married a Dumb Wife.* "That decor," as the drama critic of *Stage*, Ruth Woodbury Sedgwick, wrote, "with its colors as loud as gongs, its vitality, its absolute purity of design . . . dwarfed, for the moment, the reputations of Shaw and Granville Barker [who directed the play] and made Jones."

He went on to revitalize the decor of modern ballet with his setting for Nijinsky's *Tyl Eulenspiegel.* "The Jones blue" became a topic of controversy at theatrical dinner tables. He left his stamp on every major theatrical innovation. The Theatre Guild got an early impetus from Jones. So did the Washington Square Players, the Provincetown Players, the Greenwich Village Theatre. He was among the first to introduce the American Negro actor into serious drama.

A friend described Jones at this phase of his career as "a tall, young man with a red beard on his chin, some red paint on his finger and a red fire burning inside, so that you can see it when he talks." He later reduced his facial adornment to a pencil-line mustache.

A Jungian analysand who spent three years exploring his psyche in Switzerland, he resumed his work in the theater with a reinforced concept of how the unconscious informs art. "All art moves inevitably towards this new synthesis of actuality and dream," he wrote. "Our present forms of drama are not adequate to express our newly enlarged consciousness of life. But within a decade a new dimension may be added to them, and the eternal subject of drama—the conflict of Man and his Destiny—will take on a new significance."

Later, with the advent of Technicolor, he became the screen's first great colorist, developing his own technique of painting with lights. He saw how "amber and rose could intensify romance; how greens and blue heighten terror and gloom . . . the tragedy in violet."

"If you are fortunate to work with a Robert Edmond Jones,"

said Arthur Hopkins, "you will know that the casting angels are with you."

Robert Edmond Jones, Margaret Carrington, an imperious, statuesque woman with hair the color of red gold, and her husband, William, were virtually a platonic *ménage à trois*, each devoted to the other two. Carrington, a native of Toronto, had amassed a fortune as a grain merchant, enabling him to lavish every luxury upon his wife. Not long after the marriage, while horseback-riding, he was thrown and fractured his hip. The accident left him a cripple, confined to a wheelchair. Loving music, he dedicated himself to the American Opera Company, which produced operas in English only, financing it and serving as its president.

Margaret Carrington, née Huston, a sister of the actor Walter Huston, also grew up in Toronto. Her family, a mixture of Scottish and Irish blood, derived a comfortable income from farming. Even as a child Margaret Huston was famed throughout the Toronto area for her singing. To cultivate her mezzo-soprano voice, she journeyed to London, where she had useful connections in the musical world. She became one of the foremost interpreters of Debussy and Hugo Wolf. "A majestic voice [so the worshipful Jones described it]. I never heard a sound like it. It always seemed to me to be the most beautiful singing I ever heard. She sang somehow out of the heart of music."

At the peak of her career Margaret Carrington suffered a ruinous accident. She choked on a fishbone, damaging her vocal cords so that she could not sing again except at rare intervals and then only with severe difficulty. She finally renounced the concert stage altogether.

She had meanwhile made a study of phonetics, from which she developed a novel teaching system. Voice projection, she contended, involved many muscles, but most people used only a few. To bring this latent power into play, she devised what she termed "a litany of vowels," consisting of a nonsense sentence that contained them all: "Who knows aught of art must learn and then take his ease."

But her theories went far beyond the mechanism of speech. According to Jones, "She had come to believe that it was possible to free the speaking voice to such an extent that she could hear, not the speaker's intention or his personality, but his inner essence, the self, the soul speaking through him. Only a child or a saint or a genius could hold such a belief and Mrs. Carrington was all of these."

The performers whose voices she undertook to train were almost all men, among them Orson Welles and Alfred Lunt. Women rarely interested her as pupils. An exception was Lillian Gish, whose small voice she built into one of considerable volume. Miss Gish remembered her as "a handsome and important woman—handsome in build, manner and knowledge." She charged no fee. For her, teaching was a labor of love.

The lessons took place either in the huge red-and-gold living room of the Carringtons' Park Avenue apartment or at Denby, their Greenwich, Connecticut, estate. (They owned a third property in Santa Barbara.) At work Margaret Carrington was a compelling figure, with a gaze that pierced and the command presence of a five-star general. One of her students, Day Tuttle, an actor and director, recalled a typical Carrington exhortation as follows: "You must be more obedient. Stand at the end of the room next to the Bechstein and do it again—'O what a rogue and peasant slave am I . . .' And take your time. Nobody is hurrying you. Deepen your voice. Remember to breathe through the vowels, elongating them with downward inflections. Eventually we are going to find your basic sound, the basic sound you have never spoken, the sound that *is* Day Tuttle."

The *New Republic*'s respected critic, Stark Young, placed Margaret Carrington among "the half-dozen most distinguished and brilliant figures of the last two decades."

During a busman's holiday abroad before the war broke out, Hopkins was hugely impressed by a Viennese production of Tolstoy's murky posthumous tragedy, *The Living Corpse*, with the great Austrian actor Alexander Moissi as the protagonist, Fedya Vassilye-vich Protosov.

Unrelieved Slavic gloom envelops *The Living Corpse* like fog. Fedya, morally frail but generous-spirited, dissolute but idealistic, seeks refuge from an unhappy marriage in carousal with loose-living gypsies. When his wife, Anna, turns for solace to a former suitor, Fedya determines to free her. Shrinking from the lies and collusion necessary to establish the only grounds available under Russian law—adultery—he chooses suicide. But at the last moment his nerve deserts him. Instead he plants evidence indicating that he has drowned himself, and founders deeper into the gypsy ghetto, a drunken, degraded pariah, a living corpse. Anna remarries, only to have it discovered that Fedya lives. To save her from imprisonment as a bigamist, he musters the courage to put a bullet through his chest.

The only performances of *The Living Corpse* in America had been given in Yiddish at New York's Thalia Theatre and starred the majestic Jacob Adler, patriarch of his multitudinous acting clan, the "Jewish Barrymores." After the original 1911 production, Adler kept the play in his repertoire and frequently revived it. Hopkins resolved to produce an English version, providing he could find an actor of sufficient sensibility and power. Such an actor sought him out.

John had seen Adler's portrayal in 1916 and, profoundly moved, had gone backstage to express his admiration. When word of Hopkins' plan reached Ned Sheldon through the Broadway grapevine, he urged John to secure the role of Fedya. Hopkins was readily persuaded. *Peter Ibbetson* still occupied John, but Hopkins promised to hold the part open for him. He was, in fact, prepared to venture much further. He envisaged a classical repertory built around John, with himself as director and Robert Edmond Jones designing the costumes and sets. They would present, at the rate of two plays a year, Shakespeare, Goethe, Ibsen and the best of the contemporary dramatists. No contracts were drafted. Hopkins did not believe in contracts. It would never occur to him to shackle a reluctant performer with legalities. As for the potential profits, neither he nor John raised the question.

With the Tolstoy play the first requirement was an English version. Blanche Thomas, now in the throes of passion, undertook to have a Russian friend render a literal translation, which she would then adapt. After she submitted the result to John, he told her: "Oh, it's all right, only I want more sensuousness for Fedya. Now, have him the kind of man who, when he lies beside his wife in bed, senses her lover wriggling in under the door on his belly, and getting into bed with them. Have Fedya tortured, driven mad by the thought of that man around his wife."

"But, Jack," Blanche interjected, "remember when the play starts, Fedya has already left his wife, only hopes her lover will be able to come across, and finally shoots himself to legalize their union."

"Never mind."

"But, Jack, from the beginning Fedya is beyond the physical, and only wants to lie in a gypsy café, inviting the inconclusiveness of his Russian soul to balalaika music, while Masha, the beautiful gypsy girl, keeps on kissing him and hoping she can bring him to."

"What? Why, you can't play a fellow like that. I tell you to give me something to tear out my liver with in front of those So-and-Sos!"

With Lieutenant Thomas at the front, delicacy required that John and Blanche avoid any public association, and so the pseudonym "Michael Strange" was not to appear on the program.

John spent most of the summer of 1918 immersed in Fedya's character, determining how to project "the picture of a proud human soul in turmoil and death." By the time the first rehearsal got under way, toward late August, he had also perfected, with the aid of an aristocratic White Russian coach, a rich Russian accent. Upon hearing it, Hopkins dismissed the cast for an early lunch and took John to a restaurant. "What's wrong?" John asked, sensing disapproval.

"It's the accent," Hopkins gently explained. "You are a Russian among Russians, all of you speaking Russian. An accent makes you seem a foreigner among your own people."

John conceded the incongruity, yet never completely purged Fedya's speech of the accent he had striven hard to master. Blanche described it as "a slight Russian Jew accent that stood out with exotic poignancy from the simple mid-western voices that surrounded him."

Hopkins guided his actors with a light hand. Writing about John later, he recounted: "It was like watching the work of a treasure mine and occasionally, as director, detecting and revealing to him treasure that he was overlooking. All of my criticism of his work was based on his own best examples.

" 'You are not bringing to this scene the penetration that you reveal in the previous scenes. If you show your best at any time, you are obliged to show your best all the time. Otherwise, you bring proof against yourself. Your fair will never stand up against your best.'

"You will see that in this process I never attempted to give Barrymore anything that was not his own. I was a weighing machine revealing to him when his delivery was short or overweight. It was rarely short but frequently overweight.

"Despite his humor, usually a safeguard against exaggeration, there was in Jack a residue of the old bombastic theatre, the theatre that Grandmother Drew had long made her own. . . .

"The most immediately corrective criticism of Jack was the suggestion that he reminded me, for a moment, of some actor whose work he particularly despised. There was quite a list of these, and in them a fairly complete catalogue of all the offenses against intelligent theatre."

To honor the author of *The Living Corpse*, or *Redemption*, as it was retitled, Hopkins invited his son, Count Ilya Tolstoy, who had emigrated from Russia during the Bolshevik revolution and settled in Southbury, Connecticut, to a dress rehearsal staged solely for him. When it was over, Hopkins asked him what he thought of it. The Count had only one brief observation to make. Fixing the director with a glacial stare, he demanded: "Where is Fedya's beard?"

John had a special affection for the aged actress who portrayed the mother of Anna Protosova's second husband. Zeffie Tilbury, the descendant of a notable theatrical family, had once belonged to Mum Mum's Philadelphia company and had been an intimate of Georgie Drew's. Following the first-night performance of *Redemption*, Zeffie, considering her role too unimportant to warrant curtain calls, retreated to her dressing room and changed into street clothes. John fetched her. "Come along, Zeffie," he said. "It doesn't matter about your street clothes. Come and take a bow." He led her back to the stage and, as the curtain rose again, was warmly embracing her.

The critical reception of the play, which opened at the Plymouth Theatre on October 3, 1918, was sharply divided. The *Sun*, for example, concluded that "the attempt to act his [Tolstoy's] play showed that he can be just as tedious on the stage as between the covers of a book," whereas the *Tribune* pronounced it "thrilling and interesting . . . an important work of true dramatic worth." But the critics almost unanimously lauded John's performance: "There is probably not another actor on our stage who has the temperament so fine and spiritual, an art so flexible and pure. . . . the character is conceived with splendid breadth and dignity. Perhaps with his seeking, ineffectual hands, as much as through any other medium, Mr. Barrymore achieves the most telling effects. . . . no one will ever watch Barrymore in the scene in which he attempts suicide without gripping both sides of the seat until the pistol comes down."

One night Jacob Adler returned the compliment of John's visit two years before. As he entered a box with his fifteen-year-old daughter, Stella, the audience gave him an ovation. After the last curtain, father and daughter went to John's dressing room. At sight of the kingly old actor, John, humble, close to tears, turned his face to the wall, saying: "How could you do this to me?"

The intensity of John's portrayal exacted a nervous toll which, combined with alcohol, occasionally manifested itself in irrational outbursts of fury. A stage electrician once mishandled the controls, illuminating John's feet instead of his head. Next day, as John arrived for a matinee, his senses somewhat muddled by liquor, the blunderer greeted him with a "Good afternoon, Mr. Barrymore." John's response was to flatten him with a haymaker. When his victim could stand up, he informed the stage manager: "I'm not going to fight him. I'm going to take him to court and show people how the bastard acts backstage." The manager hastened to John's dressing room to reproach him.

"Did I knock him down?" said John. "In that case, I shall go and apologize."

He approached the electrician, hand outstretched, reflectively gazed at him a moment, then: "By God, I was right the first time!" and felled him again.

The resulting damage suit plus legal fees cost John several hundred dollars to settle.

Among his chief aversions were the heavy coughers in the audience. Fedya's last line, after shooting himself, is "Ah—happiness." One night, at the sound of hacking, John raised himself from the dead and added: "Happy indeed to leave a world of barking seals."

Dr. George Washington Colby was an inveterate first-nighter with a large theatrical practice. On a balmy Saturday afternoon in spring, Hopkins asked him to talk to John, who was behaving so strangely that the matinee might have to be canceled. Colby found John half made up, pacing his dressing room and wringing his hands. "I'm going to give up the theater," he announced. "It's too much responsibility for one man. That goddam audience, they should be outdoors playing golf on a day like this."

"You're perfectly right, John," the doctor agreed, "but it's too late to do anything about it now even if they wanted to. Suppose you give your performance, then after the matinee you can make a curtain speech and tell them they'd be better off getting some exercise."

John did precisely that.

Soon after the run of *Redemption* began, the drama editor of Hearst's New York *American* borrowed from the reportorial staff a new young recruit from Denver named Gene Fowler to interview the star in his dressing room. What had drawn the drama critic's attention to the outlander was his custom of composing verse while chewing tobacco.

Gene Fowler (born Eugene Parrott Devlan; he took the name of his mother's second husband) came to New York in August 1918, a tall, lean man of twenty-eight with a Western drawl and an urbane manner. The circumstances of his journey were already legendary among his colleagues. Though the *American*, impressed by his colorful reportage for the Denver *Post*, sent for him, it neglected to provide traveling expenses, and Gene had no cash to spare. A sympathetic local undertaker solved his predicament. An old lady had died in Denver and her body was consigned to relatives in New York. By law some custodian had to travel with it. The undertaker offered Gene train fare East in exchange for his chaperonage.

When the train paused at Chicago, Gene, craving a little fresh air, left it to take a walk around the neighborhood. A suspicious policeman asked to see his draft card. Gene had mislaid it and the policeman hauled him off to the station house, the old lady's corpse, meanwhile, proceeding unaccompanied to its destination. Gene was finally rescued by a brace of crack Chicago crime reporters who, hearing of the plight of a fellow journalist, argued the police into releasing him. They were Ben Hecht and Charles MacArthur, then at the threshold of careers both as collaborators and as solo writers that would carry them to the summit of Broadway and Hollywood success. They remained among Gene's closest friends to the end of his life.

At the Plymouth Theatre in New York, interviewer and interviewee liked each other straightaway and after the performance went to John's boardinghouse room. One of the other tenants, fearing the passage of the Eighteenth Amendment—what John termed "the blight"—had learned to make bathtub gin, and John and Gene partook copiously. It was the first of innumerable boozy sessions together extending over the next two decades.

Standing room only was available for the 204th performance of *Redemption*. Nevertheless, Hopkins, in line with his policy of presenting two plays within a twelve-month period, terminated the run and did not even send a company on tour.

The second play required John, at the age of thirty-seven, to enact a decadent, seventeen-year-old Renaissance painter.

13

The Jest

═══════════

ON Lieutenant Thomas' first night at home after the Armistice his wife told him how matters stood between her and John Barrymore. Stunned and incredulous, he convinced himself that she was in the grip of a passing infatuation. They struck a bargain: she would not see Barrymore for six months; if then her feelings remained unaltered, Thomas would step aside. She began the prescribed term in Santa Barbara, but the chances that she would forget John had been considerably lessened by the box delivered to her at the train. It contained a spray of scarlet camellias and a photograph of John in a small jade frame embossed with diamonds and sapphires, his own design.

Later her husband took her to Europe for what he hoped would be a second honeymoon.

Ned Sheldon submitted to surgery designed to break up the calcification of his knee joints and restore their mobility. As a postoperative treatment, his legs were stretched by weights and pulleys, causing him frightful pain. But despite this torture Ned went to work again in John's behalf.

Some years earlier John had acquired the American rights to an Italian tragicomedy, *La Cena delle Beffe* (The Dinner of Jests), by Sem Benelli, which had been successfully playing all over Europe since the turn of the century. Quasi-poetic and lurid, it demanded grandiose acting. Hopkins agreed to produce it as the second play in the prospective series, but both he and John felt that for American audiences it required doctoring. Such was the task Ned undertook.

The background of *The Jest*, as Ned entitled his adaptation, is Renaissance Florence under the rule of Lorenzo the Magnificent. The plot opposes two disparate Florentines—Giannetto Malespini, a young painter of Madonnas, physically weak and craven, and Neri Chiaramentesi, a coarse, rough, brawny captain of mercenaries. Neri and his brother, Gabriello, have been bullying Giannetto for the pleasure of watching him quail. To compound the outrage, Neri has stolen his paramour, Ginevra.

In the opening scene Giannetto describes the latest humiliation he has suffered at the hands of the Chiaramentesi brothers. With their stilettos they pricked grotesqueries upon his skin and tossed him, bleeding, off the Ponte Vecchio into the Arno. He admits his frailty: "I am a coward. . . . I have no courage and I never will have. . . ." What ensues is the triumph of brain over brawn.

Giannetto spins an intricate web to entrap his tormentors. At the climax of *The Jest* Neri is tricked into thinking that the cape-enfolded figure who enters his darkened abode is Giannetto come to win back Ginevra. He stabs him, only to discover that he has killed his brother, Gabriello. He lapses into babbling madness as Giannetto intones: "*Ave Maria gratia plena* . . ."

When rewriting this scene, Ned was momentarily stuck for wild, semi-coherent yet poetic lines to put into Neri's mouth. He then vaguely recalled something that had recently caught his eye and he consulted the source for verification. In the final version of *The Jest* Neri raves: "Why is the sky blue? Why do stars twinkle? Why do we dream? What made the mountains . . ." One of the play's most effective passages, Ned had lifted it word for word from an ad for *The Book of Knowledge*.

Nobody connected with *The Jest* had any doubt as to who should play Neri. Pitted against each other again, it was agreed, the Barrymore brothers would almost certainly repeat their success in *Peter Ibbetson*. This time Lionel did not demur. "It was a lusty romp. Neri was a thankful role to me."

John's most serious flaw as an actor was his voice. Rasping, limited in range, with overtones of the New York streets, it was good enough for the kind of farce and melodrama he formerly played, but inadequate for higher flights of language. Fully aware of this, he took lessons, at $20 an hour, from a voice teacher, Robert Hosea, to whom he later wrote:

> My dear Mr. Hosea—I trust you will not be surprised by this letter for I feel I must tell you of the unprecedented success of "the Jest"—how much I owe you—for whatever small share I might have in it.
>
> Of all the many defects there might be in my acting—the salient one was my speaking voice—which in a long part was almost sure to be monotonous and unvaried in character—as I did not know how to use it properly—and in remedying the defect for me as you have done I feel I owe you a debt of gratitude that is impossible to repay—as it will naturally last the rest of my theatrical career—I think your method is extraordinary in its simplicity and its almost immediate effect—Believe me—Yrs. most gratefully John Barrymore.

Robert Edmond Jones designed the sets and costumes for *The Jest*, as he did for every production in Hopkins' repertory project. The calf of John's right leg, it was found, measured fifteen inches in circumference, the left eleven and seven eighths, a disparity which his Renaissance body hose would emphasize. He was fitted by Dazian's, the leading New York costumer, with "symmetricals"—that is, tights padded to equalize the shape of legs or buttocks. The peerless specialist in this tailoring was one James Osborn, who, working with a dummy with ideal measurements, would obtain the desired proportions by stuffing the tights with lamb's wool.

Heywood Broun, who covered the opening of *The Jest* on April 9, 1918, for the *Tribune*, wrote: "John Barrymore . . . was at his best in the love scene, in which he managed to convey every shade of a compound of subtle emotions and yet lost nothing of a big sweep of passion. Lionel was at his best in the second act in a glorious moment in which a hostile crowd has come to arrest Neri, the warrior. He fairly preened himself for the fight and finally, with great hops like a gamecock, rushed out to meet the foe. A thrilling rough and tumble battle follows, in which Lionel goes through the supers like Samson in an all Philistine cast. No play we can remember has afforded such remarkable stage pictures."

The *Times*' John Corbin had reservations about the play, but none about the Barrymore brothers: "Lionel Barrymore illumines it with a touch of genius. . . . Except for the white flame of beauty, half spiritual, half decadent, with which [John Barrymore] invests the part, there is no phase which is not inward and subtly complicated. It is only on a second hearing that its involutions become clear. To the future of such actors it is impossible to set any limit. Some day we shall see them, perhaps, as Othello and Iago."

Overseas Giannetto had been played by women, Sarah Bernhardt in France, Duse in Italy. John managed to convey the character's effeminacy, his effeteness, without alienating the women in his audience. They predominated, women of every age, size and condition. Many of them returned to the Plymouth three, four times or more. An elderly paralytic had herself wheeled down the aisle in a hospital chair. When John made his first-act entrance in a fire-red wig and green tights copied from the portrait of a twelfth-century falconer hanging in the Metropolitan Museum (which, as Blanche noted appreciatively, "left no faint fragment of his anatomy to the imagination"), sighs and gasps would greet him. Hedda Hopper, then a fledgling actress and later a Hollywood gossip columnist, attested: "I am able to understand those fans who worship film stars. To the day he died I was that way about John Barrymore."

At one performance of *The Jest*, the exquisitely mannered Jane Cowl, who had no equal in the theater as a manipulator of fans and handkerchiefs, sat in a stage box. At the final curtain her frantic applause, her gesticulations, the piercing timbre of her bravos! outdid everyone else in the audience and fixed all eyes upon herself. John finally motioned for quiet, then said in a curtain speech: "I want to thank you on behalf of myself and my co-star, Miss Jane Cowl, for the wonderful reception you have given us."

One woman who remained impervious to John's appeal was his then press agent, Ruth Hale, the wife of Heywood Broun and the founder of the feminist Lucy Stone League, whose members retained their maiden names. There came a torrid June matinee when John flatly refused to leave his dressing room, where, to keep cool, he shed every stitch of clothing. As curtain time approached, Miss Hale marched determinedly to his door and knocked hard. "Come in," John called to her in impish glee. "Now listen, Jack," she told the naked actor, "I see big Heywood and little Heywood like that every day. It's no treat for me. You stop being foolish and get into your costume."

He obeyed.

*   *   *

John's involvement with Blanche Thomas did not inhibit him in his pursuit of women. There was Margaret Case, the clever, attractive daughter of Frank Case, who owned New York's Algonquin Hotel, a theatrical and literary celebrity haunt favored by the Barrymores. At the time she came to know John she imagined herself enamored of Percy Marmont, an English screen actor. "I prayed about him exhaustively," she recalled years later.

One evening, in front of the hotel, she found herself standing beside John while they both waited for a taxi. "You're in love, aren't you?" he said. She admitted she was. "I knew it. That lovely, lost look, that exquisite, forlorn look, that roseleaf cheek that is not quite a blush, that brightness in the eyes that is not yet a tear— Tell me, who is the man?"

She named Percy Marmont.

"That *ham?*"

A taxi pulled up and he propelled her into it. "We will talk this over," he said and to the driver: "Tottenham Court Road, Tibet."

As they drove through Central Park, John entreated her to dismiss the Englishman from her thoughts. "I didn't have the heart to tell him I had never met Percy Marmont."

Ethel introduced John to a striking nineteen-year-old belle from Alabama named Tallulah Bankhead, who was living at the Algonquin while striving to make her mark on the stage. "I met that most beautiful of all men, Jack Barrymore," she wrote in her autobiography, "and to my surprise and delight he fancied me. . . .

"It wasn't for his acting skill alone that John was famous or notorious . . . he was the contemptuous conquerer, the outrageous brigand, to whom the girls paid homage. Homage? What a euphemism!"

Not long after meeting Tallulah, John, who was to start work for the Famous Players company on a movie version of *Dr. Jekyll and Mr. Hyde*, summoned her to the Plymouth to discuss a possible role for her. In his dressing room it quickly became clear that he had a different purpose in view. "Though I was flattered when he made a determined attempt to 'take my virginity,' I was—despite make-up that made me look like a tart—very much of a pure girl. . . . I felt that I must decline his offer. . . . Jack took this in stride. Then he started to make little animal noises. Freely translated these indicated his desire to shred the seventh commandment. He rose and took my hands in his and started to lead me to a convenient couch. With such dignity as I could simulate under these fiery circumstances, I declined. With difficulty I understood his pleading . . . shaken and seared."

According to John's recollection, "For the good part of a season I wore myself out trying to impress Tallulah. I felt like a bullfighter who makes his kill and is then publicly given the boot. . . . In all truth, I must report that our relationship was loathsomely platonic."

Not that Tallulah was unmoved. She kept John's photograph by her bed.

In October of 1919 Blanche Thomas was vacationing in Paris, and on the 4th John wrote to her:

Saturday—after the matinee—

My darling my own tiny fig—my baby—

Oh my weariness before the matinee I sent you a tiny letter Enclosing yours—asking about a tiny phrase in it my own love—I'm sure you meant that the deceit of other people regarding us—to *each other*—would roll off our love like frogs off a crystal mountain—and leave us shining and smiling with our tiny hands grown together like a lovely tree and the brown earth—Isn't that what you meant my own beloved? and am I a stupid tiny fish for not knowing it before?—I am so *terrified* that you will ever say "I mustn't tell tiny one *this*—as he perhaps couldn't bear it yet!" that I see or am apt to see occasionally a meaning where none was meant—I suppose its because I *know* I can *never* be happy til my tiny soul is sitting on the pinnacle— the *utter* top—with *nothing* above it but the sky! and no initials carved on trees by people who have been there before—I want to sit beside you in a place where no foot has ever been and the wind that fans our faces is virginal as off a hitherto unseen and undiscovered snow—Oh my own *darling* beloved I love you so terrifically like a spark from Vulcan's forge purified by centuries of unsatisfied desire— There is more quivering strength in one slender attenuated line of my love for you than in the bulk and surge of all the lovers that have ever lived my darling—It is like Astarte and the horn of Isis wrapped in the light of some white-flaming cross—or a saint's heart with a burning snake in it —or the pallid breathless soul of moonlight dipped in blood!

My beloved am I going to lie down now and close my eyes
and think of resting my passionate head in the Lethe of
your body—and forgetting everything but its fragrance
and the soul-rest of your lovely skin—Good by my darling
I love you—tiny one.

And three days later:

Monday night

My weeny beloved my own darling fig—

Am I writing you this from the tiny restaurant near the
theatre my own tiny wife—Having had a divine nap and
a naughty dream about you in the dressing room. A beloved
wire *just* came from you—weasel—I called up the postal
telegraph place about it as it seemed a trifle late but they said
it had to go quarantine and was then *mailed* via the Suez
Canal or Afghanistan!! Anyway I *got* it and I *loved* it my
own weeny fig—I saw Ethel's dress rehearsal last night
with Lionel & Doris—If I hadn't gone she would never
have spoken to me again Doris said Lionel and I looked in
the taxi cab like "two heiffers led to the slaughter" I saw
Katharine She came and sat with us during an act when
she wasn't on the stage—and asked me about you and I
said "I am more fond of her than anything I've ever known
and I hope you are glad and wish me well" She was really
terribly nice and not even pathetic about it because she
seems to have gotten hold of herself and is making—it
would seem something for herself out of her own life—
I shook hands with her and wished her luck and I know
perfectly well—as well as I am sitting here and writing
you my beloved my tiny soul mate—that she will never
dream of trying to see me or have me see her or come into
my life if she is sick or well—*ever* again—I was *very* glad
I had seen her because every single nuance of the meeting
was *what* you would have *wished* for and from both of
us—oh my darling do I love you in the worst *divine* way
in the world incomparably more wonderfully than I ever
thought was in my nature or capacity—I don't suppose
anyone has *ever* been so stupid about themselves as I have
been—There has never since the inception of mankind
been anyone to whom you could trust your happiness and

love to like you can to me my darling little Genius Fish—
I am getting so devilishly tired of being separated from you
darling—I am dieing [sic] to hear all about the tiny place
your living in my weasel—Has it a lovely view my baby—
and will you be happy there—dear one—write me all about
it darling—I am going to day to get you a divine surprise
my beloved to bring you in Paris—Do I adore getting you
things my tiny baby wife—write me when your mother
is coming back from Newport darling and what her address
will be—so I can see her my fish—I have your tiny scapu-
lar around my neck on a long black ribbon—That is divine
so it is next to my tiny body all the time—oh my love
these days must pass quickly—For God's sake send for me
tiny one if your tiny soul or body needs me near you—I
am so close to you all the time and need you so terribly
darling—if Nellie Mackay *isn't* there—wouldn't it really
be better perhaps if I came over earlier and stayed with you
longer dear—I can't *bear* to think of you alone for all *kinds*
of reasons—darling—write me about it quickly dear one—
I love you so my little wife—my fig

By the fall of 1920 Leonard Thomas had acknowledged defeat
and Blanche went to Paris for her divorce. The Oelrichs clan was agi-
tated. For the sake of her two sons, they argued, she must not break
up her marriage, certainly not to wed the likes of John Barrymore.
They nearly prevailed. Blanche had exacted a promise from John that
he would give up liquor, yet, according to a letter from home, he was
seen staggering in the street. The lovers had been writing or cabling
each other almost daily. Now, for a week John received no word from
her. Desperate, he cabled:

OH MY BABY WHAT IN THE NAME OF GOD COULD MAKE
YOU SO COLD TO ME I HAVE BEEN SO WRETCHED I HAVE
WRITTEN YOU LETTERS THAT WERE LIKE THE LAST WAIL
OF THE DAMNED IN THE VALLEY OF THE DEAD AND TORN
THEM UP OH MY BELOVED MY DEAREST BELOVED I HAVE
WAITED AND LONGED AND PRAYED AND CURSED FOR YOU
ALL MY LIFE LIKE A MAROONED SOUL ON A DESERTED
COAST PLEASE FOR THE LOVE OF HEAVEN BELIEVE THAT
YOUR FUTURE IS STREWN WITH LITTLE PIECES OF MY
HEART FOR YOUR FEET TO WALK ON SO THEY NEED NOT
TOUCH THE EARTH I LOVE YOU I LOVE YOU I LOVE YOU

Blanche capitulated. Upon returning to New York she confided her intention of marrying John to her friend Mercedes de Acosta, a fellow member of the International bon ton and, like herself, a dabbler in the arts. "When you do," Miss de Acosta commented, "I wonder who'll kill the other first."

"What do you mean by that?" Blanche asked.

"You are both such egomaniacs that you will some day start a fight to the finish, and one of you will do the other in. I'm not sure which one."

Blanche laughed. "I can tell you that right now. It will *not* be me."

Ned Sheldon never saw *The Jest*. He never again saw John in any play. He was gradually turning to stone, forced, much of the time, to lie on his back in bed. He had walked eight steps, he wrote to a Harvard classmate. "It took five minutes and two nurses, but I am as proud as if I had had twins."

The Jest ran from April 9 to June 14, closed for the summer, reopened in September and was still going strong on the last day of February when Hopkins took it off to make way for his second production of the season. John welcomed the decision. Boredom, tinged with self-disgust, had set in. He thought of himself as "a patchoulied neurasthenic . . . a stained glass window of a decadent string bean."

John chose the next play. He had had it in mind for some time. Doting on animals, like his father, he had once visited the Bronx Zoo with Ned. Among the specimens that fascinated them was a tarantula, hairy, with a gray patch on its back, reddish eyes and eight legs, "sinister and evil looking," said John, "the personification of a crawling power. . . . He looks just like Richard the Third."

"Why don't you play him?" said Ned.

"All right, I will."

14

Richard III

A NOTHER woman whom Margaret Carrington once accepted as a pupil was Blanche Thomas, then writing a play of her own and entertaining the possibility of appearing in it herself. They had worked together briefly in Santa Barbara during Blanche's bootless cooling-off sojourn. When John, after reading *Richard III* aloud to himself, realized that his vocal equipment needed further training to handle Shakespeare's iambics, Blanche, back from Paris with her divorce decree, took him to Margaret Carrington.

Only six weeks remained before the scheduled opening of the play, scarcely enough, so the voice teacher thought, to build a new voice. She nevertheless agreed to try. Every day of that interval John spent five hours or more in the Carrington apartment, and between intensive coaching and Arthur Hopkins' direction he not only developed perhaps the finest vocal instrument in the American theater, but also arrived at a perception in depth of Richard's motive force.

A side of his teacher's multifaceted nature that must have attracted John was mystical. "Mrs. Carrington," Robert Edmond Jones explained, "was a person of great physical vitality and psychic intensity. Although she detested and (I think) feared anything that savored of the occult, I think it was not an accident that in her expression she was not unlike Madame Blavatsky.* Jack always said

* Helena Petrovna Blavatsky (1831–1891), founder of the Theosophical Society.

151

she was a witch. She was in a way, a white witch. Her intuitions were always uncanny. Many people were in awe of her."

Twenty years later Margaret Carrington began a book about John's acting. She died after she finished the first chapter, according to which:

"It has been said of Sarah Bernhardt that she was courageous, arrogant, dangerous and beautiful—that Calvé before her entrance in the first act of *Carmen* had to be held by two stage directors—that Melba's singing was bold, perfect—that her intonation was faultless —that Chaliapin 'appeared' on a scene. No one ever saw him 'walk' on. He came in on the air. The only conclusion one can come to about these great personalities of the theatre and opera is that they were born possessed of a dynamo energy, to startle, to remind us that there is a power in certain people which defies analysis. Great personalities stand alone and aloof, above praise or censure. Their power has essentially to do with performance. They do not thrive in seclusion. . . .

"Working with John Barrymore was like playing on a harp with a thousand strings. . . . He worked as he walked in the streets, prolonging his vowel sounds until he acquired the muscular control required to read through to the end of a sentence on one breath. . . .

"The role of *Richard III* was a challenge to Barrymore's mordant and rapier-like mentality. It is a superhuman test of an actor's ability to play a villain like Richard and project the beauty and significance of Shakespeare's text and not fall into theatric or realistic interpretation of a role fraught with pitfalls for actors without creative or poetic imagination. Richard's lines in the first scene give us a complete key to his character: 'I that am curtailed by fair proportion, cheated of feature by dissembling nature, deformed, unfinished, sent before my time into this breathing world half made up, and that so lamely and unfashionable that dogs bark at me as I halt by them . . .'

" 'And therefore, since I cannot prove a lover to entertain these fair well-spoken days, I am determined to prove a villain. . . .'

"There is more in this speech than mere villainy. It is perhaps the greatest written revelation of human frustration. . . . [Barrymore] was the living incarnation of Shakespeare's Richard. . . ."

To allow John the widest possible scope, Ned Sheldon, in his sickroom, prepared an expanded text, preceding the standard version with passages from *King Henry VI*, in which Shakespeare introduced Richard.

Jones spent weeks at the British Museum studying fabrics for the medieval costumes, weapons, banners, jewelry. John spared no pains either to ensure the authenticity of Richard's trappings. In Newark, New Jersey, he learned, there lived an old German metal-worker, something of a medievalist, whom museums and private collectors entrusted with the restoration of damaged armor. To John's specifications he forged a many-jointed suit of armor, all black, another of copper, and a two-handed sword after a drawing John made of a type wielded in Richard's day. The fittings for the armor kept John hopping to and from Newark for months. When seated on the throne, brooding, spiderlike, after the murder of the two little princes, King Richard would wear robes of scarlet and gold lined with silver, a blazing contrast to the austere gray walls of the Tower of London which Jones' designs called for as the background of every scene.

Hopkins deliberately chose actors who, like John, had no previous Shakespearean experience. At the first rehearsal he handed them their lines typewritten with the stage directions omitted. He conjured them to refrain from consulting printed copies of the play and not to treat Shakespeare with the kind of awed reverence that so often cast a mortuary pall over the proceedings. *Richard III*, as Hopkins saw it, was a melodrama and should be played accordingly.

John derived a peculiar satisfaction from roles in movies as well as on the stage that required him to disguise his good looks by makeup or facial contortion, as if they embarrassed him, as if they somehow lessened his manhood. "I want always to play character parts," he said. "I feel very bald and a little naked in my own face. I do not want ever again to find myself in the position of saying, in effect: 'You have paid two dollars to look at the face of John Barrymore, and here it is.'" In roles like Peter Ibbetson, what he called "pansy roles," he described himself as "a marshmallow in a blond wig." Of his famous profile: "The right side of my face looks like a fried egg."

Thus, it was with zest and glee that he assumed the persona of Richard III, that "lump of foul deformity," that "abortive, rooting hog," crookbacked and halt, long, crow-black hair falling to his shoulders, mouth twisted in a sly, cruel smile. With the play still in rehearsal, John went before the Famous Players' camera filming *Dr. Jekyll and Mr. Hyde*. In the first stage of transformation from high-minded physician to monster he applied no special makeup, but simply turned away from the camera, hands covering his face, then spun around to reveal hideously twisted features. At that moment the camera focused briefly on his clawlike hands. When it returned to his face, makeup had completed the transformation into a pointy-headed, fanged horror.

None of the six earlier Jekyll-Hyde cinematic portrayals,* not even Richard Mansfield's celebrated stage impersonation surpassed, in the estimation of many critics, either the silken suavity of John's doctor or the frightfulness of the alter ego.

After the release of the film in April 1920, John visited his sister and her three children summering in Easthampton. A local theater was showing *Jekyll and Hyde* and they all attended. During the more gruesome scenes Ethel placed her hands on the heads of the children beside her and shoved them down below the line of vision. That night little Ethel Colt could not sleep for terror until Uncle John finally calmed her by explaining how the mutation was achieved.

Tickets for the opening night of *Richard III*, on Saturday, March 6, 1920, cost $5, thereafter $3.50 for the first ten rows and $3 elsewhere, an unheard-of scale for a non-musical production. With its expanded text (later trimmed), the play lasted four and a half hours to one a.m. But nobody in the audience budged.

"People like this man," said John of Richard, "because he is on the level with his iniquity. The audience is his only confidant, and that is the secret of the play's success."

In accordance with this view, John and Margaret Carrington between them had devised a number of gripping innovative effects. For example, after Richard, by the subtlety of his serpentine tongue and the force of his eloquence, has softened Lady Anne's heart toward him even as they stand beside the coffin of her husband whom he murdered, he gloats: "Was ever woman in this humour woo'd? Was ever woman in this humour won?" The lines and the long speech following were customarily delivered as an aside, an interior monologue. But John would single out a member of the audience, transfix him with his gaze and address him directly, finishing with a cackle of sardonic laughter.

* According to Leslie Halliwell's *The Filmgoer's Companion*, "There was a Selig version in 1908 and a Danish one in 1909. James Cruze directed a Universal version in 1912, and in 1913 King Baggott appeared in a rival production. 1919 brought Sheldon Lewis as the doctor and . . . in Germany Conrad Veidt, directed by Murnau, had had an equally splendid shot at the character."

The vigor of Richard's last-ditch combat with the avenging Richmond stunned the audience. The stage manager, William Seymour, had learned theatrical swordplay from John Drew and, bounding all over the stage, imparted the fine points to John. Seymour, unfortunately, was short and fat, and the exertion led to a stroke. So heavy was John's copper armor that when he executed a backward fall, landing on his spine, he sustained contusions, and so hot from the spotlights and footlights that it had to be hosed with cold water before his dresser could remove it.

At the final curtain the audience stood and cheered. The critics to a man extolled John's performance. "All in all, a magnificent achievement," wrote Alexander Woollcott in the *Times*. "It ranks with Forbes Robertson's Hamlet and Ada Rehan's Katherine . . . the highest point reached in the precipitous and electrifying ascent of John Barrymore to his present commanding position in the English-speaking theatre."

To the *Tribune*'s Heywood Broun it was "the most inspired performance which this generation has seen," and to the *Globe*'s Kenneth Macgowan, "the finest moment in the American theater."

In the memory of Arthur Hopkins, John was "unforgettable. He had fire, beauty, humor, cajolery, chilling cruelty. Shakespeare tragedy, for the first time in our day, became vibrantly alive. Here again it had the wide popular response that it must once have had to have survived. This was no play requiring special knowledge for appreciation. Here was no work to be shunned because of its tragic content. Here was exaltation, a brief, dazzling sojourn in the high heavens of emotion. Here was an experience for all people, an experience that made them one."

The only dissenter was John himself. As usual, achievement brought in its train boredom and the conviction that acting had no importance. "It was a meticulous and not very inspiring performance," he said.

But it was no fault of John's that the run of *Richard III*, playing to packed houses, had to be ended barely a month after the opening. The stress he imposed upon himself proved intolerable. In addition to his nightly work as Richard, he spent the day at the Famous Players studio on West Fifty-sixth Street enacting *Jekyll and Hyde*. To cap it all, as soon as he shed his armor at the Plymouth, he would taxi to Pennsylvania Station and board a train for Atlantic City, where Blanche had retired to work on her play in seclusion. The result was that John suffered a physical and nervous collapse.

"If there is a tragedy in his short run of *Richard III*," Margaret Carrington lamented, "it was because a man of his temperament and talent could not physically sustain so high a standard as he achieved in his performance under the pressure of influences surrounding him at that time. His performances were electrifying as well as being a demonstration of demoniac talent used at its highest pitch. . . ."

William Muldoon, the former wrestling champion and friend of Maurice Barrymore, now operated a sanitarium near White Plains, and John committed himself to his care. Every morning Muldoon obliged him to rise at daybreak, an hour when, on the outside, he had often just gone to bed. A cold shower followed, then, in a gym suit, he tossed a medicine ball. After breakfast, a two-hour rest. No smoking or drinking ever. He tried to persuade cronies like Jack Prescott to smuggle liquor to him, but Muldoon always foiled him and finally denied him the telephone altogether. The major feature of the day's program was a five-mile afternoon hike, with Muldoon riding horseback alongside to make certain John did not slacken his pace.

While at Muldoon's John rendered a pen-and-water color caricature depicting the duality of his own nature. An ethereal, Peter Ibbetson–looking figure represents his romantic, idealistic self, a monster, part spider, part octopus, his wild, aberrant self. He inscribed it to another Muldoon inmate, a man named Henry Hunt King.*

The free verse that gushed from the pen of "Michael Strange" at about this period doubtless reflected her relationship with John:

> During the night-tide of my departed love illumining beside me
> And his words like the hiss of approaching flood
> Across droughted places—
>
> And his embrace washing my fatigue
> As of a draught of orchard perfume
> Stealing through dishevelled city curvage
>
> O the splendour of his dream-felt touch . . .

* In 1971 the National Portrait Gallery, Smithsonian Institution, purchased it from King's widow.

O comrade, in that strange illicit dialogue
Of our perfectly matched fancy . . .

Then my thoughts of you pressing upon your mouth—
Your evasive—flippant—tragic mouth
A kiss—sharp—evanescent
And drawing you for ever after its insinuation
That you should know yourself further—
Upon tasting it again . . .

O the cool fragrant breathing of this night
Savouring my breast—
And becoming the caress of my bridegroom's
Ivory and scented fingers . . .

Leave your mouth well over into the moonlight
So that I may kiss it full, O chance—
Press me into your pungent arms . . .

A batch of these poems was eventually published by Alfred A. Knopf under the title *Resurrecting Life*. John contributed some drawings to the volume in his Doré-esque manner. The frontispiece, showing a nude female figure soaring heavenward above a tangle of earthbound human and animal grotesques, was intended to illustrate the lines

And a flashing want of supreme melody—
Furling back all space
Before the great vibrating empty
Of an eternal union . . .

As a believer in astrology who consulted the stars when facing an important decision, John, an Aquarius, might have taken warning from a curious circumstance. His former wife Katherine Harris, and his wife to be, Libras both, were born in the same city, Newport, on the same day, within an hour of each other, and delivered by the same obstetrician. But John's ardor was not to be cooled by the inauspicious coincidence. The wedding took place in the Ritz-Carlton suite of one of Blanche's friends, with Lionel as best man and Ethel a witness. She was then seven months pregnant.

15

Clair de Lune

===

DURING the first year of the marriage John eschewed the theater to devote himself wholly to his new wife. As a wedding gift he had purchased a small white farmhouse near White Plains, New York, surrounded by lilac bushes and fifteen acres of field and woods. It moved Blanche to poeticize:

> Our hidden house
> As an haunted reflection thrown in the subterranean
> Circlet of a well—
> A mound of mischievous plaster set in a gnarl of
> Still strange green—
> Built by sprites by angels in an elfin mood
> To be seen by lightning moonlight never forgotten
> Perfect for memory.

The enraptured couple proceeded to convert their snug retreat into a mini-museum of medievalism. According to Blanche's description, "The hearth was typical of both of us, of a kind of crazed spirituality that crept very early into our relationship; for the andirons tapered into Holy Grail cups that were sheathed in wings, and drawn down at the ends into serpent's claws, while above the fireplace, to seal the bewilderment of the visitor, was printed in the stone, 'Behold I send my angel before thy face.' "

The first professional stint to interrupt the idyll came in 1921 when John played the lead opposite Colleen Moore in a First National romantic comedy directed by Marshall Neilan, *The Lotus Eater*. The main location was Miami, from which the hero flees civilization in a balloon, landing on a remote Pacific island. A toothsome native girl (Miss Moore) bewitches him. He tries to break away and give civilization another try. It's no use; he flies back to Miss Moore and the primitive life.

First National chartered a boat, the *Virginia Bee*, to sail the company four miles out to sea. Everybody became horribly seasick except John, who had taken the precaution not to eat beforehand. In addition to nausea, the cast was tormented by a blistering sun. Then the *Virginia Bee* blundered into a sandbar and hung there. An SOS to First National brought a two-seater plane for John, but he insisted on sticking it out with the company. As the hovering plane turned back, he shouted to the pilot: "If you've got any New York newspapers, for the love of Mike drop them down."

Blanche finished the play she had begun in Santa Barbara. Entitling it *Clair de Lune*, she appended a program note explaining: "Suggestions for the play, also the names of the mountebanks and villain are taken from *L'Homme Qui Rit* [The Man Who Laughs] by Victor Hugo." This admission somewhat scanted the truth. She also took from the Hugo novel the basic story line, that of Gwymplane, a hideously disfigured mountebank, and Dea, the blind girl who loves him.

Literary originality was not Michael Strange's forte. An earlier attempt at a short story, which she called "Isaroff" and sold to the New York *Sun* for its Sunday fiction section, she modeled on Turgenev. Among the dramatists she emulated were J. M. Barrie, Bjørnstjerne Bjørnson and Ibsen. Not long after *Clair de Lune* an American dramatist, Sophie Treadwell, who was residing in England, submitted to John a play about Edgar Allan Poe. It failed to interest him and he returned it. Blanche presently turned out a play, *Dark Crown*, dealing with the same subject. John showed it to Miss Treadwell, who thereupon charged Blanche with plagiarism, repeated the accusation to the English press and threatened a lawsuit. The London solicitor whose advice Blanche sought concluded: ". . . we were of the opinion that . . . having regard to the fact that certain scenes in your play and certain characters were similar in setting to those in Miss Treadwell's play that subconsciously you might have had Miss

Treadwell's play in mind. . . ." Blanche consigned *Dark Crown* to oblivion.

Stylistically, however, Michael Strange owed nothing to Victor Hugo. A decided individuality marked her dialogue, which in *Clair de Lune* ranged from strained metaphor to utter obfuscation.

"How calm the water is!" exclaims 2d. Courtier at the start of the play. "It makes the swans look exactly like topaz clouds reflecting in a titanic mirror."

"Yes," A Lady agrees. "The sky is just as clear as the Queen's ear-rings of aquamarine. A storm could hardly blow up out of such blueness, so the masque is bound to be heavenly."

A little further along, The Queen bafflingly remarks to 2d. Courtier: "I hope you are not hiding a mud-sling in your silk swallow-tail."

No greater proof of devotion could John have tendered his wife than his willingness to portray Gwymplane and deliver such lines as "I am kissing your little white feet. It is like brushing sprays of silken flowers."

John did much more. He designed the sets and costumes, selected the rest of the cast and persuaded Ethel to play The Queen. Required in his guise of mountebank to make his entrance somersaulting, followed by a balletic *pas seul*, he retained a famous ballet master, Maurice Koslov, to show him how.

John also found a producer. He had initially offered the play to Arthur Hopkins, who wanted nothing to do with it. He turned next to Alf Hayman, who ran Charles Frohman, Inc. For Hayman the opportunity to present two Barrymores in the same production overrode every other consideration, and he scheduled the opening for April 18, 1921, at the Empire Theatre on Broadway and Fortieth Street.

On March 3 Blanche presented John with a daughter. By her choice, the name inscribed on the birth registration was Joan (after Joan of Arc) Strange Blythe, but in the taxi en route to the christening at St. Ignatius Church she had second thoughts. "It sounds too much like John," she said (according to what she later told her daughter). "This child must be an individual, not an echo of her father."

John bridled. "It may sound like John in that bastard British accent they use in Newport, but it doesn't sound like John to me. What name are you giving her?"

Blanche chose "Diana."

John assented, but at the same time bestowed a nickname upon the infant by which he alone would call her—"Treepeewee" or "Treepee" for short. What, if anything, it meant remained as inexplicable as "Fig."

Barely a month after Treepeewee's birth John took an astonishing legal step. From impenetrable motives of his own, without any request by Michael, he waived his paternal rights of guardianship then and forever, conferring upon his wife, whatever the course of their marriage, sole control of their daughter until she reached her majority.

Before the first-night curtain rose on *Clair de Lune*, John assured Blanche: "Now you'll show those sons of bitches, those society friends of yours, what you are made of. This is your justification. Now they have to accept you for what you are."

As a newsworthy event the opening was a howling success. Sizable contingents of both Social Registerites and theatrical luminaries turned out for it. Reporters besieged the stage door. A feature writer, preparing an article on the Drew-Barrymore clan, managed to interview Ethel in her dressing room. Among sundry details, he wanted to know with what play John Drew had most recently toured. Ethel called out to her brother next door: "What was the last piece Uncle Jack was in?"

John's bawdy reply resounded through the backstage corridors: "Mary Boland."

To gawk at the celebrities debouching from their limousines, crowds waited under a pelting rain in lines that stretched the length of the block and out into the street. The best seats, $5 at the box office, had been sold by scalpers for as much as $50. But the critical reception of the play was catastrophic.

Next day the theatrical pages were peppered with such pejoratives as "flimsy and trivial . . . bombastic . . . empty . . . formless and inchoate . . . amateurish." Even Alexander Woollcott, a Barrymore booster, could find few comforting words for the second Mrs. John Barrymore's maiden dramatic effort: "The play itself, feeble much of the time and incorrigibly pretentious always, was wanting. . . . the program acknowledges grudgingly, in the manner of a reluctant debtor, what the play owes to *L'Homme Qui Rit*, which is nearly all of what is good and interesting in its six scenes."

Heywood Broun wrote: ". . . it did not seem to us that there was any very great demand upon the powers of the two stars or opportunity for them. . . . One of the characters remarks, 'Before the rain can fall it is necessary for the mist to gather,' or words to that effect. We think Michael Strange has been a little too intent on assembling the mist."

John, love blind, trailing clouds of wrath, stormed into Ethel's dressing room to announce that after the next performance he would go before the curtain and deliver a speech denouncing Woollcott and Broun. Ethel implored him to do nothing so unprofessional. When it appeared that she could not deter him, she went in search of Uncle John Drew. She found him at the select Racquet and Tennis Club (one of the rare few actors ever admitted there; among the others: Fred Astaire, Robert Montgomery). No self-respecting actor, he told his nephew, would stoop to take notice of critics. John was adamant. Ethel then sent for Lionel, who added his remonstrance.

"My mind is made up," said John. "I know what I propose doing is unusual. That is the reason why you can't dissuade me. I am going to talk about that pair of vultures in such clear and vigorous language that the story will make the front page of every paper in the country."

"You're mistaken," Lionel said. "The item on the front page will read 'Lionel Barrymore strangles his brother Jack in the dressing room before the performance.' "

In the end John yielded, but he vented his ire by posting identical letters to the two most offending newspapers:

> Upon reading Tuesday those notices of *Clair de Lune* written by the gentlemen of the *Times* and *Tribune*, I became inclined to wonder if a malice so stark should be permitted to pass without comment, or such unauthenticity of statement to circulate without contradiction.
>
> I am forced reluctantly to the conclusion that the gentleman of the *Tribune* is either jaded from forced attendance at the theatre throughout a long season, or that in his job he, like Melisande, is not happy.
>
> As for the *Times* reviewer, one cannot help wondering, while reading his odd cacophony of words, if he has ever dualized those two functions—which the public daily expect of him as a critic—of thinking and writing at the same time.
>
> In perusing these two strangely inaccurate reviews,

one wonders if the dignity and beauty of honest labor should be froufroued away by these acidulated whirlwinds of lame invective, and if the time is not ripe for that laughter, which has been held rather long in one's sleeve, to appear upon one's face while asking one's self and the public —whose servants they are as much as we of the theatre— a sensible account of what is incumbent upon them to witness in a spirit of mental alertness and fair play.

Neither newspaper published the letter.

Despite the poor press, the excitement, the glamour generated by the Barrymore image kept *Clair de Lune* going for sixty-four performances.

John and Blanche were on an emotional roller-coaster, now manic with passion, now depressive, exchanging terrible insults and threats of violence to each other or themselves. Leonard Thomas had remained friendly with his ex-wife, sometimes advising her in financial matters, and when, following a particularly savage altercation, she asked him to act as peacemaker, he complied and effected a truce.

Iris Tree, who was also privy to the Barrymore bouts, compared them to "a tennis game in hell where nobody misses a ball."

A major source of discord was John's boozing. Blanche hid or destroyed what bottles she could find in the house. Thus deprived, John once drank the alcohol out of her curling iron. Another time, after she smashed an entire case of champagne, he downed a flacon of her perfume.

One winter day Blanche telephoned Mercedes de Acosta. John had vanished after a row. Would she come for dinner and stay the night? Blanche felt sure, she said when Mercedes arrived, that John had fled to New York "to pour out his woes to his nanny—Ned Sheldon."

After dinner the two women sat before a log fire while Blanche read an adaptation she was writing of Edmond Rostand's play *L'Aiglon*. A strange noise issuing from the cellar interrupted her. A cat or skunk? Perhaps a burglar? Arming themselves with pokers and kitchen knives, they crept down the cellar steps. At the foot sprawled John, barely sentient, amid a wreckage of gin bottles. They managed to get him upstairs to his bedroom. In the morning he explained penitently that his scrap with Blanche had so distressed him that he had pretended to leave the house, slamming the door behind him, but had stolen back to the cellar. "I only meant to drink enough for a few hours of forgetfulness."

When Mercedes left, husband and wife were standing close together, holding hands, wreathed in loving smiles.

It was neither the first nor the last marital combat Mercedes witnessed. As a guest in a house they rented one summer in Normandy, she was torn out of her sleep by Michael's screams—"Help, Mercedes, help!" She found the couple rolling on the bedroom floor, John clutching a knife. Plunging into the fray, she wrested the knife from him and planted herself between them. John backed away, picked up a kerosene lamp and flung it at the women, missing them, but messing up the wall behind them. All three then realized that Mercedes had cut herself on the knife. Submerging their animosity, the couple hastened to her aid, bandaging and petting her. The scene ended with all three kissing each other, Michael calling her mate "honey bun" and he responding with "my beautiful Fig." To both of them Mercedes was a "wingèd meadowlark."

Thirty-six years later Diana Barrymore wrote: "Their intense egos galled them: they were in competition with each other as artists, as lovers, as parents; each insisted on being the only focus of attention in the home, on the street, at parties; each had an uncontrollable temper—madly theatrical, they could explode in a rage at the turn of a word. Both seethed with jealousy; it was no secret that women shamelessly pursued Daddy or that there was hardly a gentleman acquaintance of Mother's who hadn't felt impelled to try his charms on her."

In New York the Barrymores leased a brownstone near Madison Avenue. Their cook, Martha, awakened at two o'clock one morning by an uproar beneath her window, glanced out to behold Blanche, clad only in a nightgown, tearing along the street toward Madison, screaming: "I'll throw myself under the first streetcar!"

Marital strife sometimes left the couple's bedroom furniture in splinters and assorted porcelain art objects in shards. One night as Blanche bent over Diana's bed to kiss her good night, the nurse, Mary Dempsey, saw that she carried an arm in a sling and an eye had been blackened. Blanche grandly explained: "I stumbled over a case of champagne in the dark."

During the summer of 1921 John and Blanche traveled to Paris, commending five-month-old Diana and the two Thomas brothers to the care of servants. They stayed first at the Hotel Crillon, then for two weeks occupied a flat overlooking the Seine loaned to them by a friend of Blanche's, Mrs. William Astor Chanler. Amid *le tout Paris* the couple occasioned a good deal of *oh*ing and *ah*ing by the singularity of their dress, which prefigured the unisex style of a later generation. They chose the same black silk or black velvet for John's trousers and Blanche's skirts. Pleatings and flutings, duplicates of those on Blanche's skirts, embellished John's trousers. Blanche ordered a dozen copies of John's shirts with their wide, pointed, Byronic collars and both wore flowing black cravats. John let his hair grow long. They affected identical felt hats, cocked at the same rakish angle.

But the ferocity of their quarreling did not abate. As Blanche observed, "If ever two egotists crashed down in one field it was Jack and I." John climaxed a squabble in the riverside flat with the announcement that he was going to drown himself. "Go ahead!" cried Blanche, and he burst out of the flat. As her anger cooled and remorse seized her, she dashed out after him and ran along the river. Finding no sign of him, she retraced her steps, emotionally drained and fearing the worst. In the flat John lay on his bed, peacefully sleeping.

In one of her fake suicide attempts, Blanche wailed behind a locked bathroom door that she had swallowed iodine. John threatened to bash in the door with his head unless she opened it. An impact like a thunderclap, followed by deathly silence, drew her forth. John was stretched out on the floor, playing dead until he could hold his breath no longer and had to sit up—a scene straight out of *Twentieth Century*, the movie comedy made twelve years later about a guileful producer who gets his way by pretending heart failure.

What triggered these set-to's was often trivial. One evening at dinner the conversation turned to Walt Whitman, Blanche's favorite poet. "So," said John, outraged, "you do not care that a poet whom you admire above all others is rumored to have had homosexual relationships?"

"Why not?" riposted Blanche.

"Why not? Is there nothing ridiculous to you in the idea of a venerable poet with a long white beard—and a bus-boy?"

"What have his pleasures to do with his greatness? What concern are they of mine? I'm not the bus-boy! I'm his reader!"

"You are a poet and no doubt you feel that a poet should follow his emotions wherever they might lead him."

"Of course!"

"Then in God's name," said John, sweeping all the glasses off the table, "what security is there in life with such a person?"

They continued to travel together as far as St. Moritz, where Iris Tree joined them. Blanche then insisted that she must have a period of separation from John. Accordingly, she and Iris proceeded on foot to Italy, while John wandered west to Chamonix. Confronted by Mont Blanc, the highest peak of the Alps, almost three miles above sea level, nothing would do but that he climb it, though he had no previous mountain-climbing experience whatever. He reached the top, tearing a ligament in his hand on the way. The Compagnie des Guides acknowledged the feat with a certificate issued to "Monsieur John Barrymore de New York," the sixty-first climber to be so honored. Just as he had abandoned Association Football after distinguishing himself on the playing fields of King's College, so, having conquered Mont Blanc, he felt no urge to attempt another mountain ascent. One challenge met sufficed; now that he knew he could do it, repetition would only bore him.

In Venice, where, according to Blanche, "you must be with your lover or obsessed by him," she was introduced at a dinner party to "a blond young man with a pale poetic face, who carried his head thrown back and his chest pushed out, as if he had been running against a wind to deliver tidings of sacred moment." She identified him in her memoirs only by his first name—Terence.

"I saw you crossing the Piazza this morning," he told her, "and I said, 'There goes an angel crossing the Piazza.' "

Blanche did not discourage him when he professed to love her. " 'Let him,' I thought. 'Here is really something for Jack to endure!' "

When her husband arrived and she spoke of Terence, he took it calmly enough. "Is he in love with you?" he asked.

"I'm not in love with him," replied Blanche, "and that's the only part of it that concerns you."

"I wonder," said John, staring bleakly at the Grand Canal.

Back in their Paris flat, they received a surprise visit from Terence. He had come, he explained, to beg John to set his wife free. John assured him that he wished only for her happiness. As they vied with each other in self-sacrificial protestations, Blanche broke in to announce that all she wanted was to sail home. Since John, some weeks before, had signed a contract to portray the title role in the sixty-fourth Sherlock Holmes movie, to be shot partly in London, partly in Switzerland, he let her depart alone, himself proceeding to London.

The producing company belonged chiefly to Samuel Goldwyn,

Warsaw-born ex-glove salesman and malapropian ("a man who goes to a psychiatrist ought to have his head examined") who in August 1912, immediately after viewing *Bronco Billy*, a nickelodeon two-reeler, started his first movie studio with Jesse L. Lasky and Cecil B. De Mille. The other principal actors awaiting the arrival of the director, Albert Parker, included Roland Young, cast as Dr. Watson, Gustav von Seyffertitz, one of filmdom's chief bogeymen, as Professor Moriarty, "the Napoleon of Crime," and Carol Dempster as the heroine, Alice Falkner. Minor roles were to be filled by Hedda Hopper, Reginald Denny and William Powell.

When Parker reached London, John was not to be found. He was finally traced to a small attic room at the Ritz Hotel. John was sitting up in bed, stoned. Gin bottles lay everywhere, even inside his shoes. Drunk during most of the filming, wrangling continually with Parker, he yet managed a flawless impersonation of the imperturbable, infallible sleuth.

The world-renowned co-founder of the Moscow Art Theatre, Constantin Stanislavsky, was then visiting London, occupying a two-room flat, and he invited John there for dinner. Over coffee and brandy John asked him how he chose his actors.

Stanislavsky picked up a pin. "I choose them by means of this. Don't look surprised, my friend. You will understand in a minute. You go into the next room. I will hide the pin. You come and find it."

He watched intently as John lifted plates and glasses to peer under them, ran his hand along the tablecloth, finally raised the corner nearest his host and uncovered the pin.

Stanislavsky applauded. "Very good. You are engaged." He then explained. "I can tell a real actor by the way he looks for a pin. If he prances around the room, striking attitudes, pretending to think hard, looking in ridiculous places—in other words, exaggerating— then he is no good. Do you understand, my friend?"

John did and the lesson stuck.

Following the location shots, the Sherlock Holmes company returned to the States for the interiors. By then Parker's nerves were frayed. He upbraided John, warning him that he was killing himself with drink. Contrite, John abstained for the rest of the shooting. One scene required him to disguise himself as the malign Professor Moriarty. This he joyously accomplished on camera without special makeup, simply turning aside briefly while he mussed his hair and contorted his face.

"The film got marvelous reviews," Parker recalled. "It broke records in New York. . . . After that Jack and I became great friends. I was very fond of him and I think he was fond of me. But he was absolutely crazy, mad as a hatter, not good for himself at any time, but lovable."

Among those who would be welcomed into the frolicsome little coterie that later revolved around John was Roland Young. "When the modest, self-effacing Roland appeared on my horiozn," John told Gene Fowler, "I took a great liking to him; so much so that I began to feel sorry for him during our scenes together. For once in my life, I decided to be somewhat decent toward a colleague. I suggested a little stage-business now and then, so that such a charming, agreeable thespian might not be altogether lost in the shuffle. When I saw the completed film, I was flabbergasted, stunned, and almost became an atheist on the spot. That quiet, agreeable bastard had stolen, not one, but every damned scene! This consummate artist and myself have been close friends for years, but I wouldn't think of trusting him on any stage. He is such a splendid gentleman in real life, but what a cunning, larcenous demon when on the boards!"

When, in 1922, Charles MacArthur moved from the Chicago *Tribune* to the New York *American*, his presence added immeasurably to the gaiety of Manhattan's literary-theatrical community, especially to John's extrovert entourage. How could John not take to his heart a reporter who, while waiting in Otto H. Kahn's library to interview the great patron of the arts, took down a volume of Greek tragedies and inscribed it: "To my friend Otto, without whose help this could not have been written—Socrates"?

A minister's son, he rejected most ministerial values. Elfin, dreamy-eyed, skeptical, he quickly became a knight of the round table at the favorite watering hole of Manhattan's ink-slinging wits and wags, the Algonquin Hotel. Helen Hayes was starring in a George Kaufman–Marc Connelly comedy, *To the Ladies*, at the time of MacArthur's arrival, and they met at a party. MacArthur, who had a bag of peanuts in his hand, uttered one of the most often repeated gallantries in the history of courtship. Tendering the peanuts, he said: "I wish they were emeralds." After their marriage, it was so often quoted, MacArthur got so sick of it, that upon returning from a World War II army assignment to India with some real emeralds, he told his wife: "I wish they were peanuts."

Ben Hecht, who with Fowler and MacArthur enlarged the Barrymore circus, came to New York some years later, and from their common reportorial experiences among the cops and crooks of Chicago he and MacArthur distilled the powerful newspaper melodrama *The Front Page*.

16

Hamlet

===

Most people went to White Sulphur Springs, West Virginia, for sports and social activities, a few for the mineral waters. With John the visit was a first step toward the realization of the loftiest goal that his "Board of Regents" had envisioned for him. He went there to explore *Hamlet* in tranquil solitude. He brought with him the Temple edition, a duodecimo bound in red cloth,* and for weeks pored over the text, having never before approached it with a professional eye.

"I was amazed to find how simple *Hamlet* seemed to be, and I was no little bewildered that anything of such infinite beauty and simplicity should have acquired centuries of comment. It seems to me that all the explanation, all the comment that is necessary upon *Hamlet* Goethe wrote in *Wilhelm Meister*. These simple words . . . are more illuminating than all the commentaries:

" 'And to me it is clear that Shakespeare sought to depict a great deed laid upon a soul unequal to the performance of it. In this view I find the piece composed throughout. Here is an oak tree planted in a costly vase, which should have received into its bosom only lovely flowers; the roots spread out, the vase is shivered to pieces.'

* One of forty volumes edited by Sir Israel Gollancz between 1894 and 1896 and published in London by J. M. Dent Sons.

"*Hamlet* to me in the theater, no matter who plays it, will never be quite the play that it is in the theater of the cerebellum. . . . Perhaps one of the reasons so many people write about *Hamlet* and do not write about other simple things of great beauty, like the Sermon on the Mount and the Gettysburg Speech, is merely because they feel they can add something to the character which no one else has done. They see themselves playing the part. . . ."

He ranged the countryside around the resort, hurling the mighty lines at the trees. When he had done all he could do by himself, he knew he must turn again to Margaret Carrington for help.

She was eager to give it, providing Arthur Hopkins would schedule no opening date until she had worked with John at least a month and not even then unless she felt confident that he would be ready. John became a guest at Denby, the Carringtons' Greenwich, Connecticut estate, in June of 1922, and stayed there two and a half months.

"What a happy summer that was," Mrs. Carrington recalled; "we worked six, eight hours a day—sometimes into the night. In the garden—and the woods. The day he arrived, he was carrying an armful of books. The *Hamlet* variorum, histories of the play as interpreted by actors of the past. I suggested that we put the books away and find out for ourselves what the play was about. We . . . studied the play as we would a modern script that had never been performed. I think this accounted for his spontaneous reading and acting throughout the various scenes and helped to banish any natural fear he might have had appearing for the first time in a part that has been the high spot in every actor's experience. To face the potential 'back seat' actors, those kibitzers of the theatre—the critics who seem sure that there can be nothing original in a contemporary *Hamlet*—the elderly Shakespearean first-nighters whispering to their neighbors how Booth, Barrett and Mantell interpreted the part in their day! Surely this is enough to intimidate any actor. . . . we had a good time discovering *Hamlet* by ourselves. . . .

"Barrymore is the only actor I have ever known in America who was willing to polish every phrase of a play until he was satisfied that the deepest meaning of Shakespeare's text was completely revealed and understood, just as a great musician like Toscanini reveals the mind and soul of the composer. His artistry lies in the fact that he does not impose an interpretation on the music. With Toscanini it is only what the composer has set down. This is the distillation of music and applies equally in the reading of Shakespeare. This process is not so easy as it may appear. It depends on the most intensive study of every sentence in a play. . . ."

She told John that if he could forget for a few weeks everything he had ever learned about acting, he might accomplish within a relatively brief span what took less gifted and less malleable actors months or years. Among the requisites she stressed was a further refinement of the breath control he had developed for *Richard III*, enabling him the more easily to sustain Shakespeare's long, unbroken lines.

After leaving Denby, John continued to practice breath control whenever he found himself alone, even as he walked the streets of New York—to the consternation of a patrician acquaintance, the Wall Street magnate Oliver Harriman, whom John passed one day while emitting eerie sonorities.

When Mrs. Carrington informed Arthur Hopkins that her pupil was now equipped to undertake the great adventure, the taciturn little producer picked an opening date six weeks ahead—November 17, a Friday. For the role of Ophelia he engaged, at $175 a week, a twenty-one-year-old former showgirl, Rosalinde Fuller. Blanche Yurka, a Bohemian-born blonde, would play Gertrude (though she was seven years younger than her stage son), receiving $300. Tyrone ("Fred") Power the Second, a bibulous theater veteran who had once portrayed Frederick in a production of *As You Like It* starring Maurice Barrymore and knew John as a boy, drew $675 as Claudius. Hopkins paid John $1,000 a week.

As the central background throughout the play, Robert Edmond Jones' designs called for an immense flight of stairs rising from the stage to a vast arch through which appeared the sky, varying in shades of blue according to the predominant mood of the scene. The action would proceed against a painted drop or tapestried arras on one of three platforms at different levels of the staircase, with a fourth jutting out over the orchestra pit. Jones dispensed with footlighting in favor of overhead and side spots. Some viewers would find all this distracting, particularly when the actors had to dash up and down the stairs, while others pronounced it masterly, the artist's crowning work.

The player who enacted Bernardo, John Lark Taylor, a native of Nashville Tennessee, kept a log of the entire run.* He described the first rehearsal as follows:

---

* The unpublished typescript was donated by his heirs to the Special Collection of the Joint University Libraries in Nashville.

"After an exchange of greetings, we all waited about expectantly. Pretty soon Arthur Hopkins came in—greeted every one in a self-conscious sort of way—sat down near the footlights and also waited expectantly. In a short while, Barrymore came strolling in—there was a short confab in undertones. Barrymore greeted various ones—I not included—then we were told to draw our chairs close in a semi-circle —all given small books of the play—told to read our parts—and make cuts as we read."

The books were all Temple editions, and John, referring to his marked copy, called out the cuts decided upon between himself, Mrs. Carrington and Hopkins. As rehearsals progressed, he would enter in his copy marginal reminders to himself, indicating the tone, expression and movement relevant to the adjacent line. For example:

Act I Scene 2. "How weary, stale, flat, and unprofitable
Seem to me all the uses of this world!"
(*gesture*)
"Frailty, thy name is woman!" (*surprise*)
Scene 5. "O all you host of heaven! O earth! What
else?" (*sincerely, pitifully*)
Act II Scene 2. "What's Hecuba to him, or he to Hecuba
That he should weep for her?" (*down*)
". . . Bloody, bawdy villain!
Remorseless, treacherous, lecherous,
kindless villain . . ." (*crescendo*)
Scene 2. "What a piece of work is a man!"
(*look out*)
"He that plays the king shall be welcome . . ."
(*In a sort of dream-like voice*)
Act III Scene 2. "Why, let the stricken deer go weep,
The hart ungallèd play;
For some must watch, while some must
sleep;
Thus runs the world away . . . (*high*)

In the margins John sketched Hamlet, Marcellus, the First and Second Players, the Gravediggers and, on the last page, the dead Hamlet.

He later gave the volume "To Margaret Carrington—with love & gratitude for her very great helpfulness & kindness." Below the inscription he added: "This is the copy we worked from. It's a small copy—but God how we worked!!"*

Lark Taylor went on: "I rather dreaded rehearsing with Barrymore—for I'd heard, from all sources, that he was a 'Perfect Fiend'—absolutely impossible at rehearsals and to act with.

"I must say he proved quite the reverse—he was more 'Angelic' than 'Fiendish'—a kinder, more considerate person at rehearsals I've never been associated with. He seemed to go out of his way sometimes to be kind and courteous. He rarely directed any one; occasionally he would make a suggestion, and always a good one. His efforts, always, so far as I could see, were to get the best effect for the whole thing, and he seemed to want each individual actor in the cast to get the most he could out of his part.

"He and Hopkins both rather harped on the company not being 'Shakespearian'—meaning, of course, the old, conventional, ranting way of doing Shakespeare. . . .

"One day Barrymore let himself go in one of the long speeches. He made us all jump—it was positively electric—and I think made some of the company realize for the first time that this Hamlet was going to be something quite unusual. Tyrone Power came over to me, during the rehearsal, and said 'By God! He's going to be great. He's going to make the hit of his life in this part. . . . '"

According to Hopkins: "Of all the actors I have known he was the most conscientious and untiring in preparation. Nothing was too much trouble. He would go to the costumer, the bootmaker, the wigmaker, the armor maker, twenty times each, forty if necessary to get everything right. He was the first to know his part. He would rehearse each time as though it were a performance. He was never late, never made excuses. He would rehearse scenes with other actors as long as they wanted. He never grew tired. To him perfection was the aim and its attainment could not be too much trouble. He loved creating a part. . . ."

John was determined to incarnate a Hamlet less "sicklied o'er with the pale cast of thought" than "a man, take him for all in all." He told Hopkins: "I want him to be so male that when I come out on the stage they can hear my balls clank." (Asked many years later his opinion of Maurice Evans' uncut Hamlet, he replied: "You've got to have balls for Hamlet.")

"Barrymore is a curious sort of person, many-sided, moody," Lark Taylor noted, "but he was particularly well-behaved at re-

* It has since been acquired by the Players Club Library.

hearsals and pretty well-behaved all the run of the play. He has a fine, lovable side, and seems very shy, almost diffident at times. At times I used to look at him and wonder if he was really what he appeared to be. I have been told that he had run the gamut of vice and emotion— that he is cruel, bitter, heartless, and yet he seems so sort of innocent at times—almost child-like—at other times, and sometimes I've seen an expression in his eyes of awful sadness and old-age disillusion."

John and the actor who played Laertes, Sidney Mather, had some difficulty staging their last-act fencing match effectively. They took lessons from a fencing master. Then Douglas Fairbanks, a Barrymore family friend, dropped in during a rehearsal and spent the rest of the day showing them how to make the fight more acrobatic and exciting.

The entertainment page of the New York *Times* on November 16, 1922, carried ads for ninety-one attractions. At the Cort Theatre it was Jeanne Eagles as Sadie Thompson in *Rain*, a dramatization of W. Somerset Maugham's story, *Miss Thompson;* at the Republic, Anne Nichols' *Abie's Irish Rose*, which had opened the preceding May and, inexplicably, would set a new long-run record of five and a half years. *The Cat and the Canary* led the mystery thrillers; *Sally, Irene and Mary*, the musical comedies; the sixteenth edition of the *Ziegfeld Follies*, the revues. At the Metropolitan Opera House the soprano Lucrezia Bori was singing Fiora, the heroine of Montemezzi's *L'Amore dei Tre Re*, and the Canadian tenor Edward Johnson, the Met's future general manager, was making his debut there as the hero, Avito. Other musical prodigies to appear within the next few days included John McCormack, Mme. Schumann-Heink, the Flonzaley Quartet, Josef Hofmann, Rachmaninoff, Rubinstein and Paderewski.

Amid this abundance the modest notice was almost lost:

> Arthur Hopkins announces the opening performance of John Barrymore in "Hamlet" at the Sam H. Harris Theatre Tonight at 8 o'clock sharp. First Matinee Saturday at 2:15. Seats now on sale. Prices after opening, $3.30 to $1.10.

Hopkins had rented the Harris Theatre on Forty-second Street, a step from Times Square, because his own Plymouth Theatre was occupied by his production of Don Marquis' comedy hit, *The Old Soak*.

The evening was cool and fair, with a light wind blowing from the north. By six o'clock the approaches to the Harris, its 1,400 seats and standing room sold out, were choked by swarms of celebrity-watchers, autograph hounds and the idly curious, hushed and edgy, intuitively sensing that a momentous event was about to take place. A canopy stretched from the theater marquee to the street curb as protection for the carriage trade against the caprices of weather. The ticket-holders streamed through glass doors and across an outer foyer, its floor marble, its walls mirrored and embellished by marble pilasters and leafy terra-cotta dadoes. Gleaming metal doors opened into a second foyer and the orchestra, the decor here predominantly gray and black. Inlaid on the lip of the balcony were white plaster disks, each depicting the profile of some notable performer.*

As the curtain rose on *Elsinore. A platform before the castle*, Jones' Gothic-gloomy set drew a salvo of applause. During the first scene the audience waited in tense, anticipatory silence. . . . Darkness momentarily covered the stage. When the lights went up again for *Scene 2. The same. A state room of the same*, John, clad all in mourning black, sat apart from the assembled court in a Dante chair, one hand resting on an arm, the other cupped under his chin, his sculptural profile turned toward Ophelia. "A little more than kith and less than kind." A sigh rippled through the audience. The voice was resonant, melodious and natural, devoid of those fluted vowels and trilled consonants affected by many Shakespearean actors.

Ethel Barrymore was then playing six blocks away at the Longacre Theatre in another Hopkins production, Gerhart Hauptmann's *Rose Bernd*, yet she managed to get to the Harris, along with her supporting cast, during the third act by the simple expedient of accelerating the tempo of the Hauptmann text. But it was not her first view of her brother as Hamlet. The day before, in the afternoon, the company had staged a special run-through, enabling Ethel to see the entire play before she had to appear at the Longacre. "Jack didn't dress for it. He was just in his ordinary street clothes, and I suppose it was the greatest experience I ever had in the theater. He was superb, magnificent, unforgettable, and had in some mysterious way acquired that magical ease, as if he really were Hamlet. It was for me the fulfillment of all I had ever hoped for him and more."

The *World*, Saturday, November 18, 1922
"The Conning Tower"—F.P.A. [Franklin Pierce Adams]
The Diary of Our Own Samuel Pepys
    All day at my desk and so in the evening to see Ham-

---

* The Harris Theatre is today a movie "grind house," with continuous daily showings from eight a.m. to three the following morning.

let and J. Barrymore acting of it the finest I ever saw, and all about it as close to perfection as ever I hope to see, and when my grandchildren say to me, This or that is a great Hamlet, I shall say, Ay, but not so fine as Barrymore's. And I will disinherit those babes.

The rest of the critical fraternity were scarcely less enthusiastic. To Woollcott, John was "a Hamlet re-born and one that, for all its skill and graphic artfulness, is so utterly free from all that is of the stage stagey. Issuing from his lips, the . . . soliloquies . . . seemed to have been spoken for the first time." To Broun, "He excels all others we have known in grace, fire, wit and clarity." To the *New Republic*'s Stark Young, John "seemed to gather in himself all the Hamlets of his generation, to simplify and direct everyone's theory of the part . . . his Hamlet was the most satisfying I have ever seen." To the *Tribune*'s Percy Hammond, "Mr. Barrymore's Hamlet . . . was so beautiful a picture, so clear an analysis, so untheatrical an impersonation, and so musical a rendering of Shakespeare's song."

But, for all the clarity and simplicity of John's performance, he introduced a complex and controversial interpretation.

The English psychiatrist Ernest Jones, a close friend of Sigmund Freud and the first to practice psychoanalysis outside Austria and Germany, speculated in an essay, *Hamlet and Oedipus:*

"I would suggest that . . . Shakespeare's extraordinary powers of observation and penetration granted him a degree of insight that it has taken the world three subsequent centuries to reach. . . . It is now becoming more and more widely recognized that much of mankind lives in an intermediate and unhappy state charged with what Dover Wilson calls 'that sense of frustration, futility and human inadequacy which is the burden of the whole symphony' and of which *Hamlet* is the supreme example in literature. This intermediate plight, in the toils of which perhaps the greater part of mankind struggles and suffers, is given the name of psychoneurosis and long ago Shakespeare depicted it with faultless insight. . . .

"How if, in fact, Hamlet had in years gone by as a child, bitterly resented having had to share his mother's affection even with his own father, had regarded him as a rival, and had secretly wished him out of the way so that he might enjoy undisputed and undisturbed the monopoly of that affection? If such thoughts had been present in his childhood they evidently would have been 'repressed.' . . . The actual realization of his early wish in the death of his father at the hands of a jealous rival would then have stimulated into activity these 'repressed' memories, which would have produced, in the form of depression and other suffering, an obscure aftermath of his childhood conflict. This is at all events the mechanism that is actually found in the real Hamlets who are investigated psychologically. . . .

"As a child Hamlet had experienced the warmest affection for his mother, and this, as is always so, had contained elements of a disguised erotic quality. . . . Nevertheless Hamlet appears to have with more or less success weaned himself from her and to have fallen in love with Ophelia. . . .

"Now comes the father's death and the mother's second marriage. The association of the idea of sexuality with his mother, buried since infancy, can no longer be concealed from his consciousness. . . . Feelings which once, in the infancy of long ago, were pleasurable desires can now, because of his repressions, only fill him with repulsion. The long 'repressed' desire to take his father's place in his mother's affection is stimulated to unconscious activity by the sight of someone usurping this place exactly as he himself once longed to do. . . .

"Was ever a tragic figure so torn and tortured!

"Action is paralyzed at its very inception, and there is thus produced the picture of apparently causeless inhibition which is so inexplicable both to Hamlet and to readers of the play. This paralysis arises, however, not from physical or moral cowardice but from that intellectual cowardice, that reluctance to dare the exploration of his inmost soul, which Hamlet shares with the rest of the human race. 'Thus conscience doth make cowards of us all!' "

Hamlet may also have evoked memories in John, conscious or unconscious, of his seduction at fourteen by his father's wife, an encounter that aroused a lifelong mistrust of women and perhaps love-hate feelings toward his father. Whatever the genesis of his interpretation—the first of its kind ever ventured in *Hamlet*—John's treatment of Gertrude in the closet scene left no doubt as to its underlying meaning. He behaved toward her more like a lover than a son, shifting abruptly from anger to loving solicitude, seizing her roughly by the shoulders, the next moment all tender amorousness. Kneeling, he would lay his head in her lap, against her breasts, would caress her cheeks, touch her breasts and thigh. . . .

Such physical contact once nearly caused the actors hideous embarrassment. While fondling Blanche Yurka, John caught the point of his sword in her skirt. A burgeoning young actor named Spencer Tracy was in the audience, saw what had happened and, as he told his beloved friend Katharine Hepburn long after, wondered: "How's he going to get out of that? What's he going to do?" What John did was to kneel at Gertrude's side, raise the hem of her skirt and kiss it, thereby freeing his sword.

Discussing the closet scene with Lark Taylor, John pointed out: "There's an unusual thing, something that's never been done before, and not a single critic noted it." He was referring to the moments when he acted as though his father's spirit possessed him and spoke to the Queen through him. As he uttered the lines

> Nay, but to live
> In the rank sweat of an enseamèd bed;
> Stew'd in corruption; honeying and making love
> Over the nasty stye . . .

a shaft of light from overhead enveloped him. He went rigid, his eyes wide and staring, his voice hoarse like the voice of the Ghost. When the light left him, he dropped to his knees, as though released from the grip of the spirit, shrieking: "Save me, and hover o'er me with your wings, you heavenly guards!"

In an experimental variant of the episode, attempted later while on the road, a light representing the Ghost was projected onto John's body, a literal rendering of spectral possession. John disliked the terrible accusations Hamlet flung at his mother—so he told Taylor. Letting his father's spirit use him as a medium, he felt, "took the curse off the scene. . . . It makes Hamlet so much more decent." Then, after a moment's reflection, he burst out: "God, how I'd love to talk to Shakespeare about the play!"

In the presence of his father's spirit, Taylor wrote, "there was a spiritual beauty about him which was really stirring. His eyes would overflow with tears, and, on the line, 'I think I see my father,' his voice would grow tremulous, and his whole face would express a tenderness and love that was rarely beautiful."

Gene Fowler put several questions to John concerning his interpretation of the Dane, among them what Fowler himself considered "one of the shrewdest questions ever asked by a reporter of an actor." He omitted the answer from his biography because "I did not want my book barred from libraries, nor did I want to destroy my protagonist's character utterly in the opaque and intolerant public mind."

"Do actors have a subconscious, or an unconscious, when they are on the stage reciting?" Fowler asked John. "By that I mean—"

"I know perfectly well what you mean, you inquisitive police reporter bastard! Does the actor think beyond the line he is saying. Does he have a mind within a mind, or rather a mind within another mind?"

"Yes, would Barrymore on the stage, when reciting, say a Shakespearean line, and at the same time think as Barrymore, as Shakespeare, or, let us say, as Hamlet?"

"It all depended on my mood during a particular performance. If I was 'into' the part (which I was during the first weeks at least) I thought as Hamlet."

"All right. Could you now, years afterward, recreate the subconscious flow of ideas, associations,—or let us call them backdrop thoughts—while you were declaiming in the presence of your stepfather, whose name escapes me?"

"Yes, I could, and, if you will wait until we have this can of beer, I shall do it. If the dear old schoolteachers, who used to come to the Sam Harris Theatre, knew what was going through my mind while I was saying my lines, well, they would have run screaming into the street, either to escape what was going on, or to hunt a sailor."

"Now give me, not Hamlet externally, or merely in a thespic scene, but repeat as nearly as you can Hamlet's stream of consciousness or unconsciousness, the association of ideas, etc., when in the presence of his stepfather on the stage."

"It wasn't merely when I was in the presence of my stepfather. It was *most* of the time. The thing I like best was the second soliloquy, which closes with my determination to put on the play for the king. That is the soliloquy I remember best, and I can best remember what went through my mind while reciting it. 'That dirty, red-whiskered son-of-a-bitch! That bastard puts his prick in my mother's cunt every night.' "

In summary Fowler wrote: "Now, in like language, he held forth for perhaps two minutes on his own jealousy of his mother when in the arms of his hated stepfather. The language was obscene, yet one began to forget its actual filth as against the powerful and unique performance. . . ."

John's response to the New York *Evening Post*'s drama critic, Rankin Towse, won the admiration and affection of the entire cast. Towse praised John's performance, but concerning the company, wrote: "We feel certain that the other players will agree their performance can hardly be mentioned in the same breath with Mr. Barry-more's."

The next day John posted on the callboard a letter to his colleagues. After quoting Towse's comment, he wrote:

I cannot tell you how *utterly* the idea is repudiated by everyone I have talked to since last night, and how entirely and absolutely foreign this is to the manner in which the entire performance was genuinely received.

The thing that makes this play go over the way it does is the extraordinary teamwork and brilliant and sincere projection of the company as a whole, and, believe me, this is not false modesty—which brings it to life in a fashion that is unprecedented.

Everyone is speaking of it, and is thrilled by it, and I cannot resist the opportunity of saying that the comment of this critic is entirely at variance with the facts, and that every message I have received—and I have received many —has said that the beautiful performance of the company had been more than half the battle, and is a thing of wonder and delight.

Lark Taylor echoed the sentiments of his fellow supporting actors in a letter he left for John:

You have done one of the most graceful and generous things I have ever encountered in more than twenty years in the theatre. I am certain that your sincere and earnest work in this play has been an inspiration to the rest of us. Never have I read such fine and well-deserved notices. I am proud to have a part in so fine a performance.

For several days John showed no sign of having received the letter. Then one evening, shortly before curtain time, he sat down in the wings beside Taylor. "I sent your letter to my wife," he said shyly.

Taylor, astounded, could only murmur, "Thank you."

"She'll be tickled to death with it," John said.

"I envy her the pleasure she will have in seeing you do Hamlet."

John sighed. There was nothing he wanted more than for Blanche to see his Hamlet, but she had gone to Paris with the children and did not propose to curtail her visit. "Mrs. Barrymore cared nothing about his work in the theatre," **Taylor** observed, "and urged him every day, by cable, to join her."

During the early performances a crusade was in progress to purge the Broadway theater of immorality. At the behest of Supreme Court Judge Cornelius Collins a grand jury conducted an inquiry. The License Commissioner meanwhile received a complaint characterizing *Hamlet* as obscene and accordingly dispatched Police Sergeant Stewart DeWitt to the Harris. The latter reported: "It's okay. I used to recite *Hamlet* myself when I was a kid and it wasn't any worse tonight than it was then."

America's most celebrated acting couple, E. H. Sothern and Julia Marlowe, attended a performance. When the stage manager, William Adams, so notified the cast, John asked him to bring them to his dressing room afterward, then, in panic, countermanded the request. "He tried his best to play well that night," Taylor recalled, "but I think perhaps he gave the worst performance of the season." Adams stopped by the Sotherns' seats to pay his respects. They made no mention of the play, but their silence was eloquent.

John also failed to impress favorably the members of the Moscow Art Theatre, then playing in New York prior to a national tour, when they accepted Hopkins' invitation to a matinee. The visitors included Constantin Stanislavsky, and the actress Olga Chekova, widow of the playwright. In his eagerness to compel their admiration John overacted to the point of bombast and hysteria. Introduced to him after the final curtain, the dumfounded Russians could not muster up appropriate words, but stood with forced smiles in awkward silence. At length Mme. Chekova ventured: "Do you really do this eight times a week?"

Stanislavsky wrote to the other founder of the Moscow Art Theatre, Vladimir Nemirovich-Danchenko: "John Barrymore's Hamlet was far from ideal, but very charming."

Not many weeks elapsed before John was chafing again under the tedium of repetition. Now and then he sought relief by inflicting practical jokes upon his fellow players. A favorite butt was Whitford Kane, the First Gravedigger, a portly Englishman who had enacted the role in eighteen *Hamlets* and buried thirty-five Ophelias. One night, when Kane caught sight of the dummy representing the drowned Ophelia as he and the Second Gravedigger lowered it into the grave, he nearly went to pieces: on the dummy's head John had painted a lurid caricature of Rosalinde Fuller. Blanche Yurka also saw it and barely managed to choke back her laughter, while John, too, was convulsed by his own prank. " 'Twas a jolly funeral that night," Taylor noted, "and I wondered what the audience must have thought of it all."

In the same scene, just before Hamlet appears, the First Grave-digger sings the quatrain:

> But age, with his stealing steps,
> Hath claw'd me in his clutch,
> And hath shipped me into land,
> As if I had never been such.

John would sometimes deliberately delay his entrance, whisper-ing from the wings: "Sing it again, Whitford, you ought to be in opera." Occasionally the hapless Kane had to repeat the verse two or three times.

But John was contrite when he inadvertently committed a cardinal thespian sin against Kane and he had a note of apology delivered to the First Gravedigger's dressing room: "I'm damned sorry I forgot my bally lines last night and amputated two of your best laughs. I must have been in Paterson—instead of Denmark!"

By January of 1923 John felt he could not endure the monotony much longer and he notified Hopkins that he had decided to quit after the 101st performance. Why the 101st? Because it amused him to best Edwin Booth's record of 100 consecutive performances as Ham-let at the Winter Garden Theatre in 1865.*

Though the Harris was jam-packed at every performance and could probably have continued so for many more months, though most of the audience came primarily to see Barrymore, not Shake-speare, and thus no substitute was feasible, Hopkins did not protest. No contract bound John; he was free to leave whenever he chose, and Hopkins announced February 9 as the closing date. Still, John felt guilty not only for causing Hopkins financial loss, but for throwing about sixty show people out of work. By way of excuse he pleaded domestic anxiety. "God, I'm nearly crazy, I'm so worried about my kid!" he said.

He was more worried by what, in his jealous imaginings, he conceived to be Michael's loose behavior while thousands of miles away from him. He had sent her a long cable taxing her with infideli-ties. ". . . innocent as I was of any offense [she wrote], it was im-

* Actually, the actor to beat was one John E. Kellerd, who, during the 1912–13 season, chalked up 102 performances, beginning at the Garden Theatre and finishing, oddly enough, at the theater where John was to appear ten years later—the Harris.

possible for him to trust me. . . . And looking back, I believe, although we still had some years left together, that any genuine vitality of hope I had towards a mutually happy, successful life, fled on that day. . . ."

On the night of John's farewell performance the Harris box office turned away more than 1,000 people. John somewhat alleviated the company's distress by promising to resume his role in the fall and then go on tour.

Blanche Yurka was married to Ian Keith, a young actor with a faintly Barrymoresque cast of features and a lofty opinion of his own histrionic ability which was not justified. When he learned that John was leaving, he hurried to his dressing room to suggest himself as a replacement. John answered with exquisite tact: "But you see, Keith, if you proved better than I am, it would be very bad for me. If I proved better than you, it would be bad for you. I don't think it's a good idea, old man."

Before John's defection Jack Warner came east to sign him up for the title role in a film treatment of Clyde Fitch's drama *Beau Brummel.* A crafty, everlastingly grinning, cigar-chomping potentate, Jack Warner, with his brothers Albert, Sam and Harry, had parlayed a nickelodeon theater in Newcastle, Pennsylvania, the Bijou, into a multimillion-dollar show-business empire. He was among the most hated, feared and ridiculed figures in Hollywood. He himself once claimed, not without a certain pride: "I don't have a single real friend."

Beginning on April 17, 1921, at the Broadhurst Theatre, Lionel had starred in another Hopkins production, *The Claw*, a translation of the French playwright Henri Bernstein's violent tragedy *La Griffe.* The cast included Lionel's wife, Doris, as well as Irene Fenwick, with whom John had had one of his numerous affairs years earlier shortly before she married James O'Brien. After observing Lionel and Irene together, Doris said: "I have been married to Lionel Barrymore for seventeen years, but I would gladly give several years of my life if I could truthfully say that in all the seventeen years he looked at me just once in the same manner as I saw him look at that woman."

She divorced Lionel. At about the same time Irene rid herself of O'Brien, then announced her engagement to Lionel. John was appalled. "Don't do it," he pleaded with Lionel. "I've fucked her. She's nothing but a whore." Irene's past, Lionel retorted, did not matter to

him. In June 1923 he took Irene to Rome, where they were married
a week later. But gradually John's brusque disclosure began to prey
on Lionel. A coldness developed between the brothers. For a long
while they scarcely spoke to each other.

As soon as John had taken his last curtain call at the Harris, he
repaired to his cabin on the liner due to sail him to France next morning. Before his first day in Paris ended, he and Michael were locked
in combat. Throughout that spring and early summer they alternated between discord and gusts of passion.

In July, John headed west to enact *Beau Brummel*, the Regency
dandy who won the Prince of Wales' favor by his wit and elegance
and by his arrogance lost it and died in squalor, alone and forgotten.
It was John's first Hollywood assignment and one perfectly suited to
his romantic flair. The Warners greeted him with a copy of an ad they
proposed to circulate, proclaiming him "the world's greatest actor."

"In some cities you might put a question mark opposite that
line," said John.

"Is it all right?" Jack Warner asked him.

"It's great. The photograph is flattering. If you'll lend me two
of them, I'll walk up and down the street with them like a sandwich
man."

They introduced him to his leading lady, a lovely little starlet
who styled herself "Mary Astor." Her real name was Lucile Langhanke and she was seventeen years old. "You are so goddamned
beautiful," John whispered in her ear when a test shot required him
to hold her close, "you make me feel faint!"

During the first day on the set, Mary Astor recounted thirty-six
years later, "my awe for this great man made me confused and awkward. Mr. Barrymore broke through my shyness by talking about
everything under the sun but the picture; he made me laugh about
something, and he gradually and skillfully made me feel that I was
his contemporary as an actor and as a person."

She told him her age. "It seems so long ago that I was seventeen
—I'm forty now," John confessed, dropping a year.

"*That's* not so old," said the adolescent.

Then and there, she later claimed, they fell in love, "and I am
sure he was even more startled than I. . . .

"The romance flourished, quietly and unobtrusively, under the
unseeing eyes of . . . my parents [Otto Ludwig Wilhelm Lang-

hanke, formerly of Berlin, and Helen Vasconcells, a Kansan, a classic Hollywood mom-and-pop team who relentlessly exploited their only child's potential as a movie actress]. In the filming of the many romantic, delicate love scenes of *Beau Brummel* we could stand in each other's arms. . . . We whispered softly, or just stood there, quietly loving the closeness. . . . Between scenes, Jack had the prop man place two camp chairs together just off the set, and we sat side by side."

The romance followed the usual pattern of John's love life. He ingratiated himself with his inamorata's parents, praising Mother Langhanke's cooking when invited to dine in their apartment and discussing German politics with Pop. "He used all his charm on them, and he had more of it than any other man I have ever known." He schooled Mary in the art of acting, reading scenes from Shakespeare with her in the Langhanke parlor and trying to purify her Midwestern diction, while Mom kept vigil from the adjoining dining room. "The tawdry little living room vibrated with magnificence," Mary recalled.

When Margaret Carrington was summering at her Santa Barbara estate, the Villa Riposo, John persuaded her to take on Mary as a pupil, and every Sunday afternoon he would drive her to her voice lesson. Mrs. Carrington referred to Mary as "Jack's little protégée."

Mrs. Langhanke could scarcely contain her delight at the attentions John lavished upon her and Mary, whom she seldom let out of sight, chaperoning her even at the studio. When John used coarse language, as he often did, the protective mother would hustle Mary away from the set beyond earshot. John and Willard Louis, a fun-loving character actor who played the Prince of Wales, would occasionally spice the dialogue with obscenities, there existing as yet no sound camera. When *Beau Brummel* was released, the studio received a good many scandalized letters from deaf lip-readers.

John's manner on the set, his gaiety and fellow feeling deeply impressed Mary. She had never before met a star without affectation and condescension. John was on first-name terms with all the workmen and enjoyed long, technical talks with them. Yet he preserved an unassailable dignity, letting nobody forget that he was a Barrymore. Once, when a cameraman yelled: "Hey, Jack!" John spun around, eyed him coldly and said: "Why so formal? Call me kid."

When a fellow actor, whether known or unknown to him, showed talent, John was quick and generous in conveying his appreciation. After seeing D. W. Griffith's *Way Down East*, with Lillian Gish, he wrote to him:

Any personal praise of yourself or your genius regarding the picture I would naturally consider redundant and a little like carrying coals to Newcastle. . . .

I have not the honor of knowing Miss Gish personally and I am afraid that any expression of feeling addressed to her she might consider impertinent. I merely wish to tell you that her performance seems to me to be the most superlatively exquisite and poignantly enchanting thing I have ever seen in my life.

I remember seeing Duse in this country many years ago, when I imagine she must have been at the height of her powers—also Madame Bernhardt—and for sheer technical brilliancy and great emotional projection, done with an almost uncanny simplicity and sincerity of method, it is great fun and a great stimulant to see an American artist equal, if not surpass, the finest traditions of the theatre.

I wonder if you would be good enough to thank Miss Gish from all of us who are trying to do the best we know how in the theatre.

(Lillian Gish said in her old age: "I never wanted to meet him after that. I had plenty of opportunities, but I avoided him. I was too afraid of disappointing him. I didn't want to risk saying something that might displease him.")

Authors of books that John admired were also likely to receive an accolade. "My dear Miss Stern," he wrote after reading a talking-dog fantasy by the English novelist G. B. Stern,

The Dark Gentleman is not only superlatively the most delightful book I ever read about dogs—It is almost the most delightful book I've read about anything!

To coin a phrase—it was sheer enchantment from start to finish! The drunken Italiano singing his way home in the night is one of the loveliest things ever written—and *all* the dogs are simple Heaven. . . .

At length John told Mary's parents that he must work with her alone. "I feel she's too self-conscious," he said, "she's too afraid of what *you* are thinking, instead of listening to me." Mom and Pop hesitated and John, reading their minds, added, the sly rogue: "Don't be ridiculous! This is a *kid!*"

And so, reluctantly, they allowed Mary greater freedom. She herself had no qualms. "Not for a moment was I concerned with the violation of moral laws or the breaking of a commandment. The only moral law I knew was the law proclaimed by my father, and it had been many years now since I had had any faith in his laws. . . ."

Mary kept a diary and later, as her experience of men became more extensive, she would confide to it an assessment of each lover's sexual capacity. The story is apocryphal, however, that she included John in these revelations and that she wrote: "He is a scoundrel, but so sweet!" What she did write, not in her diary but in her memoirs, was:

"He gave me love, affection, humor and, above all, beauty. He always had flowers in his rooms, and inevitably a bowl of tuberoses in the window. He encouraged me to think out and talk about ideas— often some rather abstract ideas. To help feed my growing mind he gave me books on philosophy, art, music, drama, poetry. He collected rare books, and he showed me beautiful samples of the art of printing; he picked up an ordinary-looking volume, flexed the front edges, and showed me the beautiful fore-edge painting—which I had never heard of before. He taught me about manners, consideration for others. Social conduct, he explained, was not designed to 'impress' people; but by considerate behavior 'we acknowledge their existence, which everyone needs to be assured of.' He stretched my mind in all directions."

When November came, John was expected in New York for the reopening of *Hamlet*. Ensconced in his stateroom aboard the eastbound Twentieth Century, John sent for two Pullman porters, old friends from previous trips. Handing one of them a book, he explained: "Now, this is really the skull of Yorick and you are the Gravedigger." And to the other: "You are Polonius." Fed his cues in this fashion, he rehearsed himself all the way across the continent.

The Plymouth Theatre being still occupied by *The Old Soak*, Hopkins secured the Manhattan Opera House for a run of three weeks prior to the cross-country tour.

A movie to be shot in New York brought Mary Astor and her parents there shortly after John's *Hamlet* reopened. For two weeks, while Mary awaited her call to the film studio, they spent every afternoon except matinees alone in John's suite at the Ambassador Hotel on Park Avenue. Mary would slip into a pair of burgundy satin lounging pajamas that he had had tailored for her, with the initials "M.A.B." over the breast pocket, returning them to a closet when it was time to leave. Once again Mom and Pop Langhanke swallowed (or pretended to swallow) John's taradiddle that Mary's attention must not be diverted by the presence of a third party if she was to concentrate on his teaching. Those afternoons Langhanke would drive his daughter from Jackson Heights, where he had rented a flat, to the Ambassador, and call for her at six.

Her parents' complacency puzzled Mary, but it did not puzzle John. She recorded a discussion they had one afternoon:

Mary: "I can't believe that they think that every day for six hours we act out bits of Shakespeare together, that all you do is teach me how to speak and move and think in terms of a character in a play. . . . But they seem satisfied with what I report to them."

John: "And I think they're satisfied with what you *don't* report to them at night."

Mary: "I don't believe *that!* Why, if they had an inkling, they'd—"

John: "They'd what? Now let me tell you something. They have no intention, no intention whatever of losing you, of allowing you to get married and get away from them."

Mary: "How do you know that?"

John: "I felt out your old man one night, and I got nothing but a fishy stare. I put it to him in his own cold-blooded idiom. I told him that I thought so much of your potential as a great actress—oh, I said I thought he'd done a hell of a job so far, but now I thought it was time for you to emerge from your little cocoon. That I would like to take over—I would even marry you, keep you in my protection, train and develop you as a person and an actress."

Mary: "What did he say?"

John: "He said he wasn't quite ready to relinquish his job. It was out of the question. Absurd. I asked him, 'Doesn't she have anything to say about that?' and he answered, 'Nothing, nothing whatsoever.'"

Mary: "Of course not."

John: "You don't have the guts, the vitality, to be an individual, do you? It would be an impossible thing for you to say, 'I want to be with my beloved—I want to go with him, and the hell with you.'"

Mary: "Not just now."

John: "They are damn foxy, you know? They are shutting their eyes to what is really between us—it's their way of letting you out on a rope but keeping you feeling guilty, so they've got you."

Mary: "I just don't believe that. They're very strait-laced, truly."

John: "My ass!"

*   *   *

The *Hamlet* company went on tour shortly before Christmas. On the eve of separation, as they clung to each other, weeping, John besought Mary to remain faithful to him. "You have become wise at deception," he said. "Don't use it against me. I need your fidelity. I need to know that there is someone in the world who can be faithful."

In Washington, D.C., the first stand, President and Mrs. Calvin Coolidge attended the opening night and invited John to the White House.

"Have you seen many Hamlets, Mr. President?" John asked.

"Two," replied Coolidge, whose laconism furnished humorists with an inexhaustible source of jokes. "You and E. H. Sothern."

"And which performance did you like better?"

Coolidge reflected a moment. Then: "Well, Mr. Sothern's clothes were prettier than yours."

(According to Ethel, who was playing in the capital and dined at the White House shortly after John did, "Silent Cal" was not quite that dim. She quoted him as saying: "Saw your brother the other night in *Hamlet*. Very good. He made a speech between the acts, a very funny speech. Told some stories about his Negro valet, right in the middle of *Hamlet*. That's a good way to make speeches—funny stories. I know some funny stories, but I think the American public likes to think of their President as being a sort of solemn ass and I think I'll just go on being a solemn ass.")

In Boston, where *Hamlet* cracked all American box-office records for Shakespeare (one evening performance took in $3,348.88 and one Saturday matinee, $5,938), John booked a suite on the top floor of the Copley-Plaza Hotel. The elderly Anglo-American artist John Singer Sargent occupied another suite nearby. Twenty years earlier, when Ethel came to Boston in a Frohman production, *Cousin Kate*, Sargent, who was supervising the installation of the first panels of his murals for the Boston Public Library, wrote to her: "Would it be possible to give me an hour or maybe two? I would like to do a drawing of you and I would be so honored to present you with the drawing afterward." He was a guest at the time of a Proper Bostonian, Mrs. J. Montgomery Sears, and Ethel sat for him on the top floor of the Sears mansion, all of which had been converted into a studio for his use. He now offered the same opportunity to John, who delightedly accepted it. The resulting full-face crayon portrait so pleased the subject that he had a quantity of reproductions made to give to friends.*

* The original hangs in the San Diego Museum.

He gave one of them to Blanche Yurka, inscribing it: "To my mother from her wildly incestuous son."

Not long after the touring *Hamlet* left New York, boredom beset John again and in Cleveland he announced his departure, with apologies to the company. As compensation for their loss of employment, he distributed gifts and cash among them. The wardrobe mistress received $100 accompanied by a note:

> Dear Miss Madlyn—Do not I beg you regard this as the price of our shame! That—is—believe me—priceless —but it has been splendid having you with us, and I wish you a very great deal of luck—and hope we'll get together soon—most sincerely—John Barrymore.

Lord Castleross, who was plump and pigeon-breasted, leaned forward, exerting a pressure against his shirt front that popped a stud and sent it whizzing across the dinner table to smite the swarthy Spanish portraitist seated opposite. His Lordship struggled to his feet to beg the Spaniard's pardon. The latter assured him no harm had been done, then, turning to the orchidacious American woman next to him, said: "I am Zuloaga and I would like you to pose for me." Michael Strange happily agreed. A few days later she presented herself at the London studio of Ignacio Zuloaga y Zabaleta, who proceeded to paint her full-length, wearing a medieval black doublet and hose, a dagger dangling from her belt. The portrait was subsequently exhibited in New York with the title *Hamlet*, giving rise to the rumor that Miss Strange would alternate with her husband in the role of the Dane. Though groundless, it hardly calmed the couple's stormy relationship.

They were now spending as much time abroad as at home, sometimes together, more often separately. John was not much taken with Michael's modish, cosmopolitan acquaintances, such as Princesse de Polignac—"Winnie" Polignac to Michael—the Duke of Alba, Oswald Mosley (later Sir Oswald and the leader of the British Union of Fascists), Mrs. William Randolph Hearst, Vita Sackville-West, the author George Moore, whose attitude toward sex, according to Michael, "was really very Latin, extremely un-English. . . . [He] asked me if I would mind undressing!"

John's liaison with Mary Astor did not lesson his sexual jealousy of his wife. While he was still playing Hamlet, Michael had rented from Elsie de Wolfe (Lady Mendl to be) her *bijou* of a London town house, together with her secretary and servants. John had barely entered the place, upon his arrival in London, following the *Hamlet* tour, before he began to voice his suspicions. "He . . . cried out to the white satin walls of my bedroom, 'Who is he! Who is your lover! You might as well tell me!'" On the infrequent occasions when he escorted Michael to a dance and saw her in the arms of some man, he would glare at her and silently mouth the question, "That's him, isn't it?" In Michael's view, "He seemed condemned to look forever and feverishly for his peace in the last possible place that he, as he was, would be able to find it, in the moral conduct of people with whom he was in love."

When in New York, John never failed to visit Ned Sheldon, and when away, he wrote to him frequently, cabled and telephoned. Ned at thirty-eight was now a prisoner in his bed, almost every joint ankylosed, scarcely able to change position without help, and so he would remain to the end of his life twenty-two years later.

Among the specialists who examined him was Dr. George F. Draper, a pioneer in the field of psychosomatic medicine.* He speculated that rheumatoid arthritis in the rare extreme form that afflicted Ned might have an emotional basis because he seemed to worsen under emotional stress and to improve slightly when some happy event raised his spirits. This indicated, Draper surmised (and Ned's regular physician, Dr. Carl Binger, who was about to shift from regular practice to psychiatry, tended to agree), "if not a subconscious retreat from life, at least a sort of self-immolation, of not moving forward into life."

Mercedes de Acosta, a friend of both Ned and John, and a lesbian, perceived a homoerotic element in Ned's plight. "I believe," she wrote, "Jack was the love of his life and the suffering and emotional frustration he went through on account of it caused his illness." None of the doctors ever found the faintest grounds for such a hypothesis. In the improbable event that Ned's condition derived from a repressed sexual desire, a far likelier object would have been Doris Keane, who had rejected him.

John was not through with Hamlet after all, for there remained a supreme challenge—namely, to play it on Shakespeare's own ground, London, there to compete against such British Hamlets past and present as David Garrick, Edmund Kean, Charles Macready,

---

* Who coined the term "psysomatic," later changed to "psychosomatic."

Beerbohm Tree, Sir Johnston Forbes-Robertson, Sir Henry Irving, Sir John Martin Harvey. John had already tried to persuade Arthur Hopkins to take on the production, but when Hopkins sought the advice of an English colleague, he was told: "If Barrymore has the audacity to come to London in *Hamlet*, they'll assassinate him." This was all John needed to fortify his resolve.

Hopkins pledged the loan of his head carpenter, his head electrician, his stage manager and the Jones costumes and sets. John traveled to England twice in 1924, seeking financial backing. He could find nobody willing to gamble with him, for recent London productions of Shakespeare had proved poor investments. Nor could he find a theater. Eventually, Constance Collier, who was to play Gertrude, put John in touch with the lessee of the Haymarket Theatre, Frederick Harrison, who agreed to sublet it for six weeks. The Theatre Royal, Haymarket—to give the full name—was the second oldest in London, the original building having been completed in 1720. (The oldest was the Theatre Royal, Drury Lane, dating back to 1672.) It was at the Haymarket that Herbert Blyth supposedly saw the name William Barrymore on a playbill and took it for his own, and he later performed there himself. To meet the initial costs of his *Hamlet* production, John set aside $25,000, his entire cash reserve, and managed to borrow the rest.

Toward the end of the year John settled in London with Michael and the children. He rented a house at No. 2 Cheyne Walk in Chelsea, once occupied by James McNeill Whistler, and in January 1925 he began rehearsals. No member of the American cast of *Hamlet* had been retained. Malcolm Keen was Claudius; Herbert Waring, Polonius; Fay Compton, Ophelia. Margaret Webster, whose parents had kept an eye on John during his English schooldays, filled the walk-on role of A Gentlewoman. The year after, Tyrone Power wrote John a reproachful letter:

> I think you know that I have always admired your art, on occasions I have called in your dressing-room & expressed my admiration of your performance. Though I disliked the part of the King in Hamlet, believing—as I still believe— that it is a difficult and thankless role, still when I undertook Claudius in your production I did all I could with it, it may not have been very much yet it was the best I could do. I played through your entire run, never missed a single performance, never slighted my work or played with in-

difference. It was all uphill work for me, but I was loyal in my effort to assist you, and to please your audience. Surely you will subscribe to this? I arrived here in London after an absence of twelve years, eager to again see my oldest and dearest friend Edmund Footman,—in whose house you have been. Naturally we spoke of you. . . . I was deeply wounded, hurt beyond measure when he said, "Fred, in this room, sitting in this very chair, I was asking Barrymore about you, & he said 'I didn't bring Fred over because he is absolutely unreliable—through drink, & not to be trusted.' " I cannot believe that you whom I have known since you were a boy, who was a friend & fellow-player with your father could have made such a statement. Uttered by an actor of your standing, it bears the stamp of authority, & calculated to ruin me in my profession. . . . Until I hear from you I absolutely refuse to believe you would injure a man with a story without foundation of truth. . . .

He heard from John by cable: DEAR FRED YOUR LETTER THIS INSTANT RECEIVED IMPRESSION CONVEYED ENTIRELY ERRONEOUS I FAIL UTTERLY TO UNDERSTAND IT WRITING FULLY.

The follow-up letter read:

In the first place, it is impossible for me to talk about any other actor in such a fashion, and in the second place I have far too much affection for you personally, as an old friend of my father's and myself to indulge in such an absurdity. The only thing that could possibly have been peculiarly misconstrued that I can imagine having happened, and I say this in order to palliate what was evidently a misconception on the part of Mr. Footman whose hospitality was kindly tendered me, was some allusion intended to be humorous, in what I considered practically the bosom of your family (at least warm and loving friends of yours) to an occasional mutual potation we enjoyed together in the sanctity of my dressing room as the performance was in progress. Inasmuch as Shakespeare did the same with Burbage,* that seems to establish a pretty good precedent for both of us, in whichsoever capacity either of us might wish to cast himself.

* Richard Burbage, the Elizabethan actor who created many Shakespearean roles.

I think we are both old enough to realize that these *contretemps* happen in the best regulated domestic circles for varieties of reason, and should make no difference to friends of such long standing as ourselves. . . .

During an early London rehearsal John exhorted the supernumerary women who formed Ophelia's funeral cortege: "A little more dignity, ladies. Try to be virginal."

An aged pallbearer endeared herself to John when she remarked: "My dear Mr. Barrymore, we are not character actresses."

While the extras were trying on period shoes, John noticed that one of them seemed close to tears. Calling her aside, he asked her why. Crimson with embarrassment, she explained that her stockings had holes in them. Such a condition, John hastened to reassure her, was not unique. "Many a time I have had all my toes out at once." He asked the costumer to fit her in his dressing room, and to put her completely at ease, he took her to dinner that evening.

The rehearsals were regularly attended by the Haymarket house cat, a huge tom who had inhabited the theater for as long as anybody could remember. At odd moments he would pad across the stage, tail erect, head high, sniffing. He seldom failed to do so during Hamlet's soliloquies. ". . . it was very disturbing. Nor did I quite like the way it looked at me. It seemed to say: 'I've seen them all—what are you doing here?' "

Following the dress rehearsal, John assembled the entire cast onstage and to each tossed a little verbal nosegay. "Miss Compton, you will be the most adorable Ophelia since Ellen Terry. God bless you and thank you very much. . . . My dear Constance, I can't tell you how magnificent you are. God bless you and thank you very much. . . . Mr. Waring, you will make a triumph that will be unprecedented as Polonius. God bless you and thank you very much. . . ." And so on down to the humblest spear-carrier. He did not neglect the tomcat, who had meanwhile emerged from the wings. "As for you, my dear fellow," said John, bending down to stroke him, "you are going to make a hell of a hit in one of my soliloquies."

The opening night audience, on February 19, 1925, glittered with celebrities. Mayfair was represented by Princess Bibesco, Lady Violet Bonham Carter, Lady Oxford, Lady Diana Manners (who attended several performances and wrote to John from France: "It's terrible to have seen the play for the last time. I'd sooner be in Denmark than here"); politics by the Earl of Oxford and Asquith

(Herbert Asquith); Thespis by Sir Squire Bancroft, the dean of English actors, Gerald du Maurier, Mr. and Mrs. Ben Webster, Lilian Braithwaite, Gwen Ffrangcon-Davies; opera by Dame Nellie Melba (who sent John a wreath of laurel); dramaturgy by Henry Arthur Jones and Alfred Sutro; fiction and poetry by John Masefield, Lord Dunsany, Somerset Maugham, Arnold Bennett, George Moore, Anthony Hope. Michael Strange saw her husband as Hamlet for the first time in the company of George Bernard Shaw.

She owed her introduction to Shaw, in December of 1923, to the editor of the *Fortnightly Review*, Henry Massingham, who had sat beside her at a luncheon party given by Cynthia and Oswald Mosley. When Massingham asked her whom in London she especially wanted to meet, she answered eagerly: "Of course, Bernard Shaw!" The next morning she found a message from Shaw, shoved under her door, inviting her to lunch at his Adelphi Terrace house. She immediately canceled an appointment with Lady Colefax, one of England's great hostesses, and en route to the playwright she stopped at a pub to bolt a noggin of gin for her nerves.

As lunch progressed, Michael expressed her dislike of certain writers with such vigor that her host clapped her on the shoulder, exclaiming delightedly: "But you have a fine sense of invective yourself! You ought to be in the House of Commons!"

As she was leaving, he asked her: "Why on earth did you marry an actor?"

They lunched together several times before he escorted her to the London opening of the Barrymore *Hamlet*.

While none of the critics considered John superior or even equal to the revered native products, nearly all granted him high marks. "On the whole, then," concluded the *Morning Post*, "Mr. Barrymore's Hamlet, if not ranking with the very greatest, may be declared the best now before the public." James Agate, the astringent critic of the *Sunday Times*, found it "magnificent . . . we know ourselves to be in the presence of a fine and powerful mind," yet faulted John for failing to give the lines their full, poetic value. The *Times*: ". . . every moment of his work is of the highest interest." The *Daily Telegraph*: "The wonderful voice of the poet could not have been delivered with finer intelligence or more charming music."

One of the few harshly dissenting judgments, leveled not so much against the actor as against his textual cuts and interpretation, came from Michael Strange's escort. Shaw published no critique, but conveyed his opinion to John in a letter, dated February 22, 1925.

My dear Mr Barrymore

I have to thank you for inviting me—and in such kind terms too—to your first performance of Hamlet in London; and I am glad you had no reason to complain of your reception, or, on the whole, of your press. Everyone felt that the occasion was one of extraordinary interest; and as far as your personality was concerned they were not disappointed.

I doubt, however, whether you have been able to follow the course of Shakespearean production in England during the last fifteen years or so enough to realize the audacity of your handling of the play. When I last saw it performed at Stratford-on-Avon, practically the entire play was given in three hours and three quarters, with one interval of ten minutes; and it made the time pass without the least tedium though the cast was not in any way remarkable. On Thursday last you played five minutes longer with the play cut to ribbons, even to the breath-bereaving extremity of cutting out the recorders, which is rather like playing King John without little Arthur.

You saved, say, an hour and a half on Shakespear by the cutting, and filled it up with an interpolated drama of your own in dumb show. This was a pretty daring thing to do. In modern shop plays, without characters or anything but the commonest dialogue, the actor has to supply everything but the mere story, getting in the psychology between the lines, and presenting in his own person the fascinating hero whom the author has been unable to create. He is not substituting something of his own for something of the author's: he is filling up a void and doing the author's work for him. And the author ought to be extremely obliged to him.

But to try this method on Shakespear is to take on an appalling responsibility and put up a staggering pretension. Shakespear, with all his shortcomings, was a very great playwright; and the actor who undertakes to improve his plays undertakes thereby to excel to an extraordinary degree in two professions in both of which the highest success is extremely rare. Shakespear himself, though by no means a modest man, did not pretend to be able to play Hamlet as well as write it: he was content to do a recitation in the dark as the ghost. But you have ventured not only to act Hamlet but to discard about a third of Shakespear's script and substitute stuff of your own, and that, too, without the help of dialogue. Instead of giving what is called a reading of Hamlet, you say, in effect, "I am not going to read Hamlet at all: I am going to leave it out. But see what I give you in exchange!"

Such an enterprise must justify itself by its effect on the public. You discard the recorders as hackneyed back chat, and the scene with the king after the death of Polonius, with such speeches as "How all occasions do inform against me!" as obsolete junk, and offer instead a demonstration of that very modern discovery called the Oedipus complex, thereby adding a really incestuous motive on Hamlet's part to the merely conventional incest of a marriage (now legal in England) with a deceased husband's brother. You change Hamlet and Ophelia into Romeo and Juliet. As producer, you allow Laertes and Ophelia to hug each other as lovers instead of lecturing and squabbling like hectoring big brother and little sister: another complex!

Now your success in this must depend on whether the play invented by Barrymore on the Shakespear foundation is as gripping as the Shakespear play, and whether your dumb show can hold an audience as a straightforward reading of Shakespear's rhetoric can. I await the decision with interest.

My own opinion is, of course, that of an author. I write plays that play for three hours and a half even with instantaneous changes and only one short interval. There is no time for silences or pauses: the actor must play on the line and not between the lines, and must do nine tenths of his acting with his voice. Hamlet—Shakespear's Hamlet—can be done from end to end in four hours in that way; and it never flags nor bores. Done in any other way Shakespear is the worst of bores, because he has to be chopped into a mere cold stew. I prefer my way. I wish you would try it, and concentrate on acting rather than on authorship, at which, believe me, Shakespear can write your head off. But that may be vicarious professional jealousy on my part.

I did not dare to say all this to Mrs Barrymore on the

night. It was chilly enough for her without a coat in the stalls without any cold water from

yours perhaps too candidly,
G. Bernard Shaw*

As to the box office, it sold out the house for the entire run, which was extended to nine weeks. John not only recouped his $25,000, but netted $10,000 more.

On the third night his old enemy, the cougher, turned up in a row close to the stage. He hacked and hawked at frequent intervals through the first three acts until John managed to stare him into silence. At the end, when four of Fortinbras' captains bore off the dead Hamlet, he sat up and, freezing the offender with an icy look, muttered between his teeth: "Now you may cough, you bugger!"

But few disturbances so infuriated John as the British theater custom of serving tea in the orchestra at matinees. The spectators would give their orders beforehand to the ushers, who would deliver the tea to their seats during intermissions. The sipping and the clatter of cups and saucers being collected sometimes continued after the curtain had risen again. John once stopped in mid-soliloquy, roared at the audience, "Tea! Tea! Tea!" and, his anger thus assuaged, went on with the play.

The celebrated tragedienne Dame Ellen Terry, an Ophelia of bygone days, honored John with her venerable presence in a front box. She was then seventy-eight and deaf. Knowing the lines by heart, she proceeded to recite them in what she thought was an inaudible whisper, but, unable to hear her own voice, she spoke loudly enough for the players to hear. She also kept ten lines or so ahead of them. John, beside himself with fury by the time he fought the fatal duel with Laertes, began hurling rapiers all over the stage. Calming down after the curtain calls, he sent someone to bring the grand old lady backstage. But Dame Ellen was too deeply affected by his performance and she left the theater in tears.

The writer Hilaire Belloc was John's host at dinner one evening before the performance in a Regent Street seafood restaurant noted for its whitebait, small, delicate fish cooked and eaten whole. It was not a food that normally agreed with John, but courtesy compelled him to yield to Belloc's insistence that he try it. About two hours

* By permission of The Society of Authors on behalf of the Bernard Shaw Estate.

later, as he launched into his favorite soliloquy, "O what a rogue and peasant slave am I!," nausea seized him. He hurried off the stage, still speaking, relieved himself and quickly returned to finish the speech. Next day a critic credited him with a strikingly original way of delivering the speech. "He did not know that it really required speed," said John.

Among the most intent spectators was the seventeen-year-old son of a country clergyman, a pupil at Elsie Fogerty's Central School of Voice Training and Dramatic Arts, named Laurence Olivier. Twelve years later as Hamlet at the Old Vic, Olivier adopted a good deal of John's stage business as well as his Freudian interpretation. Latterly, Lord Olivier acknowledged his debt to John: "He was stunning, so exciting, his voice, his high jumps. I modeled my Hamlet on his, and people said, 'Why is Larry always leaping about? . . . I must have been the most gymnastic Hamlet anyone has seen—not more than Barrymore, I suppose. I emulated him."

Few foreigners in London were more handsomely feted than John during the run of *Hamlet*. The Garrick, the Savage, the American clubs tendered him an honorary membership. The Garrick, the English-Speaking Union, the Dramatic Circle, the Old Players, the Lyceum all gave Lucullan luncheons or dinners in his honor. The Garrick menu listed *Tortue Claire, Soles Diable, Steak Garrick au Cresson, Haricots Verts, Pommes Sautées, Glace Pralinée, Os à Moelle, Café*, accompanied by *Grave Postillion 1916, Veuve Cliquot champagne, 1915*, Barley Wine, No. 1, Dow's Port 1908. At the Old Players, which had similarly entertained Irving and Booth, among other Hamlets, it was a "dinner of welcome," presided over by the novelist and playwright Israel Zangwill and consisting of eight courses, each with an appropriate potation.

At the Lyceum, an international women's organization dedicated to the advancement of literature, music and art, the president, the Marchioness of Aberdeen, reminded the gathering that the son of Maurice Barrymore was "after all one of us." Said John in response: "They [England and America] are only disconnected by water, which I fear is becoming our national drink, and I sometimes wonder to which country I belong. I remember when I was in Venice, seeing against St. Mark's at night the astonishingly beautiful figure on the summit of an animal with the wings of the American eagle and the body of the British lion. My only hope is that this may be more a fact in the future."

At one of these functions a studious Englishwoman put the

question to him: "In your opinion, Mr. Barrymore, did Hamlet ever have sexual relations with Ophelia?"

"Only in the Chicago company, madam," he replied.

Some of John's most uproarious late nights were spent tippling with Ethel's erstwhile suitor Winston Churchill, with Edward, Prince of Wales, with the prodigious Russian basso Feodor Chaliapin, who was singing at Covent Garden.

Into a huge leather-bound album John pasted a collection of reviews and stories about him carried by the London press and inscribed it "For my daughter—Diana—with much love." Diana was then four and she was not to see her father again until her tenth year. Her parents' competing egos led to a decisive battle. John moved out of the Cheyne Walk house to the Ritz Hotel, and, soon after, Michael sailed back to New York with the children.

John played his last Hamlet on the evening of Saturday, April 18, 1925. A week later he wrote to an English friend, Golding Bright:

> I am sailing Thursday [the twenty-ninth]. When I closed on Saturday I went pleasantly and instantly to bed— entirely alone for five blissful days. . . . These—my first significant days as an actor in England have been reasonably intensive. What with labour, exhaustion, fatuous public utterances, the Flu, and eight or possibly nine times a week of this snappy Scandinavian farce, whenever I had a moment to myself, I occupied it by sitting down on the nearest thing at hand, however hard, and wondered vaguely through the accruing coma why I had taken up the theatre as a profession. There are so many other forms of endeavor equally lucrative and dishonest. . . .
>
> I am far too weak to hold a pen, a glass is the best I can manage. . . .
>
> I shall be back in a few months when before I start indulging in the absurdity of painting my nose, for God's sake let's get together and find out definitely if Clos Veugeut [*sic*] is as good now as it used to be when we were younger. . . .

John disembarked in New York with an English valet, William Blaney, formerly employed by Beerbohm Tree, and perched on his shoulder, a small, chattering female monkey called Clementine, a gift from the English actress Gladys Cooper. Within a month he and Michael had signed a separation agreement. It required John to pay Michael $18,000 a year for her support and Diana's, whether or not reconciliation, divorce or remarriage should eventuate. She was to retain custody of Treepee (or "the Rabbit," or "Binky," as her father also called her). John later gave Michael the White Plains house and its contents. The agreement embodied a false statement designed to forestall a divorce on the grounds of adultery, which, if granted, would, under New York State law, place the blame entirely on the transgressor, who might then be exposed to far greater financial penalties. "The parties mutually recognize and declare that neither has been guilty of misconduct which would entitle the other to an absolute divorce under the laws of the State of New York [that is, guilty of adultery]. . . ."

After *Hamlet* Robert Edmond Jones had written to John: "You can do anything you want to do any way you want to do it. There is nobody else in that position in the theatre today. There is Arthur, and Margaret, and me, and all the big roles that have ever been written. It is a great happiness to have something like this to look forward to."

Jones was doomed to disappointment. *Beau Brummel* having achieved a critical as well as a commercial success ("One of those artistic celluloid efforts that come along none too frequently," said the New York *Times*, ". . . sparkling . . . John Barrymore delivers a performance that is a delight to the eye"), Warner Brothers signed John to a three-picture contract incorporating some of the most alluring clauses ever offered to an actor up to that time. John was to receive $76,250 a picture. Should the shooting of any of the pictures last longer than three weeks, payment would be augmented by $7,625 a week. Each script and each co-star had to have John's approval. The perquisites included a suite at Los Angeles' Ambassador Hotel, all meals and a chauffeured limousine.

And so, toward the summer of 1926, John, Blaney and Clementine entrained for Los Angeles (where Mary Astor was eagerly waiting). "Most critics compare me to Irving," John, in self-mockery, told the reporters seeing him off. "They all agree he was better."

With a single sorry exception fifteen years later, John would never again set foot on a stage.

Among drama critics and the theater-loving public there were a sizable number who could not forgive John for what they considered a crass betrayal. None mounted a bitterer attack than the

New Republic's Stark Young. "They [John's movies]," he generalized with wild exaggeration, "are rotten, vulgar, empty, in bad taste, dishonest, noisome with a silly and unwholesome exhibitionism, and odious with a kind of stale and degenerate studio adolescence. . . . the little measure of superiority over most movie acting, in sophistication and technical expertness, is only another way of saying how low Mr. Barrymore has fallen. . . . in Molière's play about Don Juan, Sganarelle, the valet, has a remark that sums up the whole case of what Mr. Barrymore is doing to his art, to the theater and the public. 'A wicked great lord is a terrible thing,' Don Juan's valet says . . . by which Molière means to say that it is a terrible thing when a man brings to the exercise of his lowest desires the added power and persuasion that derives from prestige, from the inherited physical and cultural endowments, and the insolence, ruthlessness and spoiled wilfulness, the callous and grasping cynicism, the self-confidence and glamor, possible to his station. . . ."

Others imputed a diversity of ignoble reasons to John's desertion, such as dissipation, sloth, greed. But Arthur Hopkins, who had good cause to deplore it, viewed it with understanding and sympathy. "He loved to create, but once that had been accomplished, he was like an artist who could not bear to look again upon a finished painting, or a writer who was nauseated by a glimpse of some past operation. . . . It is something akin to those forms in the animal world who must be restrained from devouring their young. That he would have had an unparalleled career there was no doubt, and he knew it. He did not forsake undreamed-of realms. His renunciation was with the full knowledge of what he was leaving. He did not want the slavery that continuous service in the theater demands. . . . He was in no sense what the theater knows as a trouper, what his forebears had been, what his uncle John and sister Ethel were. The creative part of the theater he loved. Its repetition was unbearable. . . .

"He knew that the theater was his, and he knew that he ought to want it, but his sickened heart was not in it. . . .

"His theater flights were like the nuptial flight of the bee—a glorious ascent into high, rarefied air, momentary exaltation and then quick death.

"It is a mistake to think that Barrymore left the theater for Hollywood money. His theater earnings were much more than he wanted or could use. His short nine weeks' road tour of *Hamlet* netted him over Fifty Thousand Dollars.

"The lure of Hollywood was the absence of repetition. Once a picture was finished, succeeding performances were neatly wrapped in cans. . . ."

But probably the greatest, the overriding reason for John's renunciation of the theater was, to his mind, the dearth of other, equally inspiring challenges. After a Hamlet considered by many the greatest of his generation—and perhaps of any generation—what new worlds were left to conquer?

HOLLYWOOD AND NEW YORK
1925–1935

17

From Ahab to Villon

========

U PON John's return to the West Coast he renewed his romance
with Mary Astor, who confided to her diary in the first entry,
dated March 7, 1925: "Cable from J.B. Says he'll be back the
middle of May. Haven't seen him since December 1923." Every entry
was "cautious and restrained. It had to be. The whole book was open
to inspection at any time; it is very cryptic, filled with code words
and symbols that no longer have meaning for me. But I haven't forgotten my transport of joy when that 'cable from J.B.' arrived."

At the Langhankes' new home John met a couple who were to
involve themselves deeply in his career. Mary's increasing income
from movies had enabled her parents to acquire a showy house on
Temple Drive in Hollywood, a maid, a gardener, a chauffeur and a
Pierce Arrow limousine. The house, a many-chambered, East In-
dian-style fantasy with lotus-flower cupolas, stained-glass windows
and ogee archways, was one of a cluster of similar structures built
by a real-estate developer named Henry Hotchener, who had traveled
widely in India with his wife, Marie, and lived on the property adjoining the Langhankes'.

A graduate of the College of the City of New York, a law student at both Georgetown University and the University of Southern
California, Hotchener had served his apprenticeship under various
industrial titans before establishing himself as a canny operator in the

207

realty field. He later became chairman of the Bank of America. Of chalky complexion, moon-faced, his thinning hair plastered to his skull with pomade and parted precisely down the middle, his eyes like ice cubes behind steel-rimmed spectacles, Hotchener habitually wore blue serge suits of ultra-conservative cut, the pockets bulging with business memoranda. At home he affected Indian garb of the finest silk and linen, the toes of his slippers turned up.

Marie Hotchener was fifteen years older than her husband, bulky, her head ringed by a corona of snowy hair, her customary expression one of seraphic sweetness. She often meditated for several hours a day, lying supine on a marble slab. She preferred the appellation "Helios" (after the Greek god of the sun), conferred upon her many years earlier by Annie Besant, the international president of the Theosophical Society, under whose well-meant but naïve leadership a good deal of mediumistic fraud was perpetrated.

Few forms of occultism were strange to Helios. She practiced astrology, claimed to have experienced out-of-body journeys, purportedly witnessed the comings and goings of the astral beings known to the society as "the Mahatmas" or "Masters." Described in its organ *The Theophist* as "a courteous and amiable lady . . . of respectable American parentage," she was a native San Franciscan, the daughter of the Chief Justice of the State of California, Judge Allyn Barnard. A graduate of Oakland's Mills College and a music student, Marie Barnard enjoyed a transient fame in her young womanhood as an operatic soprano, a career she abandoned in favor of psychic studies. She had meanwhile married a California millionaire named Russak, who died leaving her financially secure for life.

Marie's mystic pursuits took her to Adyar near Madras, the headquarters of the Theosophical Society, founded in 1883 by a Russian psychic, Helena Petrovna Blavatsky, and her American disciple, Colonel Henry Steel Olcott, a Civil War veteran. In 1889 Annie Besant, a former British socialist militant, joined the society after reading Mme. Blavatsky's *The Secret Doctrine*, the bible of Theosophism, and two years later, upon the founder's death, became its most influential member, eventually succeeding Colonel Olcott as its president. Convinced that in most of her previous incarnations she had been Indian (also the beauteous ancient Greek philosopher Hypatia as well as the Renaissance Italian philosopher Giordano Bruno), she adopted Hinduism. Among Mrs. Besant's myriad activities as a Theosophist was her sponsorship of a Hindu boy, Jiddu Krishnamurti, whom she proclaimed "the World Teacher and vehicle of the new Messiah." To weld together all those who shared her belief, she established the international Order of the Star of the East.

Marie Russak won Annie Besant's gratitude—and the sobriquet Helios—by her testimony concerning Colonel Olcott's last moments. Left to attend his deathbed, she swore, she saw the Mahatma Morya and the Mahatma Koot Hoomi hovering around the dying man and heard them command him to appoint Mrs. Besant his successor as the society's president. ". . . he sprang from his bed," Helios deposed, "knelt before [Koot Hoomi] and clasping his arms about his feet, kissed them. . . . the Blessed One put his arms around him and placed him once more upon his bed. . . ."

As recompense for her helpful testimony, President Besant elevated Helios to a position of leadership within the society, even though the dead Colonel's physician discredited it, pronouncing Helios "an emotional or hysterical person."

In London, following the coronation of King George V, which Helios witnessed alongside Mrs. Besant in the Admiralty grandstand at Whitehall, her stock rose higher still in the society, for she was among the few votaries who had supposedly been privileged to witness an extraordinary spectral phenomenon. According to her account, as the royal procession passed the grandstand, Hindu divinities known as devas demonstrated their approval of the coronation by assuming visible forms and creating a vast electrical display. Dazzling light rays, Helios reported, emanated from both King and Queen.

Helios met Henry Hotchener after she returned to California, where she published the Hollywood *Theosophist*, and recognized in him a kindred spirit as well as a shrewd businessman. They were married in 1916 and proceeded to explore together various arcana, with particular attention to astrology, Oriental occultism, survival after death and reincarnation.

These areas held inexhaustible fascination for John. He accepted the validity of psychic experience, of prophetic intuition, dreams and visions. He subscribed to Llewellyn George's *Astrologica Bulletina*, the oldest periodical in the field, and his library included such occult works as the *Chaldean Oracles* and Mme. Blavatsky's *The Secret Doctrine*.

Within a short time of meeting the Hotcheners John retained the husband as his business manager and the wife as his "court astrologer," whom he consulted whenever facing a major decision, such as whether to sign a movie contract with a new studio or take another wife. (Hotchener's brother Maurice, a New York lawyer, who dropped the first "e" from the surname, shortly became John's Eastern legal representative.) Helios and Llewellyn George between them constructed his astrological chart, covering his past and present and projecting his future. Chiefly an exercise in hindsight, it read:

> *Gemini ascending*—Ambitious, aspiring, active, dexterous, capable of engaging in several pursuits at the same time, intuitive, imaginative. At times the Gemini mind is very restless, anxious, high-strung, diffusive, irritable, excitable, inclination for change and diversity. Must be constantly moving or busy to be happy. The Planetary Significator is Mercury.

> *Mars* is in the first house in the ascending sign of Gemini. This endows the native with a quick, keen intellect, plain-spoken, forceful, combative, active and nimble, good at repartee, a dexterous fencer with words and with swords.

> *Mars in the first house*—Assertive, confident, aspiring and skillful. Creates a great deal of his own fate by impulsiveness and strong desire-nature. Loves liberty and independence. Danger and injury through cuts, burns, scalds, falls, bruises and other accidents. Not averse to fist-fights or quarrels with brother or sister or family.
>
> At this time the birth sign Leo (the lion) occupies the third cusp, which marks the house designating brothers and sisters. He had a brother named Lionel, and a sister Ethel, who was born in the sign of the lion, Aug. 15, 1879. As the *sun*, which rules the sign Leo, was in the midheaven of his chart, it indicates that this brother and sister would rise to public prominence; and as the sun was in good aspect to Mars in the ascendant, from signs of the same triplicity, it denotes that he, too, would rise to prominence in the same profession.

> *Uranus in the fourth house*—many ups and downs, a checkered career, occasional poverty through peculiar circumstances.

> *Venus, ruler of the fifth house*—fondness for a sociability and pleasure, ability to make friends easily, especially with the opposite sex. Secret alliances, and strange, remarkable, sudden and unexpected experiences in love. A union with

one of Uranian nature; possibility of marriage in later years to one widely separated from him in age. A royal entertainer, "tops" in honors and prominence in the theatrical profession.

Mercury in the tenth house in Pisces—He might attempt literary or newspaper work. Gains knowledge not so much by deep and profound application to study as by intuitive perception; possessing understanding not acquired from textbooks, seeming to know things in a peculiar manner through inner perception. Rarely at a loss to explain any condition or circumstance.

Neptune in the twelfth house—has strong bearing on motion-picture activities but, besieged by Saturn and Jupiter, denotes his losses and his recoveries in that field.

Jupiter and Saturn in the twelfth house—Related to hospitals, rest homes, or other places of confinement, accidents, over-indulgence; called the "house of self-undoing."

Pluto likewise in the twelfth house—If Pluto is taken as the ruler of Scorpio, the sign on the sixth house ruling food and drink, we see that Pluto in the pleasure-loving sign Taurus indicates a fondness for fiery stimulants and lack of discretion as to dietetics, which may have caused much of the "self-undoing."

Moon in the eighth house—shows a death which would receive great publicity. His career hectic and spectacular, great ability which kept him in the spotlight by sheer merit.

The 17th degree of Gemini—which ascended at his birthtime is described as follows in *Degrees of the Zodiac Symbolized*. "A broken pitcher lying on the ground with spilled fruit all around it." Denotes one who will come to a broken body end. Loss of powers during lifetime and some loss of faculties.

His stars show he possessed many most lovable, admirable qualities, and great brilliance of mind and personality. He was his own worst enemy, and many of his best attributes he kept submerged or hidden from the world in general.

The Hotcheners were not the only Theosophists to come within John's purview. In the Ojai Valley, eighty miles north of Los Angeles, some California devotees of Krishnamurti had bought land and a cottage to serve as his American base and later, with additions of hundreds of acres, as a camp, school and ashram. Now, at thirty-one, a darkly handsome, charismatic figure, the World Teacher traveled widely on lecture tours in both hemispheres. John met him through the Hotcheners and took an enormous liking to him. The feeling was reciprocal. In October 1926 the guru wrote to the actor from Chicago during a theosophical convention:

> I am returning to Ojai, in a few days, as the doctors have told me I must take six months complete rest [recurrent bronchitis had weakened his lungs]. So I hope I may have the pleasure of seeing you again. I shall be in Hollywood on the 5th of Nov. I am really looking forward to seeing you & hope we shall see each other often. . . .

They did. The following March John sent a wire to Arya Vihara ("Noble Monastery" in Hindustani), Khrisnamurti's new, larger headquarters at Ojai:

> DEAR KRISHNA CANNOT MAKE IT CLEAR TO YOU IN A TELEGRAM PRECISELY HOW I FEEL ABOUT YOUR SENDING ME THE LOVELY THING YOU HAVE [probably some of Krishnamurti's voluminous theosophical writings] I SHALL ATTEMPT TO DO SO WHEN I SEE YOU WHICH I HOPE WILL BE VERY SOON WITH LOVE TO YOU AND MANY THANKS JACK.

And in September another gift from the oracle of Ojai moved John to write:

> Dear Krishna: Thank you a thousand times for the books and your charming letter. I hope, and feel sure, that all is going well with you. I am, as always, looking forward to seeing you on your return to Hollywood. Things have been rather at a standstill with me, but now seem to be progressing. We will have some grand talks when you get back. . . .

For the first film under his new Warner Brothers contract *Don Juan* was proposed, but in John's opinion "sweet-scented Don Juans

affect movie audiences like a rough crossing of the English channel."
He nevertheless agreed to it, providing one of his favorite novels take
precedence. This was *Moby Dick*. "It appeals to me and always has.
It has an especial appeal to me now, for in the last few years, both
on the stage and screen, I have played so many scented, bepuffed,
bewigged and ringletted characters—princes and kings and the like
—that I revel in the rough and almost demoniacal character such as
Captain Ahab becomes . . . after his leg has been amputated. . . .
what we are going to do for a love interest I don't quite know. He
might fall in love with the whale. I am sure, however, Hollywood will
find a way."

The screenplay entitled *The Sea Beast* bore but the dimmest
resemblance to the original. In fact, the only major element of Herman Melville's novel that the scenarist Bess Meredyth retained was
Ahab's pursuit of the white whale. She not only injected love interest,
but contrived a happy ending. Among the new characters she invented were Esther Wiscasset, a New Bedford belle whom Ahab
adores and with whom Derek, his evil half-brother, is in love. Derek
tricks Ahab into believing that Esther is a faithless jade, thereby
sending him, embittered, back to sea in a whaler.

What John liked best about Miss Meredyth's script were the opportunities it offered to conceal his Byronic features behind masks
of pain and horror, as when, for example, under his misapprehension
regarding Esther, he obliterates her name tattooed on his forearm
with a red-hot iron. Still more gruesome is his agony when, Moby
Dick having torn off his leg, he submits the stump to cauterization by
fire. The scenario called for John thereafter to hobble around on a peg
leg, prematurely aged, his hair long, gray and dank with sea spray,
his eyes mad, a snarling monomaniac sworn to harpoon the monster
that maimed him. The happy ending comes after Ahab, learning that
it was Derek who shoved him overboard in the path of Moby Dick,
kills him, and returns to New Bedford to discover that Esther loves
him alone.

To play Esther, the casting office picked a promising starlet,
Priscilla Bonner. She failed to pass muster with John. He wanted
Mary Astor in the feminine lead, but during his absence she had
contracted to make a series of films for First National. Day after day
John and the director, Millard Webb, viewed test films of other actresses. None suited John. One morning he was pacing the balcony
outside Jack Warner's office, pleading with him to postpone production of *The Sea Beast* until Mary Astor, whose First National com-

mitments had taken her to New York, returned to Hollywood. Chancing to glance down at the studio entrance, John beheld a matronly figure descending from a taxi, followed by a young brunette and a golden blonde. His gaze was riveted to the blonde, "the most preposterously lovely creature in all the world"—so he proclaimed her. Staggered, he turned to Jack Warner. Who was this divinity?

Dolores Costello, age nineteen, and her sister Helene, twenty-two, were comparative newcomers to Hollywood. The year before, under the chaperonage of their mother, May, a former vaudeville trouper, they had been touring the country as chorus girls with George White's *Scandals of 1924*. In Chicago a Warner talent scout caught the show, thought the sisters outstanding and arranged a screen test. The result was a contract which paid them each $75 a week.

Long before John Barrymore ever faced a camera, their actor father, a curly-haired, cleft-chinned beau ideal, was flourishing as both a matinee idol and the hero of romantic movie melodramas produced by the Vitagraph Studio of Brooklyn. The Costellos then inhabited an estate on Long Island. The daughters began their acting careers early, usually in their father's films. Dolores graced five Vitagraph features before her eighth birthday. In December of that year—1912—a troupe billed as the Vitagraph Globe Trotters set sail from San Francisco aboard a Japanese liner, the *Tanyo Maru*, on a round-the-world cruise, stopping at various ports to make movies. The Costellos were the cynosure of the troupe. Nine months elapsed before they got back to New York.

In adolescence the sisters also modeled for commercial illustrators, among them James Montgomery Flagg, who painted Dolores in a one-piece bathing suit for a popular magazine serial by Adela Rogers St. John, *The Skyrocket*. She was, he recalled, "very slender with no bones showing."

Maurice Costello attained the pinnacle of his success as the archetype cinematic romantic during the first decade of the century. Then his star began to sink. Gradually, he went out of style, the studios offering him mostly bit parts and those less and less often. Always a hearty drinker, he became a desperate one. By the time the family moved to Los Angeles, he was a sodden has-been, subject, in defeat, to Vesuvian eruptions of rage.

The sight of Dolores close up, when Jack Warner introduced John, the sound of her mellifluous voice as they exchanged amenities sufficed to relegate Mary Astor to a remote corner of his heart. "I fell in love with her instantly," he said afterward. "This time I knew I was right." The same day he informed Warner that he had found his leading lady for *The Sea Beast* and would consider no other. Accordingly, Dolores—whom the studio had thus far assigned to a single insignificant role in a comedy melodrama, *Bobbed Hair*, by Alexander Woollcott, Louis Bromfield and others, and loaned to Paramount and Fox for equally trifling parts—was cast as Esther Wiscasset. Priscilla Bonner thereupon brought suit against Warner Brothers for breach of contract, eventually accepting a settlement.

John's subsequent attentions to "Winkie," or "Shrimp," or "Small Egg," as he variously called Dolores, precipitated a crisis in the Costello household. Mrs. Costello, like the mothers of his previous loves, was charmed by him and he by her. "She was just my age [forty-three], a remarkable woman, sweet-natured, simple, and kind. Never in the theater or in the movies had I met anyone like her." Helene Costello, a divorcee who was about to marry Lowell Sherman, a screen actor many years her senior, shared her mother's fondness for John.

But Maurice Costello strongly disapproved. "I am going to step out of character for a moment," he announced.

"What character?" Mrs. Costello asked.

"The character of minding my own business. John Barrymore is no man for Dolores. In the first place, he's old enough to be her father. Why, he is of *my* generation. In the second place, he is a married man."

Said John when apprised of these objections: "It is ridiculous to be prejudiced against a man because he is married. The divorce courts are made to take care of trivialities like that. As for the difference in our ages, an actor is no older than he admits."

Costello had a third objection. "I am something like Barrymore myself and that is the reason I do not want him for the husband of my baby."

The climactic domestic battle took place in John's presence. Costello called him a blackguard and ordered him to leave his house at once, whereupon Mrs. Costello fetched her husband a slap across the face. He stormed out of the house, never to reenter it. Divorce followed, with Costello the plaintiff. "When my daughters were shoved into success," he told the court, "I attempted to guide and advise them from years of experience. My suggestions were met with scorn and rebuffs from my wife and both my daughters. They gave me to understand I counted for nothing."

NEW YORK JAN 16 1926 JACK L WARNER WARNER BROS
STUDIOS HOLLYWOOD CALIF TREMENDOUS TURNOUT
PLUS UNPRECEDENTED AUDIENCE ENTHUSIASM AND
UNANIMITY OF PRESS PRAISE STAMPS SEABEAST ONE OF
MOST POPULAR PICTURES EVER SHOWN ON BROADWAY
LAST NIGHTS PREMIERE HUGE SUCCESS WITH MANY NO-
TABLES IN ATTENDANCE ADVANCE SALE GROWING WITH
LEAPS AND BOUNDS AND EVERYTHING POINTS TO SUC-
CESSFUL LONG RUN STOP HEARD MUCH PRAISE FOR . . .
BARRYMORE AND COSTELLO STOP EVERYONE HERE TRE-
MENDOUSLY ENTHUSIASTIC AND BENDING EVERY
EFFORT POSSIBLE TO GIVE IT THE SUCCESS IT DESERVES
STOP AMONG THOSE IN ATTENDANCE LAST NIGHT WERE
. . . MENJOU KIRKWOOD LILA LEE RICHARD DIX JOHN
DREW LOUISE DREW MEIGHAN PAUL BERN LOIS WIL-
SON. . . .

HARRY ALBERT AND SAM WARNER

NEW YORK JAN 20 1926 JACK L WARNER WARNER BROS
STUDIOS HOLLYWOOD CALIF ADVANCE SALE ON SEA-
BEAST STRONGER DAILY EACH MATINEE AND NIGHT
PERFORMANCE COMPLETE SELLOUT PLUS STANDING
ROOM STOP FIVE HUNDRED TO ONE THOUSAND PEOPLE
TURNED AWAY DAILY EACH PERFORMANCE UNABLE TO
ACCOMMODATE THEM.

AL WARNER

What greatly contributed to the popular success of *The Sea
Beast* was the final love scene between John and Dolores. Director
Millard Webb, finding himself unable to settle on any one of numerous takes, decided to splice all of them together, thereby producing an embrace of exceptional intensity and duration. When Michael
Strange saw the movie in New York, she observed: "That's not acting. He's in love with the girl."

The whale gave Webb a good deal more trouble. At a cost of
$12,000, the studio's prop department fashioned a life-size rubber
behemoth enclosing machinery which, when operated by two men
from inside, was meant to cause it to leap, dive, roll over and spurt
water through its blowhole. During a trial launching in San Pedro
harbor—undertaken, happily, without the two operators—it sank like
lead. A resourceful prop technician then carved a rubber specimen

the size of a cake of soap, inserted shoe buttons for eyes and floated it in a small tank of water, with an electric fan stirring up waves. But, enlarged on the screen, this Moby Dick decidedly lacked realism.

Bess Meredyth's scenario contained a stage direction which John felt merited some kind of award. Ahab, thrown from the longboat while hunting Moby Dick, is struggling underwater. "His lips are seen to move as he recites the Lord's Prayer, and his eyes fill with tears."

DEC 24 1926 MICHAEL STRANGE 142 EAST END AVENUE NEW YORK CITY
DEAR FIG MERRY CHRISTMAS AND THE BEST ALWAYS FIG

DEC 25 1926 BARRYMORE HOTEL AMBASSADOR LOS ANGELES CALIF
THANKS FOR YOUR WIRE SAME TO YOU BABY DELIGHTED WITH PRESENTS FIG

The exchange typified their post-separation relationship. Now that they were a continent apart, now that their rampant egos no longer had a battlefield on which to clash, a calm mutual fondness developed. They were in frequent communication by phone, telegram and letter. Several times, when Michael was financially embarrassed, John forwarded money in excess of what their separation agreement called for. From Michael came this appeal:

URGENT NECESSITY STOP IF YOU COULD CREATE A FUND OF TWELVE HUNDRED DOLLARS TO BE SENT TO YOUR ATTORNEY FOR PURPOSE ONLY OF KEEPING UP WHITE PLAINS [the house which John had given her]. . . . OTHER ALTERNATIVE IS TO ACCEPT THE BEST OF THE OFFERS I AM NOW BEING MADE PLEASE WIRE IMMEDIATELY ANSWER EVERY GOOD WISH FIG

John replied the same day:

DEAR FIG AM SENDING TWELVE HUNDRED DOLLARS FRIDAY ONLY TOO GLAD TO BE OF SERVICE IN PRESENT DIFFICULTIES STOP NATURALLY DO NOT WISH TO SUGGEST ANY PROCEDURE REGARDING YOUR OWN PROPERTY BUT HEARD FROM STERN [Henry Root Stern, a New York lawyer who formerly had represented both their interests] VALUE OF IT HAD GREATLY DIMINISHED THROUGH CONDEMNATION FOR ROAD PURPOSES AND PRESUMED

SALE WOULD BE JUDICIOUS AS SAVING YOU ANXIETY AND
HEAVY CONTINUOUS MAINTENANCE EXPENSES STOP
FEEL SURE YOUR OWN JUDGMENT WILL FIND PROPER
SOLUTION ALL THE BEST FIG

John warmly encouraged Michael in her new pursuit—acting —and whenever she managed to land a part, he would wire his congratulations. She made her debut with a Salem, Massachusetts, summer stock company as a minor character in Clyde Fitch's *Barbara Frietchie*. The next production planned was Oscar Wilde's *The Importance of Being Earnest*, Michael to attempt the leading feminine role of Gwendolyn. Then the manager found himself short of the needed cash by $1,000, so Michael proceeded to raise that sum among vacationing members of the Boston elite. "To have persuaded [them]," she wrote years later, "nearly all of them strangers, to give me a thousand dollars to avert a crisis in my acting career, I still consider to have been a major feat."

On the opening night, shortly before curtain time, Michael announced that she could not go on because she had yet to master her lines. After keeping the audience waiting for an hour, she changed her mind and, with the aid of a prompter, muddled through the play.

Her first Broadway portrayal, that of the mentally deranged heroine of Strindberg's *Easter*, drew this comment from the *New Yorker:* "The kindliness with which the press looked upon Miss Michael Strange's . . . latest adventure behind the footlights . . . is one more testimonial to the power of her exotic personality. Definitely, she is one of the group which publicity has established, one of those women . . . with an unquenchable desire to get on in the world. When one writes of Michael Strange, there is much to say. Her brusque, vigorous energy, her flashing eyes, are outward, visible signs. Whatever else, she is a personality. . . ."

Michael next appeared at the Metropolitan Opera House in Sophocles' *Electra*. Margaret Anglin played the title role and Michael played her sister Chrysothemis. "John wired me his pleasure at my good notices." She went on to impersonate Lady Anne in *Richard III*, then the nameless heroine of Shaw's *Man of Destiny*. The latter role required her to disguise herself as an army officer. "You were perfectly terrible!" said Helen Westley, an actress and member of the Theatre Guild's board of directors. "That is, my child, you were awful when you played the girl, so awkward. No one could hear you either! But when you dressed as the young man everything went splendidly. . . . My dear, if I were you, I would play nothing but boys' parts!"

Neither John nor Michael felt any urgency to obtain a divorce. John, in fact, relied on the status quo to save him from himself, for he knew that if free he would marry "Winkie" and from past experience he had come to fear that marriage would kill romance.

Disquieting rumors about John and Dolores reached Mary Astor in New York. "I hear that Miss Costello is really lovely," she ventured one day when John telephoned.

"She is," John said. "She's divine," and quickly added, using his nickname for Mary, "Don't worry, my goopher, she's just a chicken."

He was in no rush to sever his relationship with a mistress as young, beautiful and loving as Mary Astor, and when she returned to Los Angeles, having fulfilled her commitments in the East, they took up again where they had left off. She tried to discount the rumors that reached her ears about John and Dolores, but "several times when Jack was coming over for dinner he telephoned to say 'something had come up' and he couldn't make it. Or he would have someone else call and announce that he had been 'detained.' I began to be frightened."

She derived some solace from a revelation by Helios. The mystic maintained that she had known John and Mary in a previous life. Mary, she said, was the reincarnation of the eighteenth-century tragedienne Sarah Siddons and John had been her brother, John Philip Kemble, actor-manager of the Drury Lane Theatre.

No sooner had the last reel of *The Sea Beast* been shot than John reluctantly began to enact another "scented, bepuffed, bewigged and ringletted character." As Don Juan he scaled stone walls, leaped off balconies, swung on vines with rapier and poignard at the ready, breasted the Tiber, dueled enemies to the death and, according to a press agent's count, bestowed 191 kisses upon such love goddesses as Estelle Taylor, Myrna Loy, Phyllis Haver, June Marlowe, Mary Astor. At the end he galloped off toward the sunset on a white charger, holding Adriana della Varnese (Mary Astor) in his arms.

"I thought you made Don Juan for satire," said an interviewer.

"I made it for money," John rejoined.

He had wanted Dolores Costello to play Adriana, but the studio, having already signed Mary Astor for the role, was disinclined to risk another breach-of-contract suit.

The critics tore *Don Juan* apart, some calling John's performance the worst they had ever witnessed. But the grace and elegance of his bearing, his Fairbanks-like gymnastics, his steamy love-making combined to captivate audiences and made another packet for Warner Brothers.

In one respect *Don Juan*, together with the short features preceding it at the first showing in New York's Warner Theatre on August 6, 1926, was undeniably unique. As the New York *Times'* Mordaunt Hall reported: "A marvelous device known as the vitaphone, which synchronizes sound with motion pictures, stirred a distinguished audience . . . to unusual enthusiasm. . . . The natural reproduction of voices, the tonal quality of musical instruments and the timing of the sound to the movements of the lips of singers and the actions of musicians was almost uncanny. . . ."

It was during the filming of *Don Juan* that the full painful truth about John and Dolores burst upon Mary Astor. Arriving at the set for the first takes, she found the pair sitting side by side, just as she and John used to sit between takes of *Beau Brummel*, heads close together, whispering and laughing. "And then all my hopes and dreams died, and I wanted to die with them." When she later taxed John with his inconstancy, he said: "Dear Goopher, I'm just a son of a bitch."

"I had wanted it drawn, diagrammed, and signed before I could be convinced," Mary said later. "Now I was convinced. And this final, flat knowledge brought with it a strange sense of relief. Now, at least, I knew, after eight long months of the torment of not being sure. . . . I felt relief, and the beginning of bitterness. I looked for something, someone, to blame; and since I could never have thought to blame myself, I blamed his drinking, I blamed my parents for their failure to give me freedom, and finally I blamed him. I decided he was—what he said he was."

Upon completing *Don Juan*, John entertained the notion of sweeping Dolores out to sea in some private craft. From the producer Hal Roach he chartered the *Gypsy*, an eighty-foot, diesel-powered cabin cruiser, with its captain and five-man crew. The prospect thrilled Dolores. But John had reckoned without Mrs. Costello. She forbade her daughter to go near the boat. So John sailed south to Baja, Mexico, accompanied by his valet, Blaney, and Clementine, who wore a yachting cap made specially for her. On this and later sea voyages John kept a log full of vivid description and romantic musings. According to Dolores, this log was, in intent, a series of letters to her.*

" 'Winkie' saw him off," he wrote in the third person on the day he set sail, December 27, 1925. "Only she is the very dearest smallest cat, and he is crazy about her, and hopes and truly believes they will be the very happiest things, if they have *any* sense at all! Wrote that small thing the longest letter, and went to bed after looking at its own curled up picture, and after praying that they both may be happy together for always. . . ."

And on the following days: "Always think of the dear 'small egg' last thing before going to sleep. . . . [Quoting Marlowe's *Dr. Faustus:*] 'Oh, thou art fairer than the evening air, clad in the beauty of a thousand stars.' [And Ben Jonson:] 'O so white! O so soft! O so sweet is she!' . . . A slightly wheezy gramophone played . . . 'Pal of my childhood days,' which reminded me of my 'Winkie,' and the last shots of *The Sea Beast*, and I wished so that 'Cat' was sitting on my lap like a sailor's sweetheart . . . he kisses his dear small 'Wink' good night and closes this very journal for the day. . . . Thought how heavenly it would be if 'Wink' was along. . . . If that ever comes off, and it *must*, it will be simply wonderful and unforgettable and eminently *sane!* . . . Every evening I look at the fat, lovely, healthy, ever-young, ever-bright, ever-poised beacon of a star that is the symbol of 'Winkie's' and my life together, and, like the Angelus, say a gay, lifting, happy, husky, tiny spout of a prayer to it. It is as if the bottom of my soul, that has had so damned much happen above it, were stirring awake and saying, 'Hello,' like a child at something. . . ."

He was gone three weeks, returning to begin his third Warner picture as Chevalier des Grieux in *When a Man Loves*, an adaptation of Abbé Prévost's lachrymose eighteenth-century tale of star-crossed lovers, *Histoire du Chevalier des Grieux et de Manon Lescaut*. Deferring to John's demand, the studio engaged Dolores to play Manon, and John, in his eagerness to advance her career, went so far as to underact that she might shine the brighter.

For convenience John, who still lived at the Ambassador Hotel a good many miles from the shooting, and Dolores, whose home was

---

* What ultimately happened to it remains a mystery. Dolores had it for several years before it unaccountably vanished. It turned up again, after John died, in the possession of Henry Hotchener. He sold it for $20,000 to Gene Fowler, who quoted it extensively in his biography. Whoever acquired it after Fowler's death in 1960 is unknown.

also distant, each took a nearby apartment. John invited Krishnamurti to visit them and he stayed three days. He struck a sympathetic chord in John when, strolling under the stars one evening, he paused in the midst of a religious discussion, gazed skyward and murmured: "That's all you need."

Not long after, Krishnamurti horrified Annie Besant and other devout Theosophists by shedding the messianic mantle with which she had clothed him. He dissolved the Order of the Star, saying during a broadcast address in Holland before an audience of thousands: ". . . Truth is a pathless land, and you cannot approach it by any path whatsoever, by any religion, by any sect. . . . you have the idea that only certain people hold the key to the Kingdom of Happiness. No one holds it. No one has the authority to hold it. That key is your own self and in the development and the purification and in the incorruptibility of that self alone is the Kingdom of Eternity."

Finally, he resigned from the Theosophical Society to pursue a spiritual teaching devoid of dogma and cultism.*

At about this time James Montgomery Flagg arrived in Los Angeles to paint portraits of movie celebrities. One afternoon John summoned him to his Ambassador quarters, explaining that he was having Krishnamurti to tea. Flagg already knew him. He had met him with Annie Besant in London when Krishnamurti was only twelve and found them both so attractive that he persuaded a friendly foreign correspondent for the Associated Press to publicize their activities.

As John opened the door to him, Flagg saw he had been drinking. "But, Jack, Krishna hates liquor," he reminded him.

"Think nothing of it," John replied. "Krishna says some of his best friends are drunks."

Krishnamurti was sitting for Flagg in Indian robes at Ojai when the artist ran out of Chinese white. The sage dispatched his gardener, Peter, to the nearby town of Ventura to fetch some more. Peter returned empty-handed and was told to search further. Upon his reappearance with the needed pigment, Krishnamurti remarked: "Ah, the second coming of Peter."

Flagg would sometimes ply Krishnamurti with formidable questions, as when during a promenade together in New York they passed a pair of apparent homosexuals and Flagg asked: "What makes pansies?"

"Lack of control," Krishnamurti shot back.

---

* At the age of eighty-two, as I write this, Krishnamurti, still based at Ojai, is continually on the move, lecturing in America, Europe and Asia.

Another time: "What is God?"

"Man purified."

In late 1926 Cecil B. De Mille was directing his super-colossal life of Christ, *The King of Kings*, when Krishnamurti visited the set. An alert studio press agent had him photographed between De Mille and H. B. Warner (no kin of the brothers), the actor who played the Savior. "I left soon after this," he told John, "as I thought three Saviors on the same lot was perhaps a little too much."

Michael Strange did not allow her theatrical ventures to divert her from her literary endeavors. With John in mind she wrote a cinematic treatment of the life of François Villon. John, who had left Warner Brothers to sign a three-picture contract with United Artists for a total of $352,000 plus a share of the profits, was already contemplating such a film and, after reading Michael's script, he wrote to her:

> When this scenario was first devised . . . it was before I had perpetrated such arrantly "romantic" movies as *Don Juan* and *Manon Lescaut.* . . . I now wish, for this new firm I am with, to do something totally different, that I have greater sympathy with, and can get much more fun out of, and I believe achieve a more significant result, and that is with the extraordinary figure of Villon as a vehicle to rather burlesque the whole idea of romance. He was a creative artist, a poet, and everything happened in his *head*. When he is caught by life in these movie situations, which always demand a rather asinine, heroic activity, he is frightfully up against it, and only by his amazing dexterity and imagination can he elude them, maintain a certain whimsical integrity, and prevent himself from looking like an ass, the audience being the only person he takes into his confidence. I think the picture of Villon skipping, bounding, and crawling on his stomach through a Gothic dimension of a dying chivalry and a brutal and slightly sacerdotal materialism till almost the very end of the movie, when he is forced, through the reality of suffering, his mother's death, etc., to a different attitude, always, however, flecked by a sort of pinched gaiety, is something that I can have genuine fun with and accomplish something real in the movies whose possibilities interest me exceedingly. . . .
>
> I am writing to you right off the bat, just as I feel, for

as you have expended a certain amount of time and energy on the formulation of a scenario, you most certainly deserve to have it explained to you clearly why the general scheme of it is not in line with the thing I have the urge to do at present. . . .

We are utilizing a nuance out of Tyl Eulenspiegel, with which the latter part of your scene in the Square at Rouen might very well fit in, as Joan of Arc died the day Villon was born. It at any rate gave me a handle on which I could base the assumption that the author of "The Days That Were" [possibly an unpublished manuscript of Michael's] should receive some compensation. Also, the title about "They Shall not pass," although "free and clear," which seems to be the anesthetic slogan for all scenario writers, has been evolved by yourself in this instance, and I honestly believe it might be eminently utilizable.

The most the Producer was willing to pay for these two points was $700, but I jacked him up to $1250., which offer I have wired to Miss Marbury [Elizabeth Marbury, Michael's literary agent]. . . .

Hope everything is well with you and the Rabbit [Diana]. . . .

United Artists imported the German actor Conrad Veidt to play Louis XI. When he met John, who was awaiting him at the railroad station, Veidt knelt and kissed his hands.

The New York première of *The Beloved Rogue*, as the Villon film was entitled, which took place on March 13, 1927, at the Mark Strand Theatre, proved a far cry from what John had envisioned. ". . . a fanciful affair," wrote critic Mordaunt Hall. "Alan Crosland [the director] . . . delights in extravagancies, exaggerations that are presumed to have popular appeal. . . . As the ridiculously painted 'fool,' Mr. Barrymore reminds one of a comic character in a Sunday colored supplement. It is indeed almost incredulous [*sic*] that this Gaston-like creature is the handsome John Barrymore. But seeing is believing, for Mr. Barrymore with the aid of artificial snow gradually rubs off the coloring, straightens the nose that made him look a bit like Cyrano De Bergerac, cleans off his Mephistophelian eyebrows, wipes away the smudgy whiskers, and then appears as the romantic Mr. Villon. . . ."

Compared to the verdict of Hall's colleagues, this was laudatory. Most of them disliked the film. John loathed it. During one of the first public screenings he stole into the theater, climbed up to a rear balcony seat and watched awhile in dismal silence. At length, unable to contain himself any longer, he startled the audience by shouting: "Call yourself an actor? My God, what a ham!"

On December 27, 1927, John telephoned Michael to wish her good luck in a daring new venture. The same John Williams who had produced *Justice* ten years earlier had somehow been persuaded to put on, at New York's huge Cosmopolitan Theatre, Edmond Rostand's *L'Aiglon* (The Eaglet) with Michael in the title role. A poetic tragedy based on the short life of the Duc de Reichstadt, Napoleon's son by the Austrian Archduchess Maria Louisa, it had been written for Sarah Bernhardt and played since by a good many actresses of note. Michael, untrained as she was, merited high marks for audacity if not for performance. "Ned says they all say you're all right," John told her comfortingly.

The critics were not quite as indulgent. The *Times:* ". . . there was a curiously non-professional aspect to this latest presentation . . . a haphazard, amateurish quality as if a group of eager and talented guests had responded graciously to a social invitation which read, 'Come as your favorite character from Rostand.'" The *World:* ". . . it was a scanty but devoted house which hailed each costumed entrance with the courteous acclaim of spectators at a social masquerade." The *Tribune:* "Michael Strange . . . declaimed her lines with praiseworthy earnestness, but at no time did her eaglet get his feet far above the earth."

The eighth performance was the last. By way of consolation John, having heard that the supporting cast had offered to accept half-pay to keep the play going, told Michael: "That is the greatest tribute you could have had."

Renouncing the stage, Michael sought alternative outlets for self-expression, such as writing poetry, plays and novels, socialist politics, lecturing on art, the theater and life, and giving readings from classic poems and the Bible to the accompaniment of a harp.

During her childhood Diana never connected her shadowy absentee father with John Barrymore, the film superstar. Michael prevented it. If the subject arose, she changed the conversation. She enrolled Diana in her first school under the name of Blythe. The child dreamed constantly of the dim, faceless figure without identity. Then, at six, she chanced upon a photograph of a remarkably handsome man holding an infant in his arms and the caption: "John Barrymore and his daughter." She taxed her Nanny with it, who reluctantly, tearfully, told her the truth. Thereafter Diana badgered and bribed the servants to take her to movies starring her father. Her dreams became more complex, more fantastic. At school, ashamed to admit how seldom she had seen her father, she concocted fictions to demonstrate otherwise, basing them upon newspaper stories—about her father's epicurean way of life, about her Aunt Ethel and Uncle Lionel and the theatrical royalty she had met through them. She saturated herself in Barrymore family history. Every few days, she pretended, she received another letter from her father.

John seldom forgot Diana's birthday, he often wrote to her and sent her gifts, but Michael did not encourage and he did not insist upon frequent visits. The latter was the right he had mysteriously renounced shortly after the child's birth and, in any case, his professional commitments would have kept them apart.

Ethel fumed. Not only was the comedy about a theatrical dynasty named Cavendish a patent take-off on the Barrymores, but Edna Ferber, who wrote *The Royal Family* with George S. Kaufman, had the effrontery, as Ethel saw it, to submit the script to her with the proposal that she undertake the leading feminine role of Julie Cavendish, in Ethel's view an insulting caricature of herself. "The legend has it that we artists are wild, careless, tousled and immoral," she objected. "We live en famille and such a famille! An organization of idiots, chaotic, arty, self-conscious, thinking theater, breathing theater, smelling theater. To those half-baked intelligences a theatrical family is only a theatrical family, not an association of normal, healthy human beings."

Actually, *The Royal Family*, which opened at Broadway's Selwyn Theatre on December 28, 1927, was a gentle, affectionate spoof, depicting the Cavendishes as warm, loving, charming people from the septuagenarian Fanny Cavendish, a matriarch in the grand tradition of Louisa ("the Duchess") Lane of the old Walnut Street Theatre, to Gwen Cavendish, her granddaughter who is ripe for ingenue parts as Ethel's daughter, Ethel Barrymore Colt, would soon be.

Bewildered by Ethel's displeasure, the playwrights piously entered a disclaimer of any intent to parody. Edna Ferber explained later: "George Kaufman and I had decided to write a play about a glamorous theatrical family—no particular theatrical family, I hastily add—but an imaginary one that might be any family wedded to the stage." She confessed, however, that they did draw upon certain aspects of John Barrymore in delineating the character of Tony Cavendish, Julie's irresistible scapegrace brother, "not as a whole . . . he was, of course, too improbable to copy from life. . . .

"Casting was a nightmare. We couldn't get anybody to play Julie Cavendish. We had hoped, in our innocence, that Ethel Barrymore would play it. She would have been perfection. . . . Ina Claire, approached, had announced that she wasn't going to be a walking ad for the Barrymores. . . ." In the end a lesser-known actress, Ann Andrews, portrayed Julie. *The Royal Family* ran for more than a year.

Ethel's overreaction was to consult the famed trial lawyer Max Steuer as to the feasibility of suing the authors. After Steuer attended the play, it was his opinion (for which he supposedly charged Ethel $1,000) that she had no case, but John might have.

For five years Ethel declined to speak to the playwrights. At the outset of World War II Kaufman asked her to take part in a Bundles for Britain benefit. It was to be held on the second Sunday in February, many weeks ahead. She crushed him with a paraphrase of one of "Julie Cavendish's" lines. "I'm sorry," said Ethel glacially, "but on that night I expect to have laryngitis."

John did not see *The Royal Family* until a road company brought it to Los Angeles. Fredric March played Tony Cavendish and he emphasized John's mannerisms—the jauntily held cigarette, the quizzically raised eyebrows, the sardonic grin, the left profile turned toward the audience. He suffered some qualms one evening when he learned that John was out front and planning a visit to his dressing room. "I had heard of his athletic prowess," March said later. When John appeared, March braced himself for a set-to. John walked around him thoughtfully, eyeing him from head to toe, then burst out with a roar of laughter: "Christ, you were great!"

Fredric March went on, with John's friendliest encouragement, to impersonate him in the movie version of *The Royal Family*.

18

Bella Vista

═══════

I⊤ was John's triumph as Hamlet, leaving him no greater worlds to conquer, that had led him to quit the stage for Hollywood. Abject failure as Macbeth led to the same result in Lionel's career. An Arthur Hopkins production, and Lionel's first and only Shakespearean endeavor, opening at the Apollo Theatre in New York on February 17, 1921, it was mauled by the critics. Heywood Broun penned one of his most devastating quips. It was then the practice (now illegal) for theater-ticket agencies to buy up in advance blocks of tickets to shows that looked like hits. The leading agency was McBride's. Broun wrote: "Lay on MacDuff. Lay off McBride." It ran for only twenty-eight performances.

Lionel continued on the stage four more years, appearing in five plays, of which two, Henri Bernstein's *The Claw* and David Belasco's adaptation of an Italian drama, *Laugh, Clown, Laugh,* were moderately successful, the rest—*The Piker* by Leon Gordon, *Taps* by Franz Adam Beyerlein and *Man or Devil* by Jerome K. Jerome, catastrophes. *Man or Devil,* the only one of the five which did not co-star Lionel's wife, Irene, lasted twenty performances. Toward the fall of 1925 husband and wife followed John to Hollywood.

The breach between the brothers healed, and they saw more of each other than they had since boyhood. Lionel, no teetotaler, helped John kill many a bottle. They both loved music. "Jack knew a lot about it without knowing a lot about it," Lionel recalled. "He was particularly fond of Brahms and liked him best when he didn't have his toga on. I think we had our happiest time out here and by ourselves. We would sit up all night with refreshments, of course, and Jack would put one of Brahms' Hungarian folk songs on the Capehart and let it play over and over. Of one polka in particular, Jack said one night: 'Now this is really Brahms without his toga. Let me tell you what is actually happening. The little old fellow has got up from bed, combed his beard, had a pretty fine breakfast and a good crap, put a cigar in his kisser and is now merrily on his way to the whorehouse. Listen.' We sat up all night listening to the polka and must have accompanied Brahms thirty times to the cat house. Then we both passed out along about noon the next day and when we woke up Jack had been asleep in a chair and I was stretched out on a sofa, utterly happy."

In the spring of 1927 an arthritic John Drew went on tour as Vice Chancellor Sir William Gower in an all-star production of Arthur Wing Pinero's *Trelawny of the Wells*. At seventy-three he was the second oldest member of the company. The oldest was Mrs. Thomas Whiffen. She was eighty-two. Only to please "Whiffy," a long-standing pet of his, who wanted to play Mrs. Mossop once more, had he agreed to go along. One of his exit lines was "My box, sir . . . my box" (meaning his theater box). In Vancouver, at his last performance, he was heard to mutter, as he moved offstage into the wings: "My box . . . my wooden box."

That night he fell ill, attacked simultaneously by rheumatic fever and septic poisoning. He was taken to San Francisco's Dante Sanatorium. Various members of the Drew-Barrymore clan rallied around him, among them John and Lionel. John came with Jack Prescott, who had recently turned up in Los Angeles. Lionel soon went back to Hollywood to finish a movie adaptation of *Rain*. But John stayed three weeks, spending the better part of each day at his uncle's bedside, seeing to it that he had every comfort. After visiting hours John and his friend would divide their time between browsing through antique and rare-book shops and pub-crawling with newspapermen. Among the latter John had been something of a legend ever since the night, some years earlier, when he held his own in a drinking contest with an opponent of heroic capacity named Walter Deffenbaugh. The drama critic of the San Francisco *Examiner*, Idwal Jones, left a memoir of the encounter:

"We had on our staff a journalist of distinction, of an old stage family, who had the profile of Kyrle Bellew [a matinee idol of Maurice Barrymore's generation], manners that were the punctilio of elegance, and a voice of such modulation that Booth would have envied it. It was this prodigy, to whom I introduced Rufus Blair, then a newspaperman in San Francisco, that Blair suggested as an excellent person to meet and crack a few bottles with, when J B phoned and said he had decided to do some large-scale and ceremonial imbibing. At 10 p.m., our hero and Blair arrived at the St. Francis and J received them with his ritualistic courtesy. The meeting was a bit stiff. Both were drinkers of epochal stature. They bowed, shook hands, and our hero hung up his cane, gloves, hat and coat. They sat at a small table decked out with Scotch and the appropriate tumblers. The drinking was liturgical, done in the prescribed form, with heel-taps and profound bows, with silence and the extreme of hauteur and self-respect.

"At 4 a.m. J B suddenly relinquished the chair and consciousness. Our hero rose, and with austere deliberateness drew on his coat, hooked the cane on his arm, pulled on his hat with a finality that signified he thought mighty little indeed of J B as a drinker, gave one pitying, amused glance at J B, and made his majestic exit.

"Well, Blair later phoned downstairs, but learned no gentleman had been picked up in the lobby or found dead on the stairs. Then he peered awestruck through the blinds, saw our hero crossing the street, to stand by the park railing and, swinging his cane airily, fling up a contemptuous glance at the window of the suite. His lips moved, as if to say, 'So he thought he could drink a nip, did he!'

"He moved on, with the air of a conqueror, then swayed slightly, and toppled to the sidewalk, whence he was collected by a cop and a couple of taxi-drivers who took him home."

John Drew's last words to his nephew were characteristic of the gallant old trouper: "Stake the nurses," he said. He died on July 8.

John wired David Glasford, a fellow member of the Players Club, of which John Drew had been president: DEAR DAVID I WISH YOU TO KNOW THAT I AM IN ACCORD WITH MY UNCLES EXPRESSED WISH THAT OTIS SKINNER BE APPOINTED THE NEXT PRESIDENT OF THE CLUB I SINCERELY HOPE THAT THE BOARD WILL BE OF THIS OPINION. It was not, preferring to elect Walter Hampden.*

When John returned to Los Angeles he was further saddened by news of a friend he had not seen nor heard from in almost fifteen years. George Foster Platt had once ranked high among Broadway

---

* Skinner, however, became vice president.

directors, with hit after hit to his credit, such as Ned Sheldon's *The Nigger* and a series of productions for the New Theatre. It was Platt who, meeting John at the Players Club bar, cast him on the spot as Anatol in the Schnitzler playlets.

At times a lone, morose drinker, Platt would disappear for long periods between plays. Following such a retreat, he went to Hollywood, one of the first important figures in his profession with a contract to direct pictures there. But he directed none. Soon after his arrival he drove with three companions to Santa Monica. On the way back, all of them drunk, the car crashed. Only Platt survived. Following a long convalescence, he departed for China and his friends lost track of him. John often spoke warmly of George Platt, of his talent, his charm, his kindness.

A pile of letters and telegrams awaited John at the Ambassador. Thumbing through them, he suddenly called to Prescott in great excitement, waving an envelope: "Do you know who this is from?" Platt had written from a Dr. Pottinger's sanatorium for tuberculars in Monrovia, about twenty-five miles northeast of Los Angeles. Packing two quarts of liquor, they hurried there to learn from the doctor that Platt was destitute, a charity-ward patient. Was he allowed to drink? John asked, indicating the liquor. One light nip only, said the doctor and led them to the ward. Before the sun set, doctor, patient and visitors were in a merry mood, having between them polished off the two quarts.

In Los Angeles John shopped for all the things he felt Platt should have, such as dressing gowns, silk pajamas, gourmet delicacies and wine, and he instructed Dr. Pottinger to move Platt at his expense to the best private accommodations. During the succeeding days he brought Dolores to the sanatorium to cheer the invalid, kept him supplied with books and put him in touch with other old friends. Three weeks later, to John's intense sorrow, Platt died. He was but one of many luckless men and women to have received John's bounty.

Mr. Ralph Hays
120 Broadway, New York City

Ambassador Hotel
Los Angeles, Calif.

July 21, 1926

My dear Mr. Hays:

After several years of considerable traveling about, I am at last settling down in a permanent fashion and am

gathering together my belongings from the four corners of
the globe. I am sure you will realize what a pleasure it will
be to have around me these particular possessions which
mean more to me from their association than from their in-
trinsic value, and I am venturing to ask your kind assistance
in connection with those articles which you have been enjoying from my Washington Square house presided over
by my friend Mrs. Nichols.

A partial list of the items is given in the attached
memorandum. I wonder if you would also have any of the
things that were on the roof? If so, would you please enumerate them for me so that I can make adequate provision
as to fire insurance, etc.? My plan is to have my New York
representative arrange for the warehousemen to call at
your residence and prepare these articles for shipment. To
facilitate this would you kindly wire, at my expense, to the
above address stating how soon it would be convenient for
you to have my representative call for them?

With kind personal regards to you,

Sincerely yours,

John Barrymore

Will you please state in the wire the address where the
things now are?

The attached list of forty-six items included "1 wooden hippo-
potamus . . . 1 picture [*Sorrows of Werther*] . . . 2 face masks
. . . 1 set fishing tackle . . . 2 daggers . . . 1 mountain icepick
. . . 1 box of cartridges . . ."

John sent similar requests to hotel managers, landlords and
friends scattered all over Europe and America, in whose keeping he
had entrusted, during the preceding ten years, a vast diversity of
objects acquired at the promptings of his curious, restless mind. The
general manager of New York's Ambassador Hotel, one Theodore
Kroell, was directed by wire TO SEND IMMEDIATELY . . . ALL MY
RUGS . . . STOP SHALL SOON ARRANGE BY LETTER TO SEND
OTHER ARTICLES BY FREIGHT BUT NEED RUGS IMMEDIATELY.
. . . To an inquiry concerning the whereabouts of John Singer Sargent's charcoal portrait of John, Michael replied that she was not
certain but thought she had last seen it in John's Ritz Hotel apartment during the run of *Hamlet*. He cabled the Ritz management and
shortly recovered the portrait.

Diana's seventh birthday fell on August 5, 1927, and John, who had not seen his daughter in almost three years, dispatched a quantity of toys. Diana wrote, decorating her letter with thumbnail sketches of boys and girls:

> Dear Daddy Thank you very much for all those nice things you sent me. How have you been? I had a very nice summer and I had swimming lessons come and see me Daddy I would like so much to see you With love and kisses from Diana xxxx

The ultimate destination of the objects John was reassembling became apparent in a letter to Michael dated September 29, 1927: "Thanks ever so much for the letter from the small egg. I am sending her a large box of crayons with which she will probably patine the entire house. I have just bought out here a small piece of property which looks like a good investment. . . ."

For this property, which had belonged to the film director King Vidor, John paid $50,000. It clung to a hillside at the end of a steep, twisting road—Tower Road in Beverly Hills—a thousand feet above sea level. Bella Vista, John named it, and beautiful indeed was the view, embracing the whole of Los Angeles and the Pacific Ocean beyond. It consisted originally of a five-room Mexican-style hacienda, relatively modest by movie-star standards, and three and a half acres of fertile land. Though John did not reside there for another year, he launched at once a grand design of expansion and embellishment so complex that it could hardly have been fully realized within a normal life span. Ten years later he was still initiating changes and additions while planning yet others. With a tall, spiked entrance gate, sixteen separate structures and more abuilding, fifty-five rooms and assorted botanical and zoological enclosures, the eventual effect was that of a citadel under construction. Many of John's projects remained forever unfinished.

He first of all acquired the four acres adjoining the northern boundary of his estate and, as his main dwelling, he built a second hacienda of two stories with six rooms above the first building, connecting them by a vine-covered arbor winding uphill. It was U-shaped with a square patio, a roof of handmade red tiles and an iron grille at every window. The interior was laid out around a central hall. Along passages radiating from this nucleus protruded hemisphere-shaped, blue-and-gold sconces. The stretches of whitewashed wall, lined with old prints, were broken here and there by weathered timbers and

Spanish mission and cantina doors. Some of the doors elsewhere in the house were museum pieces—sixteenth-century European portals, for example, and an East Indian entryway of the first century.

From one of the passages a short flight of stairs rose to a white gate opening into a formal drawing room, its walls walnut-paneled and massed with tapestries and paintings, its ceiling traversed by weathered walnut beams, the draperies gold-brocaded and, covering the pegged hardwood floor, rugs of a mulberry hue. The windows were Italian stained glass. At one end of the room stood a grand piano, the top laden with photographs of Drews and Barrymores; at the other end, an ancient refectory table. On a marble mantelpiece sat a bust of John by the American sculptor Paul Manship, a gift from Michael Strange, and nearby hung the Sargent portrait. In the woodwork framing the immense stone fireplace that once had adorned a Scottish castle John had carved the spurious Barrymore crest. (The crowned serpent also emblazoned numerous wrought-iron fixtures, the entrance gate, the post box.) Of the paintings the most conspicuous, situated over the fireplace, was a mural depicting Spanish conquistadors astride their mounts, done by John in collaboration with a boozy boon companion, the artist John Decker. In the adjoining dining room the principal illumination issued from a pink Meissen chandelier, formerly owned by an Austrian archduke, valued at $8,500.

The tiebacks for John's bedroom window draperies had been designed by Decker. At first glance the ends appeared to be large rosettes. Actually, each one was a ballet dancer in tutu which, when closely inspected from beneath, left no doubt as to the sex of the figure.

By 1928 John had bowed to the inevitability of a third marriage. Maurice Costello was no longer an impediment, his wife having obtained her final divorce decree. Mrs. Costello viewed with undisguised pleasure the prospect of John as a son-in-law, and Dolores herself would brook no continued relationship with John outside of wedlock. So in preparation for the union John arranged the entire second story of the new hacienda, what he termed "The Marriage House," as the private domain of his future spouse. The stairs to it were handhewn with marble risers, the decor predominantly blue and gold, and a balcony off the bedroom overlooked a spectacular panorama of mountain and sea.

A tower surmounted the Marriage House, and near the top John installed a study accessible only by a ladder and trapdoor. "It was my sanctum sanctorum, my monastic retreat, my blessed hide-away from the world of idiocy."

The armor Robert Edmond Jones had designed for John's *Richard III* he kept in the library behind a carved oaken door from Italy a foot thick, along with such *rarae aves* as first editions of *Alice in Wonderland, Moby Dick, Hakluyt's Voyages, Froissart's Chronicles*, incunabula, a 1572 English translation of Cicero, a 1542 atlas.

Outbuildings scattered over the seven and a half acres contained quarters for servants; a rathskeller, the floor inlaid with sections of redwood trees; a replica of an old Western saloon complete to brass cuspidors and a frontier bar from Virginia City, Nevada, pierced by bullets; a gun room with a collection that included an elephant gun, a Harper's Ferry flintlock rifle, an 1891 Springfield, early Winchesters, Remingtons and Savages, a Maxim silencer, blunderbusses, dueling pistols, antique swords, John's *Hamlet* poignard, stilettos, crossbows, armor. In a trophy room were gathered ship models, two dinosaur eggshells (the only examples outside New York's American Museum of Natural History, which the explorer Roy Chapman Andrews gave John after his 1925 Gobi Desert expedition), stuffed reptiles, birds, the skeleton of a 500-pound swordfish, a leopard skin, a giant tortoise shell.

Outdoors were a skeet range (where Clark Gable occasionally tested his marksmanship), a bowling green, tennis courts, an antique sundial, presented to John a decade earlier by McGill University in appreciation of his performance as Peter Ibbetson, which gave not only the time but the day of the month together with various astronomical calculations. There were six artificial ponds, some stocked with trout and other edible fish, fountains galore, a kidney-shaped swimming pool measuring fifty-five by forty-five feet, fed by a dozen jets and two cascades. A silken canopy providing shade on a terrace above the pool was supported by brightly striped poles in the style of Venetian mooring posts. At night multicolored lights played over the pool. The plumbing alone for the waterworks cost John $40,000.

Under the tender ministrations of a gnomish, crinkly-faced Japanese gardener named Nishimura, who directed ten helpers, the grounds of Bella Vista became a floral and arboreal wonderland. At a San Francisco fair one of the prize exhibits was a tree, 450 years old, from Osaka, where it formerly adorned an imperial arboretum. John bought it for $1,800 and entrusted the transplanting to "Nishi." Among scores of such treasures at Bella Vista were a century-old olive tree from Palestine and a dwarf cedar from Japan, the latter costing $1,100. Stands of fir and palm trees cast their shadows upon the swimming pool. The footpaths meandering through the wooded areas were paved with sunken tree trunks.

John found an additional use for Nishi. The green-thumbed wizard spoke hardly any English. So, to discourage unwelcome phone calls, John would have him answer. The caller soon gave up trying to make himself understood. When Nishi was otherwise occupied, John would take the call himself, imitating the gardener's singsong voice in a spate of Japanese-sounding gibberish.

The son of Maurice Barrymore was serenely content among the animals that freely roamed Bella Vista. In addition to nippy little Clementine, there were an opossum, a South American kinkajou, a mouse deer, Siamese cats by the dozen, nineteen dogs, including eleven greyhounds, St. Bernards, Kerry blue terriers. Three of the terriers, born during a temblor, were named Shake, Quake, and Shock.

John would sit by himself for hours at a stretch in the heated aviary which sheltered 300-odd specimens, among them a blue-and-green-feathered motmot, a pair of toucans, a pair of quetzals, a crimson-backed tanager, a blue tanager, oropendolas, three pairs of honeycreepers, green parakeets from Australia, broad-tailed wydahs, red-billed Chinese magpies, barbets, bleeding-heart doves, pearl-necked doves, dark, shiny gallinules, black-headed nuns, white-headed nuns, strawberry, saffron and fire-red finches, six birds of paradise, canaries, weaverbirds, crested Yucatan jays, jungle warblers. . . . Sometimes John would hold mealworms between his lips for the birds to snatch.

At Henry Hotchener's conservative estimate, John sank at least a million dollars in Bella Vista.

John's excursion aboard the chartered *Gypsy* had left him with a craving to own a yacht of his own, and in January 1926 he bought for $100,000 the *Mariner*, a 106-foot, gaff-rigged schooner. Built in 1922, the *Mariner*, owned and skippered by Captain L. A. Norris, had distinguished herself by setting a new trans-Pacific record in the annual San Pedro–Honolulu race, the West Coast blue-ribbon yachting event, sailing the 2,200 miles in eleven days, fourteen hours. Though she finished first of the six entrants on corrected time, she placed second to the sixty-foot schooner *Diablo*.

No sooner had John, the sometime soccer player, sometime high diver, sometime mountain climber, taken possession than he decided he must enter the *Mariner* in the 1926 race. He recruited a crew of eleven and as captain, a "Doc" P. H. L. Wilson, and on June 12 the yacht, sleek and white, glided out of the harbor, a burgee carrying the Barrymore crest. Once in the open sea, John occasionally took the helm, with Clementine in her yachting cap perched on his shoulder. At first the monkey felt queasy and refused food. But she soon acclimatized herself, jealously bit everybody who came near John, and climbed all over the rigging, unchastened by the frequent kicks the crew aimed at her.

Captain Wilson, fully aware of John's weakness, kept the key to the liquor chest on his person and every evening before grub measured out no more than one drink per man.

On the sixth day a calm befell the *Mariner*, with the result that she limped into Honolulu almost nine days later, the fourth contestant out of five. Waldo Drake, a sailor-writer, reported in the next issue of *Yachting* magazine:

". . . we enjoyed the lighter side of sailing to the fullest extent. From our veteran skipper, a Corinthian [amateur yachtsman] down to the tyro of the afterguard, every man experienced 14 of the most enjoyable days of his life. . . . the sea routine of watch and watch, the excitement of the race, the meal-time philosophy, and the fun brought out what Jack Barrymore so aptly termed the 'glittering freemasonry of the sea.' . . . Excerpts from *Mariner's* log during those 96 hours, during which we went swimming twice over the side, offer interesting sidelights on the weather. . . ."

Becalmed again off the Hawaiian coast, John dived overboard for a third swim. A sudden wind blew up and the *Mariner* luffed into it. John looked up, unperturbed, to see the boat swiftly moving downwind, waved cheerfully and shouted: "Go ahead, boys. I'll see you in Honolulu." They managed to haul him out before his strength failed.

A single race sufficed to satisfy John's taste for the untried. He never competed again as a yachtsman. The sea, however, fascinated him always and he was to spend a great deal of time cruising. He came to love deep-sea fishing as well after he landed a swordfish for the first time, a marlin seven and a half feet long, weighing 185 pounds. "That swordfish changed my whole life. I wanted to live forever where I could meet other members of his family. To this end, I straightaway became a life member of the Tuna Fishing Club, with the proud degree of S.C. (Swordfish Catcher)."

PARIS MAY 13 1929 JOHN BARRYMORE TOWER ROAD
BEVERLY HILLS CAL
(DELIVER CARE WARNER BROS STUDIO)
DEAR FIG CONTEMPLATING BUT NOT DECIDED ON CER-
TAIN STEP BUT EITHER WAY OUGHT REMAIN EUROPE
TILL NEXT JANUARY STOP IT WOULD BE DIFFICULT FOR
ME AT THIS TIME HAVE ANY DIMINUTION OF INCOME
AND WOULD HESITATE SERIOUSLY BEFORE TAKING STEP
WHICH AT ALL CHANGE PRESENT CONDITIONS. . . .
OUR CONTRACT CALLS FOR NO DIFFERENCE IN SUCH
EVENT CABLING BECAUSE WOULD LIKE LEARN YOUR PER-
SONAL VIEWPOINT . . . TOWARDS DIANAS FUTURE
MINE. . . . EVERY GOOD WISH FIG

MAY 17 1929 NIGHT LETTER CABLE MICHAEL STRANGE
DEAR FIG ANY STEP YOU MAY TAKE WOULD NATURALLY
IN NO WAY AFFECT OUR AGREEMENT AND YOU HAVE
ALL MY SINCERE WISHES FOR THE GREATEST HAPPINESS
LOVE TO DIANA FIG

The step Michael contemplated was marrying Harrison Tweed,
a socially prominent attorney who represented the Rockefeller interests.

19

"Winkie"

M<small>Y</small> hands were trembling when I rang the bell. I was afraid of I know not what—probably just afraid of Michael Strange. It was a weird situation that I had never before encountered—not even in plays. I didn't know just how a man went about arranging with his wife to divorce him so that he could marry another girl. I couldn't even guess what kind of scene to play, what my wife's reaction would be."

Dolores had consented to marry John, had accepted an engagement ring, after exacting his promise to touch no liquor for six months. Between pictures, in April of 1928, the last month of his abstemiousness, he had boarded a train for New York, telephoned Michael and told her he urgently needed to talk to her. She was about to leave for the theater with her son Leonard and asked John to drop in afterward.

When Katie, the Irish maid whom the couple had employed for years, admitted John to the chicly styled apartment on Beekman Place, overlooking the East River, Michael had not yet come home. She swept in a few minutes later, eyed John coolly and exclaimed: "My God, you've gotten gray!"

"I haven't any such thing," John protested. "It's the crazy lights you've got. You always did have funny ideas about lamps."

They were on the verge of bickering, just like old times, when Michael sank into a chair, laughing, and John laughed with her.

239

"Well," she said, "you really have improved. You've got back your sense of humor. The change has done you good."

When he somewhat nervously broached the subject of his visit, Michael, showing no resentment whatever, assured him that she would set him free at the earliest possible moment. "I must admit," John said later, "that her absolute unconcern shocked me a bit. It seemed rather immoral for *her* to be quite so indifferent." The fact was that Michael had already decided in Harrison Tweed's favor.

Michael opened a bottle of champagne and they sat drinking and laughing at the past and at themselves until the small hours. As they parted, John said: "It's been the greatest evening we ever spent together."

"It has indeed. I never knew you were such an agreeable, entertaining person."

"You really are charming. I wonder why we never found this out about each other."

"We'll never know. . . . Well, so long. Watch your step."

Michael's marriage to Tweed took place that year and John maintained the friendliest relations with both husband and wife.

During his brief stay in New York John saw something of his daughter for the first time since London. He also spent part of every day at Ned Sheldon's bedside. In addition to total immobility, his friend's field of vision was beginning to contract. Before leaving New York John wrote:

Dear, dear Uncle Ned:

I enjoyed the beautiful grapes very much and ate them one at a time. I was the more grateful for them as I am rather lonely at present, my father being such a business man—though not liking same very much, as I can hear him saying things to himself in the next room which no maiden monkey should hear. I have a feeling I shall get used to it in time, and also when he is not a business man he can be very pleasant and takes me out much more, and gives me a bath with eau de cologne, though why I cannot imagine, and lets me sit on his head while he plays the self-player piano to himself and myself.

I wish to again tender you, dear Uncle Ned, my great obligations for your kindness in the matter of grapes. I shall close now with much love and kisses.

From your ever loving niece,
Clementine Barrymore

From the westbound train came another letter.

Dear, dear Ned,

It was too divine seeing you. . . . You would love the porter. He is black as ink, rather stout—and has a gray pointed beard. He is a dead ringer for Othello, and has what you would call an old world courtesy. . . .

It is too fantastic to think that after we had talked— occasionally about myself if I remember—that we had been separated for more than a week—we felt just the same— like a divine room in the top of the house where the sun always comes in and where one went to play as a little boy when one wanted to be alone.

You have no idea how much good it did talking to you. The burrs fell out of my whiskers and must be all over the floor. . . .

Diana is adorable, and the three of us will have such fun as she grows up or gets larger, as she is quite grown up enough as she is. . . .

Ever so much love, dear Ned. It was great.

Jack

A third letter followed concerning Krishnamurti, who had set off on a global journey via Chicago and New York. John felt that his two friends had a great deal to give each other. As Eric Barnes put it, "Traveling different roads, both men had found truth in a realm outside the narrowly circumscribed self. Krishnamurti had found his way through the age-old traditions of Oriental thought. Sheldon reached the goal by the lonely path of suffering."

Dear, dear Ned [John wrote in June 1928],

. . . I gave Krishnamurti a letter to you yesterday. He is a charming person but rather shy. Coming through Chicago the newspapers and a lot of absurd women strewed his path with roses and hailed him as Messiah. . . . He is a grand little soul and I think you will adore him.

Ever so much love,
Jack

The meeting of the Hindu and the bedridden playwright proved as fruitful as John had hoped. For Ned, Krishnamurti, who thereafter seldom passed through New York without visiting him, opened the door to an appreciation of Eastern philosophy, religion and mysticism, while from Ned he received a confirmation of his belief in the power of the spirit to transcend materiality.

Some years later, in Santa Barbara, Krishnamurti was descanting upon this "possibility of a person rising completely above and beyond one's physical being to a serene and lofty plane, where the pains and turmoil of one's body were non-existent." He had known only one person in his life, he noted, who proved capable of so doing —"a friend in New York." Who but Ned Sheldon?

The marriage was solemnized on November 14, 1928, by a Unitarian clergyman, the Reverend Theodore Abel, in the rose-bowered living room of Mrs. Costello's new home in Beverly Hills. Helene Costello served as maid of honor, Lionel Barrymore as best man. The bride's father did not attend. When the minister pronounced the words "for richer, for poorer," John repeated in a stage whisper: "For richer! For richer!"

The ceremony was preceded by the kind of melodramatics beloved of audiences during the early phase of John's theater career. The day before, "a mysterious woman, heavily veiled and expensively dressed," as one newspaper described her, confronted the Deputy County Clerk of the Los Angeles marriage-license bureau and warned him against issuing a license to John Barrymore lest he commit an official blunder, for his marriage to Michael Strange had not been dissolved. In short, the prospective bridegroom was contemplating bigamy. The woman refused to identify herself. "For your further information," she added, "I will say that I know Barrymore received a telegram today from Mrs. Barrymore announcing that she had no intention of obtaining a final decree." The mysterious veiled one then disappeared, her name and motive forever an enigma.

As the nation's press carried the story under piquant headlines, Dolores calmly told reporters: "Mr. Barrymore asked me to marry him. For that reason I believed, and still believe, that he is legally free to marry," and John commented: "Even in this superb climate there are crazy people."

The brouhaha subsided when Michael, by then vacationing abroad, was heard from. Under New York divorce laws the only grounds available to her had been adultery. Not to create a scandal that might damage John's career as well as her own, she had attempted secrecy by journeying upstate to the town of Kingston and filing for divorce there as "Mrs. John Blythe." She had received her final decree on August 14. The documents detailing John's transgressions were sealed.

The contractual obligations of John at United Artists and Dolores at Warner Brothers precluded an immediate honeymoon. Not until January of the following year were they at liberty. They lived meanwhile at Bella Vista, upon whose enlargement and beautification John continued compulsively to expend huge sums on an enterprise that would never end.

They asked Michael if Diana might not spend the summer at Bella Vista. The child begged to go, wept, threatened to throw herself out of a window. Michael refused.

"The only time I received a show of affection from my mother was immediately after she hurt me," Diana recalled in later life. "It was always the slap and then the kiss."

Maurice Costello had taken a modest house lower down on Tower Road. Though relations with his daughter and son-in-law remained hostile, they did not let him live in want. "My family live just up the hill," Maurice said. "I can see their home from here. I often look up there. If the pillows in my car could speak, they would tell you a great story. I used to drive into the hills and cry myself to sleep. Sometimes I would take a newspaper and read myself to sleep. Sometimes I cried myself out of the idea of murder. I would wake up there in the hills and look at the sunshine and decide this was better than San Quentin, that after all John was not worth murdering."

The newlyweds began their belated honeymoon at San Pedro on December 29. It lasted almost three months. The *Mariner* was now skippered by Otto Matthies, a powerfully built, phlegmatic man of forty, who had forsworn liquor, tobacco and profanity upon receiving what he believed to have been a mystical revelation.

While John filled page after page of the ship's log with descriptive writing, Dolores kept a journal of her own. "Dec. 30, 1928 . . . Aboard the S.S. *Virginia* [sailing from San Pedro] on our own dear honeymoon. We are to meet our own dear yacht The Mariner at Balboa, C.Z.—"

John had instructed Matthies to take the yacht ahead to the Canal Zone, there to see to any needed repairs and replenish her stores.

"From there we are going on a fishing trip—expect to stop at Ecuador—Cocus Island—and Galapagos. I am thrilled to death—It is such fun spending a vacation of almost three months away from everybody with some one you worship."

Still aboard the *Virginia*, Dolores picked up her diarist's pen again on January 4.

"Winkie and I spent the whole day in our own rooms [Like John and Michael Strange, they called each other by the same nicknames.] —had lunch on our verandah and read—We didn't go up at all—It was a sweet lazy day. . . .

"*January 5.* My darling and I didn't get on deck until after 4 o'clock (Stayed with him in the Barber shop until he had had a shave —I adore being with him always. . . . I adore my Egg.—We watched the Masque Ball for a while—this evening—then we came down to our cabin. I adore my Egg—I love in him everything.

"*January 6.* Went for a swim today in the ships pool—It was sweet to look up and find my own dear Winkie watching her [referring to herself in the third person]. He had ordered her lunch to be served on their own verandah—It's been a heavenly day. . . . We arrive at Balboa tomorrow. . . ."

They devoted the next two days to a tour of the city. Dolores temporarily lifted her ban against drinking and they both partook, in moderate amounts, of cocktails, wine, beer and other alcoholic potables. (Later, when John reverted to excessive indulgence, Captain Matthies, like his predecessor, learned to keep liquor supplies under lock and key.)

"*January 8.* Winkie and I both love this place—We have the dearest Suite at the Hotel So old fashioned. . . ."

They set out to sea again the next day.

"*January 10.* Sailed along Panamanian coast—had a sweet day, dropping anchor at Bahia Honda about 10 P.M. . . . The phosphorus on the water tonight was the most exquisite thing one would want to see—The water looked like a black Heaven filled with the brightest stars."

"*January 11.* . . . Went ashore on the most beautiful island [Aquerita near the Colombian coast]. It has a lovely beach—Winkie and I want to buy it—We would call it Paradise Island. . . .

"*January 12.* Got up early to go alligator hunting a native played guide all dressed in his best clothes but in the most ridiculous hat I've ever seen We went up some small rivers—only saw one which Winkie shot—it sunk—so didn't get it—used my little Parker for first time—(Shot one eagle—which we are having mounted). Got a curlew with first shot and made my Winkie and Otto very proud of me

—Winkie shot two curlews & a Kingfisher—we are going to have the curlews for dinner tomorrow night.

"*January 13.* What a divine day!!—Otto rowed us ashore in the Skiff for a bath. I don't believe any two people spent such a Honeymoon—As soon as Otto left us—we took off our bathing suits & had our bath in the most heavenly small deep pool in a mountain stream—ending in a waterfall—have never giggled so much or been so happy —The natives were washing the laundry from the boat at the end of the stream—They gave us a dried cocanut shell to pour water to rinse ourselves. We later visited them in their huts—Had dinner on deck while the sun was setting. Had shark hook off stern got an enormous one. . . ." (A fourteen-footer which John harpooned.)

Here John caught some trout and taught Dolores to fish and shoot.

"*January 14.* Left the most beautiful place in the world— 9 AM —for Cocus Island [Isla del Coco, off the Costa Rican coast]—Slept most of the day—saw a few enormous porpoises playing at the bow. Winkie and I went below for awhile—I love him more today than ever if thats possible—He is a darling. . . .

"*January 15.* My Winkie and I didn't wake up until about 10 o'clock—expect to reach Cocus Island sometime tomorrow afternoon.

"Peculiar how one forgets what they do during the day while on the sea. Its heavenly. . . .

"*January 16.* Chatham Bay. Anchored Cocas Island—7 P.M.— Fished off the side of big boat after dinner—Winkie caught huge fish —Fought like mad—Winkie got into skiff—but he wound himself around anchor chain—so got away. I caught a Blue stripe Golden snoper and small Rock Bass—Sailors forward caught baby shark— 2 feet. My darling looks like the brownest Hindu and I worship my dear husband.

"*January 17.* Cocos Island [arriving finally at the correct spelling]. This has been one exciting day. Sailors called Winkie about 8 o'clock this A.M. They had seen a ray. My darling and Otto went after it in the small boat—After Otto harpooned it Winkie shot it 8 times—after they got him in dozens of small sharks came around and one large one which we got a little later. I went out with my darling Otto and Eric [a crew member] for the shark. It was thrilling—He weighed about 1700 pounds—16 ft. long. The ray weighed about one ton and was 18 ft. across. This is an extraordinary Island—It seems enchanted—very green—and has many small water falls—one beautiful cascade. Heaps of chick goonies [baby albatrosses] with the whitest feathers—in their nests on the rocks. The birds haven't any fear of people—The crew is grand—had divine talk with Cook today Says instinct is only a word—It explains nothing—But I love my dearest husband—that I know.

"*January 19*. Went ashore again this AM on Chatham Bay side of Island. Had heaps of fun. Winkie took a shower in the most marvelous Water-fall we've ever seen—all sorts of dates and names carved on rocks by old Pirate Ships found date today 1829 my darling carved our initials in beautiful cocanut tree carved Sweet Cat under it—Otto carved Mariner in another one—Went fishing in afternoon— caught my first wahoo [a large, swift game fish] about 25 lbs.—More sharks—Winkie and Otto killed another—10 ft. about. . . .

"*January 20*. Left Cocos Island. 8:30 AM. I will miss the beautiful fragrance that comes off shore—settled down to read Zane Grey's 'Tales of Fishing Virgin Seas.' Some rather interesting things in it (Interesting because they're about the places we've been and Galapagos) but he writes like Horatio Alger. . . .

"*January 21*. . . . thought of Mama & Helene a lot. Slept for ages on deck after lunch. So did my own darling but he slept in the Cabin—Came up with about two more inches of his hair cut off and looks like The Sweetest 'Salty' Mariner—

"*January 22*. 10 PM. . . . Its heavenly to sit on deck with the one you love and read and laze around. . . . My darling is up on deck and loveing it. Winkie has just called me to take my first peak at the Galapagos Islands [the southernmost point of their voyage]. The moon is out.

"*January 23*. Woke to find ourselves in Darwin Bay—Tower Island. . . . Otto seemed a bit leery about being there as the wind was against us & not a good anchorage. (We draw 14 ft.) So my darling & I spent another day just reading—taking pictures & loveing each other."

They tarried longest, from January 24 to February 6, among the islands of the Galapagos archipelago, going ashore at Albemarle, Indefatigable, Eden, Seymour and Chatham Islands, where they explored, fished, hunted, photographed and collected fauna. "I love this life and I adore my darling. . . . It all sums up to the fact that I love my Winkie. . . .

"*February 2*. . . . We went ashore at dusk took the seine made quite a haul of mullets—after dark many turtles came on the beach one gigantic one about 5 feet—Winkie rode him until he got into the water. . . .

"February 3. Left Seymour Island anchorage 5:45 AM. Arrived Chatham Island 3 PM.—My darling & Otto & I went ashore—were met by a dizzy Ecuadorian who spoke French—& My Wink surprised me very much by being very apt at the language—We brought him back to the boat and gave him a drink. . . .

"February 8. . . . My own Winkie looks like Huckleberry Finn with Funny knives very elaborately attached to his belt. . . ."

On February 10 the *Mariner* put in at Guayaquil, the principal port of Ecuador. "Many came up to the yacht to see us. . . . They took photographs for newspapers. . . .

"February 11. Found it almost impossible to get out of hotel. huge crowds. Many girls came to our room—With presents After I had told one Noisy one I can't speak Spanish I used many gestures that my darling was asleep, hoping she would desist She made more noise to make him get up. Which he didn't do right away, so she walked in the Bedroom to see him—

"February 12. . . . The theatre owners gave a dinner for us. The Hotel was packed never known to have done such business as it was during their carnival their idea of fun was to spray you with a perfume which contained Ether—a gay night in Guayaquil didn't get to bed until after two Must get up at 5 a.m.—"

From Guayaquil, John and Dolores traveled inland by train to Quito, the capital.

"February 15. My Lambs birthday. The crowds were so great when we arrived at the Hotel last night that the Manager asked us to go to the balconey. . . . Very cold—here. Altitude so great one can hardly walk went to bed about 6 I felt mean only hope my darlings Birthday will be happier next year.

"February 19 [back in Guayaquil]. . . . Winkie and I made our appearance in the Theatre in Eve—They showed—'Beau Brummel' We didn't watch the picture for Winkie is a dear considerate thing—The Theatre had never been crowded before & My darling's Spanish speech was great. . . .

"February 20. Packed . . . We sailed at 3 P.M. Its great fun to think of being alone again with my Jiggie Wink. The crew had celebrated to such an extent their last night ashore that Otto cooked our dinner. Winkie & I set the table. . . .

"February 24. My darling and I are married three months today and I only hope it will be for all our lives—

"February 26. . . . My darling has been drawing lovely pictures of Ecuadorian Indians. . . ."

And buying *tsantsas*, human heads shrunken by Jivaro tribes-men.

"*February 28.* My darling is beautifully tanned & looks mar-velous. . . .

"*March 1.* Up at 6 AM. My darling and I off for the alligator hunt. . . . got out of launch up the [Biana] river—& walked along shore—plenty mud. sank to the tops of our boots & my egg slipped & slipped & eventually landed *all* four limbs in the Air—trying to save the gun from getting muddy. Scared but he looked so funny couldn't resist laughing. Saw oodles of gators—Winkie shot 6 (I shot one with him) but only recovered three—others in 'mucho agua' first one about 16 feet long.—Left them for the natives to skin came back to boat about 6 PM, very very tired and muddy.

"*March 2.* Went to get the skins early this AM and found much to our annoyance & disappointment the tail of the largest gator miss-ing. They explained that a saw fish had gotten it while they were working on the head—so decided to hunt another—found three huge ones laying in deep mud. My lamb shot two and I shot my first alli-gator he measured just 14 ft. 6 in. [When stuffed and mounted, he would occupy a prominent place in the trophy room at Bella Vista.] . . .

"back to Balboa in the Morning—Hope their will be a cable from Momie.

So to Bed—"

In addition, Dolores and John kept a joint honeymoon diary for the later delectation of Mrs. Costello.

"Dearest Mama darling," Dolores began aboard the ship taking them to Balboa. "This is the first day of the New Year and we spent it sweetly and thought about you and Helene a lot. We are terribly happy. And I adore Winkie. . . ."

To which John appended a sketch of Happy Hooligan and a post-script: "Mama darling—The sea air is doing your bastard son in law a lot of good and Winkie Dink is the belle of the boat—much love B.S."

Next day, John: "Winkie wore her red dress and funny red shoes and looked like the meanest cherry in a Manhattan cocktail and terribly sweet—& absurdly young—We met two nice people friends of Jack Dempsey's we like better than anyone else on the boat—"

"Ditto!!!" Dolores added. "This is a divine life—it's a balmy night— I only hope Mama will take a long trip and have heaps of fun—"

January 3. Dolores: "Winkie darling has astonished me—He has asked me to dance both last night & tonight. He dances divinely. (I don't understand why he loathes it). . . ."

John: "Fat Mama—There is only one on this boat who dances as well as me—He back heeled his wife three times just as if he didn't know her! and climbed up Winkie as if she was a cliff with daisies on top of it. A Fat Man out of your past asked about you. . . . Winkie is a happy cat—I think!"

January 5. Dolores: "Dearest Mama—I have just made a discovery! Not liking Champagne etc.—I have found I like Moselblumchen very much. . . ."

"Only [John writes] she doesn't like Moselblumchen as much as she thinks—after 3 drinks of it! It is principally satisfied curiosity—! She is a dear egg and every one adores her—"

January 6. John: "Have just packed Winkie's two douche pans and given her a bite on the nose. . . ."

January 9. John: "Sailed away from harbor today for Galapagos. . . . Big crowd to see us off. They are all crazy about Winkie and call her 'Doloreth' and call me 'Don Juan' which will hand you a good laugh!"

January 10. John: ". . . We are certainly two absolute bums and this is certainly the life for us! The small egg is very happy I think—I love her more and more every day. . . ."

January 11. John: "This is absolutely the Paradise of the World [Bahia Honda]. I've never seen anything like it anywhere. Winkie is a grand fisherwoman!"

January 12. John: "I got up early to go alligator hunting. . . . Had shock of my life today when Winkie brought down a big bird we had for dinner with the first shot she ever had with a shot gun— I thought Otto would fall off the boat—he laughed so!"

January 13. Dolores: ". . . had our bath in the most heavenly small deep pool in a mountain stream ending in a water fall. I have never giggled so much or been so happy."

John: "You would have died to day seeing Winkie bathing in that stream. The natives have never seen a blonde and can't get over Winkie. . . ."

January 14. Dolores: "Miss mother and Helene terribly—Have been calling Winkie Mama for the last two days. . . . Pulled out of that heavenly place to day [Cocos Island]—feel sure we will all be there some day together. It is really enchanted. . . ."

John: "Winkie slept on and off all day on deck and looks like a little brown duck egg—"

January 18. John: "The small egg is sleeping on deck in the moonlight—curled up with its head on its' hand and looks about seven. She had a grand day. We went ashore on this Enchanted Island with long water falls all over it falling like white-silk ribbons into the sea about three hundred feet high. It is really glorious—We all have to come here some day—She caught lots of fish but the sharks got the big ones so we are going to get Mama a fish big enough to put in the dining room! She insists upon catching it herself!!"

Dolores: "I miss you & Helene terribly. Will get you a big fish yet."

January 19. John: "We tried to skin Winkie's Wahoo this evening—(that doesn't sound right somehow!!)—but the skin was too thin so we are waiting till she gets a bigger one for Mama's Dining Room. Gee—we had a good time to day—"

January 20. Dolores: "Winkie & I have been planning a marvelous Coconut Palm House . . . with you & Helene running all the nigger slaves—Then at last Helene could be the Queen of an Island. . . ."

January 24. Dolores: "Albamarle! . . . Went ashore again on other part of Island, found whole family of Sea Lions—the largest one (the father I presume) scratched his ear with his flipper in the most unconcerned manner. Winkie caught Tuna, but shark got all but his head. . . ."

January 25. Dolores: ". . . had lunch on the beach with the Iguanas, cormorants a huge Sea Lion. . . ."

January 30. Dolores: I hooked & landed 150 lb. shark—Winkie & I love this life—I only hope Mama & Helene have gone to Cuba & are having a marvelous time—I miss them terribly."

On March 17 John and Dolores ended the happiest journey they would ever take together.

If John sought guidance from Helios and astrology, as he probably did, before switching from Warner Brothers to United Artists, he was sadly misled. What the studio boss, Joseph Schenck, offered John seemed at first blush a far more lucrative arrangement—$200,000 for two films plus a percentage of the net—but it proved far less so because United took two years to complete the two films whereas at Warner Brothers, though John earned only $75,000 per film, he made three in one year, devoting no more than a few weeks to any of them, for a total of $225,000. What the Warner payments really came to was about $10,000 every week that John worked as against $2,000 at United. The United contract, moreover, omitted some of the fringe benefits John had enjoyed at Warners, such as hotel expenses and a chauffeured limousine. As for a percentage of the profits, Schenck reported none from either film.

Assuming John also consulted Helios when United submitted the scripts for his approval, she failed him again. The first film, *The Beloved Vagabond*, met a dismal fate at box offices as well as at the hands of critics. The second film, *Tempest* (scenario by Erich von Stroheim), a romance set against the background of the Russian revolution, did not fare much better. John played Ivan Markov, the young son of poor peasants, who is granted an officer's commission in the Imperial Army, falls in love with Princess Tamara and rescues her from a Bolshevik mob. The concluding screen title read: "Out of the tempest comes an enduring love and life begins anew."

As Ivan, John had the looks and physique of a man in his twenties. He was then forty-six. The illusion was created in part by the combined efforts of a makeup artist and Charles Rosher, one of Hollywood's deftest cameramen and the inventor of the Rosher Kino Portrait Lens, whose soft focus smoothed away the erosions of age. Theretofore cameramen had tended to favor John's celebrated profile. ("The right side of my face looks like a fried egg. The left side has features that are to be found in the face of almost any normal anthropological specimen, and those are the apples I try to keep on top of the barrel. If you see the right side of my face in a movie, you may be perfectly sure that there are stout steel wires attached to my protesting body and that a sixty horsepower donkey is being used to pull me into focus.") But Rosher with his magic lens flatteringly photographed John full face.

"I was the only one who could get him on the set," Rosher recalled. "He was half-stiff from drink most of the time. He used to get me in his dressing room to drink Napoleon brandy with him; I used to pour it surreptitiously into a flower vase." Rosher neglected to note that, however drunk John may have appeared before or after work, the moment he stepped in front of the camera self-control took over and he performed without a fumble.

To titillate prospective audiences for *Tempest*, a studio publicist

sowed rumors of a romance between John and his German leading lady, Camilla Horn, actually Schenck's mistress. John, who
scorned press-agentry and, unlike most Hollywood stars, never employed a personal glorifier, spoiled the game by ungallantly explaining to a covey of reporters: "Camilla is a delightful girl with a big
appetite. When she eats, it lasts forever. The reason she looked so
fragile in *Faust* was that Murnau* put her in corners and made her
think of sad things like virtue."

When detained late at United, John sometimes spent the night in
the nearby apartment complex which the studio maintained for the
convenience of its personnel. On one such occasion his next-door neigh-
bor was the screen siren Carmen Myers. The following morning, running into Schenck, Miss Myers complained that her sleep had been
disturbed by the sound of John's penetrating voice pleading with
somebody to embrace him. Like all Hollywood moguls of that epoch,
Schenck knew how adversely a public scandal involving a star could
affect the box office. He sent for John. "I am informed," he said,
"that you had a dame in your apartment last night." Hanging his
head, John pleaded guilty. But perhaps Schenck would care to meet
the dame in question? He led him to his suite. There, dangling from
a chandelier by her tail, was Clementine. As John spoke to her in
the kind of loving language Miss Myers had overhead, the simian
leaped into his arms.

John agreed to make a third film for $150,000 and a profit-
sharing bonus. This was *Eternal Love*. Charles Rosher photographed it and it was directed by the German wunderkind Ernst
Lubitsch, whose famed "Lubitsch touch" would impart froth and
sparkle to such entertainments as *The Student Prince*, *The Merry
Widow*, *Ninotchka*. His biographer, Herman Weinberg, defined the
Lubitsch touch by analogy to a sign that hung in the men's restroom
of the renowned Budapest Club: "Members may not bring their mistresses unless they are the wives of other members." But *Eternal
Love*, the last silent film for both director and star, provided meager
scope for the Lubitsch touch. A soggy tale of Swiss lovers who perish
together in an avalanche, it took a critical drubbing and once again
Joseph Schenck claimed a net loss.

By July 1929 Dolores was expecting her first child. John
wanted a son, but what concerned him more was whether her film

---

* F. W. Murnau, a German director.

career might not interfere with the obligations of motherhood and domesticity. He consulted Helios. His "court astrologer," never having drawn up Dolores' horoscope, referred him to the astrological material in his library for the general astral influences affecting a woman born, like Dolores, on September 17, under the sign of Virgo. To his relief, he read that such women were by nature homebodies, affectionate, maternal, preferring the peaceful quiet of country life to the hurly-burly of the city. If happily married, they could be expected to anticipate their husbands' every comfort—to have, for example, the husband's slippers warming before the fireplace when he came home from work.

With the unborn child in mind, John sold the *Mariner* and for $225,000 bought a bigger yacht, naming it the *Infanta*. A steel, diesel-powered, twin-screw vessel with a cruising speed of twelve knots, she measured 120 feet from stem to stern. In the master stateroom John set up a mahogany bed with a gold-threaded design and mirror glass and a hand-painted Italian landscape on the headboard. Other installations included a glassed-in sun deck, a library with wood-burning fireplace and boxes of soil in which to grow mint for juleps.

20

Talkies

====

As the trim, slight figure—so much slighter than his movie image—stepped in front of the Winter Garden's gigantic screen to introduce what was to follow, a murmur of surprise and delight greeted him.

The occasion was the New York première, on November 20, 1929, of *Show of Shows*, Warner Brothers' contribution to a brand of entertainment then the vogue among the major Hollywood studios. A movie composed of a great diversity of vaudeville acts, it utilized seventy-seven stars and more than 200 chorus boys and girls. Frank Fay served as master of ceremonies, Irene Bordoni sang "Just an Hour of Love," the retired French heavyweight prizefighter Georges Carpentier danced with a bevy of showgirls, Dolores Costello—billed as "The Belle of the Box Office"—and her sister, Helene, appeared in a song-and-dance routine featuring all the sister teams currently available in Hollywood.

John's appearance in the flesh was sandwiched between Ted Lewis tootling his trumpet on the screen and Rin-Tin-Tin barking. What came next was John's first cinematic talking role, that of the crookbacked, homidical Duke of Gloucester (later Richard III). Wearing black armor and clutching a severed head, he delivered the Act III Scene 2 soliloquy from Shakespeare's *Henry VI, Part Three*, beginning:

254

Ay, Edward will use women honorably.
Would he were wasted, marrow, bones and all,
That from his loins no hopeful branch may spring,
To cross me from the golden time I look for! . . .

"Of all the footage of prismatic [Technicolor] and black and white material," wrote Mordaunt Hall, "the most compelling stretch is given over to John Barrymore's magnificent delivery. . . . it impressed one with the marvelous control of his facial features and with his ability to deal out the full effect of the role." But in the eyes of devout Shakespeareans who had hailed John as the greatest Hamlet of his generation the *Show of Shows* bit served only as a reminder that he had sold his theatrical birthright for a mess of Hollywood pottage.

The advent of sound film wrecked the careers of stars like John Gilbert, whose natural voice was thin and reedy, while John, with his Carrington-trained vocal organs that could resonate like thunder or float whispered tones to the farthermost seat in the largest movie palaces, attained new heights of popularity. His first full-length talking picture was *General Crack*, the acronymic nom de guerre of Prince Christian Rudolph Augustus Christopher Ketlar, a fictional warrior and Lothario of early-eighteenth-century Austria who dethrones King Leopold II and makes off with an archduchess.

Leopold was impersonated by Lowell Sherman, a stage and screen luminary renowned for his enactments of unctuous villainy. "Be cruel, but elegant" was Sherman's prescription for maltreating women on camera. "Lift your eyebrows thus—while you lift the club. After you have berated them, meet their reproaches with an icy, inscrutable, irritating smile. When you have them in your power, which takes about five minutes, hurt their feelings continually, but suavely, delicately, elegantly. Scrutinize them through your monocle, then tell them they are not looking well. But smile."

Not long after the filming of *General Crack*, Sherman married Helene Costello. He and John came to detest each other. They seldom exchanged a civil word. Sherman forbade Helene to visit Dolores. "He was born a hundred years after his time," said John. "His manners and his wit were in a class by themselves. We were the best of friends until he became an in-law, then something happened. God knows what."

One thing that happened disrupted a party at Bella Vista during which the guests, Sherman among them, consumed oceans of liquor. In the course of the evening John, surrounded by admirers, fell to reciting passages from *Hamlet*. Suddenly Sherman, nose out of joint, broke in, shouting: "To hell with you and Hamlet!" John lurched toward him. Reiterating the blasphemy, Sherman fled into the night with John in furious pursuit through shrubbery and brambles, across flower beds, over fences. At length Sherman outran him and, doubling his tracks, returned to the party. When John failed to reappear, the guests fanned out in search of him. They found him, clothes tattered, passed out by a hedge.

Under John's new Warner Brothers contract, his right of approval extended to the costumes. Forced to respect the clause, Sherman grudgingly sent his dresser to John with the crown he was to wear as Leopold II. John inspected it carefully, pulled a sour face and said: "Tell my brother-in-law that I think his crown looks like a paper basket in a third-rate roominghouse, but I okay it, for nothing could be more appropriate than for him to stick his head into it."

Sickness forced John to suspend the filming of *General Crack*. Complaining of severe stomach pains, he was rushed to a hospital, where X-rays showed a duodenal ulcer. The doctor prescribed rest and a diet restricted to bland foods and liquids. For a patient who had so abused his body with alcohol and nicotine, the wonder was that he had reached the age of forty-seven without contracting any serious malady. He was back at work within two weeks, still ailing but unchastened, chain-smoking and drinking as before.

During the summer of 1929 Winston Churchill, pausing in Los Angeles during a tour of the United States after five arduous years as Chancellor of the Exchequer, visited the set of *The Man from Blankley's*, a farce in which John played a sottish, hiccuping British peer. Ignoring the studio stars and executives, John piloted his sister Ethel's erstwhile suitor past the entire awe-struck company to introduce to him a Welsh woman bit player, a Barrymore mascot known as Tiny Jones, who at John's insistence was cast in many of his films. Churchill had to bend low to shake hands with Tiny, for she stood only four feet five inches tall and weighed sixty-two pounds. That evening the actor and the statesman copiously wined and dined by themselves.

John's third film under his new Warner contract was a talking remake of *The Sea Beast*, now titled *Moby Dick*. John, as always, relished any opportunity to simulate physical suffering, insanity, death throes, whatever required him to deform his body and uglify his face, and moviegoers were chilled to the marrow by Ahab's screams of agony as he endured the cauterization of his severed leg. "Give them more torture," said John. "The public loves torture."

In the role of Esther Wiscasset, Joan Bennett replaced Dolores, who was pregnant. John chose as her obstetrician a highly reputed Dr. John Vruwink, and required him to visit her at least once a day. A few weeks before the baby was expected, John, in a paroxysm of jealousy, told the doctor as he was leaving the house: * "Good night and *goodbye*, you son of a bitch. Don't come back. If I ever find you in this house again I'll break your goddam jaw," and to his stunned wife he explained: "I don't want him around here because he's stuck on you and I don't want anybody stuck on you touching you, especially the way this guy has to touch you."

The seizure shortly subsided and Vruwink continued to attend Dolores, who entered the Cedars of Lebanon Hospital for her confinement. John took an adjacent room and every day after the last take would hurry to her side, not even stopping long enough to remove his makeup, which, as he described it, made him look "like something out of a sunken barge in the Erie Canal." Hospital staff members were somewhat discomposed when they ran unexpectedly into a disheveled, grimy apparition striding the corridors. One evening John, his face and seaman's garb stained with synthetic whale's blood, happened upon a young man whose fatherhood was also imminent. At the gory sight the young man blanched. "You look as if you needed a drink," said John.

"It'll take more than a drink," said the young man. He was, John learned, the son of President Herbert Hoover, who called Prohibition "a great social and economic experiment, noble in motive."

On April 8, 1930, an exceptionally long shooting session left John so depleted that after looking in on Dolores he went to his room and fell sound asleep. A nurse shortly roused him to announce the arrival of a daughter. John uttered the single word, "Splendid," and relapsed into slumber.

The newcomer was christened Dolores Ethel Mae Barrymore and nicknamed "Squeegee" (and later "Dede"). John sent the date and hour of her birth to the London astrologer Llewellyn George, whom he acclaimed as "the boss horoscope cockalorum of the world." Back came the prediction and a bill for $50: "Her life will be devoted to artistic pursuits, probably the stage."

---

* According to what the playwright and director Garson Kanin, in his book of reminiscences, says John told him several years later.

At the age of two Dede received a letter together with a caricature from an old English friend of John's.

Dear little Miss Dolores—

Your father tells me that a work of mine "nestles between Sargent and Zuloaga" [probably the Sargent drawing of John as Hamlet and the Spanish painter's Hamlet-like portrait of Michael Strange], and I suppose he is telling me the truth (as I hope you will always do when you are old enough to tell things). So here am I nestling between those two gentlemen. I used to live in London and I knew Mr. Sargent quite well. But I never lived in Madrid and have never met Mr. Zuloaga. I have here guessed at Mr. Zuloaga. I hope that when you are old enough to guess at people, you will refuse to do so, and I hope that, when you are old enough to read, you won't read this letter. If you did, you might say to yourself "Things are not worth reading. All my labor has been in vain."

I like the look of you in your photograph so much that I venture to sign myself,

Yours Affectionately

Max Beerbohm

Rapallo—1932*

John had written to Darryl Zanuck, then an associate producer at Warner Brothers: ". . . for our next picture . . . am willing to play the title role in Peter Ibbetson . . . provided that my wife, Dolores Costello, plays the part of the Duchess of Towers."

Warners declined, but the role they offered John instead, adapted, like *Peter Ibbetson*, from a novel by George du Maurier, could hardly have suited him better. This was Svengali, the beetling, black-bearded Hungarian Jew, musician and hypnotist, under whose sinister dominion the lovely, docile little Trilby blossoms into a great singer. Beerbohm Tree had triumphed as Svengali on the British stage, while in America Wilton Lackaye had played him with notable success.

In September 1930, before starting work on *Svengali* (the novel was entitled *Trilby*), his twenty-seventh film, John took his wife and five-month-old daughter on a cruise aboard the *Infanta* south to Central America. He had converted a cabin adjoining the master state

*By permission of Mrs. Eva Reichmann.

room into a nursery with a pink-and-white crib, the corners rounded to minimize the risk of injury to the occupant during heavy seas. Clamped to the floorboards of the dining salon, beside Dolores' place, was a highchair with wells in the tray to hold steady Aunt Ethel's christening gift of a silver spoon and the matching porringer from Uncle Lionel. A special refrigerating system had been installed for the infant's food. In anticipation of her first steps, John enclosed part of the main deck with wire mesh.

A baby's nurse and a doctor accompanied the seafarers. It was John, as it happened, who needed a doctor's services. Off the coast of Guatemala his ulcer flared up, producing gastric bleeding. The doctor and a specialist from the mainland brought him out of danger, but during the entire voyage home he was confined to his bed.

As soon as he regained his strength he flung himself into the role of Svengali with a gusto unequaled since his Jekyll-and-Hyde. Marian Marsh, a picture-pretty blonde, proved less than affecting as the malleable heroine, and Bramwell Fletcher as her distraught suitor, the Paris art student Little Billee, raised no emotional temperatures either. All in all, the film lacked the romantic Victorian glow of the original. But John's performance, aided by makeup and photographic wizardry, belongs among his half-dozen greatest screen characterizations.

Whenever John's Svengali exerted his mesmeric power over poor Trilby, the irises would fade from his eyes, leaving gaping white holes, a makeup trick that sent shudders coursing through the audience. In one memorable sequence a far-off clock strikes midnight as Svengali, alone in his musty quarters, begins to cast his spell. The camera focuses at first on the gaunt, bearded face with its blank white orbs, then travels out the window, over the rooftops of Paris, finally, in a distant part of the city, enters Trilby's room and there holds her image in close-up as she succumbs again to Svengali's will.

The last scene takes place in a tawdry Cairo café where Svengali, down on his luck, his heart weak, has brought his bewitched protégée. As he strives to maintain his control over Trilby, who is entertaining the café's rough clientele with a rendition of "Sweet Alice, Ben Bolt," he falls dying to the floor. At that instant her voice breaks, she collapses.

For the fifth and last film John owed Warner Brothers they wanted something like *Svengali*. The resulting flimsy scenario, set against a background of Russia and the ballet, was *The Mad Genius*.

The title refers to a club-footed, Svengali-like puppeteer named Tsarakov, whose deformity has frustrated his longing to become a *danseur noble*. In Fedor, a youth who has run away from a tyrannical father (played by Boris Karloff), Tsarakov finds a male Trilby. Under the puppeteer's tutelage Fedor evolves into another Njinsky and conquers all Europe. But Tsarakov, now jealous of his pupil, schemes to wreck his career and to turn against him the ballerina he loves. Before Tsarakov can wreak destruction upon both young lives, his assistant, a drug addict, kills him.

The critics reacted to *The Mad Genius* pretty much as they had to *Svengali*. They found little to commend in either the drama itself or the supporting cast, but they lauded John's portrayal.

The box-office returns from John's recent films, the Warner accountants concluded, scarcely justified the thumping sums he had been paid, and after *The Mad Genius*, a commercial flop, the studio did not tender a new contract with the same attractive terms. John, in fact, never appeared in another Warner film, nor did he ever equal his 1931 income of $460,500. But by dint of completing eleven pictures during the next two years he grossed more than $700,000.

The best offer John received after leaving Warner Brothers came from Louis B. Mayer, the squat, thick-spectacled, lustful product of a Russian ghetto who rose from junk dealer to the helm of Metro-Goldwyn-Mayer, where Lionel had become a star of the first magnitude. When John accepted, a minor executive asked him if he would like to have a portable dressing room. "Certainly," John replied. "I want one with swinging doors and over the top a big sign reading: 'John Barrymore—Ales, Wines, and Liquors.'"

Alert to the publicity value, MGM set the brothers, shameless scene-stealers both, against each other in five films. The first of these, from which John earned $83,500 under a non-exclusive contract, was *Arsene Lupin* (directed by Jack Conway), Maurice Leblanc's debonair Parisian master thief who steals the Mona Lisa from under the nose of Chief of Detectives Guerchard, played by Lionel.

The second film, yielding John $66,750, was an economic experiment conceived at a time, in the depths of the Great Depression, when attendance at movie theaters was dwindling. If a movie with two or three big stars could still attract audiences, the studio reasoned, then a movie with a slew of them should attract bigger ones.

As a galactic vehicle, MGM chose the sturdy old workhorse of a plot which assembles disparate characters in a single environment and intermingles their destinies. The cast of *Grand Hotel*, adapted by Vicki Baum from her play and directed by Edmund Goulding, included, besides the Barrymore brothers, Wallace Beery, Joan Crawford, Lewis Stone, Jean Hersholt, Greta Garbo. John played the gallant Baron von Geigern, whom high living and gambling have ruined; Garbo, the world-weary ballerina Grusinskaya. They fall in love at first sight.

The two Great Ones approached their first encounter warily. From all John had heard and read, he foresaw himself making screen love to a cold, disdainful misanthrope, while Garbo was resigned to coping with an egomaniacal poseur. John reported for work the first day at 8:45 a.m., fifteen minutes earlier than the customary starting time. Nine o'clock came and went without a sign of the Swedish divinity. Exactly what he had expected, a display of temperament. He was smoldering when a prop boy ran up to him, saying: "I didn't know you were here, Mr. Barrymore. Miss Garbo has been waiting outside the door since nine o'clock to escort you onto the set. It was an honor she wanted to pay you."

Close behind the prop boy followed Garbo. "This is a great day for me," she said. "How I have looked forward to working with John Barrymore!"

John melted. He lifted her hand, kissed it and told her: "My wife and I think you are the loveliest woman in the world."

Throughout the filming of *Grand Hotel* they behaved toward each other with a thoughtfulness and magnanimity rare in the savagely competititive world of Hollywood. Grusinskaya was a dominant role and John would often modify his performances in a way to enhance Garbo's. When, during a particularly difficult sequence, he sensed that she felt insecure, he would embolden her by repeating in a whisper: "You are the most entrancing woman in the world." Following such a sequence, the company was dumbfounded when the normally diffident Garbo flung her arms around John and gave him a lusty kiss, crying: "You have no idea what it means to me to play opposite so perfect an artist."

Aware of John's aversion to his own right profile ("It has all the expressive play and subtle nuance of a morbid deep-sea fish"), she spent an entire lunch break rearranging the couch on which they were to enact a passionate love scene. "I was touched," John said later, "to think she would make that generous effort so the camera could wander up and down my left or money-making profile."

The chief cameraman, William Daniels, Garbo's favorite, who was retained for *Grand Hotel* at her demand, proved equally solicitous of John's preferences. "How do they light you?" he asked him. "How do you want to look?"

"I have no more idea how they light me than I have how they light a firefly's tail," John replied. "But I know how I want to look. I'm fifty years old and I want to look like Jackie Cooper's grandson."

It had been Garbo's practice at the end of the day's shooting to retire immediately to her dressing room, not speaking a word to anybody. With John she would linger on the set, earnestly discussing movies and movie actors. "There are no good actors," he once told her, presumably excluding her from the generalization. "There are only bad ones who try to make themselves and others think they are good. Some bring it off. Others don't. That's the only difference."

Garbo detested posing for publicity stills, but to oblige John, who had no such aversion, she would meekly submit when studio press agents wanted them photographed together.

John frequently arrived at the set hollow-eyed and shaky after a night of carousal. One morning the hangover symptoms were so evident that Garbo led him gently to her dressing room to partake of what she claimed was an infallible restorative. An order to Ellen, her black maid, produced a potion she called "Irak punch." "You will feel good in a few minutes," she promised John. He not only recuperated, but pronounced the concoction the most palatable he had ever tasted. For MGM it was also the most expensive. Every minute the pair tarried cost thousands of dollars.

During a crucial love scene Garbo, who could not bear the gaze of outsiders when she was at work, froze as she noticed a broad-browed, heavily spectacled man watching her from the shadows behind the camera. She murmured a protest in John's ear. John passed it along to the director, Edmund Goulding, and the stranger was escorted to the exit with profound apologies. Did she have any idea who had been ousted? John, amused, asked Garbo. None other than the autocratic boss of his newspaper days, now a journalistic potentate, Arthur Brisbane.

"Holy yumping!" said Garbo.

On May 17, 1933, after *Grand Hotel* had established box-office records all over the country, John wrote to Greta Garbo:

I don't know precisely what has been indicated to you from the studio concerning the part that I have been approached to play in your next picture.* . . . I read the manuscript and was delighted with the whole idea, not only for the very important reason of acting with you again, but because the part was definitely sympathetic to me and I had a distinct feeling that in the scenes between us, with your help and your artistry we could evolve something whimsical, touching and very lovely in the first part of the play, and something most significant and tragic in the latter part of it.

There were certain elements of time when I was first approached in this matter, which I have put completely in abeyance as my desire to play with you is so great. . . . I am completely in your hands, and gladly so. Naturally I would like to know what your reactions definitely are toward my playing the part, because that is of more importance to me than anything else. . . .

Whatever your decision is, please believe I will most perfectly understand it, and it can in no way affect my very great admiration for you as an artist and my affectionate regard for you as a personage. I have such faith in your human understanding that I am writing you this letter merely to know where I am at. I don't like to bother or harass you with telephone calls, so possibly you can evolve some way of communicating to me what your feelings are in the matter. . . .

But *Grand Hotel* was the only film they ever played in together.

Years later, when asked his opinion of Garbo, John said: "She is a fine lady and a great actress and the rest is silence," and Garbo described John as "one of the very few who had that divine madness without which a great artist cannot work or live."

John's letters to Ned Sheldon now had to be read to him, for by 1931 he was blind as well as paralyzed, a victim of iritis or inflammation of the iris. Ophthalmologists knew there existed a con-

---

* Don Antonio de la Prada in MGM's *Queen Christina?* If so, the producers changed their minds, for the role went to John Gilbert, one of his last.

nection between iritis and certain rare cases of rheumatoid arthritis, but they did not know what the connection was, let alone how to save the sufferer's sight. Thus Ned was to abide in darkness, supine, rigid from head to toe, for the remaining fifteen years of his life.

Yet he never surrendered to despair, never railed against his lot or even referred to his affliction, never withheld himself from the countless friends who drew strength from his invincible spirit. "He gave abundantly," said Anne Lindbergh, a frequent visitor, "advice, encouragement, stimulus, criticism. . . . So perfect was the spell he cast over his bedroom that you ceased to think of him as an invalid. You had almost the impression, as a small boy once expressed it after a first visit, that he was a 'prince under an enchantment.' He spoke of 'reading' books, 'seeing' friends, and 'meeting' people in a way that was physically impossible for him. But he spoke like this not out of any vanity, I am sure, but simply not to burden his friends with the constant awareness of his difficulties. . . .

"If you should ask them why they came, what was the compelling force that drew them, I believe many would say, in one form or another, 'He understood me; nobody understood me so well. This was true . . . he had the most uncanny powers of perception. . . . he seemed to have developed other senses of apprehension unknown to the normally endowed individual. The minute you walked into the room he knew all about you, inwardly and outwardly. . . .

"After all, as Saint-Exupéry's *Little Prince* says, 'The eyes are blind; one can only see with the heart.' Edward Sheldon saw with the heart."

Before *Grand Hotel* was released John changed studios again. He went over to RKO, where Gene Fowler, in collaboration with Rowland Brown, adapted for him from a short story a script entitled *State's Attorney*. John's characterization was Tim Cardigan, a shady criminal lawyer who reforms, becomes a district attorney and brings to book his former racketeering client.*

The RKO director George Cukor had never seen an actress quite like the newcomer who, on July 6, 1932, strode into his office with an almost military bearing. Nobody in Hollywood had. Tall, taller than a good many male stars, thin, broad-shouldered, with reddish hair, high

---

* The writers cribbed a famous quip of Maurice Barrymore's. A speakeasy operator and Sunday painter shows Cardigan a winter landscape from his brush. "Winter," comments Cardigan, "is not as bad as it's painted."

cheekbones and a wide mouth, she seemed all planes and sharp angles, a misleading impression conveyed by her erect, taut stance. A little later, when she moved relaxedly, Cukor saw the grace and beauty of her body. Her speech, throaty and precisely articulated, suggested New England finishing-school influence. On the train from New York she had caught a steel filing in her left eye and it was still inflamed.

Shortly, John entered, saying: "Miss Hepburn, I've seen the test. You are going to be a great star."

Following her first Broadway success, at the age of twenty-two, as Antiope, Queen of the Amazons, in Julian Thompson's comedy *The Warrior's Husband*, RKO had brought Katharine Hepburn to Hollywood to play John's daughter (test films depending) in a film version of the drama by Clemence Dane, *A Bill of Divorcement*. John, noticing her reddened eye, drew her aside, fished a vial and an eye-dropper out of his pocket and explained: "This is what I use when *my* eyes are bloodshot after a gay night."

A foreign body, not revelry, she protested, had caused the injury.

"Put the drops in anyway," said John.

The ensuing relationship engendered some of the hardest-dying figments in the entire Barrymore mythos. According to Garson Kanin's biography, *Tracy and Hepburn*, John invited the novice to his dressing room for special coaching. No sooner had the door closed behind her than he whipped off his dressing gown and advanced, stark naked. When she recoiled, Kanin continues, citing John himself as the source, he asked: "What's the matter?"

She is alleged to have replied: "My father doesn't want me to have any babies."

According to another account, they supposedly bickered throughout the filming and at the end she vowed: "I'm never going to act with you again."

The story goes that John shot back: "I wasn't aware you had."

No such dialogue took place. Nevertheless, the latest Hepburn biography, Charles Higham's *Kate*, published in 1975, repeats the old canards and adds a few new ones. Higham puts into John's mouth words wholly out of character—"My dear, any young girl would be thrilled to make love to the great John Barrymore"—and later has him pinching her bottom.

It is true, Miss Hepburn says, that John summoned her to his dressing room and that she promptly went. "I felt honored and flattered. What actress making her first movie would pass up a chance to be coached by John Barrymore?" True, too, that he received her in a bathrobe with a distinctly libidinous gleam in his eye. But after a brief, polite exchange, he said: "I see I've made a mistake."

John ventured no further attempt upon the novice's virtue during the weeks it took to complete *A Bill of Divorcement*, but proved unfailingly kind and helpful. With her inexperience, for example, she tended to turn away from the camera. John would hold her in such a way as to compel her to face it.

His role was Hilary Fairfield, a musician and war veteran who escapes from the insane asylum to which he had been committed years before, a victim of shell shock. There were people close to John who thought they detected in the anguish and pathos of his performance a reflection of his own haunting terror that he would end insane like Maurice Barrymore. "Am I, too, to suffer an inheritance of madness?" he once asked Helios.

The fugitive mental patient returns home, unwanted, an embarrassing intruder from the distant past, to learn that his wife has divorced him and is about to remarry. In vain he pleads with her to take him back. (Billie Burke, who played the wife, said that to reject convincingly a man as attractive to her as John was the most difficult piece of acting ever demanded of her.) The only members of the household to feel sympathy for Fairfield are an old aunt and his daughter, Sydney (Katharine Hepburn), who was an infant at the time of his commitment. Sydney, too, is engaged, but upon discovering that a strain of insanity runs through the paternal branch of her family, she dismisses her fiancé, urges her mother to marry immediately and resolves to stay with her father. In the final sequence father and daughter, sitting side by side before a piano, begin to compose a sonata.

"I'll never forget the first day she worked," says George Cukor. ". . . she was required to look at her father, and she looked at him with this infinite compassion, and then her eyes filled with tears, and Jack Barrymore winked at her. He said: 'She's okay.' "

In another highly emotional scene, when Sydney recognizes Fairfield as her father, the actress, for all her inexperience, discerned in John's delivery a lack of conviction, a weariness, which he was covering up with facile tricks, with overacting. John sensed her disapproval and after the take, cupping her chin in his hand and turning to Cukor, he said: "I'd like to do that one again." Miss Hepburn remembers the retake as "the most shattering acting I've ever seen."

She also remembers the indecorous japes that John would ad lib when he blew up in a line. "Do you know what the dead do in Heaven?" Hilary Fairfield asks his wife when pleading with her not to leave him. "They sit on their golden chairs and sicken for home." Flubbing the answer, John said for all to hear: "Do you know what the dead do in Heaven? They sit on their golden chairs and play with themselves."

In Miss Hepburn's memory John remains "a gentle, thoughtful, decent human being."

In June 1932, John once again sought a glimpse of the future through astrology. On the fourth of the month, under the sign of Aquarius, John Blyth Barrymore, Jr., was born, an event the father greeted with a good deal more enthusiasm than he had shown at the birth of his second daughter. "Have you ever been kissed by a movie actor?" he asked the nurse who brought him the tidings. "No? Well, you're going to be," and, to her happy confusion, he suited the action to the words.

". . . the boy will be quick in speech and action, with a tendency to accidents," the proud parents learned from the stars. "He will be alert, forceful, positive, but inclined to be suspicious and cynically sarcastic like his father. Perhaps he will also have the same critical and penetrating mentality and rise to no little fame." Chemistry and surgery, according to the prophecy, would attract John, Jr. He was unlikely to become an actor.

21

Siblings

━━━━━━━━

Not since childhood, when they staged their version of *Camille* at home, had all three Barrymores acted together. Now in MGM's *Rasputin and the Empress*, Lionel and Ethel were to play the title roles and John, the Czarist prince who murdered Rasputin. The idea of thus casting the trio originated with the dynamic young producer Irving Thalberg, the protégé of Louis B. Mayer, the husband of Norma Shearer and the model for F. Scott Fitzgerald's *Last Tycoon*, and it added no little luster to his reputation. Obtaining Ethel's services especially was hailed as a maser coup, for the cinema was not a medium she cared for.

Ethel's distaste stemmed partly from her experience in early silent films when "on location" meant some New York sidewalk open to the gaze of curious crowds. Once, while portraying an Italian street singer, she learned, to her horror, that a sequence was to be shot in front of the Madison Avenue mansion of her aristocratic friend Mrs. Whitelaw Reid and she balked until the director shifted the setting to another part of town.

But the protection from gawkers afforded by studio sets failed to lessen her distaste. As John sardonically explained the difference in attitudes between the brothers and their sister, "Lionel and I see no debasing of our so-called art when we allow our histrionic antics to be recorded on celluloid and packed in tins like pineapple, to be shipped to all parts of the world. We feel it better to appear in five thousand movie houses at once, before a million patrons, than in one theater before a thousand. But Ethel doesn't see it that way. She can't stand just having a cameraman and his satellites for an audience."

Three years before *Rasputin and the Empress*, Ethel's first talkie, a tour in Martinez Sierra's convent drama, *The Kingdom of God*, brought her and her actress cousin Georgie Mendum to Los Angeles. At dinner before the performance, on one of John's Tower Road patios, Ethel fell to deriding her brothers for debasing the lofty theatrical ideals of their forebears by selling out to tawdry, tinselly Hollywood. Midway through her tirade she glanced at her watch and jumped to her feet, exclaiming: "We'll be late for the theater, Georgie! Hurry!"

"At least you can wait for a Benedictine," John ventured.

"Not a second. We're late!"

As the brothers saw them into their limousine, John turned to Lionel in mock sorrow. "What a tragedy it is that you and I have become bums and have deserted the glorious theater for the utterly low in movies. Here are these two women who are going to work, carrying on the traditions of the family. They'll go downtown to recite lines that they have been reciting for weeks and have a magnificent evening, while you and I, having become shovelers of trash, will be forced to sit on a patio under the stars and sip genuine Benedictine."

"Aye," said Lionel, "let us return to our Benedictine and try not to be envious."

"Go to hell, both of you!" said their sister, slamming the car door.

Ethel could ill afford to turn down Thalberg. His offer of $100,000 for eight weeks' work (John and Lionel each got roughly half again as much) came at a time when she had depleted her capital, a plight familiar to both brothers, who, like her, kept squandering more money than they earned. To compound Ethel's dilemma, the Internal Revenue Service was demanding additional payments for the years 1921 through 1929. Haphazardness in the face of taxes due—indeed, of any debts—was a tendency Ethel also shared with her brothers.

A ruse sometimes adopted by Hollywood-bound stars from the East who wished to avoid premature exposure to the press, particularly when they looked a bit frazzled after the cross-country railroad trip, consisted of detraining at Pasadena instead of Los Angeles and traveling the rest of the way by car. The press, however, was not so easily eluded and had learned to cover both stations. Ethel, arriving at Pasadena with her three children, was greeted not only by reporters and news photographers, but also a tangle of movie notables and celebrity-watchers.

The crowd gazed upon the touching family scene as John enfolded Ethel in his arms and, pressing his cheek to hers, murmured something in her ear. What he murmured was not, as the beaming onlookers might have assumed, "Hello, Ethel" or "How are you?" but, bluntly, "For God's sake, get Bill Daniels!"

"Who is Bill Daniels?" Ethel asked.

"He's a cameraman. One of the best. He takes all those sweetbreads away from under my eyes. Garbo won't make a picture without him."

Among Ethel's first imperious words to Thalberg were "Where's Bill Daniels? I want him." Thalberg saw to it that she got him.

For her relatively short sojourn Ethel chose a Beverly Hills estate with tennis court and swimming pool. The cost doubtless figured in her 1932 tax returns, for she reported $57,500 as her MGM earnings that year (presumably the rest of the $100,000 was payable in 1933) and claimed deductible professional expenses of $60,000.

Ethel's contract specified eight weeks as the maximum length of her services because she had promised Arthur Hopkins to star in his opening production of the 1932–33 season—a fantasy called *An Amazing Career*. The first three days of the eight weeks passed in inactivity because none of the five scripts submitted to Thalberg satisfied him. Charles MacArthur had recently arrived in Hollywood with Helen Hayes, not to work but to rest in the Hollywood bungalow they owned. "He's just the man," said Thalberg, "but he won't do it."

"I'll make him do it," Ethel promised, hurried to the bungalow and, seizing him by the shoulders, informed him: "You are going to write *Rasputin!*"

Never, MacArthur swore, ducking behind his wife as behind a protective barrier.

"You lazy, cowardly, incompetent, loafing, good-for-nothing ass!" said Ethel. "You are going to write *Rasputin*."

Helen Hayes intervened. "Charlie, no woman ever talked to you like that. What are you going to do about it?"

Nothing, said he, could induce him to work on the script.

Sweeping a pile of books off a table, Ethel threatened to wreck the whole place. "I'll throw that lamp right through the wall," she threatened.

"Look out, Charlie," Helen Hayes warned her husband. "She's going to do it."

He capitulated. "All right, I'll do your damn show. What's it about?"

Ethel stayed until dawn, telling MacArthur what she knew about the Romanovs and "the Mad Monk."

With MacArthur's script, the sixth, quickly completed, shooting at last began. The Czarina herself could scarcely have been accorded greater deference by her court than the regal Ethel Barrymore when she first swept across MGM's Stage 21. Noblesse oblige. She embraced Edward Arnold, a Broadway colleague of long standing, who had been cast as Dr. Remezov, the Romanovs' family physician, and she told the director, Charles Brabin, how happy she was to be working with him.

The benign atmosphere was soon shattered. Ethel, eager to get back to her natural habitat, found Brabin's pace too slow. From a studio telephone on a wall near the set, she said to Louis Mayer in tones audible to the entire company: "See here, Mayer, let's get rid of this Brahbin or Braybin or what's his name." Brabin immediately left the set and, at Ethel's suggestion, was replaced by Richard Boleslavsky, a Polish author reputedly knowledgeable about Russian royalty. Then Ethel flared up one morning when an assistant director reprimanded her for tardiness. Asked to reenact a sequence for the fourth time, she refused and protested to Mayer. He managed to placate her, and friendly feelings prevailed again until a former official of the Russian imperial court, whom Thalberg had hired as a technical consultant, ventured to correct Ethel's impersonation. Bridling, she informed the impudent fellow that she, too, had known both Nicholas and Alexandra, having met them several times in London through the Duchess of Sutherland.

At luncheon in the MGM commissary Lionel remarked in jest to the waitress serving him: "The three Barrymores are going to be together in one picture. Can you imagine what will happen to the poor director?" John also spoke lightheartedly when, in response to Thalberg's explanation of how he was going to kill Rasputin in the last reel, he said: "The way Lionel is going to steal this picture, I ought to shoot him in the *first* reel." Taken seriously and widely circulated, such comments prompted rumors to the effect that the studio had become a battleground with the Barrymores ferociously assaulting each other and the director.

"They seem to think the three Barrymores are just three damn fools!" John said afterward. "They say we are jealous of one another, that we won't do what the director tells us, that we want to change the story, each for his selfish glorification. . . . Ethel has been marvelous. Lionel, who loves his sarcasm, has never been in better humor. I have, ladies and gentlemen, conducted myself magnificently. . . . our business is to put on the best performance of which we are capable. We fence, between ourselves, because it is amusing. But we are quite sure of ourselves before we lunge at one another, for we have great respect each for the other. Ethel has a quick and withering and delicious wit. Lionel can cut you down with scorn. And now and then I can take care of myself in an exchange of good-humored hisses."

The scenes in which Ethel appeared were shot out of their natural order so that she might get back to New York within the eight weeks. (Upon viewing the early rushes, she observed: "I look like Elsie Janis's burlesque of me.") During the rest of the shooting the film fell, at an astronomical cost, weeks behind schedule.

Asked her opinion of Hollywood when she reached New York, Ethel said: "The place hasn't been thought in. There is no sediment of thought there. It looks, it feels as though it had been invented by a Sixth Avenue peep-show man. Come to think of it, it probably was."

Thalberg, meanwhile, had received forewarnings of grave trouble. They came from Mercedes de Acosta, now in Los Angeles, trying, with meager success, to write screenplays. Because of her acquaintance with the White Russian set abroad, Thalberg had put her under contract to prepare background material on Rasputin and the Romanovs, to be followed by a scenario. As she began the scenario, he instructed her to insert a sequence in which "the Mad Monk" seduces Irina Youssoupoff, a niece of Czar Nicholas II and wife of the prince who killed Rasputin. To her knowledge, Mercedes objected, Irina never met Rasputin; such a scene would not only lack historical authenticity but invite a libel suit.

"I don't need you to tell me a lot of nonsense about what is libelous [so Mercedes quoted him in her memoirs]. I want this sequence in and that is all there is to it."

She wrote to Prince Agoutinsky, a Czarist émigré living in

Paris, explaining what Thalberg wanted and asking him to discuss it with Prince Youssoupoff. Back came the word: "If Irina appeared in the film at all, Youssoupoff would file suit." But Thalberg could not be dissuaded.

Mercedes was not alone in her misgivings. Ethel shared them and told Thalberg so. His only concession was to give the Youssoupoffs a fictitious name—Chegodieff. John himself spoiled that feeble dodge by telling interviewers that his portrayal was, of course, based on the real Prince.

Rasputin and the Empress had its première at the Astor Theatre in New York on December 23, 1932. The reviews were so inconsonant that one wonders whether all the critics had seen the same film. At one extreme was the *Times'* Mordaunt Hall, who found it "an engrossing and exciting pictorial melodrama . . . further distinguished by the knowledgeful guidance of Richard Boleslavsky," while at the other extreme the *Herald Tribune's* Richard Watts, Jr., condemned it as "a heavy-handed, hard-working drama which never succeeds in being convincing either as narrative or chronicle."

(It is interesting to compare the *New Yorker's* critical estimate then with the magazine's review of a rerun in 1975. In 1932 John McCarten wrote: "In my amiable opinion not all the praise has been given 'Rasputin and the Empress' that it deserves. There is Ethel Barrymore's Czarina, for instance, and I don't think it nonsense to present this lady with a few more bouquets than she already has and to welcome her to the screen with a hullabaloo of boyish enthusiasm. . . . It is largely her performance which gives verisimilitude to this film; but in the presentation also, in the settings and in the cast in general, there seems to be a historical scrupulousness, and some reflection of the magnificence of that court and of the drama of its downfall, given here for your republican contemplation. . . ." And in 1975, according to a brief, unsigned review: "The only film with all three Barrymores . . . and they all seem to be at their worst. John had played the mesmerist Svengali the year before, so Lionel was decked out in a beard to play Rasputin. The hammiest actor in the family, Lionel, who doddered even in his youth, is so unhypnotic that Ethel, as the Empress, seems less mesmerized than bored stiff. John finally gets to choke his brother to everyone's immense satisfaction.")

Princess Youssoupoff, who, with her husband, had acquired English citizenship, sued MGM for libel in an English court. The

case came to trial on February 27, 1934, and led to the largest recovery ever won by a libel plaintiff. First, the jury awarded the
Princess £25,000 (at the time equivalent to about $125,000). Then,
faced by the likelihood of similar judgments in each of the scores of
countries where *Rasputin* would be shown, MGM paid the Princess a
blanket settlement. The exact figure was never officially disclosed,
but it came close to a million dollars.

A substantial profit from *Rasputin* would have afforded MGM
some consolation. According to its general counsel, J. Robert Rubin,
however, "The damn thing stinks. Audiences won't go near it." The
film cost more than two million dollars to make, and the net loss
was nearly a million.

The years 1932 and 1933 were the most productive of John's
Hollywood career. He made ten films during that period, six for
MGM, three for RKO and one for Universal. They included three of
his finest portrayals: in *Topaze*, Marcel Pagnol's satiric comedy, he
played the timid, gullible schoolteacher of the title, who undergoes
a radical moral transformation when he discovers that crime does
pay; in an adaptation of the Kaufman-Ferber Broadway hit *Dinner
at Eight*, Larry Renault, a faded, destitute ham actor who tries
and fails to keep up appearances, then kills himself; in Elmer Rice's
Counsellor-at-Law, George Simon, a brilliant Jewish lawyer, up
from the ghetto, who faces ruin when an unethical deed of his distant
past comes to the knowledge of an enemy.

None of those three films or, in fact, any of the fifty-seven
Barrymore films ranks among the classics of the medium. Some are
unmitigated trash. Yet in nearly all, good, bad and mediocre, John
rivets the attention with at least a scene, a moment, perhaps only a
gesture. No contemporary performer surpassed him in virtuosity, in
the sheer range of his characterizations from the horripilating Mr.
Hyde to the insouciant, amatory Archduke Rudolph von Hapsburg,
the hero of Robert E. Sherwood's Theatre Guild success *Reunion in
Vienna*, and few actors could convey such nuances of meaning
with such economy of means—a crooked index finger, the lift of an
eyebrow, an ironic half-smile, an intonation.

George Cukor, who directed *Dinner at Eight* and became a
warm, understanding friend of John's, said afterward: "His ability
to project himself into a dramatic character and then let that character completely transcend his own individuality; and then, to inter-

pret it down to the last fine shade of mood—that genius is possessed by no other actor on the screen today."

Dinner at Eight followed much the same formula as *Grand Hotel*, bringing together a miscellany of characters, played by Grade A stars, to interact within the same framework, in this instance a prospective dinner party. Besides the Barrymore brothers the cast included Wallace Beery, Jean Harlow, Marie Dressler, Edmund Lowe and Billie Burke.

Cukor exclaimed over John's portrayal of Larry Renault: "Oh, that is wonderful, Jack!"

"Well, it ought to be," said the actor. "This is a combination of Maurice Costello, Lowell Sherman and me."

In the course of a 1973 television series, *The Men Who Made the Movies*, Cukor recalled: "The very first shot, he is on the telephone . . . pretending to be very grand to a society woman. He said [to Cukor], 'Let me put this phrase in. "Yes, yes, yes, dear lady." ' He was being very grand and hambola. His speech was very well observed and accurate. When he wanted a drink and he talked to the bellhop, all this grandeur, all this fake suavity left him. And he played an ignorant actor and he found out that another actor got the job he desperately needed. And he'd say, 'I can be English. I can be as English as ahnnybohdy.' Then he'd say, 'Ibsen, Ibsen. I can do Ibsen,' and he had just heard vaguely of Ibsen, and he would strike this absolutely inappropriate pose and he said, 'Mother dear, give me the moon.' Whereas the Ibsen line was, 'Mother, give me the sun.' "

The manner of Larry Renault's death was largely John's concept. After sealing the door and windows of the hotel room he can no longer afford, he turns on a gas jet, seats himself by the fireplace in an armchair and, ham to the last, so positions his profile that the rays from a nearby lamp illumine it like a spotlight.

The Barrymore brothers' fifth and last film together was *Night Flight*, adapted from the prize novel by France's great aviator and author Antoine de Saint-Exupéry. (The cast also included Clark Gable, Helen Hayes, Robert Montgomery and Myrna Loy.) John readily conceded Lionel's superiority in their game of scene-stealing, but this time John's role, the tough, autocratic director of a small airline, so dominated both action and dialogue as to afford Lionel, who played the much smaller part of chief foreman, scant opportunity for larceny. In their longest scene John berates Lionel for eating with the pilots; superiors, he insists, should not mingle with inferiors. Lionel stands wordlessly before the martinet's desk, finally turns, humbled, and shuffles out the door. The director, Clarence Brown, bet John ten dollars that Lionel could never steal that scene. "Taken," said John. "He will snatch it if he has to hang from the chandelier."

As Lionel approached the door, back to the camera, with few seconds left before the sequence ended, he reached a hand around and scratched a buttock.

"Now there, sir, is a brother to be proud of," said John to Clarence Brown. "Pay me the ten dollars instanter!"

William Wyler had barely begun his career as a Hollywood director when Universal Studios assigned him to *Counsellor-at-Law* with a scenario adapted by Elmer Rice from his Broadway hit starring Paul Muni. John set out to put Wyler at his ease. "You've heard a lot about the Barrymore temperament," he said, throwing an arm around the director's shoulder. "It's not true except maybe about Ethel and she's full of prunes."

Feeling somewhat miscast as a self-made, fast-talking Jewish dynamo bred on New York's lower East Side, John told Wyler: "I'm glad you're directing this picture. You'll be able to help me play the part right." Following Wyler's suggestions for certain overtones of speech and manner, he played it masterfully. Many critics considered *Counsellor-at-Law* his greatest portrayal.

The film was all but finished within three weeks. John had already gone to work in a low-budget RKO comedy, *Long Lost Father*, when Wyler called him back for the retake of one scene. As John stepped before the camera to repeat lines that he had spoken several times before, his memory failed. He could not summon up a single word. A second retake produced the same result. After half a dozen tries, the baffled director postponed further shooting until next day. John then breezed through the scene without a hitch.

John saw no reason to seek medical advice about his lapse of memory, the first of its kind he had ever experienced. Had he done so, he might have learned that intermittent amnesia is a common effect of alcoholism.

On April 14, 1932, Theresa Helburn circulated among her fellow members of the Theatre Guild's directorial board a telegram from John Barrymore:

MANY THANKS FOR YOUR CHARMING WIRE AM AFRAID
THAT THE IMPRESSION THAT I AM ABOUT TO RETURN
TO THE THEATRE IS SO FAR MERELY A RUMOR BUT I
DEEPLY APPRECIATE YOUR INTEREST.

Miss Helburn sent John a seond message:

THANKS FOR YOUR PROMPT AND VERY KIND REPLY IF
THE IMPRESSION WHICH HAS GOT SO FAR EVER GETS
BEYOND THE RUMOR STAGE WONT YOU CONSIDER THE
POSSIBILITY OF RETURNING TO THE THEATRE IN AS-
SOCIATION WITH THE GUILD I ASK YOU TO KEEP THIS
CONFIDENTIAL.

There was no dearth of producers striving to entice John back to the legitimate stage. Paul Bonner wanted him to portray Pericles in Robert E. Sherwood's *Acropolis*, which was to open in London. The Shuberts wanted him in any play he fancied. Alexander Pantages offered him fifty percent of the gross receipts to tour the Pantages theater circuit in a vehicle of his choice. Sam Howard, a Broadway agent, wired:

OFFERED TWELVE THOUSAND FIVE HUNDRED FOR
PALACE THIS IS FIVE THOUSAND MORE ANY STAR RE-
CEIVED JOLSON OFFERED TEN THOUSAND CANTOR GET-
TING SIX THOUSAND CONSIDER HOUSE CANNOT DO MORE
THAN TWENTY THREE THOUSAND CAPACITY TWO SHOWS
DAILY I AM SURE AFTER PALACE APPEARANCE WE WILL
BE ABLE TO NEGOTIATE FOR REAL MONEY STOP BARRY-
MORE AT THIS SALARY ESTABLISHES RECORD SALARY
NEVER PAID ANYONE YOU MUST CONSIDER THIS.

A bizarre plan germinated in the perfervid brain of the producer-director Jed Harris, at the time Broadway's golden boy with a succession of resounding hits to his credit, including *The Royal Family*. As Harris outlined it to John, he proposed to hire the Metropolitan Opera House for one night, there to present John in a single appearance as King Lear, the price of tickets to range from $200 to $500 each. John, one eyebrow arching, contemplated the prodigy a moment in stupefied silence. "You are crazy," he said.

But, fantastic or feasible, no proposal could tempt John to quit Hollywood. Not that he viewed the film capital with unqualified affection. He referred to it variously as "that dermoid cyst," "Hollywoodus in Latrina," "the flatulent cave of the winds," "this goddamn sinkhole of culture."

The only theatrical role that John did now and then consider was *Hamlet*. He spoke of staging it himself at the Greek Theatre of the University of California in Berkeley. Later he got as far as reserving the Hollywood Bowl for a week. But the project never materialized.

John came closest to re-creating his greatest portrayal during the late winter of 1933 when the multimillionaire and diplomat John Hay Whitney, who had bought fifteen percent of Technicolor, Inc., and organized Pioneer Pictures, agreed to finance a cinematic *Hamlet* using the new process. David Selznick was to produce it. Margaret Carrington, whose husband had died three years before, arrived to supervise the actors' speech. With her came Robert Edmond Jones, now her second husband, to design the sets and costumes. The venture progressed no further than a series of test films.*

Not only did John's memory black out when he was reciting one of the soliloquies in a test scene, not only were these lapses at times accompanied by a pounding headache, but his general physical state had markedly deteriorated. At fifty-one he had grown too heavy, too jowly, his ankles swollen with a form of edema stemming from damage to the liver by alcohol, to impersonate convincingly the young prince of Denmark.

The fear of some hereditary taint assailed John with redoubled force. Were his spells of amnesia the precursors of a disease that would lead to madness like his father's? The thought was so intolerable that he chose to attribute his father's condition to an altogether different, non-heritable cause. When Maurice Barrymore fought his last amateur bout in England, his son claimed, he took a powerful blow behind the right ear. Ever after he suffered from periodic loss of memory and headaches of such intensity that he advised John against pugilism. Curiously, so John maintained, he too sustained an injury behind the right ear. He said it happened during the silent-film era when he performed hazardous stunts himself rather than leave them to a double. Required to take a high leap on horseback,

---

* The only surviving audible or visual evidence of John's career as a Shakespearean actor are a few recordings of soliloquies, MGM's *Romeo and Juliet*, in which he played Mercutio, a short strip of the *Hamlet* test film consisting of the soliloquy from Act III Scene 3, when Hamlet considers killing Claudius at his prayers ("Now might I do it pat . . ."), his Act I Scene 5 soliloquy after meeting his father's ghost ("O, all you host of Heaven! . . .") and the Duke of Gloucester's soliloquy in *Show of Shows*.

he was thrown and landed on the back of his head. During the years 1924 and 1925, while making movies in New York and living at the Ambassador Hotel, he supposedly endured frequent headaches, which he would alleviate by fishing a piece of ice out of a pitcher and applying it to the site of the injury.

Scarlet Sister Mary, Julia Peterkin's Pulitzer Prize novel of life among the Gullah Negroes of South Carolina, so touched Ethel that she commissioned a playwright, Daniel Reed, to adapt it to the stage. She proposed to play the title role herself in blackface. Her nineteen-year-old daughter, Ethel, nicknamed "Sister," was to make her stage debut as Mary's daughter Seraphine, also camouflaging her face with burnt cork. Before opening in the Shuberts' Broadway theater which they had named after Ethel, *Scarlet Sister Mary* was tried out on the road toward the end of September 1931, first at the Shubert-owned Empire Theatre in Cleveland. A week earlier Henry Hotchener wrote to a Mrs. Helen Chaittin of the production staff:

> Confirming telephone conversation, here are details of what Mr. John Barrymore wishes:
>
> In Cleveland, on Sept. 29th (better send wire several days in advance), at the theatre where she is appearing that evening, deliver to Miss Ethel Barrymore Colt, *one* big red apple in a nice box, the apple wrapped in cotton and the box wrapped and tied as if it contained flowers. In the box have a card as follows:

> > Dearest Sister—
> > Knock 'em cold to-night.
> > Uncle Lionel and Uncle Jack.

> Same evening, same time, deliver to Miss Ethel Barrymore Colt, 2 doz. Hadley roses, with a card saying

> > Dearest Sister—
> > We shall be thinking of you so hard to-night.
> > Ever so much love.
> > Dolores and Uncle Jack.

> At same time deliver to same theatre 2 doz Pernet roses with card to Miss Ethel Barrymore, as follows:

> > Dearest Ethel—
> > Hope everything is grand to-night. Lots of love.
> > Dolores and Jack

(Mrs. Chaittin: Please note the peculiar spelling on the card to Ethel Barrymore, EETHEL. As the Western Union is apt to get this wrong, please ask your florist in Cleveland and New York to wire you a confirmation of the whole message.)

About Oct. 9th or 10th—get exact date from N.Y. florist,—they appear in New York theatre. On that night send a doz. white and a doz. red roses to Miss Ethel Barrymore Colt, with a card

> Dearest Sister—All our thoughts tonight.
> Dolores and Uncle Jack.

And at the same time and place 2 doz Talisman roses to Miss Ethel Barrymore, with card

> Dearest Ethel—Hope everything will be wonderful tonight. Ever so much love.
> Dolores and Jack

If anything in this is not clear, please phone Mr. Hotchener OXF 1434 about 12 o'clock noon; or at OXF 6219.

The critics agreed that Ethel should never have attempted to talk like a Gullah Negro, let alone look like one. According to *Theatre Arts Monthly,* "The barriers between the actress and her goal in *Scarlet Sister Mary* were not less than appalling. . . . her personal quality sometimes emerged from the burnt cork and more often did not."

The misfortune presaged a long spell of artistic and financial reverses for Ethel. On January 3, 1934, she wrote to John from her country home in Mamaroneck, New York:

Dearest Jake—

Will you be an angel and lend me quite a big sum. . . . I will ask for $25,000—I know it sounds fantastic but my state is fantastic. I have a chance of going to London and sort of starting all over again—but I have to set my house in order here. . . . Oh Jake—I don't want to be maudlin . . . don't think I don't realize about your family and everything—I am going to have my life insured tomorrow which will cover this loan—in case I die

—before I can pay it back, but please help me get away from this dreadful palace [*sic*]—You must know how humble I feel when I am afraid you don't like me any more & still I am doing it . . . and I can't ask anybody else and I will promise to pay you soon—and will you send me a wire and relieve my mind—love—Ethel.

What she pinned her hopes to was a revival, at London's famed music hall, the Palladium, of *The Twelve Pound Look*, Sir James Barrie's feminist playlet in which she had year after year toured American vaudeville circuits. Whether John advanced the money no existing record indicates, but almost certainly he gave her part if not all of it, despite his own chronic financial disarray, for he had never forgotten her devotion to him and to Lionel, her encouragement and generosity, when they stood on the low rungs of their careers. "Ethel Barrymore," John said, "is the most magnificent, most brilliant, loveliest, kindest sister that a man ever had. In my early life I was utterly worthless. I was always in trouble, always in need of money. And when I wanted help, I went to Ethel instantly, no matter where she was, and a thousand times out of a thousand, she helped me, cheered me, straightened me out for another whack at my crazy, foolish, often misdirected efforts to make something out of myself. She's the grandest sister, the grandest sport that God ever created, and if it hadn't been for her, I'd be shining shoes for a living, or in jail, or dead."

Ethel sailed for England in the late winter of 1934 only to meet defeat. ". . . an astonishing thing happened. They didn't like the play! They hated it! They said it was old-fashioned—I don't know what they didn't say about it. I had banked on it for so many years, had thought it practically a classic, and it was a shock to discover that as far as England was concerned its day was past."

There followed a long, dark period—six years of infrequent engagements, and those unrewarding, an occasional tour in one of her old stand-bys, now poorly attended, a few radio readings. She even considered teaching. It was during this period that Ethel succumbed to the family weakness for liquor. She managed to control it, though, far better than John or Lionel, and shortly she gave up drinking altogether.

On Christmas Eve of 1936 Lionel's wife Irene, who had destroyed her health by excessive dieting, suddenly died. Every Christmas Day for years Lionel had portrayed old Scrooge on a radio broadcast version of Dickens' *Christmas Carol*. This time John replaced his sorrowing brother.

Not only did Lionel lose his wife, but soon after he suffered the second of two accidents that threatened his position as one of MGM's topflight, highest-salaried stars. Early in 1936, while sketching at home, he leaned too heavily on his metal drafting board, overturned it, tripped and fell, fracturing his hip. Long hospital treatment enabled him to move his body within limits, but not to walk around freely. Louis Mayer, however, did not propose to lose so valuable an attraction, and he instructed studio writers to accommodate character and story lines to Lionel's disability.

By the spring of 1937 Lionel was sufficiently mobile to journey to England and, with the aid of a cane, to get around the set of *A Yank at Oxford*. Upon his return to Hollywood he joined Clark Gable and Jean Harlow in *Saratoga*. As the film neared completion, he stumbled over a cable, fell heavily and broke the same hip again. Thereafter, to his dying day, Lionel was confined to a wheelchair except for rare occasions when he could hobble a few steps on crutches. Yet his acting career continued to flourish. In addition to several sedentary roles, notably Grandpa Vanderhof in *You Can't Take It with You*, there was MGM's Dr. Kildare series. "Nothing greater, of course, could possibly have been contrived for me than the character of the grumpy but likable old physician in the wheel chair. . . . I liked the part so much that I subscribed to *The Lancet* and other medical journals, and have as a result become a second-class quack and a first-class hypochondriac. . . ."

"Turn him loose," said Harry Cohn, the former garment-center cutter who rose to the presidency of Columbia Pictures, after signing up John for a single film, "give the public an eyeful, and we'll see acting as we've never seen it before."

Legend names Cohn as the target of one of John's sharpest barbs. When during an argument, the story goes, Cohn shook his finger in John's face, John said: "Don't shake that thing at me. I remember the days when it wore a thimble."

Cohn had commissioned Hecht and MacArthur to adapt their Broadway comedy hit *Twentieth Century* to the screen. If George Simon, in *Counsellor-at-Law*, was the finest of all John's serious film performances, Oscar Jaffe, the egomaniacal impresario of *Twentieth Century*, proved by far the funniest. "There's enough ham in me to let me imagine that old fellow," he said. "I didn't have to act to be Jaffe. I needed only to close my eyes and live over again the happiest days of my life. The character was so cleverly written that I could actually feel the peculiarities of such a man—a humbug, a faker, and a ham, but through it all, a man with a heart and soul."

Twentieth Century had the added distinction of starring Jane Alice Peters, better known as Carole Lombard, on her ascent to the top echelon of stardom. Though Paramount had been paying her $1,000 a week, the roles it gave her brought her only minor popularity. Loaned to Columbia, she received five times her Paramount salary to play Mildred Plotka, the hare-brained movie novice whom Jaffe takes as his mistress, renames Lily Garland and, Pygmalion-like, transforms into an actress of note. The hilarious denouement unfolds on the Twentieth Century express between Chicago and New York. Learning that his Galatea, now a Hollywood star, having freed herself from his domination, is aboard, Jaffe fakes a heart attack. His deathbed act so arouses Lily's compassion that to gladden his last moments she yields to his pleas and signs a contract, placing herself once again in his power. The entrapped Lily emits a howl of rage as Jaffe leaps to his feet, gloating and flourishing the contract.

Inhibited, possibly, by the prospect of playing opposite John Barrymore, Carole's acting in rehearsal the first day was so wooden that John, conferring privately with Howard Hawks, a soft-spoken, conservative director, held his nose. The problem, as Hawks saw it, was Carole's efforts to imagine a character and then act according to her imagining.

"You've been working hard on the script," Hawks told her as he walked her around the set.

"I'm glad it shows," she said.

"Yes, you know every word of it. How much do you get paid for the picture?"

Five thousand a week, she told him.

"That's pretty good. What do you get paid for?"

"Well, acting."

"What if I would tell you that you had earned all your money and don't owe a nickel and you don't have to act any more?"

She stared at him, stupefied.

Then, to relax her further, he asked: "What would you do if a man said such a thing to you?," mentioning an insult called for by the script.

"I'd kick the son of a bitch right in the balls."

"Well, Barrymore says it to you. Why didn't you kick him? Now we're going in and make this scene and you kick him, and you do any damn thing that comes into your mind that's natural, and quit acting. If you don't quit, I'm going to fire you this afternoon. You just be natural."

"Are you serious?"

"I'm very serious."

"All right."

During the ensuing take Carole aimed a blow not at the organ she originally indicated, but at John's shins. John roared with pain and Carole roared with laughter. "Cut and print it," said Hawks happily. Nursing his smarting ankle, John told Carole: "That was marvelous. What have you been doing, kidding me?"

She began to cry and ran off the set.

"What's happened?" John asked Hawks.

"You've just seen a girl who is probably going to be a big star, and if we can just keep her from acting, we'll have a hell of a picture."

John helped Carole throughout the filming, feeding her pointers at every turn, and a hell of a picture it proved to be. It is today the Barrymore film most often rerun on both theater and television screens.

22

Breakdown

I WENT to Hollywood to ask him to come back to the theater,"
Margaret Carrington said. "When I climbed the hill to his house
and saw how he lived in the sunshine, saw his collection of tropical
birds and fish, his library of rare volumes—he was then married to
Dolores Costello; they had two beautiful children—my heart sank.
I knew I had come on a lost cause. However, I pleaded with him to
come back and build a Barrymore theater where . . . he, Ethel
and Lionel would act singly or together. . . . I still believe if this
could have happened, the New York theater would have been different to what it has become. They, the Barrymores, would have accepted a large share of their natural heritage in perpetuating a
theater of elegance and distinction established by their forebears.
. . . This theater has waned and vanished because these three most
gifted of all the children of the American theater chose otherwise.
. . . When one remembers the individual performances of the
Barrymores strewn along the years, surely it is just such stuff as this
that theater dreams are made of."

But if Margaret Carrington imagined that domestic felicity was
what kept John away from the stage, she was deluded. In the last
two years his marriage had been disintegrated by the same cor-
rosives that had eaten away at his previous marriages—his tainted

view of women as betrayers, his pathological jealousy, his alcoholism.

Even before the marriage there had been a period of almost two months when he would neither see nor speak to Dolores, having fancied that she smiled encouragingly at another man. Later he installed iron gratings at the windows of Bella Vista lest some admirer of his wife's attempt to sneak into the house in his absence. Liquor fueled his jealousy and in drunken rages he would sometimes strike her.

In the spring of 1934 Worthington Miner, a young director working for RKO, undertook to make a silk purse out of a sow's ear. The film foisted upon him, *Hat, Coat, Glove*, was twaddle. Yet he felt that with John Barrymore playing the lead, a debonair swindler named Robert Mitchell, it stood a chance of popular success. Miner had venerated John since the age of eight when he was taken backstage at the musical comedy *A Stubborn Cinderella*. Eager to meet him again and to hear any suggestions he might offer to improve the script of *Hat, Coat, Glove*, he sent it to Bella Vista and followed it there a few days after.

John proposed a number of changes, which Miner had the writer incorporate into the script, and three weeks later, sitting with John by the Bella Vista swimming pool, he showed him the final version. Shooting was scheduled to begin in ten days.

In the first scene, a department store, Mitchell purchases the three articles of the title. As John faced the salesman, his memory suddenly faded. He could not even pronounce the name of the character he was playing. After a ten-minute break, he tried again. He had only seven lines to speak, but not a single word came to him. Efforts to get through the first scene went on for three working days, while the producer, Kenneth Macgowan, chewed his nails in anxiety over the extra cost to RKO.

Dolores consulted a physician who had formerly treated her, Dr. Samuel Hirshfeld. He thought chemotherapy might restore John's memory and he asked Macgowan to suspend shooting for a while. When John returned to the set, he managed to speak a word or two, stumbled again over his character's name, then bogged down completely.

"Come to my dressing room," he commanded Miner and Macgowan. "I'll show you I know the whole thing." They spent an hour with him while he struggled in vain to recapture his lines. At length, in a burst of fury, he turned to Miner. "I know what's going on here," he shouted. "With a few successes under your belt, you're delighted to be in on the fall of John Barrymore." He accused both men of exulting over his misfortune. "It would never have happened but for the antagonism you made me feel."

RKO refused to spend any more money beyond the budget allocated to the picture. A settlement of John's contract was agreed upon and his role given to Ricardo Cortez.

"It was one of the most painful experiences of my life," Miner says today. He wrote to John, expressing his admiration and regret. He received no reply. "I realized his anger was torn out of an inner anguish over his belief that he had reached the end, and, indeed, nearly every film he made after that was junk, a travesty of himself. It was a shattering blow for me. I had so looked forward to working with him. The appalling recognition of his own deterioration—it was awesome, terrible, harrowing to observe. For a long time I could not remember it without a shudder."

With his entire future as an actor in jeopardy, John let Dolores and Hirshfeld take him to Good Samaritan Hospital to determine whether some cause other than alcohol underlay his lapses of memory and his headaches. Two weeks of tests precluded two possibilities—a brain tumor and paresis. At the same time Hirshfeld tried to dry out the patient by putting him on a regime of ever decreasing daily doses of liquor. The pangs of withdrawal maddened John. He became violent, hurling obscenities at the nurses and assaulting them physically. Dolores, who occupied the adjoining room throughout his hospitalization, could not pacify him. Hirshfeld advised her to have him committed to a sanitorium for the mentally ill. Knowing John's obsessive fear of ending like his father, she could not bring herself to it. She lived to regret her reluctance. "I sometimes think it was my fault that all that happened afterward happened," she said.

She proposed to John that they take a sea voyage until he felt rested in mind and body. He needed no urging. Nothing had so lifted John's spirits, during intervals between pictures, as his adventures at sea and remote spots ashore. He had fished salmon streams in Juneau, Alaska; hunted Kodiak bear, once stopping a huge specimen that charged him with two shots fired at a range of about twenty-five yards (the creature's head eventually adorned the trophy room of Bella Vista); frolicked with elephant seals in the shallows off Guadelupe Island near the coast of Southern California (a private movie of the excursion shows John in a boyishly joyous mood as he jumps up and down, flapping his arms in imitation of their capers);

collected specimens for his Bella Vista zoo and exotic pets, among them an exceptionally repulsive king vulture he named Mr. Mahoney, who would enfold him in its wings and hold up its beak to be kissed.

With Captain Matthies and crew John sailed for Canadian waters on the *Infanta* in early June, while Dolores, the children and a young nurse, Margaret Hastings, traveled overland by train to board the yacht at Vancouver. Before they embarked, Matthies and Dolores scoured the vessel for liquor, jettisoning every bottle they could find. But just as desperation once drove John to drink the alcohol out of Michael Strange's curling iron, so during the cruise he consumed Dolores' perfume, some mouthwash and a pint of spirits of ammonia. His general behavior, however, remained relatively passive until, two months later, they anchored again in Vancouver harbor. There John struck a blow that would lead to the end of the marriage contracted seven years earlier, the same span of time his two previous marriages had lasted.

John went ashore and stayed all night. Dolores was awakened in the morning by the chugging of a motor launch and John calling to her to remain below, evidently not wanting her to see him in his disordered state. He was standing unsteadily in the prow of the launch, wearing evening clothes. As he climbed aboard, Dolores and Margaret, the nurse, appeared on deck. "Oh, Mr. Barrymore—" Margaret began. She got no further. John hit her, breaking her nose.

That evening Dolores with her children and the wounded nurse (who would presently collect $3,000 in settlement of her lawsuit against John) caught a train to Los Angeles. John came home toward the end of August. When Dolores announced that Dr. Hirshfeld had arranged a consultation for him with a neurologist, he concluded they were plotting to have him committed, which was not the case. He never saw the neurologist. After instructing a trusted factotum at Bella Vista to secretly pack and send him a trunkful of clothes, he flew to New York on the first leg of an escape route that would take him halfway around the world. Hotchener accompanied him as a kind of travel manager and, at John's invitation, took along Helios. Lest Dolores suspect his intention to flee the country and attempt to stop him, he telephoned from the airport to tell her he had received an irresistible offer from a New York broadcasting corporation, necessitating his immediate presence, but he would keep her abreast of his movements. As soon as his trunk arrived, he booked passage for England.

Once more, and for the last time, John considered a film portrayal of *Hamlet*. Encouragement to do so came from the managing director of the London Film Company, Alexander Korda. Soon after reaching London John signed a contract with the company for six weeks of work at $60,000, the film or films as yet unspecified. Korda proposed *Hamlet*.

John had preserved at Bella Vista the black habiliments he had first worn as the Dane twelve years earlier. The servant who packed his trunk somehow decided to include them. John tried them on before his hotel mirror, but they no longer fitted his once gracile figure. With the Hotcheners as audience, he then tested his memory of the soliloquies. Line after line eluded him. He knew finally that he would never attempt *Hamlet* again and he later canceled his London Film contract.

From Helios, whose spiritual home was India, John learned of the ancient healing art called Ayurveda. Among its prominent practitioners was a Dr. Srinivasa Murti of Madras, who, Helios assured John, could restore him to mental and physical health. John prepared to go with the Hotcheners to India. The prospect held an additional appeal for him: he hoped to visit Fort Agra, the scene of his father's boyhood.

Before leaving London John wrote his will, instructing the executor to convert his entire estate into U.S government bonds, the income from them to be divided equally among his three children. He bequeathed nothing to Dolores because, as he set forth, her own movie earnings together with $50,000 worth of bonds he had given her constituted a substantial fortune. He later appended a curious codicil: the executor was to cooperate with "any person who wishes to ascertain that I am, in fact, dead and not in any other state having the semblance of death, in order, so far as possible, to avoid all risk of my being buried alive."

John's fame as an actor had long before spread to India and he was welcomed and opulently entertained by state officials, rajahs and intellectuals. He found himself fascinated by Mme. Sarojini Naidu, a poet, orator and nationalist. She was married to a rajput ("son of a king")—that is, a member of a caste tracing its origins to the Rajanya warriors described in the sacred Hindu writings collectively known as the *Veda*. Like John, Mme. Naidu had attended, at age twelve, King's College in Wimbledon. A disciple of Mahatma Gandhi, she had served a term for civil disobedience in a British prison and was to do so again.

John reached Madras in November and, while Helios looked up old colleagues among the native Theosophists, he submitted to Ayurvedic therapy. Under Dr. Murti's supervision a team of physicians scattered flowers upon a portable altar, burned sacred oils and incense, chanted magical Sanskrit incantations, massaged the patient from head to toe for an hour at a time, bathed him in aromatic liquids, fed him rare herbs and confined his diet to vegetables. The treatment was supposed to take six weeks, but midway through it John vanished, not to be heard from for a month. What happened during that interval was a sexual adventure with an account of which he would later divert various Hollywood social gatherings, adding variants and embellishments to each retelling. Thus, at a birthday party Ben Hecht gave for him he cited as the initial reason for his disappearance a desire to commune with a renowned holy man living in Calcutta. According to Hecht's reconstruction of John's narrative:

"I always dreamed of meeting a saint and learning from him the true secrets of Heaven. . . . I never met him. On the morning I arrived in Calcutta, eager for spiritual communion with the young saint, I was picked up by a pimp and led to an amazing whore house. The most delightful I have ever seen to this day. . . . I would like to describe this pelvic palace so that you will not think me totally an idiot for giving up my saint in its favor. It had a great central room with a floor of pink and white marble which was covered with fleets of pillows. You have never seen such pillows. They cooed at your buttocks. There were tall silver columns, and clouds of colored silks ballooned from the ceiling, giving it the look of a heaven of udders. Incense pots gave forth smells capable of reviving the most dormant of Occidental phalluses. And music came from somewhere. . . . Gentle music that went directly to the scrotum and cuddled there. . . . A gong sounded. Bong! Ahzee-zee-zee. Beautiful women appeared in twos and threes. They moved slowly and their bellies were like serpents. I recall that they were hung with little bells and when they moved they made a noise like a swarm of bees. These delightful creatures sang and danced for me and then draped themselves around me in artistic clusters until I felt like a public chandelier. . . .

"I remained on the pillows for four busy weeks, never leaving them except to make use of a small plumbing contrivance within staggering distance. I lived and slept on those wonderful pillows and was fed like Elijah, but by ravens bearing a superior type of food. I would be happy to describe the dainties that were supplied me—but there are ladies present. . . .

"And so I never met my saint. I met only dancing girls and singing girls, all of them devout students of the Kamasutra, which teaches that there are thirty-nine different postures for the worship of Dingledangle—the God of love."

"Catkin," Michael Strange wrote to her thirteen-year-old daughter at the Garrison Forest School, "your father has just returned from a trip to India. I've given him permission to visit you on one condition—you are not to leave the grounds with him. I want that understood."

Diana disregarded the enjoinder. She was ecstatic when the Misses Marshall and Offut, the co-principals, agreed to let her father, whom she had not seen in seven years, take her and any schoolmate she cared to invite to dinner off campus, providing they return by midnight. Diana invited a senior four years older than herself named Pamela Gardiner. John escorted them to a Baltimore restaurant, where he ordered for Diana a brandy Alexander cocktail, the first liquor she had ever tasted. She drank two of them, while John stuck to straight brandy. Somebody in the restaurant must have alerted the press to John's presence, for a flock of news photographers appeared to snap pictures of father and daughter.

Dinner over, John asked the girls what they would like to do next. They would like, they said, to go to the Century, a movie palace which was showing *Les Misérables* with Fredric March. In the Century, Diana recalled, "Daddy sat with his arm around Pamela and, as I watched, kissed her. I thought, horrified, 'Why, they're smooching! How disgraceful of Pamela, even if she is nearly eighteen!' "

Though it was almost 11:30 when the movie ended and they faced an hour's drive back to the school, John insisted they drop in at a nightclub for a few last nips. Neither Diana nor her friend wanted anything stronger than sarsaparilla. "Good God, do they permit it?" John gasped in mock horror. "Did that not go out with Prohibition? Why, Treepee, don't you know that sarsaparilla erodes your kidneys, gives you pyloric spasms, and turns your liver the color of ochre? The greatest savants of India told me so." He drank double brandies.

Finally, past midnight, they boarded a taxi for Garrison. John sat between the girls, one arm encircling "this lovely vision," as he called Pamela. Diana dozed off. When she awoke at the school entrance, her father and Pamela were fast asleep, their heads touching. John's face was smeared with lipstick. Diana wiped it off with a handkerchief. Pamela shortly came to, but John slumbered on. After trying in vain to wake him, Diana kissed him on the cheek, murmured, "Good night, Daddy," and asked the taxi driver to deliver him to his hotel. But John had neglected to say where he was staying. Reluctantly, Diana roused Miss Marshall. That stalwart woman ordered the girls to bed, shook John awake, restored him to a degree of sobriety with quantities of hot black coffee and sent him on his way.

Next day the New York newspapers carried photos of John and Diana in the Baltimore restaurant. Michael, infuriated by what she deemed the headmistress's abominable permissiveness, transferred Diana to another select school—Fermata in Aiken, South Carolina.

"Two parents like mine would discourage anybody," Diana said.

A New York doctor whom John consulted about his deteriorating health prescribed a truce to "wine, women and song."

"Do I have to do it all at once?" John asked.

"No, you can taper off."

"Well, then, I shall quit singing."

He continued to drink enormous daily amounts of liquor. It nearly killed him. When Hotchener, who had gone ahead to Los Angeles with Helios, rejoined John at the New Yorker Hotel, he found him near total collapse. The doctor he summoned reserved a room for John at New York Hospital, where he stayed a month, deprived of liquor, and under treatment with medication, an invigorating diet and radiothermy.

It had been clear to both John and Dolores for almost a year that their life together was over, and when Hotchener told him what was going on at Bella Vista, John wrote to William Neblett, the Los Angeles lawyer he had retained to represent him in the forthcoming property settlement and divorce:

> A trusted friend has just informed me that Mrs. Barrymore's sister, Helene Costello, and "another blonde," have just arrived at my Beverly Hills home and are being entertained as guests by Mrs. Barrymore. Now I do not know why Helene has come to California, for her last marriage (her third) was to a Cuban whose home is in Havana. She would naturally side in with Mrs. Barrymore and, if her marriage has fizzled out [which it had], she

would be without funds. I see no special reason why she should be entertained, with another friend, in my home or at my expense (if it is being done at my expense), and I feel uncomfortable that my home and many valuable and salable possessions of mine should be at the possible mercy of unfriendly people who *may* be in need of funds and may possibly be driven to advise Mrs. Barrymore to a course of action which she herself might not make if not badly advised. . . . And as, for the moment, we have decided not to send any more money to Mrs. Barrymore until she realizes that she cannot keep on spending money at the old rate (as I am not working and cannot supply it), she will probably not only resent this and be furious, but she may possibly try to strike back by attempting to cash some of these valuable items which I have mentioned. I may be entirely wrong about this, but I do get the strong feeling that an immediate effort should be made to safeguard my property there. . . .

CODE WORDS: If you have occasion to telegraph, I suggest that you use the word "Seymour" for the name "Mrs. Barrymore"; and the word "Smith" in the body of the telegram in any matter referring to my name. This will give us secrecy by telegraph. . . .

Among John's visitors at the hospital were Michael Strange, their daughter, Diana, and Michael's husband, Harry Tweed, with whom John had established a cordial rapport. "I need to take Treepee with me on a cruise," said John, whose yacht Captain Matthies had moored at Miami. "I mean it, Fig. It will be my salvation. It's time I knew my own daughter."

Treepee added her plea. Michael reluctantly agreed on condition that Harry go along, for since the Baltimore escapade she felt John could not be trusted to treat his daughter as a father should. John gladly accepted the proviso and made plans to sail when he regained his strength.

John's visitors during his convalescence included the producer Al Woods, Jack Prescott and Herbert Bayard Swope, now at the pinnacle of his journalistic career, who brought his son, Herbert, Jr. One day a total stranger managed to get into the sickroom—with devastating consequences.

23

Rose of Sharon

======

Now King David was old and stricken in years; and
they covered him with clothes, but he gat no heat.

Wherefore his servants said unto him, Let there be
sought for my lord the king a young virgin: and let her
stand by the king, and let her cherish him, and let her lie in
thy bosom, that my lord the king may get heat.

I Kings 1: 1–2

On March 11, 1935, the New York *Daily News*' Broadway
columnist, Ed Sullivan, informed his readers that John Barrymore
lay ill at New York Hospital. Among them was a stagestruck Hunter
College sophomore of nineteen named Elaine Jacobs. Ever since she
had seen *Svengali*, at the age of fourteen, John had been her idol, the
predominant figure of her fantasies. "When he said that Hebrew
prayer and died," she recalled, "he broke my heart." She was determined to meet him.

Elaine's curriculum included a course in journalism. According
to what she wrote to John, her teacher had instructed each member
of the class to interview a celebrity for the college newspaper. In
reality, she had received no such assignment, but the fiction served
to gain entry to John's hospital room. Sick and lonesome, his professional standing at a low point, he was vulnerable to the adoring
tone of Elaine's letter and he agreed to see her.

Unlike most of the women in John's life, Elaine was far from beautiful, but she had youth, a shapely body, big, dark, lustrous eyes, vivacity and brass. Five feet four inches tall and weighing a trim 120 pounds, she dressed colorfully. Her large, thick-lipped mouth was bright red. She wore her fingernails long and painted red.

In defiance of his nurse, who told Elaine she could stay only three minutes, John kept her at his side for three hours as they talked about books, Shakespeare, the theater, acting. Elaine was not a complete stranger to the stage. She had participated in amateur theatricals at Julia Richman High School and at Hunter. For two weeks one summer she had played a walk-on maid in a strawhat production at Mount Vernon, New York, of Sir James Barrie's *What Every Woman Knows*. The leading lady, Pauline Lord, commented: "You will go far. You have stage presence."

Ambition and infatuation in about equal degrees colored Elaine's feelings for John. "I saw no reason why I shouldn't be lifted aloft by John," she disclosed many years later.* ". . . What was this nonsense about my exploiting him? Weren't all relationships exploitative? We use each other in this world. . . . With mutual respect and adoration, Barrymore would give me my deserved entrance into the Establishment. I would give him the enchantment of my youth, my curiosity, the empty slate on which he could sketch my fate."

The hospital visit ended with John's suggestion that they read *Richard III* together next time, his promise to telephone her at nine o'clock that evening and a kiss on the cheek. Elaine floated home.

She shared with her parents a one-bedroom apartment at Riverside Drive and Eighty-sixth Street. When her father was in town, she slept on a day bed in the living room. Louis Jacobs spent many months a year as a traveling salesman in men's wear. Kindly, mild, unassertive, he was overawed by a strong-willed wife and their strong-willed daughter.

After Elaine had breathlessly recounted the events of the afternoon, Mrs. Jacobs asked her whether John was as handsome as when she had seen him sixteen years before in *The Jest*. "He was a god," she said.

"He still is," said Elaine.

She could eat no supper, but waited beside a clock, watching the minutes drag by. On the stroke of nine John telephoned. He asked to

---

* In *All My Sins Remembered*, her version of the relationship, written in 1964 with Sandford Dody.

speak to Mrs. Jacobs. "What an enchanting daughter you have!" he told her, adding that he looked forward eagerly to meeting the mother. Edna Jacobs began to share Elaine's excitement.

The second time Elaine visited the hospital, next day, John kissed her on the mouth. The third time, when she brought her mother, he declared himself enamored of the daughter. Elaine came every day thereafter during the remaining week of John's confinement, and between protestations of love the convalescent tutored her in the actor's craft.

Elaine Jacobs presently began calling herself Elaine Barrie, "getting as near to Barrymore as I dared." Her mother also adopted the surname Barrie.

Upon his discharge John left New York for the promised cruise with Diana and her stepfather. From Miami he sent Elaine an amorous telegram, addressing her as "Ariel" and signing himself "Caliban." During the next several years those linked sobriquets were to recur ad nauseam as the press reported every dizzy twist and turn of the improbable romance. "I am sick to death of hearing that name," Elaine said later. "I wish Shakespeare had never written that play."

Back in New York after a fortnight at sea, Caliban took a suite at the Hotel New Yorker and danced attendance on the Jacobs-Barrie women. He bought Mrs. Jacobs a radio and a white fur jacket and in the weeks ahead spent more than $6,000 on gifts and entertainment for mother and daughter. "Elaine was a nice girl," he recalled, "and would go nowhere without her mother. But her mother would go anywhere." He took them to restaurants, theaters, nightclubs. He invited Elaine's journalism teacher, Kate Rochmis, for lunch at the Tavern-on-the-Green in Central Park, where he ordered a bear carved out of ice, holding a bowl of caviar. "I can't tell you how much I have enjoyed your work," Miss Rochmis said.

"Please tell me," John urged.

A few days later he vanished. There was no answer when Elaine called his hotel. The management had no idea where he had gone. Neither had Henry Hotchener, who now practically commuted between Los Angeles and New York as he struggled to bring order to John's increasingly chaotic affairs. Elaine and her mother were frantic.

Late the following night they answered the doorbell. John stood swaying on the threshold, stuporously drunk. "It may be difficult

to believe now," Elaine said later, "that I hadn't the slightest sus-
picion until then that John had a drinking problem." He also had
flu and a high fever. Giving up her day bed to me, Elaine passed
the rest of the night on a cot set up in the kitchen. When Lou Jacobs
shortly returned from the road, he demurred at the overcrowding and,
in a rare display of spirit, threatened to leave the apartment for good.
But in the end his resistance melted before his wife's displeasure.

Elaine dropped out of Hunter in May to devote herself entirely
to her guest, who continued her Shakespearean education. "He
astonished me and in a contagion of fever I became so completely
Lady Macbeth that I took off and soared with him."

John remained at the Jacobses' for almost three weeks, the object of lively neighborhood speculation. Close by, on Amsterdam
Avenue, stood Barney Greengrass' delicatessen, then as now one of
the city's leading purveyors of such Jewish ambrosia as smoked
sturgeon, lox, bagels, gefilte fish. Sunday mornings the Jacobs
family would go there with John. One Sunday a former schoolmate
of Elaine's, Iris Segal, was dispatched to the delicatessen by her
father. There she beheld John, acutely hung over, demanding to know
whether he required circumcision before he would be allowed to buy
some pickled herring. Noticing the slack-jawed adolescent, he
bellowed at her and made a move as if to unfasten his fly. Iris fled,
her face red, and bumped into Jacobs père, arriving to see if
John needed any shopping guidance.

Thus far the Barrymore-Jacobs idyll had received scant publicity. Then Jesse Mass, a young reporter for the tabloid New York
Daily Mirror, chanced to attend a party on the West Side where he
met Elaine. "Guess who's living in my apartment," she said. "John
Barrymore."

After Mass had verified this information with the building
superintendent, he wrote his story. The subsequent fanfare so delighted Mrs. Jacobs that in gratitude she betook herself to the
Mirror offices and tipped off Mass to an imminent development in the
Caliban-Ariel saga.

To each of John's three wives, as well as to several mistresses,
he had given help in advancing their theatrical ambitions, regardless of their talent. He did no less for Elaine. When asked to read
a scene from *Twentieth Century* on Rudy Vallee's Colgate radio hour,
he accepted with the proviso that Elaine be allowed to audition for
the role Carole Lombard had played in the film. She passed the test
and on May 23 broadcast her first dramatic lines. The radio critics

refrained from odious comparisons. The majority accorded her faint praise. An exception was the *Daily News* critic, who felt that she "came through excellently."

The following day John, Elaine, and Mrs. Jacobs departed for Miami and a cruise to Havana. Just before the *Infanta* weighed anchor, word came from Lawyer Neblett in Los Angeles that Dolores had filed suit for divorce. The complaint specified "habitual intemperance and extreme cruelty." John directed Hotchener by phone to hurry back to the Coast and help Neblett arrange an equitable settlement.

Havana was the scene of the first of many violent quarrels between John and Elaine. The kisses bestowed upon Elaine's hand by the Cuban hidalgos she met, their ornate compliments and flirtatious glances inflamed John's jealousy. At a party one night he slapped her face.

Next day, full of contrition, he asked her to marry him as soon as he was free and, when she consented, bought her a nine-carat yellow diamond costing $1,800.

Another quarrel soon erupted. During a party aboard the *Infanta* John, glimpsing Elaine in a tête-à-tête with a Cuban millionaire, concluded that they were planning an assignation. He tried to throw the Cuban overboard, then chased Elaine to her cabin. Cursing her for a "common little tart," he raised his arm to strike her, but, overcome by drink, slumped to the floor. Reparations followed in the morning.

When the *Infanta* docked in Miami, Elaine wore her diamond ring, but neglected to declare it to Customs because—so she justified the omission to the press—"Mr. Barrymore was not yet divorced and it would not have looked well." Duty plus penalty cost John an additional $3,200.

He returned with mother and daughter to their apartment, where he lived until the fall. There was the obvious danger that Dolores might charge infidelity as further grounds for divorce, and at Hotchener's suggestion Elaine signed an affidavit attesting to the "strictly platonic relationship" between herself and John, one based solely on "professional artistic" interests. According to her memoirs, however, John seduced her at home in the absence of her parents. She described her surrender as follows:

"John was covering me with kisses and I felt myself lifted off my feet. I was in his arms. He was carrying me off somewhere. My God! Oh, my God.

"His lips and hands were like the sun and breeze. His voice was an echo of a dream, the collective dream of all maidenhood.

" 'How beautiful are thy feet without shoes, O Prince's daughter . . . the work of the hands of a cunning workman . . .'

"I felt his sweet breath at my ankle. This was the gentlest man ever to love a woman.

"Trembling in my awareness of sin, I was utterly incapable of sweet abandon, his tenderness was extraordinary and my fears melted away. I might have been a shivering bird, captive in his hand, warmed, safe—still eager for release.

" 'My dove, my undefiled one . . . she who is the only one of her Mother . . . O daughter of Jerusalem . . . who is she that looketh forth as the morning, fair as the moon, clear as the sun and terrible as an army with banners . . .' "

"There were those who thought of John as a tired, jaded old man. With me, he was as one and twenty. I can still hear him whispering, 'My Rose . . . my Rose of Sharon . . .' "

With consummation the intensity of John's desire increased, while Elaine, as she herself put it, "seethed with ambition." They decided to furnish an apartment of their own. Shopping at W. & J. Sloane on Fifth Avenue, they chose twin beds with mattresses and box springs. Elaine asked John to test them for comfort. As he stretched out on one, Elaine flopped down beside him on the other. At that instant several photographers popped out from concealment and snapped away. John tried to smash some cameras and flung harsh words at Elaine. The connubial scene appeared next day in newspapers.

The Hotcheners—Henry, Helios and Maurice—became Elaine's deadly rivals for control of John. Maurice engaged a high-powered colleague named Frank Aranow as a consultant and the Hotchener camp scored a signal victory. They convinced John that Elaine and her mother were predators scheming to bleed him white. In September 1935, following a violent clash, John stormed out of the Jacobs apartment, taking Elaine's diamond ring with him.

The Jacobs women also retained a lawyer, Aaron Sapiro. He gave Elaine to understand that "I did have some legal rights as his [John's] fiancée and, in an effort to create a bridge back to John, I demanded a return of my ring. . . ."

In Aranow's opinion, John should lie low for a while, somewhere beyond Elaine's reach. He tendered him the hospitality of his own commodious Wonara Lodge near Stamford, Connecticut. John accepted. He failed, however, to ingratiate himself with Aranow, his wife or their friends.

Three decades later the lawyer began an autobiography. Though he died in 1972 before finishing it, he did get through a chapter entitled "The John Barrymore Case."*

". . . he would sleep rather late, but when he got up in the morning he had to have his glass of gin. He said he couldn't possibly open his eyes until he had that gin. . . .

"Most of the evenings we spent at home because I knew that detectives had been searching for him, and my home was one mile from the main road, and I had some very vicious dogs who would not permit any stranger on the premises, so we felt safe at home. But he pleaded to go out and visit my friends. Finally we gave in to his request and we took him with us to visit a Mr. and Mrs. Engel at Wilton, Connecticut.

"Mr. Engel was a prominent stockbroker in New York, and he had a house full of people and they were delighted to meet the great John Barrymore. They gave him a very great ovation which pleased John no little. Mr. Engel, in spite of my advice to the contrary, supplied liquor and wines, and John did not observe any moderation. Among the guests was . . . a minister from the local church, and he had with him his young daughter. . . . The conversation ultimately led to love and the making of love. After John had several drinks, he went into a very minute and detailed description of how he made love; how he first undressed the female; then how he prepared her for the act of love by exposing her genitals and using his hands in order to make the female sensuous and anxious. By that time, most of the guests . . . were running out of the room with screams of laughter and apprehension as to how far he will go. But John did not stop at anything. . . . Ultimately, Mr. Engel brought out a bottle of champagne and thus we were able to inveigle John away from the minister and his pretty daughter. . . . We left the Engel house early in the morning and much wiser and more humiliated than we had been when we came. After that, John stayed in my house and we had no more parties except in our home. . . ."

Under an agreement worked out by Aranow to the satisfaction of both Maurice Hotchner and Sapiro, John was to place $5,000 in escrow to be paid to Elaine after one year "if she does not follow,

*I quote from the unpublished manuscript with the permission of Mrs. Aranow.

annoy or in way communicate with John." Secondly, neither Elaine nor her mother was to talk to any more reporters. Finally, John would return the diamond ring if Elaine acknowledged it as a gift, not an earnest of betrothal. John would also pay Sapiro's fee of $2,000. "I always wanted to be dignified about the whole thing," Elaine commented.

John then headed homeward in dark secrecy. As he left Wonara Lodge, Aranow warned him: "If you ever again have anything to do with Elaine Barrie, I will have nothing more to do with you." But the attorney reckoned without Elaine's steely determination.

On September 19 Julia McCarthy, a *Daily News* reporter friendly to Elaine, received a tip that John Barrymore was at Grand Central Station about to take the Twentieth Century to Chicago and, thence, the Super Chief to Los Angeles, the customary westward route for Hollywood celebrities. The *Daily News* building stands within two blocks of Grand Central. Miss McCarthy hastened there. She managed to board the train, only to be repulsed by the vigilant Henry Hotchener. Outraged, she telephoned Elaine to tell her that John would reach Chicago the following morning. "I wouldn't let them get away with it," she said. Elaine had no such intention. As she explained in her memoirs, "Unless the end of our relationship justified the means, unless it came to a fitting conclusion—marriage—then my involvement was catastrophic, my history merely a scandal. I alone could see the complete design, and it couldn't end this way. It just couldn't. I would see to that. I had to."

ELAINE SIGHS "HE'S BOUND TO ME," screamed the *News* headline. The city editor, eager to secure the inside track on what promised to be a serial sensation, chartered a plane for Elaine, and when it took off, Sapiro called Nat Gross, a Chicago *Herald Examiner* reporter he knew, asking him to help Elaine catch up with her man. The plane landed well in advance of the train, and Gross led her to the railroad terminal to await John's arrival. After ferreting out the number of his stateroom, Gross accompanied Elaine to the door, a host of reporters now trailing close behind. She knocked, crying: "John, this is your Ariel," and receiving no reply, turned the knob. "John, my John, I love you," she wailed as she opened the door. A strapping Negro porter confronted her. "Honey," he said, "I love you too, but I'm not the John you want."

ELAINE CHASES BARRYMORE BY AIR

OVERTAKES HIS TRAIN IN VAIN

Hotchener had spirited John out of the Twentieth Century into a westbound train other than the Super Chief. Elaine raced to Kansas City, the Super Chief's first stop. Finding no sign of John, she broadcast from a radio station one of the most extraordinary pleas in the annals of the medium:

"I address this appeal to the people of Kansas City and the Middle West who have been so sympathetic and understanding. John, dear, I know you need me now, more than ever. I realize that certain people are keeping you from me. When you were with me, I was able to nurse you back to health. I want to help you and save you from those who would destroy you. My messages to you have not been delivered. Please, please, dear John, don't think I have deserted you. I am here in Kansas City, awaiting your call. We have each other. That is all that matters."

ELAINE GIVES UP CHASE
AS JOHN OUTFOXES HER

Though she returned to New York in defeat, it was not without compensation. Notoriety had invested her with a certain entertainment worth and she began to receive offers from minor vaudeville, radio and theater entrepreneurs. At length, in the company of her mother, she went to Boston to join the Mary Young repertory company and play a substantial role in a farce with the atrocious title *Katy Did, So What?* "Mr. Barrymore's protégée gives a colorful performance," wrote one Boston reviewer. Another wrote: "Miss Barrie's value was not limited to her publicity. She was quite able to act."

Elaine never abandoned the hope of rekindling John's passion. Her faith did not go unrewarded.

On October 9, 1935, Dolores obtained an uncontested divorce. "She was too beautiful for words," said John by way of an elegy for a dead love, "but not for arguments." His obligations under the term of the settlement, while comparatively light by themselves, proved staggering when added to his disbursements to Michael for Diana's support, the upkeep of Bella Vista and the *Infanta*, his enormous pile-up of debts and his delinquent taxes. He undertook to pay Dolores $850 a month for the support of their son and daughter and to maintain the $235,000 life-insurance policy of which the children were the beneficiaries.

Nine more films starred Dolores Costello before she retired in 1942. She had meanwhile, in 1939, wed Dr. John Vruwink. It was at that time that John told Garson Kanin, who was directing him in a movie for RKO, *The Great Man Votes*, how he had accused Dolores of carrying on an affair with her obstetrician. What had led him to believe so? Kanin wondered. Nothing, John admitted, nothing at all. They were quite guiltless. Why, then, had he insisted they were in love? "They were. Only they didn't know it. I knew it before they did." Yes, but how? "I knew it because I am John Barrymore."

Free again, John wired Elaine: DEAR DEAR LOVELY ROSE OF SHARON HOLD ON TO YOUR END OF THE RAINBOW GOODNIGHT MY LOVE CALIBAN. He followed this with a plea that she come to him at once. Elaine required no second bidding. Quitting *Katy Did, So What?* she entrained for the Coast with her mother, that indispensable strategist in the campaign to recapture John. But a humiliating reception awaited them. When Elaine telephoned John on arrival, he told her he could not see her immediately. He must, he explained, heed the boss of the radio station for which he was to broadcast a play and avoid bad publicity lest it imperil his professional future. For the present he dare not be seen with Elaine. That evening, he said, he was going with Ben Hecht and Charles MacArthur to a party at the Beverly Hills pleasure dome of Countess Dorothy Taylor di Frasso, filmdom's most persistent party-giver. He would elucidate further next day. Apparently, John's interest in Elaine waxed and waned according to which state prevailed—concupiscence or rationality. Elaine and her mother decided to crash the Di Frasso festivities. A butler shut the door in their faces.

A distraught Elaine called John in the morning and he summoned her to Bella Vista, whose most valuable contents had either been taken by Dolores or placed in storage by Hotchener. "I loathed it on sight. . . . Fixtures had been stripped from the walls, loose wires were all over the place, furniture dragged across the floor already bare of rugs, walls denuded of pictures and hangings. . . . a Meissen chandelier . . . still hung in the empty dining room because . . . it had evidently been impossible to remove without destroying it. It was underneath this profusion of china . . . that Mother and I had our Christmas dinner and our first nightmare of the New Year. . . ." John moved them into a house in the Benedict Canyon section.

With the aid of Aaron Sapiro, Elaine now turned the tables on the Hotcheners. In a maneuver possible only because John's grasp of financial matters was sub-moronic, they convinced him that his business manager had been mishandling his funds. Sapiro filed suit against Hotchener for an accounting, and John recklessly gave Sapiro power of attorney. As Frank Aranow noted, this was "like telling the cat to mind the cream."

By and large, Hollywood society closed ranks against Elaine. The few who befriended her did so chiefly for John's sake. Even before her arrival the ineffable Hearst columnist Louella Parsons (to whom John once referred as "a quaint old udder") foresaw ostracism for her.

Eighteen months had elapsed since John's last film, and in his tattered financial state he gladly assented when Irving Thalberg proposed to him the secondary but perfectly Barrymoresque role of Mercutio in MGM's *Romeo and Juliet*, starring Norma Shearer and Leslie Howard. John's lines, like everybody else's, were brutally truncated, yet between Shearer's saccharine Juliet and Howard's anemic Romeo his Mercutio shone like gold among pyrites. With what airy, playful, skimmering grace did he deliver Mercutio's lovely flight of fancy (unhappily, cut by almost half): "Oh, then, I see Queen Mab hath been with you. . . ." What bubbling glee, what mischievous delight he took in snapping out for the ears of a mass audience Mercutio's ribald reply when the Nurse asks him the time of day: ". . . the bawdy hand of the dial is now upon the pr-r-r-rick of noon."

John's youthful, agile Mercutio was the more phenomenal considering his condition at the time. He had been drinking so heavily that Thalberg insisted he live for the duration of the shooting at a Culver City institution, not far from the studio, euphemistically known as Kelley's Rest Home. James Kelley and his wife, Louise, specialized in the care of alcoholics. A deceptively slight man, he was capable of subduing patients of twice his heft.

As an added precaution, Thalberg assigned a team of studio police to stand guard over John around the clock lest he escape to some bar. But with the connivance of Hecht, MacArthur and Gene Fowler, John outwitted them all. While the playwrights diverted the guards' attention with entertaining talk, John lowered from his window a bedsheet to which Fowler tied a bottle of gin.

When the call came around eight a.m. for the first takes, John was dozing after the night's excesses, on his dressing-room couch. The action, scheduled out of sequence, was to be the events leading to the duel betwen Tybalt (Basil Rathbone) and Mercutio and ending in the latter's death. The director, George Cukor, waited all morning. At last, toward midday, a studio limousine deposited John on the set, costumed and made up and looking, as Rathbone recalled, "breathtaking beautiful." He sauntered over to Cukor and in a gravelly whisper told him: "Sorry, old boy, lost me voice. Can't speak a bloody word."

So Cukor shot the wordless duel itself first. As the cameras moved into position, John drew his sword, executed a flourish and accidentally fetched Leslie Howard a nasty crack on the pate, raising a lump. Cukor dismissed the company for the day. When work was resumed, it proceeded smoothly enough up to the last moment when Mercutio, trying to find Romeo, who has just scaled the wall of the Capulet garden, reaches the line, "He heareth not, he stirreth not, he moveth not." Here John sucked in his breath, arched his eyebrows, popped his eyes and purled: "He heareth not, he stirreth not [long pause], he pisseth not."

Cukor groaned. "Jack, *please*."

"Strange how me heritage encumbereth me speech. Yet I would beg you to consider an undeniable fact. I have improved upon the text. 'He moveth not' is not so pertinent to the occasion as 'He pisseth not.'"

The buffoonery went on almost until the lunch break. Cukor sent for Thalberg, who cajoled John into speaking the line as written just once.

"Very well, just once shall I say it that thou mayest see how it stinketh." He said it perfectly in a single take, the one that Cukor ordered to be printed. John feigned anger, claiming he had been hoodwinked, and he swore to wreak terrible vengeance upon those who had played him false.

He was equally drunk when he came to the Queen Mab soliloquy, yet delivered it so superbly that the entire company applauded. "Fuck the applause," said John. "Who's got a drink?"

During the filming of *Romeo and Juliet* Elaine kept badgering John to "pave my way to the top," as he had promised, but aside from a few screen tests she got nowhere, a failure she attributed to his maniacal jealousy. When, for example, she posed for a Paramount publicity still and the photographer adjusted a fur piece she was wearing, John pushed the man aside, saying, "Don't touch her. I'll do it." In order to be allowed to take dancing lessons, she had to imply that the instructor was homosexual. When John escorted her to a restaurant and the headwaiter bent over her décolletage to take her order, John snatched the menu away and waved him back. In a nightclub, as she was following with polite interest an entertainer's act, he demanded: "Why are you looking at him?"

To a degree, Elaine felt she could understand his mistrust. "When packs of women were ready to fall on their backs for him, many of them married to important directors, how could he believe in such a thing as fidelity?"

July 16, 1936, was Elaine's twentieth birthday and she gave a party. Her maternal grandparents, Herman and Babette Rosenthal, came all the way from New York to attend. John had been drinking all afternoon. He turned up hours before the party started. She begged him to stay away. "Who is it you don't want me to see?" he asked menacingly. He left only to return when the party was under way and in the presence of the guests, a number of them film notables, slapped Elaine's face and ripped her dress. The Thalbergs were also among the party guests. Earlier in the day John somehow got the idea that during the Boston run of *Katy Did, So What?* Elaine had had an affair with a young member of the cast. Midway through dinner, after a Homeric consumption of wine, John turned to Norma Shearer. "The world has certainly changed," he said (as Elaine remembered it). "Tarts were never countenanced at a gentleman's table, amongst such a lofty congregation. . . . Can you imagine anything more disgusting? These whores who are never seen in public without their lady mothers."

Elaine and her mother fled Los Angeles.

They had barely unpacked their luggage in New York before John was on the phone. Elaine refused to speak to him. He called every half-hour or so. She stood firm. A week later Irving Thalberg telephoned. John needed her desperately, he said. Without her he could not work. *Romeo and Juliet* was stalled. She must come back.

"I think I deserve an MGM contract," said Elaine.

Thalberg promised her one and within a few hours the Jacobs ladies were en route to the Coast. When they got there, they found John still living at Kelley's Rest Home. The barred windows, the moans and cries of inmates in withdrawal, the pervasive stench of paraldehyde (the then sedative of choice) horrified Elaine, and when John tried to make love to her in his cell-sized bedroom, she turned and ran.

A studio contract was no guarantee of a role, and MGM found none for her. She returned with her mother to New York.

Such tergiversation produced a fresh outbreak of Caliban-Ariel headlines. They prompted station WMCA to employ Elaine on its *Symphony of Words*, a series of broadcasts during which she read poetry. She also played a bit part in Robert E. Sherwood's *The Petrified Forest* on what was known as the "subway circuit"—that is, far-off-Broadway spots like Brighton Beach and Jamaica Heights.

A blizzard of letters and telegrams and finally a second proposal of marriage reunited Ariel and Caliban. John was about to portray a music impresario in an MGM adaptation of the operetta *Maytime*, with Jeanette MacDonald and Nelson Eddy. The background was the Paris of Napoleon III and his Empress Eugénie. DARLING HAD A LONG TALK WITH STROMBERG [Hunt Stromberg, an MGM producer] WE WANT YOU TO PLAY EMPRESS EUGENIE IT IS A LOVELY PART, one telegram read and ended: THE LOVE I FEEL FOR YOU DOESN'T COME OFTEN TO ANY ONE I AM KISSING YOUR LOVELY EYES.

If Empress Eugénie ever figured as a character in the script, those passages had been expunged by the time Elaine arrived, and MGM offered no other role. The marriage proposal, however, held good, though Hecht and MacArthur mustered all their eloquence to dissuade John. When another friend permitted himself to ask what John saw in Elaine, he replied: "It fits," and to reporters he announced: "That little filly made a racehorse out of me again."

At the Burbank airport, where Elaine, both her parents and Aaron Sapiro deplaned, John chartered a private aircraft to fly them all to Yuma, Arizona, and there, on November 8, 1936, Elaine became the fourth Mrs. John Barrymore.

The newlyweds spent their first night in Los Angeles' Beverly Wilshire Hotel, interrupted at frequent intervals by bawdy phone calls from some of the groom's raffish drinking companions. "John and I were hardly strangers on our wedding night. My feet were already wet when we dove into marriage. I had waded primly into sex. Inhibited, prudish, not in love, I was rather aloof. But now I gave myself freely to my husband and any diffidence disappeared in the wonder of our mutual love. He made me unashamed of the natural. He made me glory in my sensuality."

Elaine later spoke of John as "a super-being sexually—at first. In the beginning it was a nightly affair, but then the need to prove himself made him try too hard and there were failures."

But the nuptial night did not pass without a resurgence of John's jealousy. The thought came to him that the skill and enthusiasm Elaine brought to love-making betokened some teacher before him, and he demanded to know who and when and where.

He returned to the *Maytime* set next morning in foul humor. No devotee of Jeanette MacDonald, he turned on the celluloid diva and snarled: "If you wave that loathsome chiffon rag you call a kerchief once more while I'm speaking, I shall ram it down your gurgling throat."

PART

VI

HOLLYWOOD AND
POINTS EAST
1935–1942

24

The Bundy Drive Boys

S o called because they held their revels most often in John Decker's studio at 419 North Bundy Drive. Decker was a portraitist who liked to render his subjects in the styles of Old Masters. Originally Leopold Wolfgang von der Decker, a German baron's son, raised in England where his father worked as a correspondent for the *Berliner Tagblatt*, Decker spent nearly all of World War I behind barbed wire on the Isle of Man, a suspected enemy spy. By his own account, his life had been a "perpetual hangover . . . I saw my friends through a fog and a haze of high spirits." He adorned his front door with what he insisted was his family coat of arms, bearing the motto, "Useless, Insignificant, Poetic."

Decker's best-known portrait, which Gene Fowler, a charter member of the group, commissioned, was of another charter member, W. C. ("Woody") Fields, his bulbous nose drink-reddened, his cheeks puffed out, as Victoria Regina. He signed it "Sir John Decker, R.A." The actor Cedric Hardwicke demanded a copy. So did Dave Chasen to hang in his renowned Hollywood restaurant. A liquor concern wanted to reproduce it in periodicals nationwide over the slogan W. C. FIELDS SAYS, "FIT FOR A QUEEN," but Fields objected on the grounds of dubious taste. Decker also depicted three nearly nude figures in the attitudes of Jesus and the two thieves on their crosses.

311

The middle figure was John Barrymore and those flanking him were women.

The Bundy Drivers could just as fittingly have termed themselves The Society of the Friends of John Barrymore, for a good deal of their talk and their activities revolved around "the Monster," as they affectionately dubbed him. In common with John, they tended toward misogyny. "The collecting sex," the Great Lover called women, "twittering vaginas." "I wish I'd been born a pansy," he once said while under pressure by Elaine and her mother. "You dames are all poison," and on other occasions, "Don't trust any of them as far as you can throw Fort Knox. . . . When a woman leaves you, she has opened the door and set you free." W. C. Fields allowed as how he loved "the little nectarines" if they were neither aggressive nor possessive, to which John rejoined: "Is there any other kind?"

For his fifty-fifth birthday the Bundy Drive boys delivered to Bella Vista a naked girl wrapped in cellophane tied with a silver bow.

"All of us tried to be profound, or entertaining, or witty," said Errol Flynn, a late joiner, who referred to the exclusively male sodality as "the Olympiads." "I think we thought of ourselves as essentially philosophic. What characterized us was the range of personal experience which we had each had, physical or mental; something unique or special. One or two might even be abysmal mentally, or bawdy; but outstanding in some particular way."

Like John, they were both cynical and sentimental. Cultivated men, most of them, they affected the mucker pose. Their terms of endearment for one another were generally scatological. To John, Gene Fowler was "piss-pot" and "horse cock." His ultimate expression of affection for a friend was to address him as "shithead."

Understandably, the women in the lives of the Bundy Drive boys did not regard the fellowship with favor. In Dolores' view, John Decker was a "beast." Elaine condemned them all as "perennial undergraduates . . . these unhappy creatures did a disservice . . . to John, their idol . . . a group of sodden children . . . Perpetuating the image of a sinking giant seemed to please the fancy of his friends who wept copiously and pushed him down a little further. . . . When . . . he fell in with these senile delinquents . . . he drank himself into a caricature, dancing to their tune, and laughing more cruelly than they at himself. John would emerge from the mist and the hangover, a bitter ailing man, while his cronies would alternate between mischief and compassion."

A cartoon by Decker reflected the sentiments of the group toward the Jacobs ladies. It showed them floating above John's bed, each carrying a bow and arrow.

The Bundy Drive boys shared John's taste for coarse humor and practical jokes. John Carradine, when a brassy young actor, long before he became a Bundy Drive regular, fell victim to the latter. He was one of a sizable number of actors who emulated the Barrymore style not only on the screen but in their private lives. They wore, like him, shirts with wide rolled collars and fedoras canted at a rakish angle. ("It likes me well," John would say when choosing a new hat.) As performers, they favored one profile over the other, in their diction leaned heavily on consonants and rolled their r's, and gave their eyebrows expressive play. Besides Carradine and Flynn, the Barrymore school included Warren William, Ian Keith, Edmund Lowe, John Emery—to name only a few.

Approaching John on the Warner lot one day, Carradine remarked: "I'm told you are very much like me." John punished this impudence with an elaborate hoax. He promised Carradine to get him a screen test for an important role in a movie about to be cast. With the complicity of some fellow pranksters, among them a cameraman, he staged a banquet scene during which Carradine, as directed, licked his chops over the food and exclaimed: "Delicious!" The resulting film strip was run off before a select audience in a Warner projection room. It first showed Carradine close up, then at the exclamation "Delicious!" the camera panned to John. He was buttoning up his fly.

Few older members of the Bundy Drive fraternity were exactly prime physical specimens. Decker suffered from ulcers and diabetes. W. C. Fields was arthritic. Gene Fowler had survived several heart attacks. He, MacArthur and Ben Hecht had ulcers. Sadakichi Hartmann, a half-Japanese, half-German practitioner of many arts, whom the group prized as "a living freak [in John's description] presumably sired by Mephistopheles out of Madame Butterfly," was asthmatic and wore a truss for a hernia. John himself, in addition to ulcers, edema, acute stomach inflammation and a persistent skin rash, was a prey to kidney inflammation and a cirrhotic liver. When the United States entered World War II, John, Decker, Fields and Fowler volunteered for home defense. The young woman behind the registration desk stared at them a moment in bemusement. "Who sent you?" she asked. "The enemy?"

When Decker developed his ulcers, John told him: "Forget 'em. I fed my own ulcers for six months, fed 'em everything the doctors advised, milk, cream, all that stuff, the best in the world, and they didn't budge an inch. So one day I just took a clean, undiluted slug of hot gin, and that scared 'em right out of my system. I've felt like a new man ever since!"

Sadakichi Hartmann's attitude toward drinking was equally unorthodox. "If you want to drink," he said, "you should do it. If you care more about drinking than you do for your work or your health, then by all means you should drink. But you should never make apologies for your excesses, and no trips to sanitariums. Just drink, and die, and leave the rest to the angels."

To thus cock a snook at death and disease further exemplified the Bundy Drive mystique. At the funeral of John Gilbert, who by 1937 had drunk himself into the grave, John noticed standing next to him an extremely aged mourner. When the ceremony ended, he could not refrain from asking him just how old he was. "Eighty-four," replied the stranger. "Well," said John reflectively, "it hardly pays to go back to town, does it?"

Sadakichi Hartmann was sui generis. Skeletal and lantern-jawed, he looked, as John observed, like "the last of the Pharaohs and nicely mummified." The father of thirteen children, each named after a flower, he wrote poetic dramas of formidable length about Confucius, Buddha, Mohammed, Moses and Christ (in which he depicted the Savior as being in love with Mary Magdalene), none of them produceable and few publishable. The dedication of the Confucius play read: "This book I hurl into the Jaws of Mammon, the Moloch of the Modern Art." He also translated, imitated and wrote voluminously on Japanese rhythms, on Tanka, Haikai and Dodoitso. His two most successful works were histories of Japanese and American art. For twenty-two periodicals, about half of which he published himself, he wrote stories and art critiques. An excursion into the occult produced a refreshing view of the human condition entitled *My Theory of Soul Atoms*. A dancer, he executed *pas seuls* choreographed by himself. His visiting card was a pen-and-ink self-portrait. A multilingual globe-trotter, he had come to know Mallarmé, Anatole France, Verlaine, Debussy, Saint-Gaudens, Amy Lowell, Mary Baker Eddy, Walt Whitman and Gertrude Stein, who said: "Sadakichi is singular, never plural." At one time he was Whistler's secretary. The critic James Huneker described him as a "strange, powerful, morbid, unrestrained talent . . . a Japanese primitive with the soul of Schopenhauer. . . . He may end in a madhouse, or he may become a great actor or an indifferent editor of some foreign paper of revolt. . . . Sadakichi Hartmann is a deep-dyed decadent and beats the lot for audacity and extraordinary plainness of speech. . . . [He] exudes genius."

Hartmann was seventy, living in a shack he had built on an Indian reservation, when Decker unearthed him and brought him into the Bundy Drive circle, to everybody's delight and amusement. He and John concealed their fondness for each other under continual banter. The exotic newcomer was an inveterate pipe-smoker, using the cheapest brands of tobacco. "Vesuvius with halitosis," John commented and appealed to Decker: "Can't you give him a cigar or even a Roman candle instead of that vile calumet?" When Fowler decided to commemorate the group in a book (*Minutes of the Last Meeting*), with particular attention to Hartmann, John told him: "His story would be a pilgrimage to the tomb of Freud."

"Your father was a sublime actor," said Hartmann, who claimed to have known Maurice Barrymore intimately. "I cannot say the same for his stupid younger son."

The wild, chaffing letters that John and the others occasionally exchanged exemplified the Bundy Drive spirit. During one Christmas season, for example, W. C. Fields composed the following:

Dear John,

I have been having a few drinks and I thought I would drop you a note. About this time of the year I usually take a moment to write a few letters to my good friends; the time when I remember all the good things and indulge myself to the extent of getting a little sentimental.

It is a blustery evening, but here in my Den it's coz-zy and comfuable. I'm sitting before a nice open fire with my typewriter, John, sort of haff lissning to the radio and sllowly sipping a nice, very dry double martini. I only wish you were here, John, and since you are not, the least I cando is to toast to your health and happyness, so time out, old pal—while I bend my elbow to you.

I just took time to mix another Martini and while I was out in the kitchen I thought of all the time I would waste this evening if I went out to mix another drink every once in a while, so I just made up a big pitcher of Martinis and brought it back in with me so I'd have it right here beside me and wouldn't have to waste time making more of them. So now I'm all set and here goes. Besides Mratinis are great drrink. For some reson they never seeme to effec

me in the slightest. and drink thrm all day long. So here
goes. The greateest think in tje whole wokld, John, is
friendship. Anebelieve me pal you are the gertests pal anybody ever had. do you remembre all the swell times we had
together "pal??/ The wondderful camping trisp. I'll never
forget the time yoi put the dead skunnk in my sleeping
bag. He ha Bow how we laughued didn we. Never did the
stin kout ouut od it. Bit it was prtetty funnya anywayh.
Nev I still laught about it onec in a whole. Not as muhc as
i used to. But what the heck & after all you still my beset
old pal john, and if a guy can't have a luaghg on good treu
friedn onc in a whiel waht the heck. Dam pitcher is impty
so i just went outand ma deanotherone and i sure wisch you
wee here old pal to help me drink these marotomi because
they are simply sdeliuccious. Parn me whil i lieft my glass
to you good helahth oncemroe John because jjhon Barry-
mroe best pal i goo Off cours why a pal would do a dirty thinb
liek puting a skunnk in nother pals sleping bagg I&m dash
if I kno. That was a lousi thing for anybodyhdy todo an
only a frist clas heel would di it. Jhon, wasn a dm dam bit
funney. Still stinkkks. And if you thininkit funny your a
dirity lous anasd far as Im concrened you cn go plum to
helll and stya ther you dirty lous. To hel with ouy.

Yours very truly,
Bill Fields

The high spot of many merry nights at the Fields establishment
was a treasure hunt, the treasure being bottles of gin, whiskey or
brandy which the host had artfully concealed under bushes and in
tree branches.

On Broadway, in their youth, when Woody Fields and John first
met, they started out not as friends but sworn foes. The bone of con-
tention was the vaudeville headliner Nora Bayes, for whose affection
the two fledgling actors were deadly rivals. John, who felt he had a
prior claim, decided to settle the issue once and for all with his fists.
But the confrontation got nowhere. "I fell in love with Mr. Fields,"
John remembered, "and didn't care any more for Miss Bayes."

John's Tower Road phone number was unlisted and there came
a time when Fields mislaid it. Desperately wanting to reach him, he
implored the operator to bypass the rules for once. Only a dire emer-

gency, she reminded him, could justify such an exception. But it *was* an emergency, Fields insisted.

"Could you state the nature of the emergency?" the operator asked.

"Locked bowels," said Fields.

Gene Fowler spent a lot of time away from California, usually on Fire Island or elsewhere in the East, gathering material for books. It was to Fire Island in the summer of 1936 that John addressed this letter to Gene from Kelley's Rest Home:

> Someone—I think it was Sam T. Jack the eminent buttock impressario [*sic*] said "God works in mysterious ways His wonders to perform." As I remember (a thing Thank Christ I'm not very good at)—it was at a farewell banquet in honor of the four Gash Sisters—large girls all —who having been—to coin a phrase—the mainstay of the troupe for many years were-laden with honors—gleet and hernia—retiring to the patchoulied twilight of the Everleigh Club.* It was a really great moment—and reminded me of Napoleon's farewell to the Old Guard at Fontainebleau (*NO*—I wasn't *there*—you bastard—I merely *heard* about it—from somebody who was a director—) I don't know why I ramble on this way but Elba is kind of quiet today and the bees are droning lazily around the one-holer —two dogs of frail parentage are lolling *stuck* in the stink weed patch and all nature seems waiting with finger on lip for some portentous event or cataclysm to occur—It wouldn't surprise me *at all* if it were "The Master of Ballantrae." Oddly enough I have always wanted to play that ophidian and fearless son of a bitch and went as far as to have a long interview with Loyd Osborne [Lloyd Osbourne, the stepson of Robert Louis Stevenson] on the subject. He said he had frequently "coquetted" with the idea (that was his expression) but something had always intervened— Then—Walker Whiteside did it and it was a bit of a flop and—why not! Whether or not Lionel can be seduced into playing it—I don't know—Of course *that* would be great— I have—more times than I can tell you—broached the subject to him and he has *always* dexterously evaded it—*You*

* A far-famed Chicago bordello.

might have better luck—even intimating it might be a bridge to Terra Firma for his little brother who is at present in a state of slightly swirling levitation. *If* however that combination which would be imperial—with you and Charlie writing the script—is hopeless and Lionel is inexorable the idea is too gorgeous to give up—and we could get some swell person to play the other brother. There *must* be more in this than meets the eye as I have thought about the damned thing so intensively for so many years—It is a quaint conceit but I have always regarded you and Charlie as two bawdy and libidinous guardian angels—a proper complement as it were—to my somewhat static and sacerdotal self—a sort of *Balance Wheel*—as it were to phantasmagoria.

I am eating my *gruel* at regular intervals and pulling my pud as infrequently as is compatible with celibacy— and while we are on the subject put aside a *little* every day in spite of your riotous living toward a stained glass window for Mrs. Kelley and Jim. Since your letter oh Ishmael —or Piss-Pot as you prefer—I live again!—love Jack

John's Bundy Drive confreres strove loyally to save him from the consequences of his liquory waywardness, such as the clout he occasionally invited from some outraged stranger, but, prone as they were to the same indulgence, they proved broken reeds to lean on. At Earl Carroll's Sunset Boulevard nightclub the Reverend R. Anderson Jardine, who had been internationally publicized when he married the Duke of Windsor and Wallis Simpson, was officiating at the stunt wedding of a pair of jitterbugs. Looking on, glass in hand, John noticed a fetching blonde nearby and passed a remark to her which, according to her companion, one Clarence Reed, "wouldn't bear repeating in polite society." John repeated it. Before his friends could intervene, Reed floored him and a bouncer threw him out.

He barely escaped demolition in Dave Chasen's restaurant. As he crossed the room, supported by Gene Fowler and Charles Lederer, a screen writer, he saw a pretty girl seated in a booth opposite an admiring man. Disengaging himself, John strode over to her with pot-valiant determination, performed a courtly bow and in majestic tones said: "If you will come to my place at midnight, I will give you the greatest lay you have ever had." Up leaped her admirer, fists clenched. Fowler and Lederer reached John in time to pull him back. "What is it?" John asked them, glancing over his shoulder at the furious man with the hauteur of a monarch referring to the lowliest of his subjects. "A peasant with a petition? Let the peasant come forward." His friends managed to get him out of the restaurant before he was torn apart.

On New Year's Eve, 1936, fifty-two days after they eloped to Yuma, John and Elaine broke up with a loud public bang. The scene was Hollywood's Trocadero nightclub; the cause of battle, Elaine's determination to go on the stage. Having yet to appear in a single film, she leaped at an offer from the producer of a poetic tragedy by "Amory Hare" (the pseudonym of a Mrs. James Hutchinson of Philadelphia) entitled *The Return of Hannibal*. The opening date at the Geary Theatre in San Francisco was February 1 and Elaine was to play the Carthaginian general's daughter Claudia, appearing briefly toward the end to speak a few words and, clad in toga, gold sandals and a black wig, to perform a voluptuous dance. John forbade it. She would, he warned her, only expose them both to ridicule. But Elaine imputed his objections to professional as well as sexual jealousy. "He was jealous of my talents as an actress. He was jealous of the actors who were to play with me in my first play in the West and jealous of the stagehands too."

The noisy argument, overheard by all the merrymakers around them, degenerated into invective. John, as Elaine remembered it, called her "vile, violent, obscene, indecent, profane and opprobrious names," threatened to "kill or seriously maim" her, twisted her wrist and stalked out of the nightclub, leaving her with the ultimatum— "*The Return of Hannibal* or the return of Barrymore."

"My career comes before everything else," Elaine proclaimed. "I'm still young and have my whole future ahead of me, but John— well— He's made his name. Now I must make mine." She retained a Los Angeles lawyer, Leo Schaumer, to institute divorce proceedings and departed for San Francisco.

The Return of Hannibal lasted one week. Of Elaine's performance, *Variety* commented: "She looks like Salome; acts like salami."

On April 24, 1937, Elaine appeared before Superior Court Judge Walter Gates to enumerate her grievances against John. "I think you are entitled to a divorce," said the judge and granted her an interlocutory decree, adding: "Better luck next time."

Undiscouraged by the debacle of *The Return of Hannibal*, Elaine joined another actor from the disbanded cast, Eduard Franz, in a skit written for vaudeville called *The Talented Talcotts*. The touring bill of which it formed part included two movie shorts and assorted live acts, but the producer capitalized on the name "Elaine Barrie Barrymore" by flaunting it in bold type at the top of posters and programs. The fury of the Barrymore clan was mild compared to their reaction when the name was next exploited.

This was in a semi-nudist one-reeler quickie entitled *How to Undress in Front of Your Husband.* It showed Mrs. Barrymore (back to camera, to be sure) changing from panties and bra to nightgown. The Barrymores tried to have the short suppressed or, at least, to have their name omitted, but without success. In New York State, however, the Commissioner of Education condemned it as "indecent and tending to corrupt morals" and there it was banned.

John had meanwhile transferred his labyrinthine legal affairs from the hands of Aaron Sapiro to those of a Los Angeles attorney named Henry Huntington. "Love is a paper chase," he said, "and the color of the paper is blue." He also reinstated Henry Hotchener as his business manager, the court having dismissed the suit instigated by Elaine upon proof that he had not mishandled John's finances. Huntington's initial step was to have Sapiro's power of attorney revoked. (In 1941 the New York lawyer was disbarred for acquiescence in an attempt to bribe jurors.)

Elaine wanted temporary alimony of $2,525 per month to maintain herself in the style to which she had become so quickly accustomed. The monthly requirements she listed were: "Chauffeur, $100; maid, $75; managing agent, $100; rent, $350; groceries, $100; gas, light and heat, $100; dairy products, $100; house caretaker, $125; personal incidentals, $125; automobile, $100; clothing and wearing apparel, $750; miscellaneous household expenses, $500."

She might as well have asked for millions. Of the nearly three million dollars John had earned from stage, screen and radio, there remained not enough to meet debts totaling, in round numbers, $162,000. In addition to alimony to Dolores and the support of Diana, these included federal and county taxes and seventy diverse bills, mainly from hotels in Los Angeles, New York and London.

Through Huntington, John filed a petition of bankruptcy in July 1937. He had no intention of defaulting. All he wanted from the bankruptcy court, and all it granted him, was a moratorium while he liquidated his assets, earned more money and repaid his creditors.

Bella Vista, upon which John had lavished half a million dollars, was put up for sale at auction. In its dilapidated state—John himself called it a "Chinese tenement"—it did not attract a single bidder. The auctioneer scheduled a new sale date and set the starting bid at $150,000. He failed to get it.* John's beloved *Infanta*, with a mortgage of $40,000 and a tax lien of $35,000, went to a New York manufacturer, E. P. Lawson, for $77,500.

In seeking more time to pay his debts, John counted on income from movies. But the immediate prospects were bleak. Drink, bad publicity and a failing memory combined to scare off most producers. He had been idle since *Maytime* the year before. At length, during the last months of 1937, John's agent found work for him in four Paramount films, not as a star but as a "featured player." They were *Bulldog Drummond Comes Back* (John played the dreary supporting role of Scotland Yard Inspector Nielson), *Night Club Scandal*, *Bulldog Drummond's Revenge* (*Bulldog Drummond's Peril* followed the next year) and *True Confession* (the only one of the four with any quality, a rollicking comedy in which John played a down-at-heel but blustering toper); he owed his *True Confession* contract to the intervention of Carole Lombard, the leading lady, who was ever grateful to John for what he had taught her about acting when they made *Twentieth Century*. Out of every $6,000 he remitted $5,000 to his creditors.

John's memory had so declined that studio assistants would chalk his lines on blackboards which they held aloft behind the cameras. He acquired remarkable proficiency at reading them surreptitiously without seeming to move his eyes. But John would never concede that loss of memory was the reason for the blackboards. "I can recite from memory three plays by Shakespeare from beginning to end," he told the journalist J. P. McEvoy. "But please listen to this [reading from a script]: 'So you see, the entire principle is the coordination of chemical, biological and dynamic influences.' Can you tell me why I should clutter my mind with that etymological ordure?"

"At that," he told some of the Bundy Drive stalwarts, "I am one of the few actors out here who can read and act at the same time."

He once mentioned to John Decker, not very seriously, that he would like to play *Macbeth* at the Hollywood Bowl.

"How would you get blackboards big enough?" Decker asked him.

"I'd have airplanes skywriting."

---

*An MGM film cutter, Hugo Grimaldi, eventually bought it. Among those who have since owned or rented parts of it are Katharine Hepburn, Marlon Brando, Candice Bergen.

Amid his emotional and financial tribulations John dashed off a note to Fowler typical of the Bundy Drive boys in its Rabelaisian tomfoolery:

> I have been giving your case much thought—particularly when I was on the can—and I had an inspiration anent your quasi-oriental collaborator S.—Suck it your self —Hartmann.
>
> As he seems to be normally in a state of alcoholic levitation—hanging by his truss—which as we all know is his [the word is indecipherable]—the obvious thing to do is to filch that unwieldy and sinister appendage—and substitute the provocative and fin-de-siecle pelvic titivator—that I enclose!
>
> It was used formerly by my erstwhile mother-in-law in lieu of a reticule for jaded foreskins. She has no further use for it—and Elaine has a set of her own!
>
> Yrs. with undiminished fervor—J. Puke.

John missed Jack Prescott, who, he had learned, was at loose ends in Chicago, the road show that took him there having folded. At about two o'clock one morning he telephoned him. "What are you doing, fellow?"

"I'm broke, sweetheart."

"Get out here. I'm wiring you tickets and cash. You leave on the Chief tomorrow."

"I'll come out only if you have a brass band to meet me at the station."

"Fellow, if that's what you want, that's what you get. Just be sure you're on that train."

Three days later, as the Chief pulled in, John was standing on the station platform with a brass band. He was costumed as Hamlet and cradled Yorick's skull in his arms.

Elaine had barely embarked on her eastward vaudeville trek before John was bombarding her with penitent, passionate letters and telegrams. He could not believe, he wrote, that all was over between them. If only he could see her and hold her hand "and talk to you sincerely as the one person in the world I've ever loved," she would understand. If she would give him the chance, he swore, he knew he could make her happy. "I've had a heartbreaking lesson, baby."

In a telegram he affirmed his resolution TO STRAIGHTEN OUT

COMPLETELY AND ABSORB ABSOLUTELY NOTHING NOT EVEN THE MILDEST THING. With her support, he was sure to win the good fight. He had but one desire—TO MAKE YOU HAPPY AND HELP YOU IN YOUR CAREER.

Elaine hurried back to him and, to the dismay of both the Bundy Drive boys and the Barrymore family, her interlocutory decree was dismissed.

During a visit to New York, John took his wife to meet his sister. "Come down, children," Ethel called up the stairs to Sister and Sammy, "your Aunt Ariel is here."

25

My Dear Children

━━━━━━━

In his resolve to pay back his creditors dollar for dollar, John labored hard under severe stress. He accepted any role, however modest, that the leery Hollywood producers were willing to cast him in. During the year 1938 he made six films and, in addition, began broadcasting over the NBC network a series of forty-five-minute condensations of Shakespeare plays. The movie portrayals, each of them far superior to the material, ranged from the aging Louis XV in MGM's *Marie Antoinette* (Norma Shearer) to a lovable old soak in RKO's *The Great Man Votes.* Louis XV's appearances were few and brief, yet with every one of them John, variously ironic, sarcastic, venomous, brought to life an otherwise leaden pageant.

The Great Man Votes was the last film starring John with any pretensions to quality. Adapted by John Twist from a *Saturday Evening Post* story by Gordon Malherbe Hillman, it concerned a widower, Gregory Vance, the father of two small children, once a Harvard history professor, who became a quart-a-day drinker after the death of his wife and now earns his keep as a night watchman. As fantasy would have it, however, he is the only resident of his district eligible to vote. Traditionally, as Vance's district goes, so go the other districts. The politicians therefore court him. They promise him the post of school commissioner. He falls in love with a schoolteacher, and between her, her adoring children and his new-found honors, he is rehabilitated and all ends in a glow of domestic warmth. The two children, charmingly played by Peter Holden and Virginia Weidler, confirmed the precaution John once urged upon Blanche Yurka: "Never try to act with a kid or a dog. They'll steal the show every time."

Three years before, Samuel Goldwyn, impressed by the talents of a young Broadway assistant director named Garson Kanin, also a former vaudevillian and actor, had brought him out to Hollywood to learn the movie business. Kanin wanted to direct, a function for which Goldwyn did not feel he was as yet qualified. They quarreled and Goldwyn finally released Kanin to RKO, for which he directed two films before he was entrusted with *The Great Man Votes*. Among Kanin's memories of John as an actor was the problem of the blackboards.

"There were, in fact, many blackboards, in varying sizes and shapes. Large ones for the long speeches; small ones for the shorter speeches; oblong ones to fit between the lights if necessary; tiny ones for single lines. . . .

"Barrymore's technique for using the blackboard was ingenious. He would position himself for reading the board. Often, this occasioned spectacular turns and twists and bends; a favorite trick was to turn his head sharply as though to scratch the back of his head. . . .

"I discussed the matter with him.

" 'It seems to me, Mr. Barrymore, that what you do to get the words off those boards is a hell of a lot harder than learning them.'

"He looked at me balefully and said, 'I've learned enough words in my time. Let somebody else do it now.'

" 'Shall I tell you what I think, Mr. Barrymore?' I pressed on. 'I think you really know your lines perfectly, and that this is just a habit you've fallen into.'

"He fixed me with his hard look again, and said, 'Of course I know my lines. I always do. . . . Have you ever been to a circus? Seen the blokes on the high wire? Even doing back flips? On the tight rope. Have you ever seen one of them fall? . . . Then why do you suppose they always have a net underneath them? Those blackboards are my net, that's all.' "

John disliked having strangers watch him at work unless they belonged to the profession. Tourists on guided visits to the studios, especially women tourists, were apt to induce his most outrageous behavior. When a chirping flock of schoolteachers approached the set of *Hold That Co-ed*, a negligible Fox film, John smiled dangerously, cocked an eyebrow and farted. "What did you expect to hear?" he asked the appalled teachers. "Chimes?"*

He was cavorting in a Paramount comedy, *Midnight*, when a contingent of arch-respectable dowager types, a particular aversion of his, invaded the studio. He heard one of them complain: "I've been in Hollywood a week now and I haven't seen anything scandalous." Whereupon he pranced over to a wall and urinated against it.

As *Midnight* progressed, John received letters from Gene Fowler and his sons, Gene, Jr., and Will, who were in New York. He answered them with a telegram:

DEAR HAIRY AINU I MADE THE APPALLING MISTAKE OF READING YOUR AND YOUR HOMUNCULUS SONS ILLUMINATED AND CHATTY SCREEDS ALSO BEN HECHTS WHILE INDULGING IN AMOROUS IF SLIGHTLY PERFUNCTORY DALLIANCE WITH ONE OF GRAUMANS [Sid Grauman, Hollywood's leading film exhibitor and theater owner] CIRCASSIAN BEAUTIES STOP I LAUGHED SO HARD I FRACTURED MY PELVIS IN TWO PLACES WHICH FORTUNATELY THE VAIN WENCH ATTRIBUTED TO HER PROWESS AS AN OSTERMOOR VIRTUOSO STOP IN FUTURE I SHALL READ YOUR EPITHALAMIUMS IN THE CLOISTERED SANCTITY OF THE ONE HOLER GIVE MY BEST TO . . . BEN HECHT AND THAT KEWPIE OUT OF THE BEELZEBUB BY THE YOUNGEST DAUGHTER OF CHAOS CHARLIE MACARTHUR AND TELL HIM NOT TO WORRY ABOUT HIS ULCER ALL SIX OF MINE HAVE BEEN BOON COMPANIONS FOR YEARS AND AS FAR AS YOURSELF IS CONCERNED CONSIDER THAT I AM DOING THE ONE THING THAT WILL EFFECTIVELY BLOW THE COBWEBS OUT OF YOUR BRAIN YOUR AFFECTIONATE BASTARD SON JOHN BEDDIBLE BARRYMORE.

For John 1938 was also a year of repeated trips to Cedars of Lebanon Hospital for the treatment of his ulcers. At his insistence, Elaine always took a room close by. ". . . his quick recovery would be attended by a violent affirmation of life . . . he would suddenly throw back the covers and stalk me insanely. My husband was a satyr until the end."

---

* The sally, though not the action preceding it, is commonly associated with Monty Woolley, who so spoke when playing a department-store Santa Claus with hiccups in *Life Begins at Eight-Thirty*, but it originated with John.

The Benedict Canyon house having been sold and Elaine hating Bella Vista, John bought and later signed over to her a fourteen-room Tudor-style farmhouse with three acres on Bellagio Road in Bel Air, which he optimistically named La Vita Nuova, and there he, his wife and his ubiquitous mother-in-law resided for a time in relative tranquility. Mrs. Jacobs shortly divorced her meek husband.

Elaine's movie career ended in 1938 on the cutting-room floor. Her professional Hollywood experience had been limited to two films. In *Midnight* she was glimpsed for a few minutes and spoke a few lines. She was excised altogether from *Hold That Co-ed*.

The pain was somewhat alleviated the following year when John had her play opposite him in six of his Shakespeare broadcasts. The first was *Richard III* and Elaine's role, Lady Anne. *Variety* combined faint praise with snideness: "Elaine Barrie flashed some 13th Century 'thee' and 'thou' lines and for a gal who got off the No. 19 Riverside Drive bus she turns out not to be a hopeless trouper. She may be a one-emotion actress, but, boys, can she handle scorn. She can call a guy a dirty-so-and-so and it rings up like a coin on said bus. It was so good people may think the trend to ventriloquism is spreading." Elaine's next radio portrayal, Lady Macbeth, drew from her doting husband an understatement. "Playing Lady Macbeth at twenty-two is a great achievement," he said.

Not for a moment had Elaine relinquished her dreams of theatrical glory. "I was not only going to reinstate John on the throne. I was going to share it with him." The wise course, as she conceived it, was first to do a light comedy together "to regain his confidence," followed by a serious drama, and then—the ultimate goal—*Macbeth* with herself as Lady Macbeth. She envisioned them as the founders of a new theatrical dynasty.

A year earlier a fledgling playwright, Catherine Turney, and a Hollywood press agent, Jerry Horwin, had collaborated on a comedy they called *My Dear Children*. The leading character, Allan Manville, is an aging, hammy Shakespearean actor with three daughters by as many marriages, of whose existence he is barely aware. The scene is the baronial hall of a small castle in the Swiss alps which Manville occasionally borrows from the owner. On the wall facing the audience hangs a full-length portrait of the actor at the summit of his career as Hamlet.

While Manville is sharing his alpine retreat with a new mistress, the three daughters, who have learned of his whereabouts from a story in the London *Times*, arrive unbidden one after another. They are shortly joined by three young men, their suitors. The ensuing plot convolutions constitute a play so light as to be virtually weightless.

My Dear Children was submitted by successive play agents to producer after producer, among them Arthur Hopkins. None could discern any virtues in it. Richard Aldrich of the firm of Aldrich and Myers pronounced it one of the worst scripts he had ever read. The surface parallels between Manville's career and John Barrymore's, however, were glaring, and Aldrich added that if John himself were to play the lead, he might consider backing it.

In 1938 a Hollywood play agent, Laura Wilck, undertook to find a producer. Informed of Aldrich's comment, she forwarded the script to the Barrymores, as she had a good many others. Elaine read it first. "[The] leading character was practically a one-dimensional portrait of John Barrymore and I knew I had found the formula. . . . The play, with all due respect to its authors, could only be enhanced by any of John's possible failings." She saw herself as Cordelia, one of the three daughters and the principal female role. "Cordelia offered me a chance to gain the foothold I so wanted."

She urged the play upon John in opposition to his representative, the William Morris Agency, who deplored it. On their next trip to New York John read it to Ned Sheldon. The thought of John returning to the New York theater after an absence of fifteen years in such a shoddy vehicle distressed him almost as much as John's marriage. But he voiced his objections with gentle tact and a little later wrote:

> You were very nice to listen so patiently to my criticism of *My Dear Children*. I know just how it feels when one is enthusiastic about something to run point-blank into disagreement. But I know, too, that you wanted me to be honest and tell you exactly how it struck me. As you said, Elaine, we are all after the same thing. Of course, my opinion is only that of one man, and I hope you will get others. I think that Charlie MacArthur, Ben Hecht, Arthur Hopkins, Robert Sherwood, Robert E. Jones, and Sidney Howard would be glad to give their disinterested, sympathetic, and valuable advice. . . .

As for *Macbeth*, Sheldon advanced three arguments against it:

> (1) the fact that *Macbeth* has never been a popular play in America, no matter who played it; (2) the fact that no actor ever made a great personal success or really hit the bull's-eye as Macbeth; and (3) the danger, which Elaine

was quick to recognize, of making her first New York appearance in such a tremendously exacting part.

John consulted all those whom Ned had named. They were, without exception, aghast. Yet Elaine's judgment prevailed and, once John had committed himself, Aldrich obtained the approval of his partner, Richard Myers. For a director they chose a young refugee from Nazified Austria, Otto Ludwig Preminger, who had cast the pre-Hollywood Hedy Lamarr in her first play.

Under the terms of the run-of-the-play contract negotiated by the Morris office, Elaine was to get a salary of $500 a week; John, twelve and a half percent of the gross and half the net, which, in a good week, could together exceed $4,500.

The tryout took place at the McCarter Theatre of Princeton, New Jersey, on March 24, 1939. The audience consisted preponderantly of undergraduate Princetonians, professors and members of the Institute of Advanced Science. The last group included Albert Einstein, who had met John eight years before while visiting the set of *Svengali.* He had remarked after a long talk with him: "Several mathematicians understand my theories, but of all persons it is an actor, John Barrymore, who discusses them the most intelligently."

At the Princeton dress rehearsal John forgot most of his lines, causing producers, director and cast acute anxiety. The first night a few lines eluded him, but now, to the hilarity of the audience, he substituted ad libs, once calling out to the prompter in the wings: "Give those cues a little louder, sweetheart. We can't hear you." Nobody laughed more heartily than Einstein. It was the first of innumerable ad libs which, together with clowning, mugging, grunts, snorts, rumbles, yawns, bleats, belches, leers, sneers, smirks, ogles, roars, squeaks, eye-rolling, eyebrow-twitching, strutting, mincing, pouncing, staggering, hop-skip-and-jumps, profanity, obscenity and general horseplay, would turn the vapid farce into a freakish smash hit unique in theater annals.

After five curtain calls, John, visibly moved, made a short speech. "I can scarcely tell you," he said, "not having heard that beautiful sound for more than fifteen years, how deeply it affects me. It is pure music to my ears. I thank you."

Neither producers nor star felt quite ready yet to brave Broadway. They decided instead on a shape-up tour of two weeks, followed by a Chicago run of another two weeks. They never imagined that almost eight months would elapse before they reached New York.

Washington, Sunday, March 26. The night before the opening at the National Theatre. John is sodden. A battle breaks out with Elaine (whose mother, as always, lurks watchfully in the background). The innocent cause is the handsome juvenile, Philip Reed, who plays one of Cordelia's admirers. What, John demands, do they do all that time backstage while he is on? Is Reed cuckolding him?

He wakes up next morning hoarse. Laryngitis. He manages to struggle through the evening's performance. He even gets off an ad lib or two. "You may take me heart," says Manville at his hammiest. "You may take me body, but, by God, you cannot have me soul." John winks at the audience: "Haven't said that in twenty years." Presently he interpolates a nonsense verse from Edward Lear's "The Owl and the Pussy-Cat":

> They dined upon mince and slices of quince
> Which they ate with a runcible spoon.

By Wednesday he can no longer speak above a whisper. The company returns to New York, not to set out again for ten days. En route to Rochester, John phones Jack Prescott. "I am going to kill Elaine," he says.

Rochester, April 3. A sob sister from the regional press asks John when he and Elaine expect a "blessed event." "Madame—and I use the word advisedly," John replies, "it's none of your goddamn business."

Buffalo . . . Cleveland . . . Pittsburgh . . .

Dayton, April 14. The Barrymores are barely speaking. They have been traveling in separate Pullman cars and occupying separate hotel rooms. The company's English manager, Captain Pierce Power-Waters, attempts to mediate between them and, failing, to conceal the rift from the reporters who meet the train. He persuades the couple to pose for the news photographers. The moment the last camera has clicked the combatants hop into separate cabs.

Columbus . . . Knoxville . . . Chattanooga . . . Birmingham . . .

Memphis, April 20. "I can't act with her," John complains and wants Elaine out of the show.

On the night train to St. Louis, Otto Preminger awakes to find Mrs. Jacobs perched on the edge of his berth, the incarnation of outraged motherhood. "If you fire my daughter," she threatens, "I'll tell the reporters that Jack tried to rape me."

St. Louis, April 24. John's edematose legs itch him, and scratching streaks them with blood. Eczema begins to torment him. Alcohol intensifies his ailments.

Power-Waters hires a male nurse for John. A towering, good-natured young Oklahoman by the name of Karl Steuver, formerly a medical student, he serves as driver, dresser and, so Power-Waters hopes, a stabilizing influence. There is no question of depriving John of liquor, but Steuver doles it out to him in small, carefully measured amounts, one ounce of liquor to three ounces of water. John appears content so long as he has a glass in his hand. As with all alcoholics, it does not take much to inebriate him.

Near the end of the second act of *My Dear Children* the ex-matinee idol turns his daughter Cordelia over his knees and spanks her. The first night at St. Louis' American Theatre, John spanks Elaine hard enough to raise welts. She bites his wrist. Following further hostilities between performances, John notifies Power-Waters that either he or Elaine must go. The manager has no alternative but to fire Elaine. She stays until the end of the St. Louis engagement in order to allow time for her replacement, Doris Dudley, to reach Omaha, the next stop, then leaves with her mother for New York, announcing that she will divorce John.

The producers dispute Elaine's right to continue drawing a salary, but Actors' Equity rules in her favor and she receives $500 a week until the end of the year.

Omaha, May 1. The one-night stand has been sponsored by the Omaha Drama League, a women's organization of a kind likely to bring out the worst in John. Before the performance he is interviewed on radio station KOIL. "I want to tell you something about your town," he says. "It is one of the most enchanting places I have ever been in." Here, for the benefit of the studio audience, he holds his nose. "I never saw so many quiet homes, well-kept lawns, trees with no dust. I can't see why you want to go to the theater at all. But, if you must, come to see it for the reason that one of your gals is in it, a gal named Dorothy McGuire [destined for stardom on stage and screen]. I met her mother today. If I met her mother earlier in my life —wow!"

He concludes with a reference to his grandmother. "She pupped a lot of mighty fine actors and there is an oddity you are about to see tonight called John Barrymore."

During a run-through in a high-school auditorium, attended by prim teachers and starry-eyed students, one of the teachers asks John if he does not agree that *The Fool*, an inspirational play by Channing Pollock which has also played Omaha under Drama League sponsorship, is wonderful. "Madam," John roars, "I think it is a goddamn abortion. If you say one more word about Channing Pollock, you will be puked on by one of the greatest, if not the greatest actor in the world."

His subsequent ad libs are couched in language no playwright of the period would venture to use. John answers the telephone while Roland Hogue, the actor playing Albert, his butler, stands attentively close behind. John suddenly wheels on him, piping: "Albert, how many times must I tell you not to goose me?"

The hapless Hogue is the butt of another jape on stage. He wears a green livery so tightly belted that it accentuates his slight paunch. "Albert," says John, apropos of nothing at all, "you look like a pregnant string bean."

Stroking his daughter Portia [Dorothy McGuire]: "You know, you have a very nice fanny."

With his arm around Tala Birell, his mistress in the play, John is supposed to lead her through a door for an amatory session in the greenhouse. Finding himself heading by mistake toward a flight of stairs instead, he ad libs: "Ah, we must go upstairs. There are no towels in the greenhouse."

Laughter rocks the audience, but some of the Drama League ladies flounce out of the theater. "Rather startling," the president comments later. "Perfectly disgraceful," says another member, and a third deplores the star's "prolific profanity."

In a curtain speech John assures the audience: "I am glad I amused you, but you have no idea how you amused me."

Dorothy McGuire quits the show, to be replaced by the company manager's daughter, Patricia Waters. "I had a great admiration for John Barrymore when we started," says Dorothy, "but I cannot watch this man make a fool of himself."

Nobody was more infuriated by John's antics than Director Preminger. He told John that he considered his behavior beneath human dignity. Fleetingly contrite, John urged him to watch the next performance. It was unobjectionable.

"John," said Preminger, "why don't you do this every night?"

"Bored, dear boy," said John. "Bored."

Sioux Falls, May 2. John proclaims to the press: "In every marital proceeding brought against me by my previous wives I have always, out of a sense of chivalry, not contested them. But this time I am taking the initiative." He had already instructed Maurice Hotchner:

> At my expense follow up all clews regarding adultery and start a divorce suit if you procure evidence. Start action against Elaine and her mother to make them account for a quarter million dollars filched from me since 1935.
>
> If you can work out some peaceful and matrimonial settlement with Elaine do so. But get rid of her.

They had abused the power he gave them to draw on three of his bank accounts, he charged, and had wrongfully listed parts of his property under the name of Barrie.

Des Moines, May 4. Box-office receipts have fallen off. The Midwestern theater owners, moreover, alarmed by the reports of John's antics, are threatening to cancel bookings. RKO tenders handsome terms to John to come back and the same to Aldrich and Myers to release him. The producers, who are about to cut their losses in any case by folding the show, welcome the offer as a way out at minimal loss. John talks them into reserving decision until Chicago, where he has always been a great favorite. There, he feels confident, he can turn *My Dear Children* into a hit.

Cedar Rapids, May 5. Not enough money remains in the till to pay bills and salaries, and the producers will risk no more. Power-Waters keeps the show afloat with $1,500 out of his own pocket.

Davenport . . . Peoria . . .

Chicago, May 8. The Selwyn Theatre.

It was no longer a play, not that it had ever been much of one. It was a sideshow with John the main exhibit, a mad circus, a carnival of lunacy in which he exploited his own weaknesses for laughs—his intemperance, his profligacy, his womanizing, a "spiritual striptease [in the words of the Chicago historian Lloyd Lewis] with himself as a kind of Gypsy Rose John." The chief appeal of *My Dear Children* derived from the unpredictability of its star. "What will he do tonight?" theatergoers would ask each other as they lined up at the box office, many of them for the second or third time. "Will he be drunk again?"

"Floozies behave charmingly on occasion," John, in the character of Manville, tells his daughter Portia, then interjects: "And nobody knows that better than your poor old father."

During one performance an actor accidentally tipped over a punchbowl. John's next line, speaking of Portia's suitor, was: "I think he's a dirty dog." Spotting the puddle, he added: "Not only is he a dirty dog, but he isn't even housebroken."

Only a comedian of John's extraordinary technical equipment could have roused an audience to shrieks of laughter with such waggery by an accompanying grimace or gesture. After seeing *My Dear Children*, Orson Welles observed that if he had a child he would send him to Chicago, chain him to a seat and make him sit through every performance. "Then I'd tell him he knew everything there was to know about acting."

By John's quick-wittedness his audience became stooges and chance street noises his props. To latecomers he would call out: "Where have you been, darling?" Let somebody cough loudly and he would interrupt himself in the middle of a line to ask: "Now, what the hell was that?" Spectators sometimes pretended to sneeze to see what buffoonery the sound would provoke. The first genuine sneeze had occurred when John began a line, "I will take you to—" and forgot the place. *Ah-choo!* "There. That's it. Thanks." He was holding Tala Birell in his arms one night when a woman burst out laughing. Glaring in her direction, he demanded with mock fury: "What are you laughing at?" He resumed his love-making, then suddenly dropped his arms, advanced to the footlights and singled out the same woman, telling her: "That's the place where you should have laughed." (Inadvertently, Miss Birell once stepped on an ad lib. John pressed a lighted cigarette into the palm of her hand.)

At the scream of a passing fire engine, he would cry: "My God, my wife!" One night when, immediately following the siren, a truck backfired, he added: "And she's got her mother with her!"

He might halt the play altogether while he recounted some anecdote from his past or a bit of Barrymore family history. He liked to imagine the shade of old Mrs. John Drew hovering in the wings and calling to her grandson: "Go on, Jack, give them everything you've got!"

It was hard on the supporting actors, who could never tell when John would stray from the script and hopelessly confuse them. He once strayed so far from it that Preminger, watching from the rear of the house, began pacing the aisle in anguish. "For Pete's sake, Otto," John shouted, "go back and sit down. We'll get through it somehow." Such vagaries so galled Philip Reed that he called the offender to account. John appeared contrite, but when he next met Reed onstage he said: "Better sit down, Phil," and proceeded to ad lib at greater length than usual.

The company found John's behavior behind the scenes equally objectionable. He would sit around, glass in hand, telling dirty stories, guffawing, belching, hawking loudly enough to distract the actors on stage. For the actresses he posed another problem. He was always trying to get them to bed, even though Power-Waters had thoughtfully provided him with three complaisant companions. There was less carnality underlying these attempted seductions than John's need for reassurance at the age of fifty-seven.

One night after the theater a group of show people joined him for drinks and a late supper at the Ambassador Hotel, where he was living. Next to him, in a booth of the hotel's famous Pump Room, sat a young actress, Anne Seymour, an ingenue in an NBC soap opera broadcast from Chicago. With her was an NBC executive named Harry Kopf. Presently, John whispered to her: "Won't you come up to my room and prove to me that I'm still attractive to women?" By way of a reply she glanced affectionately at Kopf. With sad understanding, John murmured: "Congratulations."

There came a moment at the rise of the third-act curtain of *My Dear Children* when laughter died and a stillness fell over the spectators, some with tears springing to their eyes. It happened at every performance when John, standing beneath his portrait as Hamlet (painted in 1923 by James Montgomery Flagg), began "To be or not to be . . ." He spoke only the first few lines, but in that brief span the years melted away, the marks of age on John seemed to fade. The deep-toned, vibrant voice, the majesty, the fire all resurged, then dimmed as John reverted to clowning.

The Selwyn Theatre was packed at every performance. The two weeks originally envisioned by Aldrich and Myers stretched into thirty-four and grossed more than a half million dollars, a record unprecedented for a poor play. A Barrymore craze swept Chicago. The Washington Park racetrack celebrated a "Barrymore day," naming each race after one of the actors in *My Dear Children.* There was also a Barrymore baseball day at Comiskey Park and a Barrymore circus day at Soldiers' Field when Ringling Brothers and Barnum & Bailey Combined Shows pitched the big tent there.

Many Broadway and Hollywood performers plying between the two coasts, with a stopover in Chicago, felt bound to attend *My Dear Children* and drop in on John backstage. When he spotted such colleagues in the audience, he would work them into his improvisations ("There's that old bastard Ned Sparks!" he announced on one occasion) or reach over the footlights to shake hands (as he did with

Charles Laughton) while the audience stood up to see how they reacted. Mary Pickford once visited his Chicago dressing room to up-
braid him for prostituting his art and in the process became so overwrought that she had to be given a sedative.

On May 11, for the second time, Elaine filed a divorce suit. A
little later John wrote to Hotchener:

> Dear Dear Henry—
>
> In view of our past associations—you are the first per-
> son who comes to my mind—to have the intimate—and
> unique possessions that—owing to the slightly peculiar ac-
> tivities of certain Lemurian people (who shall be nameless)
> —I fear me—Antonio!—should be protected for a decent
> posterity—! In other words I wish you to be the personal
> owner and possessor of all the articles which Mr. Scott [an-
> other Barrymore lawyer] and Nishi retrieved from the
> Bellagio Road House—(and Baby—when I say roadhouse
> —I *mean* roadhouse—!!) including the Sargent drawing—
> the Manship Bust—Lincoln's letter to my grandmother—
> all the old books—first editions, etc. Guns—fishing tackle
> —rugs—indeed Everything—and I hope you enjoy them.
> All my love to you and dearest Helios—
>
> > Jack Barrymore

Hotchener did not retain these valuables, as John's letter conferred upon him the legal right to do, but placed them in a storage
warehouse and subsequently turned them over to the lawyer Scott.
"The procedure I followed was the best for his interests and it prevented his enemies from seizing them," he said.

Despite the hostilities raging between them, John telephoned
Elaine to tender his condolences when Grandmother Rosenthal died,
then incredibly, wrote to her as follows:

> Dear Enchanting and slightly nebulous bastard,
>
> . . . It is very easy and completely compatible with
> all my other natural functions to say that I love you. I do. In
> some mysterious, Goddam fashion, you are the only woman
> I've ever met in my life I really want to take care of. . . .
>
> This is meant to tell you that I know I love you and
> you have sufficient goofiness in your sane and striving
> cosmos maybe to love me too. . . .

Think this over. For Christ's sake and your own, try try to be good and know that I really adore you. You know we really *can* have fun, dear one.

During the first weeks of the Chicago run the city's social elite lionized John. The chatelaines of mansions along the "Gold Coast" gave dinners in his honor. Fashionable clubs competed for the privilege of entertaining him. But their hospitality soon cooled, for he consistently showed up drunk, scandalized everybody with his language, pinched patrician bottoms and propositioned practically every female he met.

At a women's-club tea John's roving eye settled upon an exceptionally pretty young member. Shortly after obtaining an introduction, he led her to the seclusion of the club library, where he attempted to fondle her. After they had been gone some while, the club president came in and begged John to say a few words to the women assembled in the main room. He paid no attention. "What is it you find so interesting to talk about?" the indignant president asked. "Madam, if you must know," said John, "we were talking about fucking."

Throughout his months in Chicago—indeed, throughout the rest of his life—John was chronically sick. Besides the maladies from which he already suffered, he developed a blood clot in his left leg, a bone inflammation, piles, gout and dropsy. Though never fat, the slack of aging flesh obliged him to wear a girdle onstage. His hair was now white and he dyed it black. His hands had a tremor. On rare occasions his infirmities plunged him into melancholia, but most of the time he ignored them.

On May 30 John suffered a coronary. The Selwyn Theatre was closed while he remained in bed at the Ambassador under oxygen treatment. "It's the first time I've ever been in a tent show," he said. From his fans, women predominating, came letters, telegrams, flowers, books, liquor. One young admirer climbed the hotel fire escape to peer at him through the bedroom window. Elaine tried to reach him by telephone, then flew to Chicago. He would not see her. Garson Kanin wired a get-well-quick message from Hollywood, to which John replied: FOR A MAN WHO HAS BEEN DEAD FOR FIFTEEN YEARS I AM IN REMARKABLE HEALTH. Ethel flew from New York to stay at her brother's bedside until he recuperated. So did Jack Prescott.

My Dear Children reopened to a sold-out house a week later and continued so until sickness again laid John low. He had been complaining of a sore tooth and general debility. An ulcerated tooth, the doctors found, was infecting a sinus. An oral surgeon had to cut away part of the roof of his mouth along with two molars. But he was back at the Selwyn within ten days. During some of the succeeding performances he was so ill that he had to play sitting down from first line to last.

John's unloveliest practice was to urinate wherever and whenever he felt the need. He used open windows, sinks, lawns, automobiles. Leaving a soirée at the apartment of Mrs. Bror Gustave Dahlberg, wife of the "Celotex King" and a patroness of the performing arts, he urinated in their private elevator. The Ambassador Hotel finally evicted him for committing the same nuisance into a lobby sandbox. The long-suffering Power-Waters found a small house in the North Shore suburb of Glencoe for John and Karl Steuver, now a permanent fixture of the actor's entourage, but John so unsettled the neighbors by regularly relieving himself outside the house that he had to be moved to another suburb, Winnetka.

He seldom retired before seven or eight o'clock in the morning after a round of bars and nightclubs. He then had all day to recover abed before the evening performance—except on the matinee days, Wednesday and Saturday, when, head pounding and stomach queasy, he was convoyed to the theater by Karl Steuver. He gave his worst performances at matinees. Every Tuesday and Friday night Power-Waters would entreat John to go straight home, a futile effort. Steuver was not much help. He had become so bedazzled by his charge that he acted more as an adjutant in revelry than a restraining hand.

Chicago's black quarter fascinated John. One night in the company of Steuver, Catherine Turney and some members of the cast, he dropped into a nightclub there which, unbeknown to them, was a haunt of black homosexuals. John's presence enthralled the habitués. A pair of them decked out in sequined gowns and styling themselves "Joan Crawford" and "Dolores del Rio" invited themselves to his table. "Dolores" asked him to dance and John boozily agreed. They had fox-trotted a few steps when "Joan" made a gesture that touched John's companions. "Mr. Barrymore mustn't do that," he told them. "It's all right for us, but not for Mr. Barrymore," and he persuaded John to sit down again.

A Rush Street nightclub that John patronized was the Club Alabam. There one night he recognized, in the coarsened face and figure of the star performer, the passion of his youth—Evelyn Nesbit. They gazed at each other and they both wept and John said for everybody to hear that she was the first girl he had ever loved.

DEAREST DIANA JUST READ A MAGNIFICENT NOTICE OF
YOUR FIRST PERFORMANCE BY NORTON OF THE BOSTON
POST FEEL VERY PROUD OF YOU I AM RUFFLING MY TAIL
FEATHERS LIKE AN OLD HEN MUCH LOVE DADDY

Diana Barrymore, whom the New York *Journal*'s society columnist "Cholly Knickerbocker" named "Personality Debutante of the Year," was eighteen when she determined to pursue the family profession in order to "build bridges to my father's world." Her mother allowed her to study for two years at the American Academy of Dramatic Art while still fulfilling her social obligations such as heading the Debutante Committee for the Russian Easter Ball Benefit. She spent the summer of 1939 as a $10-a-week apprentice with the Manhattan Repertory Theatre Company in Ogunquit, Maine, attended, at her mother's insistence, by a chaperone and a lady's maid. It was as the ingenue, Alice Sycamore, in the George Kaufman–Moss Hart comedy *You Can't Take It with You* that she drew favorable notice from critic Elliot Norton. The following autumn she played another ingenue, in a road-company production of Sutton Vane's fantasy of afterlife, *Outward Bound*, starring Laurette Taylor and Florence Reed. When John learned that that the tour would bring Diana to Chicago's Harris Theatre, which adjoined the Selwyn and used the same stage door, he dispatched a second telegram:

CAN'T WAIT TO SEE YOU LETS SHARE THE SAME DRESSING
ROOM LET ME KNOW ARRIVAL YOUR TRAIN LOVE DADDY.

It was to be their first encounter in six years.

John prepared a room for Diana in his Winnetka house, festooning it with flowers. He met the train cold sober, an imposing figure in a dark overcoat and a rakishly angled black homburg. Reporters and photographers by the score paced the platform. Neither father nor daughter was indifferent to the publicity value of their reunion and, though genuinely happy and excited, they played to the press. "Isn't she lovely?" said John. "She's absolutely the most delightful person I've ever met. I worked like hell on *Hamlet* and *Richard III*, but

she is the best thing I ever produced." And Diana gushed: "Daddy
and I plan to change the dates of our matinees this week so we can
see each other act." But she declined to put up at the Winnetka
house, preferring a suite in the tony Ambassador Hotel.

They dined and nightclubbed together to the clicking of cameras
and the scribbling of reporters' pencils. John gave an extra matinee
in Diana's honor. It was the first time she had ever seen him onstage.
("How swollen his ankles were! I knew vaguely about edema, but
I failed to associate it then with excessive drinking.") Her face
turned crimson at one ad lib. "That couch reminds me forcibly of my
little daughter," he said. "How regularly she wet the sheets! I was
kept as busy as the Sorcerer's Apprentice."

Father and daughter grew disappointed in each other. Diana
was revolted by John's misconduct when drunk, while her debu-
tantish affectations—everybody was "darling" and everything that
pleased her "too divine"—combined with her premature flourishing
of the Barrymore panache irritated John. "Stop trying to be a Barrymore," he once snapped at her. "Be yourself."

In a sleazy nightspot to which he took her, a blond stranger
seated herself on his knee and began kissing and caressing him.
Diana demanded he take her home at once and she stood up to go.
Without removing the blonde from his lap, John prodded Diana
back into her chair, saying: "You will leave when your father tells
you to leave and not before. Don't get grand with me, Miss Newport."

Later that night they apologized to each other, and at the end
of the three-week run of *Outward Bound* they parted on affectionate
terms.

Hardly a day passed without one or more of John's creditors
dunning him. He and Elaine had formerly maintained a joint bank
account, and after they quarreled each drew checks on it, not
knowing or forgetting that the account had been terminated. Thus, a
check with which John paid their large St. Louis hotel bill bounced.
Elaine had also taken over the management of John's financial affairs
during Hotchener's banishment and it was she who sent Dolores the
sums due for the support of her children. When Elaine left, John
forgot to make the payments himself and Dolores reminded him with
a summons. Next, Maurice Hotchner submitted a bill for his services
to date totaling $10,600.

July 18, 1939

Hello, dear Jack!

Arthur Driscoll [Ned Sheldon's lawyer and now John's] has been very nice about keeping me informed as to your doings, and I am fairly up to date in these matters. It is on this basis that I give you the following advice. Why not close the play, return to Hollywood, get a good agent (if you are not already tied up) and make some money? . . . I see no use in continuing to play *My Dear Children* when so much has to be taken out of your salary. . . . Do a few pictures, Jack, at the best salary obtainable, get some of these immediate debts cleared up, and then come back to the theatre with another play and without obstacles. . . .

I wish you would cut through and out of this Chicago engagement, head straight for California, let Lionel find you a quiet and economical place to live, then concentrate on the best pictures, best part, and best salary available. . . . I am glad you saw Charlie [MacArthur] on his way to California. He telephoned me and said that you were looking well. He is another friend upon whose character and common-sense you can rely.

Good luck, dear Jack. Please think over this California plan very, very carefully. I hope so much that you will see fit to put it through. . . . I wish I could go to Chicago and talk with you for about five hours. Please consider that I am right beside you when you read this letter.

Yours affectionately,
Ned

After satisfying the claims against him, paying his doctors' fees, Karl Steuver's salary and his Winnetka rent, John was reduced to a few dollars of pocket money. Yet by the end of November 1939 he had managed to liquidate all his debts. He then reverted to the prodigality that would again lead to bankruptcy.

In November, too, Elaine obtained her second interlocutory decree.

John failed to heed Ned's advice. To his friend's dismay, he started for New York with *My Dear Children* on January 2, next evening played Pittsburgh (where, as he drank real liquor onstage, nausea gripped him so suddenly that he vomited into the footlights).

Cleveland, January 20 . . . *Detroit*, January 22 . . .

At Grand Central Station, John, who had been nipping steadily since the train left Detroit, kissed a cop, a dog and every girl he could reach among the teeming fans and newsmen. Ethel was there. Power-Waters, seeking restful surroundings for John away from the fleshpots of Broadway, had taken a house in Bayside, Queens, and thither Ethel whisked her brother and his male nurse. She stayed three days and with Steuver's help kept John relatively sober and subdued. Then Jack Prescott relieved her, spending the next three days at the Bayside haven.

The New York première of *My Dear Children* took place January 31, 1940, at the Belasco Theatre on Forty-fourth Street east of Broadway, two blocks from the Harris Theatre where John had first played *Hamlet*. The press reports describing his gambols on and off the stage throughout the Midwest, together with the saga of Caliban and Ariel, had whipped up public curiosity to fever pitch. The box-office queues stretched all the way around the block. The advance sale was one of the biggest in Broadway history—$50,000. For the opening night, scalpers got as much as $100 a ticket. The producers issued solid bronze memorial tickets. As curtain time approached the sidewalks and streets of the block were choked with rubbernecks. To Brooks Atkinson they "looked as if they hoped to be present at the final degradation of Icarus. Standing behind police barriers, they looked sinister. The crowds that watched the tumbrils pass in the French Revolution could not have been more pitiless or morbid."

In his dressing room, surrounded by Pathé newsreel men, John was groggily ridiculing himself and them. "You are listening to the Pathé News," he said, swaying slightly before a microphone, his speech slurred. "I would like to inform you that I am talking into this inverted cuspidor [uneasy laughter from the cameramen] which unfortunately tells the truth. I presume that is why Pathé News still exists. What in the name [coughing]—what I am going to talk about I have not the slightest idea. These guys who have brought up this loathsome instrument-t-t-t are such nice eggs you'd do anything for them [chuckling sardonically]. Now let me see— The gentlemen from the newsreel have informed me that they wish to see the Bar-r-r-ymore pro-feel, that is, as much as is left of it. Here goes—" And throwing back his head, he turned sideways to the camera.

In the audience the rich, the famous and the fashionable

clustered as thickly as raisins in a rice pudding. They included Tyrone Power, Gladys Swarthout and her husband, Frank Chapman, Constance Collier, Ernst Lubitsch, Elsa Maxwell, Herbert Bayard Swope, James Montgomery Flagg, Stella Adler, Harold Clurman, Jack Warner. . . . Diana Barrymore sat between her half-brothers Leonard and Robin Thomas, who so idolized John that he renamed himself "Robin Barrymore." Michael Strange had refused to accompany them. "I can't bear to see Jack debase himself," she said.

At John's entrance the audience stood and applauded for five minutes. Elaine, all aglitter in a form-fitting, low-cut gold lamé gown, a red-fox fur piece encircling her bare shoulders, swept down the aisle to her seat in the third row half an hour after the curtain rose, thereby ensuring maximum attention.

Confronted for the first time in seventeen years by a Broadway audience, many of whom had applauded his Hamlet, John for once felt intimidated and, to the general disappointment, moderated his mugging and ad libbing. When he came to the fragment of the Hamlet soliloquy, the veteran English character actor Dudley Digges was seen to weep. He was not alone.

The tumultuous ovation at the end reflected personal affection for John and appreciation of what he once had been rather than what he now was. His eyes wet, he had begun a curtain speech when a grotesque figure, wearing frayed navy-blue tights, a blue blouse and red kid boots, leaped up on to the stage, shouting: "Stop! Stop! This is Hamlet's ghost talking. To be or not to be is the question. I've always wanted to play *Hamlet* with you, Mr. Barrymore."

Suspecting a practical joke, such as an emissary from Bundy Drive might perpetrate, John pleasantly strung along for a while. "You took a long time getting here," he said. "You look as if you'd had a hard winter."

"I have always admired you in *Hamlet*, Mr. Barrymore," the interloper went on. "I have always admired your handling of the soliloquy."

John put an arm around his shoulders. "I say, old man, can't you come back tomorrow night?"

"I am Hamlet's ghost. To be or not to be—"

The curtain came down while stagehands removed the intruder. He turned out to be a twenty-seven-year-old unemployed actor named Bert Freeman, aiming to publicize himself.

"You may be interested to know," John told the stunned audience when the curtain rose again, "that the gentleman who just jumped across the footlights is now being sat upon by the fattest electrician in New York."

Elaine was among the first to reach his dressing room. When she knocked, Diana opened the door an inch and said: "Go away, Miss Jacobs. Nobody wants you here."

"Please allow your father to dismiss me, my dear," Elaine retorted, adding: "If he does." She stuck her foot in the door. Diana kicked it away. Elaine continued to knock until John finally let her in and Diana, furious, fled.

Jack Prescott, who had been waiting in the dressing room throughout the performance, cryptically recalled years later: "After I witnessed a scene that was disgusting, John told me I could leave, which I did."

Reinforced by friends and kin, Diana reentered the dressing room and hustled her father away. They were expected at Féfé's Monte Carlo Club, Elaine discovered, and she rushed there ahead of them. As John appeared, she flung herself at him, covering him with kisses. "All I want is twenty-four hours with you," she said. "I cannot go on without you. I don't want you for keeps, Jack, darling—just give me twenty-four hours of bliss."

"Miss Jacobs," said Diana, "you will do us all a favor if you get lost. Just go away."

"Ah, but this is like the gentle rain from heaven," John put in. "Please, my little Ariel, join us. Have a seat."

"We are Barrymores and you have nothing in common with us," said Diana. "Please go." Elaine sat tight. "Daddy, either this woman leaves or I do."

"Well, *you* leave, Treepee," said John.

She telephoned Jack Prescott, who had retired to the Players Club. "For God's sake, come and get my father," she implored him.

When Prescott arrived at the Monte Carlo, Otto Preminger was pacing outside. "Where have you been?" he said. "He's in there and Elaine has got him."

Frank Chapman ventured a last effort to rescue John. He conducted him to the men's room upstairs. But when they emerged Elaine was waiting on the landing. John beckoned to the cigarette girl, only to find he had no cash. "I'll pay for it," Elaine volunteered. "I might as well pay for your cigarettes. I paid for our marriage license."

Another bitter encounter occurred between Elaine and Doris Dudley, her replacement in *My Dear Children*, who knew that her days as such were numbered. "Well, you've won, my little conqueress," said Doris.

"Yes, I'm first now," said Elaine.

"You mean you're fourth."

"Well, you can stop counting because I'm going to be the last."

In triumph she piloted John to her room at the Hotel Navarro on Central Park South.

To the reporters who trailed them there, John said before shutting the door: "I have it on good authority that it is legal in New York State for a man to spend the night with his lawfully wedded wife. Or am I misinformed?"

And so Elaine's second interlocutory decree became null and void.

John's opening-night reticence had disappeared by the second night and thereafter *My Dear Children* became again the kind of romp the public expected. The ad libs which had raised the biggest laughs on the road, however, were ad libs no longer, but fixed features of every performance. In fact, when Random House published the play, some of them were parenthetically included. For example:

Manville: A moment later Van Betke came into the room and called me a dirty bastard. Nobody ever got away with that with me. (Barrymore ad lib: . . . except Ethel.)

Stevenson: Where's Portia? I want to thank her for a delightful week-end.

Manville: Gone. (At this point, Mr. Barrymore is pouring himself a drink. He turns, looks at Stevenson, and says: "Just a minute, I need this one awful bad." After drinking a full glass of prop whiskey he turns to the audience and says with a leer: "God, I wish that was real.")

The majority of the critics figuratively threw up their hands and rolled their eyes heavenward in pious dismay. ". . . you who have tears to shed over the loss of the American theatre's onetime leader may prepare to shed them," wrote Burns Mantle of the *Daily*

News. To Richard Watts, Jr., of the *Post*, "The recent offstage spectacle of Mr. John Barrymore and his shrinking, sensitive wife has been of such a repulsive sort that I am afraid it has destroyed most of the pleasure that came from Mr. Barrymore's long-awaited return to the theater. Even at best there was something saddening and embarrassing in the sight of the man who is undoubtedly the greatest of our actors appearing as an extravagant buffoon in a comedy of inconspicuous value, when he should have been trying out his incomparable talents after all these years in a work worthy of him." The *World-Telegram*'s Sidney Whipple pronounced *My Dear Children* "an open invitation to the public not to come and see a good play or an artistic performance, but to witness the humiliation of a fallen idol and the abasement of a once magnificent talent." "He practically slides down the bannister of his own reputation" was Stark Young's verdict in the *New Republic*. ". . . the recollection of what he was is far too valued a memory to have the present-day Mr. Barrymore force us to 'look here, upon this picture, and on this.' That erstwhile Mr. Barrymore was the most exciting male acting talent the American theatre produced in our time, the most splendidly endowed, the most magnificently magnetic, and by all odds the most pictorial. . . ."

The harshest moralistic attack was launched by the *Catholic World*, whose editorialist, Euphemia Van Rensselaer Wyatt, called John's performance "the most disedifying spectacle of many years. . . . If there is everything repellent in a man's capitalizing on his own degradation then there is something even more repellent in the public's coming to snicker at it. Mr. Barrymore's shame knows no modesty. . . ."

Almost alone of all his colleagues the *Times*' Brooks Atkinson voiced a minority dissent, rational, compassionate and laudatory. "He is still the most gifted actor in this country. During the seventeen years he has spent away from Broadway he has held his talents cheap, and the record is not a pretty one in appearance. He has aged more than seventeen years. . . . But whether he has wasted a great talent or not—and that is his own business—the fact remains that he has all the gifts an actor needs and can use them with extraordinary versatility. . . . In contrast with the Barrymore who dominated the theatre by memorable works twenty years ago, he is a ravaged figure now. But the fact remains he can still act like a man whom the gods have generously endowed and like a man who knows the art and the business of stage expression. . . . The Barrymore breeding keeps him master of silly material, and the tricks he plays on it are the improvisations of a man of sharp and worldly intelligence. . . . No doubt it would be more exhilarating to see an eminent actor in a part of dramatic eminence. Failing that, it is something to see him witty and gay. Although he has recklessly played the fool for a number of years, he is nobody's fool in *My Dear Children* but a superbly gifted actor on a tired holiday."

After the third night John collapsed, nervously and physically drained. The rest of the week's performances were canceled at a loss to the box office of about $15,000. As John trudged out the stage door, aided by Elaine and Jack Prescott, the doorman called out to him: "I hope you'll be feeling better, sir."

"Don't worry," said John. "You can cure a ham, but you can never kill one."

Elaine drove the two men in her own car to Mount Sinai Hospital, where all three spent the night. Next day, when Prescott returned to the hospital after a brief absence, he was informed that by doctor's orders the patient could receive no visitors while undergoing examination and treatment. Guessing correctly who really issued such orders, he ran around to Ned Sheldon's apartment nearby and with his permission telephoned Mount Sinai, telling the switchboard operator: "This is Mr. Sheldon for Mr. Barrymore." John was on the phone in an instant. "You sweet-scented son of a bitch," he said. "Come back here. You won't be stopped." Nor, to Elaine's annoyance, was he.

John read Brooks Atkinson's comments while at Mount Sinai and wrote to him:

> My dear Mr. Atkinson—
>
> To begin with I beg you to believe that I am not in the habit of writing to the Critical Cognoscenti in this—or any other—vein!
>
> It is difficult—I imagine—in such communications not to detect—in spite of the most ingenuous intentions —a certain coy note of speciousness! I somehow or other— do not believe—you will for a moment invest—this screed with that quality—!
>
> I wish merely to most sincerely thank you for your very charming—sane & understanding attitude—and to

tell you how deeply grateful I am to you for it—It is more stimulating than you possibly can imagine!

> Believe me to be
> Yrs most sincerely
> John Barrymore

He was back at work on February 7 and the following week Elaine reappeared in her original role of Cordelia. The audience booed and hissed her.

My Dear Children closed after a Broadway run of four months, bringing the total gross, pre–New York tour included, to almost $670,000. It might have lasted many more months, but John, financially hard-pressed as usual—his new debts exceeded $100,000 —accepted a Hollywood offer. Two studios had been angling for him. Selznick International proposed to star him in a movie version of *My Dear Children* and bid $150,000. When Elaine demanded not only that the contract include her, but that no actor except John be billed above her in the ads and screen credits, Selznick withdrew. Bowing at length to the inevitable, Elaine retracted her behest. 20th Century-Fox then signed John alone for another film, *The Great Profile*, at $200,000.

Before returning to the Coast with Elaine, John spent a last night with Jack Prescott, most of it at the bar of the St. Regis Hotel. "We left the hotel and I saw him home," Prescott recalled. "Then came the tough part of saying 'So long.' I was choked up and I guess he was also. We just kissed each other and with a big hug and a gay wave of the hand he left me and I started walking back to The Players, fighting back the tears. I never saw him again."

26

Diana

===

Producer Zanuck and members of the cast of 20th Century-Fox's *The Great Profile*, including Gregory Ratoff, with a face as malleable as putty and an extravagant Slav accent, and Lionel Atwill, an archetype of coolth and hauteur, were at the Los Angeles airport when the Barrymores' plane from New York touched down. Elaine, clutching a copy of the script, asked, as she entered the terminal: "Where is the blonde bitch who is going to play my part?" She was referring to a giddy adolescent starlet named Mary Beth Hughes.

"It was thirty days' work," Mary Beth recalled a dozen years later. "They went so fast. What a ball! I was sixteen and scared to death. I'd heard about Barrymore and Ratoff. I'd heard that when they met you they ripped your clothes off. I was so square.

"The first time Jack came into my dressing room he said: 'Are you a good sport?' I said: 'I think I am.' He then ripped the skirt off my dress and I just stood there with perfect aplomb and I replied: 'That's a good bit.' Jack broke up and said: 'I like you.'

"God, he was loaded all the time. He got there at eight thirty every morning and began drinking, and when we were ready to shoot, he was flying.

"Ratoff scared me to death. The first day of shooting I found two boxes at the door of my dressing room. One was a terrific fox fur—they were all the style then—and a diamond bracelet. I took

349

them to his dressing room, returned them to him and thanked him very much. But every damned day he had a different coat and a different trinket and every damned day I returned them to him. He was livid.

"Jack was too weak to hold me in the scene where we were acrobats. They had this ladder behind him so I could stand on it, and when I slipped my legs over his head for the shot, he couldn't hold me. As we fell, he had the strangest, wrinkled expression.

"In another scene we had a breakaway picture for me to crown him over the head with. It was all worked out to switch from the hard one to the breakaway the last minute so it wouldn't hurt Jack. But when the scene was shot, something went wrong and I crowned him with the real picture—the hard one. Well, he lost consciousness. We were scared to death. He was out cold for two hours. When they brought him around, he smiled and said: 'God, how strong you are!'

"He was wonderful."

By comparison to *The Great Profile*, *My Dear Children* had been an exemplar of dignity and discretion in its exploitation of John's frailties. The film, conceived as well as produced by Zanuck, travestied with sledgehammer finesse Barrymore the madcap, Barrymore the philanderer, Barrymore the tippler. The story, if it can be so described, was built around the tohubohu in John's dressing room on the opening night of *My Dear Children*, together with the marital disorders leading up to it. Yet, far from demurring, John plunged into the performance with manic zest, welcoming it, so it seemed, as an outlet for the expression of his self-contempt. He belched, he croaked "Eadie Was a Lady," he winked lasciviously at the actors and the camera.

John did not balk even when the studio flacks subjected him, a month before the movie's release, to a Hollywood rite established by Sid Grauman and celebrated in the forecourt of his Chinese Theatre. Here, since 1927, the prints of the hands, feet or other parts of front-rank stars, such as Betty Grable's legs and Monty Woolley's beard,* had been preserved in concrete. With John, of course, it had to be the Great Profile. At 6:30 on the evening of September 16, 1940, Grauman, a tiny, fidgety figure, propelled John

---

* A serendipitous concept that came to Grauman when Norma Talmadge, who was viewing the theater under construction, accidentally stepped into some wet cement. At last count, 155 stars had left their prints and signatures in the forecourt.

toward a slab of freshly poured concrete, illuminated by two klieg lights and hemmed in by hundreds of gawkers and newsmen. A cloth was spread to protect John's dark, double-breasted suit as he dropped down on all fours. Gingerly, he leaned over the slab, dipping his left cheek and the left side of his nose into the concrete. Grauman slipped up behind him and shoved his face down hard. A spout of muffled obscenities issued from John's concrete-clogged mouth. When he finally pulled his face free, he left a clear impression in which Grauman hurriedly scratched a few hair marks. A black attendant, still tinier than Grauman, wearing a quasi-Chinese uniform, handed Mary Beth Hughes a towel and she mopped John's face clean. As the crowd cheered, John stooped again and with his index finger scrawled his name under the imprint. Confused and somewhat shaken, he wrote "Jon Barrymore." When Grauman drew his attention to the omission, he rewrote the signature correctly. After satisfying the autograph hounds, he climbed back into the limousine that had brought him, dabbing at his left eye with a handkerchief and digging bits of concrete out of his ear. "Sid Grauman," he claimed later, "has requested my testicles to repose in cement."

The Great Profile was a financial disaster and, by critical consensus, one of the shabbiest films that ever starred John or anyone else. It exposed him to more of the scornful reproof that was heaped upon him for *My Dear Children*. "In the time of his discontent Mr. Barrymore is selling his talent at cut-rate. . . . Perhaps it would have been better, though, if one had never heard of Mr. Barrymore and his Elaine. Then the Great Profile wouldn't point such a reproachful finger at a great actor whose knowledge of Shakespeare is still supreme, but whose debt to himself apparently is forgotten."

The Barrymores' truce was short-lived. After eight months of renewed battling, John fled to Bella Vista, leaving Elaine and her mother to themselves at La Vita Nuova. Lawyer Henry Huntingdon had declined to involve himself further in the marital imbroglios of Caliban and Ariel since his client's last abrupt change of heart, and John was now represented by one Roland Rich Woolley. On the morning of November 27, 1940, Elaine, with Mother Jacobs as corroborative witness, appealed to Superior Court Judge Harry Archbald for a divorce. John, who did not contest the suit, was waiting in Woolley's office, a few blocks away, to learn the outcome. When a runner from the courthouse reported that the judge had granted Elaine an interlocutory decree, John poured himself some whiskey and said: "Ah, it's wonderful! Even if, after all, it's no new experience for me. I'm glad for her, too. It's no particular distinction being called 'Mrs. Barrymore.' There have been so many of them. Now I'm free to resume my search for the perfect mate."

Did he have anybody in mind? he was asked.

"I saw a lovely, simple child in the Christmas Day parade [he had ridden on Santa Claus' float], but she was only fifteen. I could hardly explain to her parents that I simply wanted to put her on ice for a few years. Anyhow I don't think there's enough ice in the world to keep a Hollywood girl cool. I ought to know."

Elaine had complained to Judge Archbald that her husband would sometimes absent himself for as long as three days without explanation. "He told me it was none of my business. He became exceedingly abusive. He was heartless and cruel. All of which caused me a great deal of anguish and sleeplessness and loss of weight and I had to be under a physician's care."

"Dear, dear Elaine," John observed. "The sentimental little girl. Why, just to show you how sentimental she is, she once asked me for my false tooth. I wondered why. So I took it out and looked at it and I found it contained five ounces of gold."

Under the terms of a pre-divorce agreement Elaine was to retain title to La Vita Nuova, on which John would pay off the tax liens amounting to $15,000. He would also make Elaine a cash settlement of $8,500. She demanded no alimony. For her part, she was never to call herself, privately or professionally, "Mrs. John Barrymore," though she could call herself "Elaine Barrymore" (and she still does).

This time there was no reconciliation. The divorce became final in 1941. Yet John, according to Ben Hecht, never purged his system of Elaine. One evening a group of the Bundy Drive boys were dining at Bella Vista when Elaine phoned. It was to resolve some post-divorce financial problem. John's guests heard him say, as Hecht remembered it: "Anything you want. All I ask is one favor in return. Don't hang up. Tell me how much you hate me, but keep on talking so I can hear your voice. No, I'm not drunk, my dear, but I am a man at the bottom of Hell—please keep on talking—tell me anything— about the man you're with, how much you love him, anything, just as long as I can hear your voice it doesn't matter."

But Elaine had already hung up.

On December 2, 1940, a play entitled *The Romantic Mr. Dickens* opened at the Playhouse Theatre in New York. The following day John received a telegram:

DEAREST DADDY THANK YOU FOR THE APPLE FLOWERS
AND WIRES . . . I AM WIRING TWO OF THE BEST
NOTICES THIS ONE BY OUR FRIEND BROOKS ATKINSON
SAYS . . . IT REPRESENTS THE BROADWAY DEBUT OF
DIANA BARRYMORE DAUGHTER OF THE ILLUSTRIOUS
PROFILE AND MICHAEL STRANGE MISS BARRYMORE IS A
VIBRANT YOUNG LADY WITH AN EXCELLENT SPEAKING
VOICE AS CAROLINE BRONSON [a young actress beloved
by the novelist] SHE GIVES A ROMANTIC PERFORMANCE
THAT IS SURPRISINGLY ACCOMPLISHED AND THAT LIFTS
THE PLAY OUT OF THE DOLDRUMS THE NEXT ONE BURNS
MANTLE QUOTE . . . THERE IS A SUGGESTION OF BOTH
CONFIDENCE AND COMPETENCE IN HER STAGE PRESENCE
THAT LEADS ME TO BELIEVE SHE WILL IF SHE IS AS
STRONG IN DETERMINATION AS SHE IS OTHERWISE
FORTIFIED DO HER PATERNAL LINE FULL CREDIT AS AN
ACTRESS END QUOTE SO DADDY DARLING I AM DOING MY
BEST TO CARRY ON THIS STINKING TRADITION MUCH
LOVE TREEPEEWEE.

It was a banner year for Diana. Though *The Romantic Mr. Dickens* survived a bad press by only five performances, her personal success led to better parts in better plays and eventually to Hollywood. It was also the year she fell in love with Bramwell Fletcher, an English actor eighteen years her senior who had played Little Billee to her father's Svengali. Under his influence Diana campaigned for Bundles for Britain during these early months of World War II. Her mother, who had joined the America First Committee, was indignant. "You and that middle-aged, middle-class English quince!" Maternal opposition merely strengthened Diana's attachment to the actor and they became engaged.

The Bundy Drive clan acquired a new member, the youngest in its history. Anthony Quinn, the issue of Mexican-Irish parents, had barely passed his twenty-third birthday when he attempted his first professional role at the Holly Town Theatre, a tryout enterprise under the auspices of Mae West. *Clean Beds* by George S. George (a pseudonym for a Georgian born Youacca Satovsky) was a flophouse drama of Stygian gloom. Camouflaged by a wig and layers of makeup, the novice portrayed a sixty-five-year-old, alcoholic ex-Shakespearean actor. The character was modeled on John Barrymore, and Tony Quinn imitated John's mannerisms.

The first night, to Tony's horror, John himself appeared backstage. As Tony recalled the episode thirty-three years later, John glowered at him and said: "You're a sonofabitch, you're a shit. You were marvelous out there. . . . Christ, everybody's doing a take-off on me, kid, why shouldn't you? At least you did it well."

Thus began a relationship like that of a fond father and son. With the exception of his real father, there was no man to whom Tony Quinn would ever feel closer. John profoundly influenced his life, private as well as professional. He stimulated in him a love of art and literature as ardent as his own. From John, Tony contracted the collector's fever. A substantial amount of his later earnings as one of the world's highest-paid film actors went into a library of more than 5,000 books and a collection of paintings that included a Degas, a Renoir and a Rouault. He learned to paint well enough to exhibit his work. "Sometimes I think I fell short of the high hopes Jack had for me, sometimes not," he says. "I don't know. . . ."

Introduced into the Bundy Drive circle, Tony Quinn, a paragon of robust health, came to fill a special need. Chronic invalids, most of the older members, shuttling between home and hospital, they sometimes required a blood transfusion. When such a crisis arose, the word would go out: "Get Tony." John Decker and John Barrymore were among the principal recipients of Quinn blood.

Gene Fowler's younger son, Will, also served the group in a life-saving capacity. An evening of jollification left few members in any condition to drive a car without dire peril. So as soon as Will obtained a learner's license (available in California at sixteen) he began to chauffeur his father, John and other celebrants to their night's final destination.

Early one morning in June 1941, after Will had transported his father and John from Decker's studio to the Fowler home at 472 North Barrington Avenue, John gave his last complete performance of *Hamlet*. Gene Fowler retired, leaving Will and a wide-awake John in the living room. Their talk turned to Shakespeare and presently Will went to the library, returning with an edition of *Hamlet*. John took it and read Bernardo's opening line—"Who's there?" Before Francisco speaks, he glared challengingly at Will and asked him: "Well, what say you?" Bashfully, the boy took the cue. "Nay, answer me: stand and unfold yourself." Sitting side by side, they read to the end without pause. It was dawn before Fortinbras' men *"exeunt, bearing off the dead bodies."*

John completed three films in 1941—*The Invisible Woman* for

Universal, *World Premiere* for Paramount and *Playmates* for RKO, all
in the same self-burlesquing vein as *My Dear Children* and *The Great
Profile*. During the shooting of *World Premiere* six Royal Air Force
pilots, who were about to fly some Lend-Lease bombers to England,
took a studio tour under the guidance of a young contract player,
Walter Abel. They were eager to meet John Barrymore, and Abel
arranged it. Gorgeously appareled in a bright lounging robe, John
welcomed them to his trailer dressing room. He bowed solemnly,
shook hands with each officer, poured them all a dollop of brandy and
asked: "How's my fart friend Winnie?" They were still laughing
helplessly when John handed around the brandy bottle again, and the
visit passed in spirituous conviviality.

Another Englishman who met John in Hollywood at this junc-
ture was William Somerset Maugham. He was not unduly impressed.
"Yesterday I lunched in company with Jack Barrymore," he wrote to
G. B. Stern. "What a ham! He now wears his hair dark red with a
white mèche sweeping up from the forehead, but he still has a perfect nose."

In *Playmates*, John's fifty-seventh and last screen appearance, an
almost plotless, semi-musical inanity, he portrayed a faded actor
named "John Barrymore." The script writers had spared him no
cruelty. They poked fun at his tax troubles, his debts, his marital
crack-ups, his alcoholism. "I'm dying," says John at one point, "and
you're telling jokes." He starts to declaim "To be or not to be," then
breaks off, saying: "That's enough of that," and bounces back into
the world of pratfalls and funny faces. Such feeble story line as
Playmates followed involved John and the band leader Kay Kyser in
efforts to publicize the has-been tragedian so that a manufacturer of
vitamins will hire him to do commercials. John tries to teach Kyser
how to act Shakespeare. Toward the end of the film Kyser and his
band set *Romeo and Juliet* to swing. Probably no actor of John's
stature ever made a drearier exit from the medium he once orna-
mented.

In New York, Ned Sheldon, having received disturbing reports
about John's health and his professional decline, asked Charles Mac-
Arthur if he would fly to the Coast with a note for their friend. Mac-
Arthur left the same day. He found John at Bella Vista as low in
mind and body as Ned had feared and in the company of a whore.
What the note said MacArthur never learned. John did not read it,
but tossed it into a fireplace, murmuring: "Oh, Virgil, Virgil!"

The year before, in his struggle to clear up a new accumulation of debt, John had gone on Rudy Vallee's Sealtest radio hour at $1,500 a week for the first thirteen weeks. The crooner and the producer-director, Ed Gardner, first had to convince the dairy-product sponsor and its ad agency, J. Walter Thompson, that John's reputation would not hurt the show. It was finally agreed to test him with a two-shot trial. John passed it handily, and during the eighteen months of his employment, which eventually paid him $2,500 a week, he managed to maintain a semblance of sobriety while on the air.

"I am doing the work of a whore," he told Gene Fowler, who was trying to decide whether to continue as a screen writer. "By necessity —or so it would seem—I am occupied with what is loosely called 'Radio,' and an occasional frothy picture. I have been told that no one will lock me up if I earn big money—money that nobody but my creditors get. So I do it. And I find it the work of a whore. There is nothing as sad in all the world as an *old* prostitute. I think that every artist somewhere along the line should know what it is to be one, a *young* one, but reform. Please, my friend, don't keep on working in pictures, where you most certainly don't find any real satisfaction. Get out now!"

The series opened on October 17, 1940, with the following dialogue:

> Barrymore: I refuse. Play *Hamlet?* Bah! I will not do it.
> Announcer: But it's not *Hamlet*, Mr. Barrymore. [Pause while the orchestra strikes up the first few bars of Vallee's theme song, *My Time is Your Time.*] Sealtest presents Rudy Vallee and that great tragedian, John Barrymore.
> Barrymore: Wild horses could not force me to play *Macbeth*. I will not do it. [More theme song.] Then what is this great tragedy?
> Announcer: It is the life of Rudy Vallee.
> Barrymore: I'll do it.

It took sixteen writers to provide that kind of persiflage, much of it capitalizing on John's legendary derelictions.

> Vallee: By nature I am docile, but your ego's so colossal that you force me to assume a fighting role. Let the girls show their affection in a nationwide election. John, I challenge you to meet me at the polls. I'm Rudy the cutie,

the crooning patootie, the vagabond lover
from Maine.

Barrymore: You're really very droll, sir, if we take it to
the polls, sir, I'm sure that I will win it by a
mile. I'm Barrymore the paramour, I'm John,
the great profile.

Vallee would refer to Barrymore by such pejoratives as "my sugar-cured friend . . . you old half-baked *Hamlet*," to which John would retort with a demeaning quip of this sort: "I am a man of experience—in the Hays office sense of the word. I am a four H boy —Haig and Haig, headache and hangover."

One J. Walter Thompson executive fretted lest the emphasis on John's lurid past repel listeners. "You can't keep tearing a guy down forever," he argued. "We want to have our fun by trying to build him up." But he was overruled. The listeners and the studio audiences could not get enough of John's self-abasement.

Ah, yes, reminds me of my own college days. Gad, how I used to study. Late at night with nothing but a little alcohol lamp. It was a real friend to me—that little alcohol lamp. I'd scrape together my last few pennies and buy a gallon of alcohol—and we'd split between us. Sometimes I could only afford a gallon. Then I'd have to study in the dark. You could come by my room practically any time and find one of us lit. . . . [To Vallee:] I'm going to put you in touch with a nice girl. Just call Columbus 5-2058 and ask for Elaine. . . . Women of America, I am humble in your presence because I owe you so much—my lawyers tell me.

When restive during rehearsals, John would sketch in the margins of his script caricatures of himself, leering and looking depressed.

While the radio audiences applauded and Sealtest-hour ratings climbed, to John's family, to his old admirers, to critics and artistic absolutists, the once supreme Hamlet of the age could scarcely have sunk lower. Billie Burke was an exception. ". . . he was miserably in debt," she wrote a few years later, "and his health was failing rapidly. But he rose in the stirrups, so to speak, with all his grandeur and charm, and made fun of himself on the air. I think this was the great lesson which taught good actors that they can be amusing at their own expense. Jack Barrymore did it gallantly, ill as he was, because he was a man of honor who wanted to meet his obligations. Few would have the skill or the wit to accomplish it."

DEAREST TREEPEE THE GUEST WING HAS BEEN SCOURED AND FLOWERED AND IS YOURS FOR AS LONG AS YOU LIKE

Six weeks short of her twenty-first birthday Diana left for Hollywood with a $1,000-a-week contract from producer Walter Wanger, a star-maker. As a minor, she required her mother's signature on the contract. Before Michael would agree, she stipulated a number of galling conditions. Diana must take with her as duenna a Mlle. Eloise Vittele, who was never to permit her to dine alone with a man, to attend any social event without chaperonage or to stay out later than midnight. Once a week Mlle. Vittele must report Diana's general comportment to her mother. The implications of still another condition struck Diana as monstrous and she never quite forgave her mother for it: she was not to spend a single night under her father's roof nor ever be alone with him. But since she would soon reach an age when she could do as she pleased, she bent to her mother's will.

Bramwell Fletcher was on tour and in his absence Diana went to a Broadway producer's party, where she was entranced by the flattery of a handsome, persuasive young actor. A few days later she slept with him. But when Fletcher returned on the eve of her westward journey, she accepted an engagement ring.

"Are you going to be good?" Diana was heard to whisper to her father when he met her at the airport.

"Of course not," he promised.

"Good. Neither am I."

He had arranged for her to play the balcony scene from *Romeo and Juliet* with him on the Sealtest show. A *Time* correspondent was so carried away that in his dispatch to his home office he said: "Diana's reading is the best I've ever heard, Eva Le Gallienne and Katharine Cornell not excepted."

Beaming upon Diana in his dressing room afterward, John announced to the press: "It was a damn good job, and if you don't believe that, you can kiss my ass."

Though Diana happily spent long hours with John and his cronies when not at work on her first picture for Walter Wanger Productions, *Eagle Squadron*, she observed the letter of the maternal law and occupied a suite with Mlle. Vittele at the Beverly Wilshire Hotel. John took an immense pride in his comely, talented daughter.

He had her meet Tony Quinn, hoping they would attract each other. There was no one he would have preferred as a son-in-law. But Diana meant to marry Bramwell Fletcher, and, in any event, Tony felt inhibited by his filial emotions toward John. "Marriage to Diana seemed to me almost incestuous," he says today.

When Diana told John she loved Fletcher, he telephoned him and, as Diana recalled, "roared into the instrument, 'Listen, you Englishman, the primroses are in bloom on my hill, and so is your fiancée—and she can't wait for you. Come out, peasant!'" Fletcher came and John put him up at Bella Vista. A few days later, before leaving for a short camping trip, he told Diana: "You and Bram take my room." They did.

The engagement occasioned John's last communication with Michael. He telephoned to beg her to fly out and bestow her blessing. But she was adamant: she would tolerate no actor of Fletcher's humble social credentials in the family. She and John never spoke again.

Diana once rekindled in her father for a brief moment a desire to make a fine film again, followed perhaps by a serious play. She brought him the script of such a play, Emlyn Williams' *The Light of Heart*. Her confidence so stirred him that he called Darryl Zanuck. "This is Jack," he said. Diana gathered that Zanuck must have asked: "Jack who?" for John said: "Jack Barrymore."

"I have my daughter here," John went on, "and we've both read a magnificent play which I think would make an extraordinary picture."

He listened in silence a moment. Then: "Oh, I see. Well, thank you, Darryl."

But Diana still clung to her conviction that John could, if he would, reestablish himself on the American stage as one of its foremost actors. She longed to act with him and she continually besought him to give them both a chance. "Treepee," he told her with finality, "you are going on to do great things. I am already a dead man."

Immediately following her twenty-first birthday Diana went to stay awhile at Bella Vista. Late one night, when John was sick in bed with his damaged liver, he gave her a telephone number to call for him. He wanted a woman and he did not trouble to conceal the fact from her. Diana made the call, packed her bag, opened the door to a young blonde and, as the latter tripped up the stairs to John's bedroom, left the house in righteous indignation, never to re-enter it.

27

Sans Every Thing

=========

Iᴛ had long been John's custom to stop for a drink around four p.m. at Ella Campbell's St. Donat's Restaurant on Sunset Boulevard. He was due at the NBC studio on rehearsal and broadcast days by six and he relied on Ella, an Englishwoman, to remind him when the hour approached. His usual drink was Pimm's No. 1 Cup, an English concoction with a gin base, and for a snack he had a bowl of tomato soup and a watercress sandwich. Near the bar hung a huge dartboard which Ella's clients would autograph. "I'll sign it," John once told her, "not for you, but because I've got a lot of English in me," and he spoke at length about his Grandmother Drew. When the war ended, he promised, he would take Ella back to her native land, though only on some tramp steamer so as to obviate the need for formal clothes.

On May 9, a Saturday, when there was no broadcast, John went to the restaurant with Lionel two hours sooner than usual and lingered there until past seven. Ella was in the kitchen most of the time, but some of her other customers remarked afterward how happy the brothers seemed to be together and how uproariously they laughed at each other's jokes.

Ten days later John was rehearsing for the eighty-second Vallee Sealtest program. Toward the end of the script the writers had, strangely, inserted for John three lines from *Romeo and Juliet* which bore no relevance to the clowning that preceded or followed it. How or why this happened none of the writers themselves ever quite understood. "But, soft! [John read in his still beautiful voice] what light through yonder window breaks! / It is the east, and Juliet is the sun! / Arise, fair sun, and kill the envious moon. . . ." They were the last words John ever uttered as an actor.

He had several times collapsed during broadcasts, yet though he could barely stand, he had managed to go on, thanks to the ministrations of his doctor, Hugo Kersten. John's edematose tissues were now grossly swollen with fluid, an effect of his impaired kidney function. The water accumulating in his lung tissue was exerting tremendous pressure against his heart. As the rehearsal neared its end, he swayed. Vallee caught him in time to keep him from falling. "I guess this is one time I miss my cue," John said faintly.

In shock and pain that forced tears from his eyes, he was driven by Kersten to Hollywood Presbyterian Hospital. The primary diagnosis was bronchial pneumonia, congestion of the lungs and cirrhosis of the liver. Kersten did not expect him to last more than a few hours. Lionel, in his wheelchair, undertook to replace his brother on the May 21 Vallee show.

The night of his arrival at the hospital John lapsed into a coma from which he emerged, to Kersten's amazement, the following morning, Wednesday. The first face he saw was that of an exceptionally plain nurse. "Well," he said, "get into bed anyway." With a trocar Kersten removed, under local anesthesia, four quarts of water from John's abdomen.

Lionel managed to do without his wheelchair for a short while, hobbling in and out of John's room on crutches. He did not want the news cameraman, holding a death watch along with reporters, to photograph him as a cripple, and when a group of them surrounded him at the entrance to the hospital, he cast aside the crutches and with an agonizing effort held himself erect long enough for a picture.

During the next two days, with Lionel, Gene Fowler and John Decker in constant attendance, John kept slipping in and out of consciousness. He dreamed and, dreaming, murmured: "Mum Mum."

Elaine sent flowers, telephoned, attempted to see John, but Lionel barred the way. From Michael Strange, a telegram: AWFULLY SORRY TO HEAR YOU ARE ILL HURRY UP AND GET WELL FIG. From W. C. Fields: YOU CANT DO THIS TO ME.

The wartime fate of Nishimura weighed heavily on John. The green-fingered little Japanese gardener who for years had so lovingly cultivated the botanical marvels of Bella Vista, who once hid John's crested silverware lest Elaine preempt it, had been removed, like thousands of other Japanese-Americans, with his wife and twelve children to an internment camp and was seriously ailing there.

By Friday twelve quarts of water had been drained from John's abdomen. Now additional amounts backed up into his stomach and ruptured a vein, causing massive internal bleeding. But still he lingered on.

Ethel was on tour. In the fall of 1940, at the age of sixty-one, she had returned to Broadway as Miss Moffat, the Welsh schoolteacher in Emlyn Williams' poignant play *The Corn Is Green*, making an unforgettable entrance wheeling a bicycle. After her long, bleak period in semi-limbo, it proved the glory of her autumnal years, running for fourteen months at the National Theatre, paying her $1,000 a week plus half of one percent of the gross receipts, thereby restoring her to solvency, and reaffirming her eminence as one of the great ladies of the American stage. Yet she would have left the road production without a second's hesitation, John knew, if he needed her. "Tell Ethel to go on, not to come," he ordered Lionel.

The Reverend John O'Donnell, pastor of Los Angeles' Roman Catholic Church of the Immaculate Heart and an old Barrymore family friend, went to the hospital. Through him John was received back into the Church, and Father O'Donnell administered the last rites. But John was not yet ready to go.

During a subsequent visit the priest asked him: "Is there anything else you wish to tell me?"

"Father, I have carnal thoughts," said John.

Incredulous that a man so near dissolution could concern himself with sex, he asked: "About whom?"

John glanced across the room at his new nurse, who was older and even plainer than the first. "Her," he said.

The nurse blushed happily, and Father O'Donnell could not repress an appreciative smile at this crowning gallantry of the Great Lover.

Tony Quinn, who visited the hospital daily, had begun to spend his first few spare dollars on art objects. He bought most of them from a dealer whose store he often passed at the corner of Hollywood Boulevard and Vine Street. A pleasant relationship had burgeoned between dealer and customer when Tony fell in love with a Tang Dynasty horse priced at $700. "I'm going to be famous someday," he said. "Trust me." So the antiquary promised to hold the horse for him until he could afford to pay for it. Another treasure Tony coveted was a Chinese carved-ivory boat with a price tag of $250. Oddly enough, the dealer told him, John Barrymore had once sat for an hour gazing with acquisitive lust at the selfsame boat, but had had to pass it up. Tony bought it then and there and carried it to the hospital. "You little shit," said John, "how did you know?" and burst into tears.

On Friday evening, May 29, John in delirium again murmured: "Mum Mum," and a little later to Lionel: "This is wonderful. What a wonderful place . . ."

Lionel called Dolores to tell her it was a matter of minutes. "What do you want me to do," she asked him, "bring his children?"

"No," said Lionel. "I want them to remember him as he was."

John Decker made a last sketch of John.

At about the same time Gene Fowler was talking to Diana on the phone. "Get out to the hospital right away. I believe your father is dying."

"I can't possibly do it," she said. "I have a very important appointment."

"So has your father."

The appointment was the preview of *Eagle Squadron*. Diana hurried to the hospital after the screening. But it was too late. John had died shortly after ten o'clock.

In Boston, after the final curtain fell on *The Corn Is Green*, the ovation lasted longer than usual. But this time Ethel knew it was not for her. "I am feeling—as I am sure you know—laid low," she wrote in a letter to Alexander Woollcott. "So many memories of my little brother—so long ago—when we were all so young, and knew and expected so little—and it didn't matter."

From Arthur Hopkins Lionel received this wire:

NO JACK COULD NEVER BEAR A PART AFTER HE GREW TIRED OF IT AM SURE HE HAS BEEN WEARY OF THE LAST ONE FOR A LONG TIME AM GLAD HE HAS FOUND A NEW ONE.

There is an ugly story confected by Errol Flynn in *My Wicked, Wicked Ways*, retold with variations by Raoul Walsh in *Each Man in His Time* and on television, and perpetuated by countless other mythologizers. According to this story, at the time John's body was transferred to the Pierce Brothers Mortuary, on Santa Monica Boulevard in Hollywood, a group of his friends, including Flynn and Walsh, were gathered at the Cock and Bull bar on the Strip, drowning their sorrow. Walsh, whom Flynn described as "a man with an off-beat sense of humor," excused himself early, saying he was overcome by grief. Supposedly, he recruited two accomplices and repaired to the mortuary, where he bribed an attendant with $100 to let him borrow John's body for an hour. In a station wagon the trio then drove to Flynn's house, sneaked the body into the living room and seated it in an armchair to await Flynn's arrival. "I was drunk—sad drunk . . ." Flynn recounted. "I let out a delirious scream." The pranksters then restored the body to the mortuary.

In Walsh's version the funeral parlor was the Malloy Brothers' and the caper was hatched in Flynn's home after he left to keep an engagement with his lawyer. Richard Malloy, a former character actor who had worked for Walsh, so the director claimed, let him have John's body simply for old times' sake.

The truth is nobody kidnapped the body. Gene Fowler and his son Will sat by it at Pierce's all night. There was only one visitor— an old prostitute well known in the area. She knelt and prayed and continued on her way in silence.

John was buried June 2 at Calvary Cemetery on Whittier Boulevard in East Los Angeles. Lionel later had engraved upon the marble facing of the tomb Horatio's farewell to Hamlet, which Fowler took for the title of his biography, *Good Night, Sweet Prince.*

The active pallbearers numbered Gene Fowler, John Decker, W. C. Fields, Herbert Marshall, the MGM executive Eddie Mannix, Louis Mayer, David Selznick, Hugo Kersten and two business friends of John's named Rider and Campbell; the honorary pallbearers, Charles MacArthur, Ben Hecht, Ned Sheldon, Roland Young, Thomas Mitchell, Alan Mowbray, George M. Cohan, Herbert Bayard Swope and Bramwell Fletcher. The chief mourners were Lionel, Diana and Elaine.

Fields agreed to serve as a pallbearer only under arduous suasion by Decker. "The time to carry a pal is when he's still alive," he protested. He refused to ride in one of the undertaker's black limousines, preferring his own chauffeured touring car. Driving back from the cemetery with Fowler and Carlotta Monti, his mistress, he pulled aside a lap robe to reveal a portable refrigerator stocked with all the ingredients for making martinis and a number of other potions. As they rolled through the Mexican quarter of Los Angeles, they came to a dead stop in a traffic jam. Half a dozen Mexicans, recognizing the comedian, pressed around the car, cheering. Through a window

Fields handed one of them a shaker full of martinis and some glasses. "Have a drink for good old Jack Barrymore," he said.

Tony Quinn did not attend the funeral along with the other Bundy Drive boys. "It was not that they loved Jack any less than I did," he says, "but I was too young to treat death lightly. . . . I don't believe a day has passed since that I have not thought of him."

Ben Hecht epitomized the feelings of the Bundy Drive boys in verse:

> You die in triumph if, before you die,
> You storm some wall beneath some battlecry.
> Your walls were like a hurdle race—you passed
> And cleared them all in high! All but the last!
> There was a mystery to you—wild and lone,
> But now your whereabouts are fully known.
> To Shakespeare's London and to Villon's town
> You've hied yourself, a-bellowing up and down,
> With bards and bawds around you as you go—
> Your arms a-link with Job and Cyrano.
> You'll walk with Byron and you'll draw a sword
> With bold Tevannes and battle for the Lord.
> Oh, exit Jack; the poets, lovers, kings
> Of wit stand beaming on you, from the wings.

On its editorial page the New York *Herald Tribune*, alone of the major newspapers, published a eulogy:

> It has been the inevitable and melancholy custom, for a good many years past, for the moralists to wag their dull heads and cluck their pious tongues at mention of John Barrymore, the rogue and the wastrel. An easy pastime, this. And the moralists, as always, had the weight of logic on their side. They could prove that he never achieved more than one-tenth of the fine things of which he was capable. He dissipated his talents, which were of a rare order. He was (to use the abominable word so beloved of whited sepulchers) "undignified." They said it was "sad" that in his latter years he had become a "caricature" of a once magnificent figure. But none of this was news to Barrymore, nor did he allow it to disturb him unduly. To the end he faced the world with a charming impudence—saucy, cocky, Rabelaisian and, in his fashion, as gallant a gentleman as ever trod the boards.

Perhaps it is too bad that his somewhat unconventional antics should, in the minds of many, serve to obscure the solid worth of the man and his career, although this is a consideration which would have bothered Barrymore not at all. Here was an actor. Was there ever a better in America? Tens of thousands of playgoers will swear that his virtuosity was unsurpassed anywhere, and they may be right. The memories of him are many. They furnish some of the brightest pages of our theatrical history. His natural equipment was superb. As all the world knows, he came into his remarkable inheritance as a member of the most distinguished, and the most vivid, family of our stage. The list of his great performances is long. Some may prefer to remember him as he was in Galsworthy's *Justice*. Others will let their minds wander back to how he played *Hamlet* and *Richard III* and *The Jest*. No matter what he touched, he gave it a manner and a dash. He was born to be an actor, and when he conscientiously set himself to a task he could blend his genius with a thoroughly sound and intelligent craftsmanship.

But it was not merely in his stage roles that Barrymore revealed a rich personality. There are many competent actors who are mimics and nothing more. John Barrymore happened to have a first-rate brain. Those who knew him best knew that, at bottom, he had a discriminating taste—although he would have hooted to hear himself so described. His memory was downright astounding. Even in the last months of his life, when he was obviously nearing the final crack-up, he could recall the lines of every part which he ever played. In conversation with his closest friends he disclosed a lively imagination and a highly original, even startling, gift for phrase making. It is probable, now that he is dead, that some persons will continue to think of him solely as a rather odd character who had a lot of divorces and who thought it was amusing to have a buzzard for a pet. True enough. But it is also true that he was a mortal whose head at times reached very close to the stars.

PART VII

SURVIVORS AND
REGRETS

J OHN had sixty cents in his pockets when taken to the hospital for the last time. An auction of his wardrobe and furniture was conducted a month later by J. J. Sugarman-Rudolph Co. of Los Angeles to defray personal debts aggregating $200,000. The girdle John wore in late years fetched $4.50 from a steel jobber named Edward Molen. The rest of the Barrymore wardrobe included Hamlet's shirt, which brought $7, a tuxedo vest (fifty cents), a gray sack suit ($35.50), a pearl-gray fedora ($6.50).

The more important sale, representing a lifetime of eclectic collecting, followed on August 24 by order of the U.S. District Court to satisfy federal tax liens. Not long before he died, John had changed his will to bequeath his daughter Dede, age twelve, the letter Lincoln wrote to Louisa Drew and the Sargent charcoal drawing of himself. The bust by Paul Manship was to go to John, Jr., ten, and an Afghan hound named Viola to the interned Nishi. The remainder of the estate was to be divided equally among his three children. As for his ex-wives, "I hereby declare that I am unmarried, having been divorced from four previous wives. All of my property over which I have the right of testamentary disposition is my sole and separate property. I expressly make no provision herein for any of the said former wives."

But the "testamentary disposition" was academic. The government claim took priority, and all the objects retrieved from Bella Vista or the warehouse to which Henry Hotchener had consigned them went on the block, among them 263 books, many autographed by John, many rare editions, such as the Froissart *Chronicles*, A.D. 1425, for which he paid $5,000 (it sold for $750), ancient theater programs, weaponry and sporting equipment of every description, including a medieval cross-bow, a Japanese dagger in a cloissoné scabbard of the eighteenth-century Tokugawa Period, the sword John wielded in *Richard III*, and the suit of armor, Hogarth prints, eighty-five stuffed animals or parts of them . . .

A local collector, B. H. Curtis, bought the Lincoln letter for $325. The San Diego Museum acquired the Sargent drawing for $250. Tony Quinn paid the same sum for Richard's armor. John Carradine paid $226 for a silver service. Lionel Barrymore kept the Manship bust in the family by bidding $160. John Decker bought a quantity of John's drawings and Edgar Bergen seventeen of his oil paintings. Bergen also bought for $185 a collection of shrunken Ecuadorian heads which he placed in the bedrooms of guests who overstayed their welcome.

When John's estate was finally settled in 1959, $75,000 was still owed, almost half of that to the Internal Revenue Service.

Astrologer Llewellyn George, "the boss horoscope cockalorum of the world," had fallen wide of the mark when he ventured to predict the futures of Dede and John Blythe Barrymore, Jr. For Dede he had foreseen an artistic career, "probably on the stage." She is today a housewife and mother, Mrs. Lew Bedell, living quietly in Los Angeles, and has never set foot on a stage or seriously pursued any of the arts.

For John, Jr., the London seer prophesied a "rise to no little fame" in the field of chemistry or surgery, with scant likelihood of ever becoming an actor. In 1951, at the age of nineteen, he was on the verge of a stage debut in John Patrick's war play, *The Hasty Heart*, at the Salt Creek Summer Theatre near Chicago, when he declined to fulfill his contract, which called for a weekly salary of $1,750, "because I'm not ready yet." His Aunt Ethel was appalled. "It has never happened in the three hundred years of the family's acting history;" she proclaimed. "After all, we're professionals. We don't do things like that. I feel humiliated and ashamed. . . ."

John, Jr., had completed four films and expressed the hope of making more "if this thing doesn't ruin me." The following year he married an actress, Cara Williams. A week later a domestic spat ended with him in jail. He pleaded guilty to intoxication in a public place and disturbing the peace, paid a fine of $100 and spent the next three weekends behind bars.

He was next accused, in 1954, by the entrepreneurs of a Connecticut strawhat theater, Lewis and Charlotte Harmon, of frequent tardiness for rehearsals, refusing to accept direction, changing the lines of plays, thereby unsettling the rest of the company, and insulting Mrs. Harmon. The couple complained to Actors' Equity.

In Las Vegas, pending Equity's ruling, John, Jr., was convicted of reckless driving.

By the spring of 1957 Equity had enjoined him from acting with other members of the union until restored to good standing. He was playing Romeo at the time to Margaret O'Brien's Juliet at the Pasadena Playhouse.

Two years later he incurred a suspended sentence on counts of driving while drunk and hit-and-run driving, having fled after bumping the rear end of another car. The court placed him on three years' probation providing he abstain from alcohol and "continue with psychiatric assistance." During the fall of that year he quit a road-company production of *Look Homeward, Angel*, Ketti Frings' Pulitzer Prize dramatization of the Thomas Wolfe novel. His agent explained that he was "not in the best of health."

Another charge of contract-jumping cost him an Actors' Equity fine of $5,000 and a year's suspension.

In 1960 the scene of his adventures shifted to Rome. Bearded and long-haired, the classic hippie, he faced trial for what the Italian police described as a "Wild West type" attempt to spring his prospective brothers-in-law from jail. He was then affianced to a twenty-three-year-old starlet, Gabriella Palazzoli. The fracas started when some Italian youths passed unkind remarks about his beard. During the ensuing street fight Gabriella's brothers, Ermanno and Marizio, as well as her father, pitched in. John managed to escape at the approach of the police, but the Palazzoli brothers wound up under lock and key. An even rougher melee occurred when John, Gabriella and the senior Palazzoli tried to force the prisoners' release. All received suspended sentences. Two weeks later, wearing a velvet-collared, lace-ruffled costume à la Beau Brummel, John wed Gabriella.

The marriage was of short duration. Following the honeymoon, a ferocious set-to occurred in public. John, Jr., said he could not remember the cause. They were divorced while he was facing charges of attempting to break into the Rome apartment of a former fiancée, an actress named Georgia Noll.

Back in California in 1967, John, Jr., was booked into the San Bernardino County jail, charged with possession of dangerous drugs (marijuana), following a collision with a State Highway Patrol car. He pleaded nolo contendere and went to jail for sixty days.

On March 21, 1972, the New York *Times* reported in its *Notes on People* column: "For the second time in 10 days John Barrymore Jr. was arrested on charges of possession of marijuana. Last Thursday he was arraigned on charges stemming from his arrest in a movie studio in Hollywood and Sunday in Van Nuys, Calif., police picked him up in his stalled car and confiscated cigarettes they said contained marijuana. . . . [He] was convicted of possession of narcotics in 1967 and placed on probation for three years. In 1966 and 1969 he was arrested on similar charges. . . ."

At last reports John Blythe Barrymore, Jr., had subsided into an inoffensive and comparatively pacific middle age. He had long before changed his name to John Drew Barrymore so that his son by Cara Williams could, should he elect to pursue the dynastic tradition, retain the honor of calling himself John Barrymore, Jr.

"I raged at myself, and the tears overwhelmed me," Diana wrote in recalling her last encounter with her father. "I was a bloody snob! I shouldn't have been that way about my father! I shouldn't have been such a Goddamned boarding-school bitch! When I let that girl into the house that night I should have said to her, 'All right, honey, be kind to him. I'll be here when you come down . . .' I should have realized that my father was sick and broken and lonely and old and unhappy. I thought, oh, if he were alive, I'd know how to be a daughter to him now, no matter what he did, no matter what he asked, no matter how shocking a life he led. But I'd been brought up too bloody much 'society' and too strictly and too everything else! And I could not take it, I could not take it, that my own father should ask me to get him a whore! *Oh, Daddy,* I prayed, *forgive me.*"

Two months after John's death Diana became Mrs. Bramwell Fletcher over her mother's objections. Michael divorced Harry Tweed the same year and embarked upon the first of several country-wide tours in a repertoire of readings entitled "Great Words to Great Music" to the accompaniment of a harpist.

In the course of a rocky marriage, which lasted four years,

Diana became addicted to drink, drugs and other men and through indulgence dissipated what talent she possessed. "She thought that by behaving this way she was being a Barrymore, like her father," a percipient friend of the family observed.

Drink and drugs also destroyed her younger half-brother, Robin, whom she adored. As a child of five Robin consistently spoke of himself as a girl, invented stories in which he imagined himself a princess and costumed himself as such. According to what his mother confided to Mercedes de Acosta, she finally took him to a psychologist to learn the root cause. "Madam," replied the psychologist, "evidently you never looked at yourself in the mirror. Had you done so, you could, no doubt, answer this question for yourself without wasting my time and your money." Robin was dead at the age of twenty-eight.

When, in a drunken confessional mood, Diana revealed to Fletcher the identities of some of her lovers, he walked out. She swallowed thirty capsules of Nembutal, but survived. Within a year she was living with a Hollywood tennis pro and pimp named John Howard, whom she then married. They separated six months later and eventually were divorced. In 1953 Howard drew a sentence of one year's imprisonment for white slavery. Diana's third husband was an alcoholic actor, Robert Wilcox, "who was to mean more to me than any man but my father."

In the summer of 1950 Michael Strange spent four months in Zurich's Herslanden Clinic, stricken with leukemia. The young scion of old family friends, Ted Peckham, had gone with her as a companion-secretary. He faithfully watched over her, took her for long walks during periods of remission, amused her with sophisticated chatter. In an access of nostalgia she began calling herself Barrymore again and she proposed to Peckham that they dress alike, as she and John used to, *pour épater le bourgeois.* "John Barrymore," she told him, "was the one great love of my life." Four months later she died in Massachusetts Memorial Hospital.

In 1954 the actor-director Day Tuttle was running a summer stock company at Wilmington's Strand Theatre and he engaged Diana to play Marie Charlet, the mistress of Toulouse-Lautrec, in an adaptation of Pierre Le Mur's novel about the artist. She was then only thirty-three, but bloated in face and figure. Arriving drunk, she flung herself provocatively on the bed of the hotel room Tuttle had reserved for her. Days later, in a sober moment, she put to Tuttle the same question John Barrymore had so often asked about himself: "Do you think I'll destroy myself like my father?"

Four years later, returning to her New York flat from a late party, she swallowed—whether accidentally or deliberately has never been established—a lethal combination of whiskey and sleeping pills.

"John came to me just before he died," said Dolores, "and he told me he was sorry." Her marriage to Vruwink had ended in divorce after eleven years. She lives alone today, far from the film colony, on a ranch she owns at Fallbrook, California, twenty miles from San Diego. "When I think of him, it is with great compassion."

For a time Elaine continued to storm the portals of the theater, but they failed to yield to her, and she finally understood that they never would. At heart a practical woman, she turned to an occupation for which she was infinitely better suited. The New York Institute of Finance trains employees for members of the Stock Exchange. Elaine passed the examinations with a score of ninety-five, one of the highest ever recorded, and became the first woman customers' broker with the firm of Schafer, Long and Meaney (now defunct). She fared so well that, after selling the Bel Air house, she bought a 150-year-old Colonial in Westport, Connecticut, which she shared with her mother.

In 1955 Elaine's career took another direction. Having grown fond of Haiti after vacationing together there, mother and daughter developed an export business in Haitian woven straw goods— table mats, hats, handbags, baskets—designed by Elaine and fashioned by native craftsmen. This remains Elaine's principal activity.

She lives alone at present in a one-room apartment on Manhattan's East Side, crammed with Barrymore memorabilia. (Edna Jacobs' health has declined, confining her to a sanitorium.) "If only I had been older and John younger," Elaine believes, "it would have been the romance of the century." She never remarried, though she was twice engaged. "I had two fittings for a wedding dress, but called it off. I realized that any other marriage would be anticlimactic after John Barrymore."

In her occasionally feral account of her years with John, which spares neither of them, she concludes: "He has never really left me. No matter where I am, John is there. . . . I'm not alone. My search is over. John is my buried treasure. I'll never find another."

ACKNOWLEDGMENTS

THE Library of the Performing Arts at Lincoln Center, Manhattan, is perhaps the most extensive of its kind in the United States. I am greatly indebted to Paul Myers, Curator of the Theatre Section, and his staff, for their endless patience and unstinting help to me in my research.

Gene Fowler willed his papers to the University of Colorado's Special Collections. Much of the material concerning the Barrymore family Fowler did not use, out of consideration for persons then living. I must thank William H. Webb, former Curator, and his assistant, Ms. Lyn Sheehy, for making this material available to me.

I am deeply grateful to the sons of Gene Fowler—Gene, Jr., and Will—for communicating to me additional anecdotal material as well as their personal recollections of the Barrymores.

For a wealth of source material, published and unpublished, I wish to thank Ms. Jane Thomas, Librarian of Special Collections, the Joint University Libraries, Nashville, Tennessee; Jon Reynolds, Archivist, Georgetown University; Bill Richards, Secretary of the Friends of the Theatre Collection, Museum of the City of New York; Ms. Geraldine Duclow, Librarian, the Free Library, Philadelphia; Louis Rachow, Librarian, the Players Club; Joseph McCarthy, Librarian Manager of the New York *News* Daily and Sunday; Charles Silver, Supervisor of the Film Study Center, Museum of Modern Art.

I wish also to thank the following individuals for their help: Walter Abel, Hollis Alpert, Mrs. Frank Aranow, Brooks Atkinson, Dolores Costello Barrymore, Elaine Barrymore, Mrs. Lew Bedell, Spencer Berger, Ms. Lynn Black, Carroll Carroll, Harold Clurman, Marc Connelly, Nathan Dinnes, Robert Douglas, William Everson, William Fadiman, W. C. Fields Productions, Iris Segal Gallin, Lillian Gish, Albert Hackett, Jed Harris, Katharine Hepburn, Jean Hoberman, A. E. Hotchner, Garson Kanin, Everett Raymond Kinstler, Herman Kogan, Myrna Loy, Sam Marx, James Meighan, Magda Michael, Ethel Barrymore Colt Miglietta, Worthington Miner, Jesse Mass, Kate Molinoff, Ted Morgan, James O'Neil, Ted Peckham,

Otto Preminger, Anthony Quinn, Richard Roffman, Anne Seymour, John D. Seymour, Louis Simon, Cornelia Otis Skinner, Chris Steinbrunner, Blanche Sweet, Herbert Bayard Swope, Jr., Yvonne Thomas, Catherine Turney, Day Tuttle, Rudy Vallee, Irving Wallace, Raoul Walsh, Richard Watts, Jr., Robert Weiskopf, John Hall Wheelock, William Wyler, Karen Zimmerman.

I owe my greatest debt to the skilled editorial eye, hand and mind of Herman Gollob.

New York City, January 1977

BIBLIOGRAPHY

BOOKS

Ackerman, William Buell, *The Hamlets of the Theatre Astor*. New York, n.p., 1968.

Acosta, Mercedes de, *Here Lies the Heart*. New York, Reynal & Co., 1960.

Alpert, Hollis, *The Barrymores*. New York, The Dial Press, 1964.

Astor, Mary, *A Life on Film*. New York, Delacorte Press, 1971.

————, *My Story*. Garden City, N.Y., Doubleday & Co., 1959.

Atkinson, Brooks, *Broadway*. New York, The Macmillan Co., 1970.

Bankhead, Tallulah, *Tallulah—My Autobiography*. New York, Harper & Brothers, 1952.

Barnes, Eric Wollencott, *The Man Who Lived Twice: The Biography of Edward Sheldon*. New York, Charles Scribner's Sons, 1956.

Barrymore, Diana, and Gerold Frank, *Too Much, Too Soon*. New York, Henry Holt & Co., 1957.

Barrymore, Elaine, and Sandford Dody, *All My Sins Remembered*. New York, Appleton-Century, 1964.

Barrymore, Ethel, *Memories: An Autobiography*. New York, Harper & Brothers, 1955.

Barrymore, John, *Confessions of an Actor*. Indianapolis, The Bobbs-Merrill Co., 1926.

Barrymore, Lionel, as told to Cameron Shipp, *We Barrymores*. New York, Appleton-Century-Crofts, 1951.

Berkman, Edward D., *The Lady and the Law*. Boston, Little, Brown & Co., 1976.

Billquist, Fritiof, *Garbo*. London, Arthur Barker, 1959.

Brady, William A., *Showman*. New York, E. P. Dutton & Co., 1937.

Brown, John Mason, *Broadway in Review*. New York, W. W. Norton & Co., 1940.

————, *Dramatis Personae*. New York, The Viking Press, 1963.

Brownlow, Kevin, *The Parade's Gone By*. New York, Alfred A. Knopf, 1968.

Burke, Billie, *With a Feather on My Nose*. New York, Appleton-Century-Crofts, 1949.

Card, James, *The Films of John Barrymore*. Rochester, N.Y., George Eastman House, 1969.

Carroll, Carroll, *None of Your Business or My Life with J. Walter Thompson (Confessions of a Renegade Radio Writer)*. New York, Cowles Book Co., 1970.

Carroll, David, *The Matinee Idols*. New York, Arbor House, 1972.

Churchill, Allen, *The Great White Way*. New York, E. P. Dutton & Co., 1962.

Clurman, Harold, *All People Are Famous*. New York, Harcourt Brace Jovanovich, 1974.

Collier, Constance, *Harlequinade*. London, John Lane the Bodley Head, 1929.

Cooper, Gladys, *Gladys Cooper*. London, Hutchinson & Co., 1932.

Crowther, Bosley, *The Lion's Share*. New York, E. P. Dutton & Co., 1957.

Drew, John, *My Years on the Stage*. New York, E. P. Dutton & Co., 1922.

Drew, Mrs. John, *Autobiographical Sketch*. New York, Charles Scribner's Sons, 1899.

Eells, George, *Hedda and Louella*. New York, G. P. Putnam's Sons, 1972.

Ferber, Edna, *A Peculiar Treasure*. Garden City, N.Y., Doubleday & Co., 1960.

Fields, W. C., *W. C. Fields by Himself*. Englewood Cliffs, N.J., Prentice-Hall, 1974.

Flagg, James Montgomery, *Roses and Buckshot*. New York, G. P. Putnam's Sons, 1946.

Flynn, Errol, *My Wicked, Wicked Ways*. New York, G. P. Putnam's Sons, 1959.

Fowler, Gene, *Good Night, Sweet Prince*. New York, The Viking Press, 1944.

————, *Minutes of the Last Meeting*. New York, The Viking Press, 1954.

Fowler, Will, *The Young Man from Denver*. New York, Doubleday & Co., 1962.

Frohman, Daniel, *David Frohman Presents*. New York, Claude Kendell & Willoughby Sharp, 1935.

Gaige, Crosby, *Footlights and Highlights*. New York, E. P. Dutton & Co., 1948.

Goodwin, Nat C., *Nat Goodwin's Book*. Boston, The Gorham Press, 1914.

Harding, Alfred, *The Revolt of the Actors*. New York, William Morrow & Co., 1929.

Harriman, Margaret Case, *Blessed Are the Debonair*. New York, Rinehart & Co., 1956.

Harris, Warren G. *Gable and Lombard*. New York, Simon & Schuster, 1974.

Hayes, Helen, with Lewis Funke, *A Gift of Joy*. New York, M. Evans & Co., 1965.

Hayes, Helen, with Sandford Dody, *On Reflection*. New York, M. Evans & Co., 1968.

Hecht, Ben, *Charlie: The Improbable Life and Times of Charles MacArthur*. New York, Harper & Brothers, 1957.

————, *A Child of the Century*. New York, Simon & Schuster, 1954.

Henderson, Mary C., *The City and the Theatre*. Clifton, N.Y., James T. White & Co., 1973.

Higham, Charles, *Kate: The Life of Katharine Hepburn*. New York, W. W. Norton & Co., 1975.

Hopkins, Arthur, *Reference Point*. New York, Samuel French, 1948.
————, *To a Lonely Boy*. New York, Doubleday, Doran & Co., 1957.

Hopper, Hedda, *From Under My Hat*. Garden City, N.Y., Doubleday & Co., 1952.

Huneker, James. *An Early Estimate of Sadakichi Hartmann*. New York, Musical America, 1897.

Jones, Ernest, *Hamlet and Oedipus*. New York, W. W. Norton & Co., 1949.

Jones, Robert Edmond, *The Dramatic Imagination*. New York, Duell, Sloan & Pearce, 1941.

Kahn, E. J., Jr., *The World of Swope*. New York, Simon and Schuster, 1965.

Kane, Whitford, *Are We All Met?* London, Elkin Mathews & Marrot, 1931.

Kanin, Garson, *Hollywood*. New York, The Viking Press, 1974.

——, *Tracy and Hepburn*. New York, The Viking Press, 1971.

Kaufman, George S., and Edna Ferber, *The Royal Family*. New York, Doubleday, Doran & Co., 1927.

Laas, William, *Crossroads of the World: The Story of Times Square*. New York, Popular Library, 1975.

Langford, Gerald, *The Murder of Stanford White*. Indianapolis, The Bobbs-Merrill Co., 1962.

Leslie, Amy, *Some Actors: Personal Sketches*. Chicago and New York: Herbert S. Stone & Company, 1899.

Lutyens, Lady Emily, *Candles in the Sun*. Philadelphia and New York, J. B. Lippincott Co., 1957.

Lutyens, Mary, *Krishnamurti: The Years of Awakening*. New York, Farrar, Straus and Giroux, 1975.

Magarshack, David, *Stanislavsky: A Life*. London, MacGibbon and Kee, 1950.

Marcosson, Isaac F., and Daniel Frohman, *Charles Frohman: Manager and Man*. New York, Harper & Brothers, 1916.

Marx, Samuel, *Mayer and Thalberg: The Make-Believe Saints*. New York, Random House, 1975.

Middleton, George, *These Things Are Mine: The Autobiography of a Journeyman Playwright*. New York, The Macmillan Co., 1947.

Monti, Carlotta, with Cy Rice, *W. C. Fields & Me*. Englewood Cliffs, N.J., Prentice-Hall, 1971.

Moses, Montrose J., *Famous Actor-Families in America*. New York, Thomas D. Crowell & Co., 1906.

Moses, Montrose J., and Virginia Gerson, *Clyde Fitch and His Letters*. Boston, Little, Brown and Company, 1924.

Mount, Charles Merrill, *John Singer Sargent*. New York, W. W. Norton & Co., 1955.

Nathan, George Jean, *The Magic Mirror*. New York, Alfred A. Knopf, 1960.

Nesbit, Evelyn, *Prodigal Days*. New York, Julian Messner, 1934.

Nesbitt, Cathleen, *A Little Love & Good Company*. London, Faber & Faber, 1975.

Nethercot, Arthur H., *The Last Four Lives of Annie Besant*. Chicago, University of Chicago Press, 1963.

Oppenheimer, George, *The Passionate Playgoer*. New York, The Viking Press, 1958.

Parish, James Robert, and Ronald L. Bowers, *The MGM Stock Company: The Golden Era*. New Rochelle, N.Y., Arlington House, 1973.

Pointer, Michael, *The Public Life of Sherlock Holmes*. New York, Drake Publishers, 1975.

Power-Waters, Alma, *John Barrymore: The Legend and the Man*. New York, Julian Messner, 1941.

Quinn, Anthony, *The Original Sin*. Boston, Little, Brown and Company, 1972.

Rathbone, Basil, *In and Out of Character*. Garden City, N.Y., Doubleday & Co., 1962.

Robinson, John Robert, *The Last Earls of Barrymore*. London, Sampson, Low, Manton & Co., 1894.

Rogers, W. G., and Mildred Weston, *Carnival Crossroads: The Story of Times Square*. New York, Doubleday & Co., 1960.

Schickel, Richard, *The Men Who Made the Movies*. New York, Atheneum, 1975.

Skinner, Otis, *Footlights and Spotlights*. Indianapolis, The Bobbs-Merrill Co., 1924.

Stagg, Jerry, *The Brothers Shubert*. New York, Random House, 1968.

Stevens, Ashton, *Actorviews*. Chicago, Covici-McGee Co., 1923.

Stoddart, Dayton, *Lord Broadway*. New York, Wilfred Funk, 1941.

Strange, Michael, *Resurrecting Life*. New York, Alfred A. Knopf, 1921.

————, *Selected Poems*, New York, Brentano's, 1928.

————, *Who Tells Me True*. New York, Charles Scribner's Sons, 1940.

Thomas, Augustus, *The Print of My Remembrance*. New York, Charles Scribner's Sons, 1922.

Tunney, Kieran, *Tallulah: Darling of the Gods*. New York, E. P. Dutton & Co., 1973.

Turney, Catherine, and Jerry Horwin, *My Dear Children*. New York, Random House, 1940.

Vallee, Rudy, *Let the Chips Fall . . .* Harrisburg, Pa., Stackpole Books, 1975.

Veiller, Bayard, *The Fun I've Had*. New York, Reynal and Hitch-cock, 1941.

Walsh, Raoul, *Each Man in His Time*. New York, Farrar, Straus & Giroux, 1974.

Webster, Margaret, *The Same Only Different*. New York, Alfred A. Knopf, 1969.

Yurka, Blanche, *Bohemian Girl*, Athens, Ohio University Press, 1970.

Zukor, Adolph, with Dale Kramer, *The Public Is Never Wrong*. New York, G. P. Putnam's Sons, 1953.

PERIODICALS

Agate, James, "On John Barrymore's Hamlet." *Sunday Times* (London), February 22, 1925.

Anonymous, "Justice." *The Theatre*, May 1916.

Barrymore, John, "The Method in My Madness." *Liberty Magazine*, September 7, 1940.

————, "Those Incredible Barrymores." "Blame It on the Queen." "How I Escaped a Great Lover's Doom." "My Son John." *The American Magazine*, February-May 1933.

————, "What Is a Juvenile Lead?" *Theatre Magazine*, June 1914.

Berger, Spencer, "The Film Career of John Barrymore." *Films in Review*, December 1952.

Biery, Ruth, "The Most Tragic Love Story." *Modern Screen*, September 1935.

Bodeen, DeWitt, "John Barrymore and Dolores Costello." *Focus on Film*, Winter 1972.

Boyesen, Hjalmar Hjorth 2nd, "John Barrymore's Work." *Cosmopolitan*, January 1902.

Broeck, Helen Ten, "From Comedy to Tragedy." *Theatre Magazine*, July 1916.

Broun, Heywood, "Shoot the Works." *The New Republic*, February 2, 1938.

Butterfield, Walton, "John Barrymore's Last Visit to the Club or a Bender of Titans." *The Players Bulletin*, Winter 1962.

Collins, Frederick L., "The Loves of John Barrymore." *Liberty Magazine*, September 19–November 7, 1936.

Darnton, Charles, "John Barrymore's Kick-Back." *Photoplay*, April 1936.

————, "John, the Great." *Photoplay*, February 1934.

Doherty, Edward, "The Barrymores." *Liberty*, July 28, 1928.

Drake, Waldo, "How the Honolulu Race Was Sailed." *Yachting*, September 1926.

Everson, William K., "John Barrymore's Sherlock Holmes." *Films in Review*, February 1976.

Fallon, Gabriel, "One Man's Hamlet." *The Irish Monthly*, May 1948.

Harris, Jed, "The Royal Family." *Playbill*, April 1976.

Harriss, John, "An Apple a Debut." *Theatre Magazine*, April 1931.

Hecht, Ben, "Barrymore's Last Performance." *Theatre Arts*, June 1954.

Huneker, James, "Looking Backward." *Theatre Magazine*, June 1910.

Janis, Elsie, "Jack of All Maids" *Liberty*, March 2, 1929.

Lang, Harry, "This Odd Chap Barrymore." *Photoplay*, March 1931.

Le Strange, Philip, "John Barrymore's Acting Style." *Drama Critique*, Fall 1968.

Lindbergh, Anne Morrow, "The Most Unforgettable Character I've Met." *Reader's Digest*, January 1947.

Literary Digest, "John Barrymore's New Idea of 'Hamlet.' " January 6, 1923.

————, "John Barrymore Stirs London." March 28, 1925.

McEvoy, J. P., "Barrymore—Clown Prince of Denmark." *Stage*, January 1941.

Maloney, Martin J., "The Frontier Theatre." *Players Magazine*, November 1939.

Maltin, Leonard, "John Barrymore." *Film Fan Monthly*, July-August 1966.

New York *Times* Film Reviews, 1914–1941.

Oursler, Will, " '. . . With Yorick in His Arm.' " *The Players Bulletin*, Spring 1962.

Parker, Dorothy, "The Jest." *Vanity Fair*, June 1919.

Patterson, Ada, "John Barrymore's Romance." *Photoplay*, November 1920.

Phillips, Michael J., "The Santa Barbara–Honolulu Race. *Yachting*, September 1926.

Row, Arthur William, "Why I Do Not Play Long Seasons" Being an Interview with John Barrymore. *The Professional Bulletin, Stage and Screen*, July 1925.

St. John, Adela Rogers, "Hollywood Can't Exist, but Does." *Photoplay*, December 1926.

Sedgwick, Ruth Woodbury, "Colorist." *Stage*, July 1935.

Shore, Viola Brothers, "What Makes a Matinee Idol?" *Liberty*, September 6, 1924.

Simpson, J. Palgrave, "Honour." *The Theatre*, London, November 11, 1881.

Smith, A., "Barrymore Pays His Annual Visit." *Photoplay*, August 1925.

Snyder, Louis L., "This Was Barrymore." *Coronet*, September 1951.

Sumner, Keene, "The Hidden Talents of 'Jack' Barrymore." *American Mercury*, June 1919.

Tracy, Virginia, "The First of the Barrymores." *The New Yorker*, October 11, 1930.

Waterbury, Ruth, "Barrymore Ballyhoo." *Photoplay*, August 1928.

Wheeler, Daniel Edwin, "As I Remember Them." *American Mercury*, August 1957.

Wyatt, Euphemia Van Rensselaer, "Moral Disarmament." *Catholic World*, March 1940.

Young, Stark, "Reflections on the Death of Margaret Carrington." *The New Republic*, August 4, 1942.

———, "A Terrible Thing." *The New Republic*, September 14, 1927.

Zeitlin, Ida, "The Miracle at the John Barrymores'." *Photoplay*, March 1938.

UNPUBLISHED SOURCES

Aranow, Frank, "The John Barrymore Case," 1972. A chapter of an unfinished memoir.

Barrymore, Dolores Costello, her honeymoon diary.

Dolores and John Barrymore. Their joint honeymoon diary.

Carrington, Margaret, "The John Barrymore I Knew."

Decker, John, "Heroes with Hangovers—Candid Confessions of a Famous American Painter" as told to Irving Wallace.

Fowler, Gene, letter to Dr. Harold Thomas Hyman (unexpurgated), January 18, 1944.

Hughes, Mary Beth, notes on filming of *The Great Profile*, 1962.

Sircom, Arthur, letter to the author on *My Dear Children.*

Taylor, John Lark, "My Season with John Barrymore in *Hamlet.*"

Turney, Catherine, letters to the author on *My Dear Children*, May 6 and 18, 1975.

Vallee, Rudy, 1942 radio programs.

INDEX

JOHN KOBLER

In addition to writing biographies, John
Kobler has contributed a wide range of
articles to most of America's leading maga-
zines, among them the *New Yorker*, *Life*,
Saturday Evening Post, *New York*, *Sports
Illustrated*. He was the star crime reporter
for the famed controversial newspaper *PM*,
a foreign correspondent for International
and Universal News Service, editor and
writer for *Time* and *Life*, and a staff writer
for the *Saturday Evening Post* during the
twelve years preceding its demise. Mr.
Kobler and his wife, Evelyn, an artist,
share an apartment overlooking Manhattan's Lincoln Center for the Performing
Arts, giving them easy access to opera and
theater, his favorite pursuits.